The SEPARATRIX Project

Katharina Grosse
Alexander Kluge

Spector Books

Katharina Grosse
Alexander Kluge

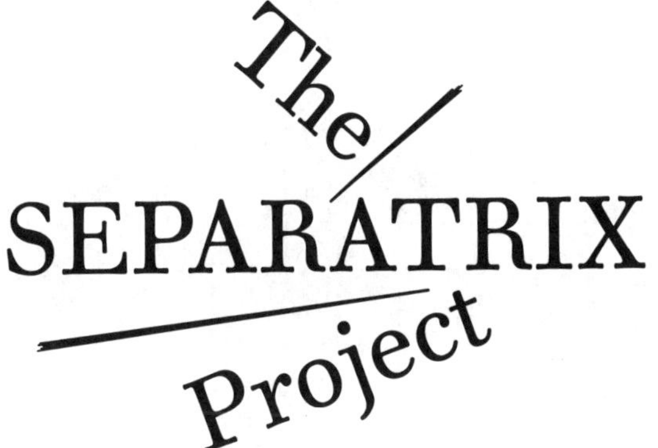

The SEPARATRIX Project

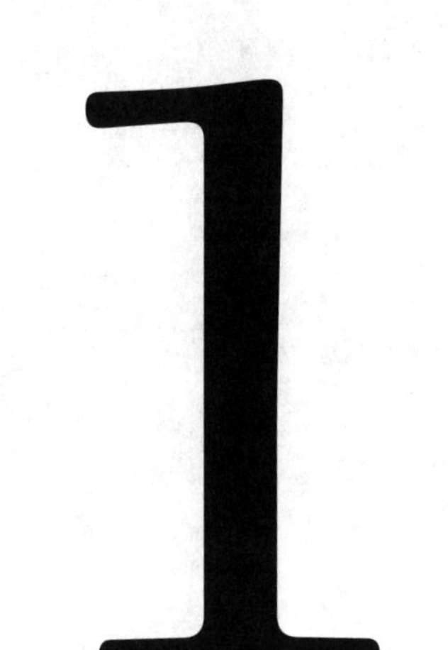

Watercolors

I

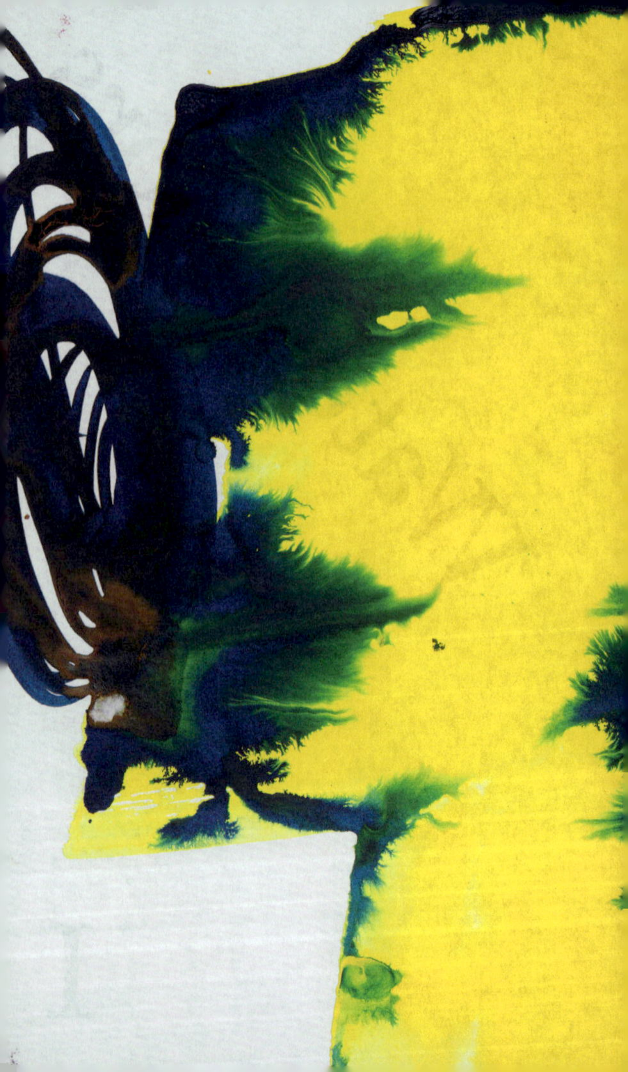

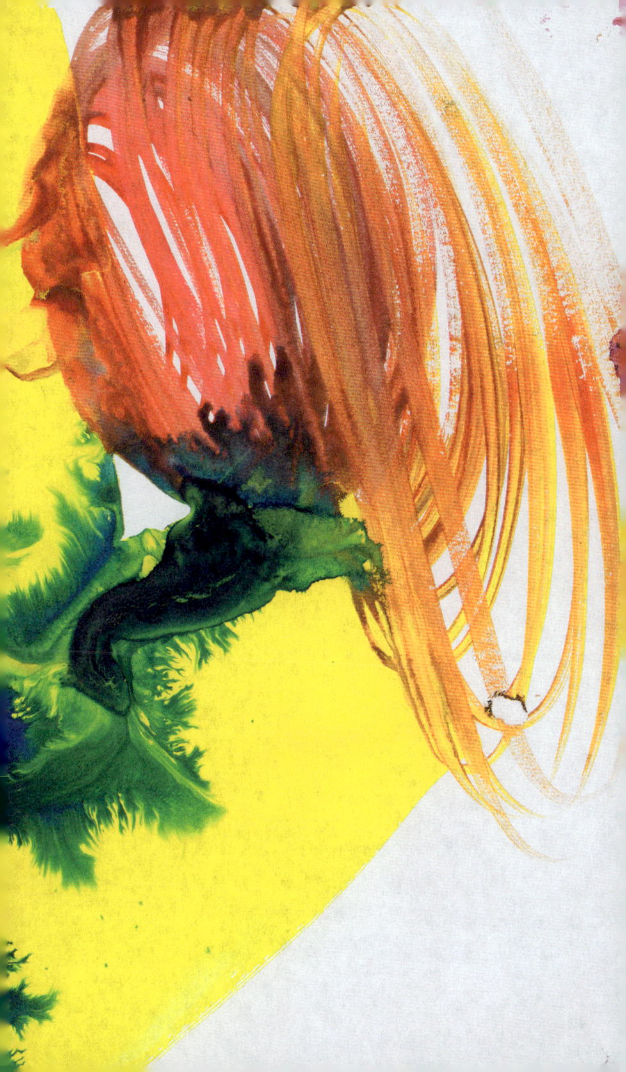

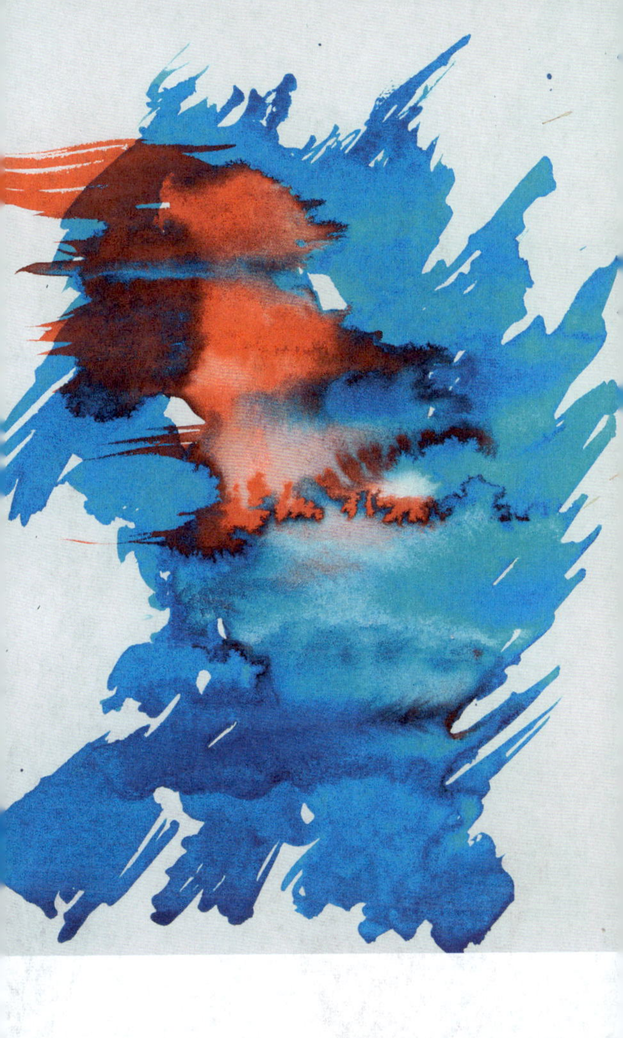

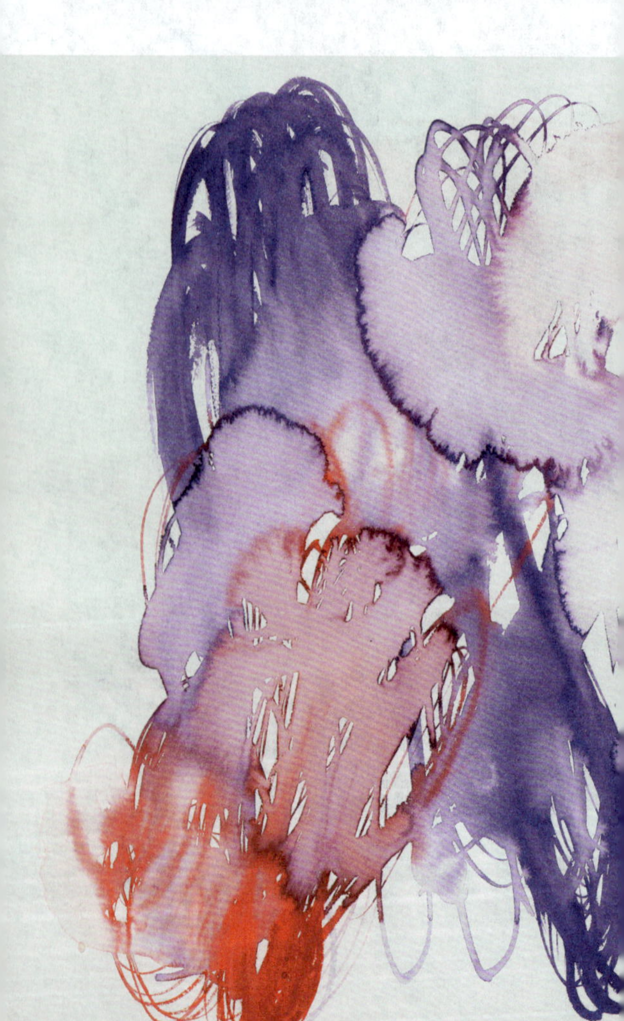

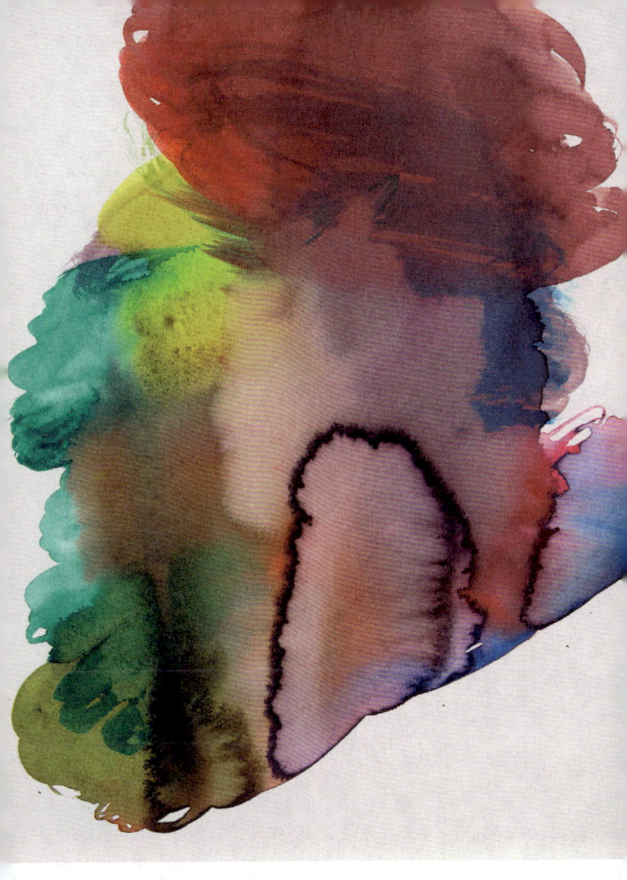

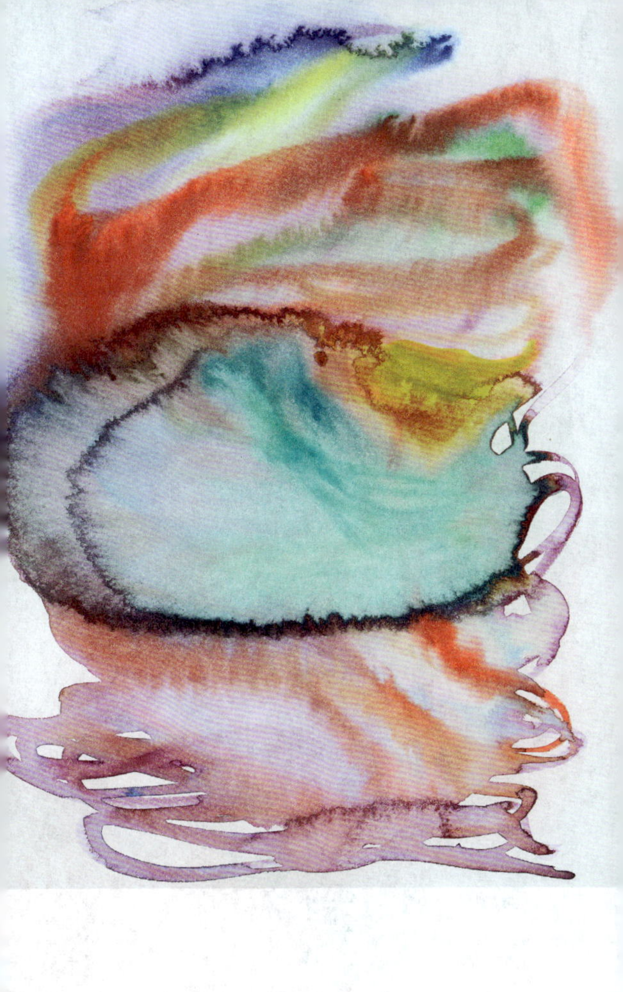

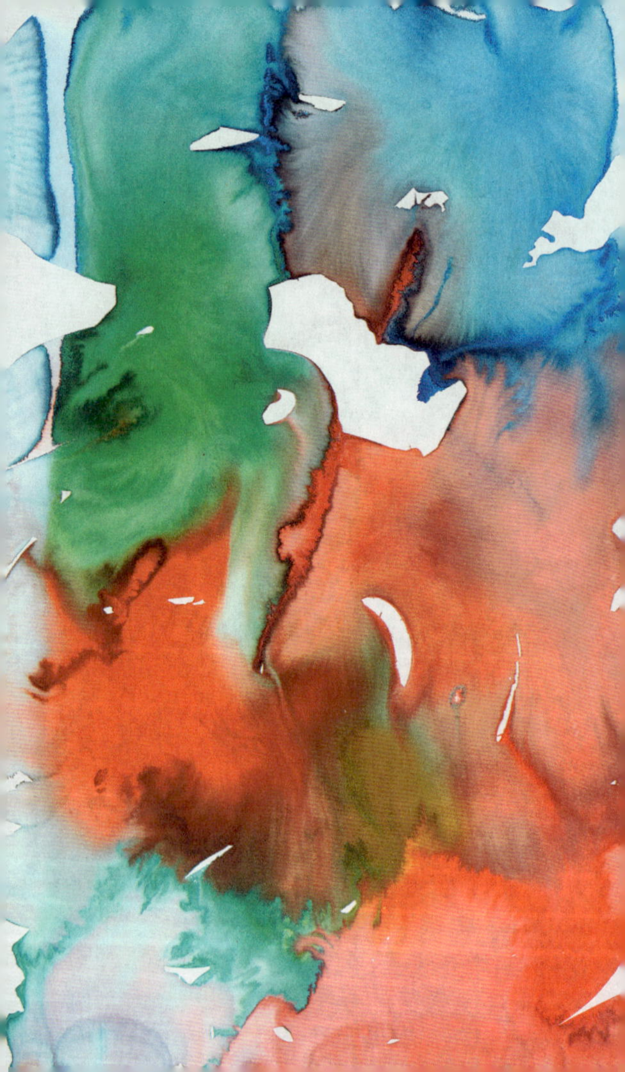

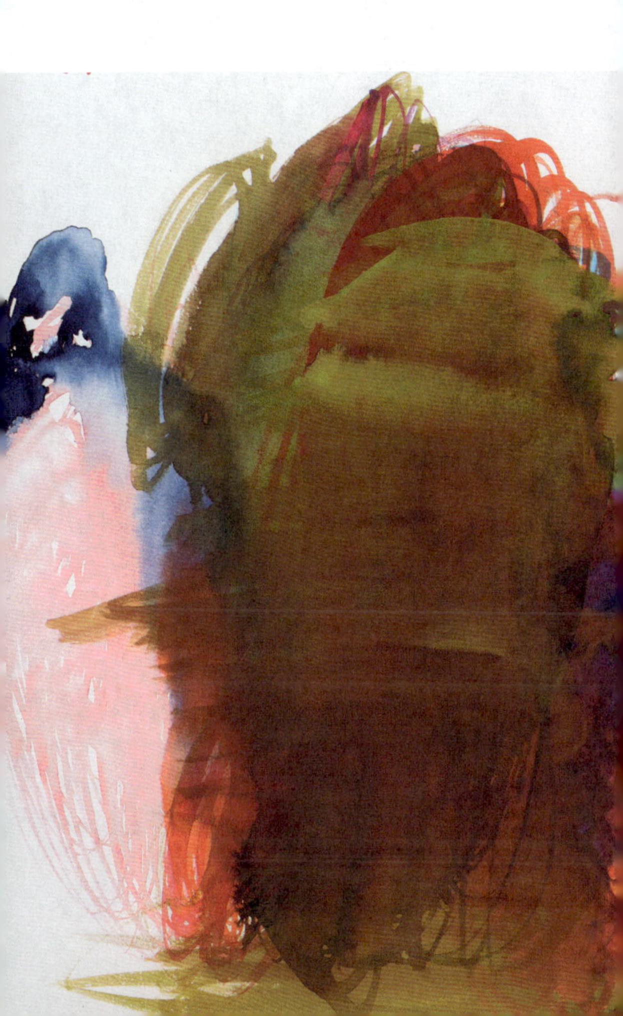

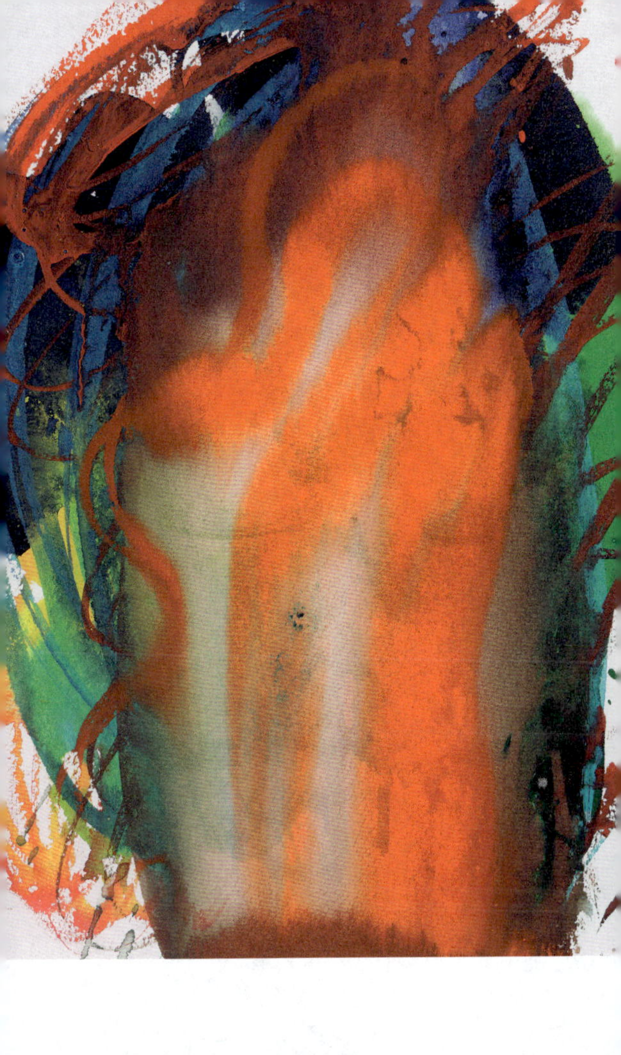

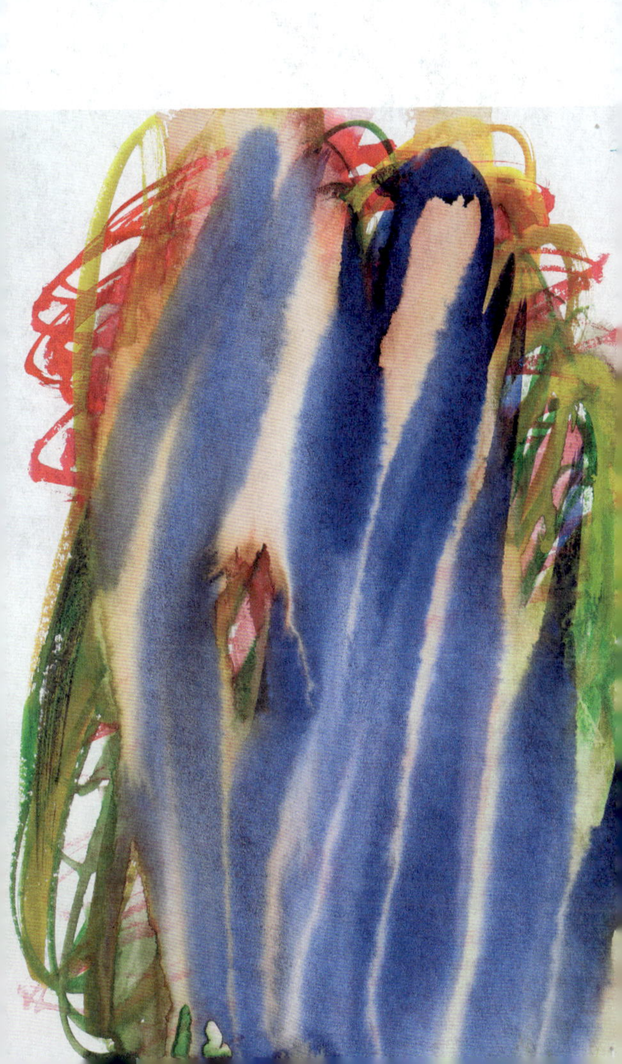

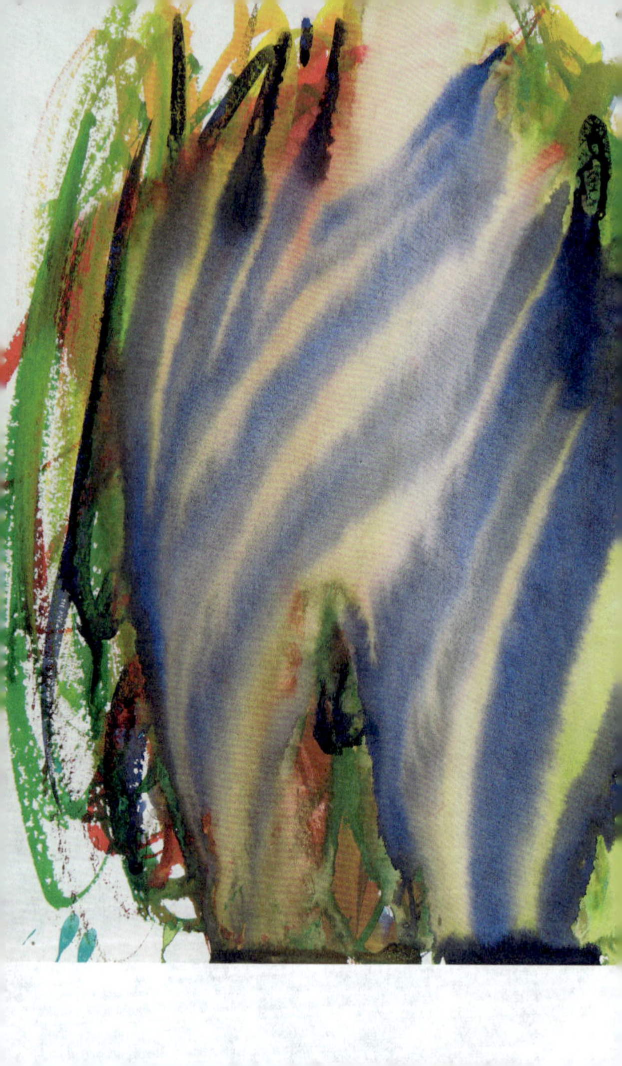

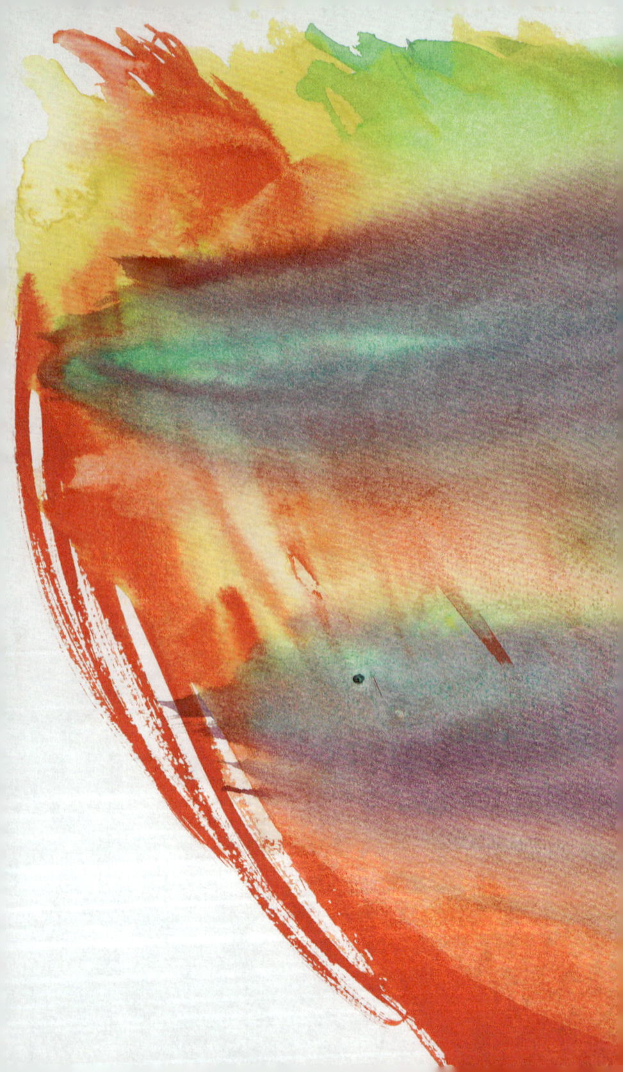

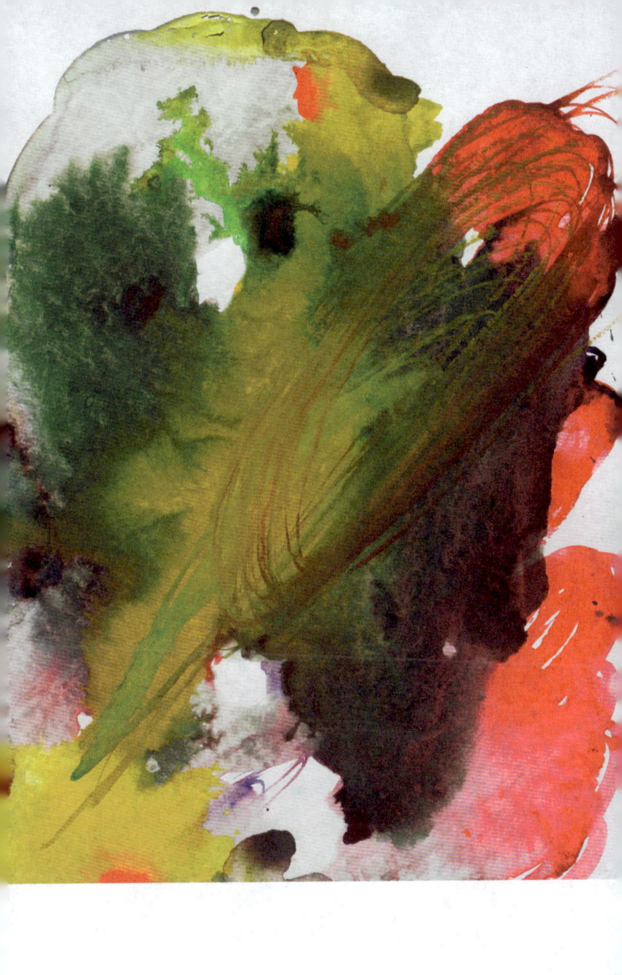

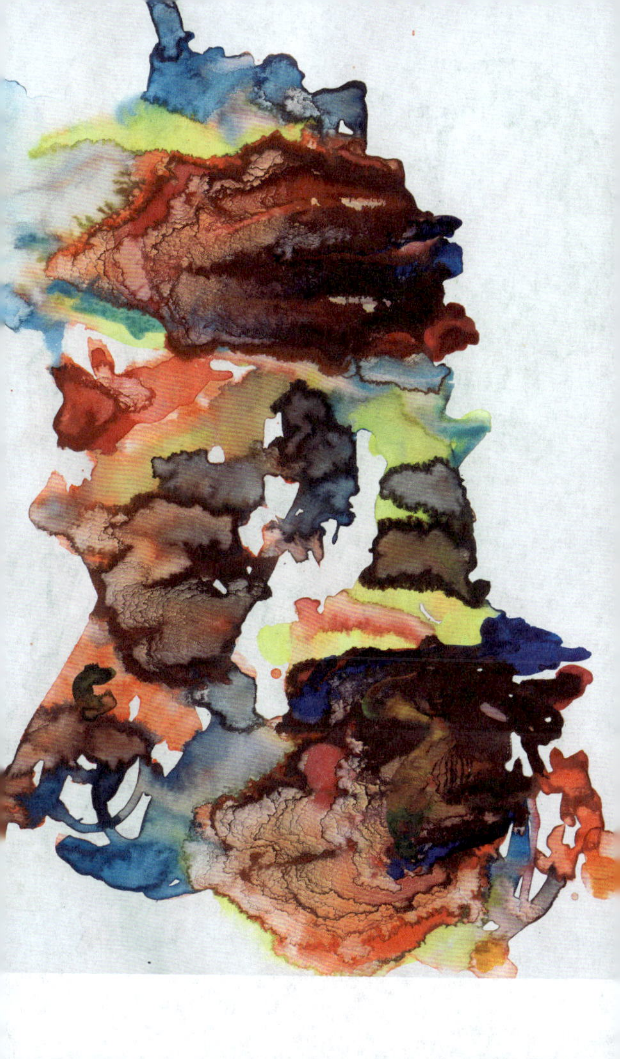

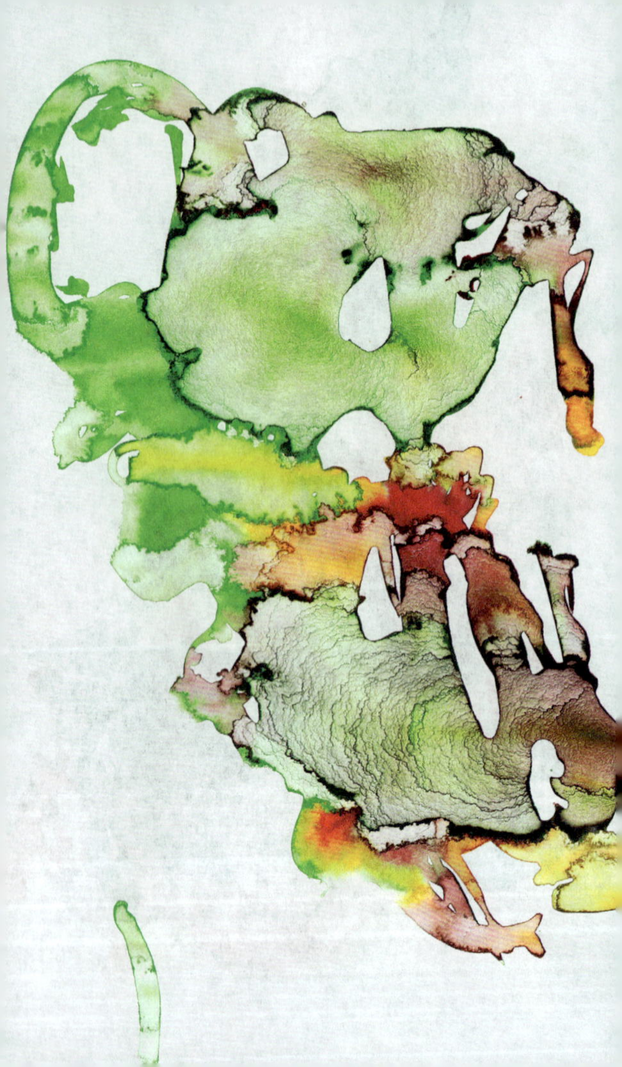

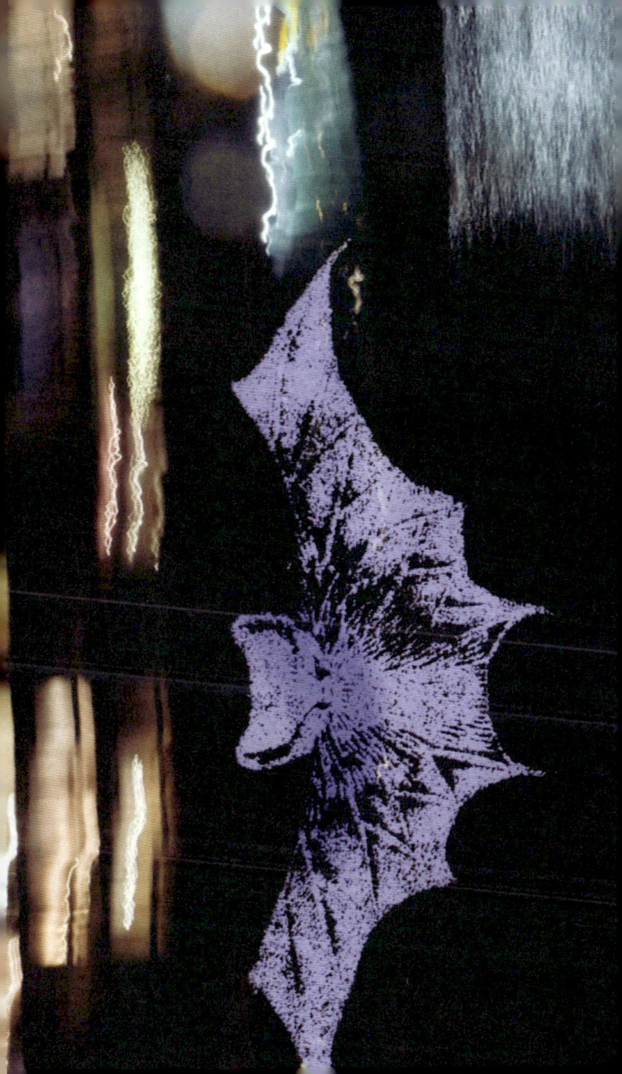

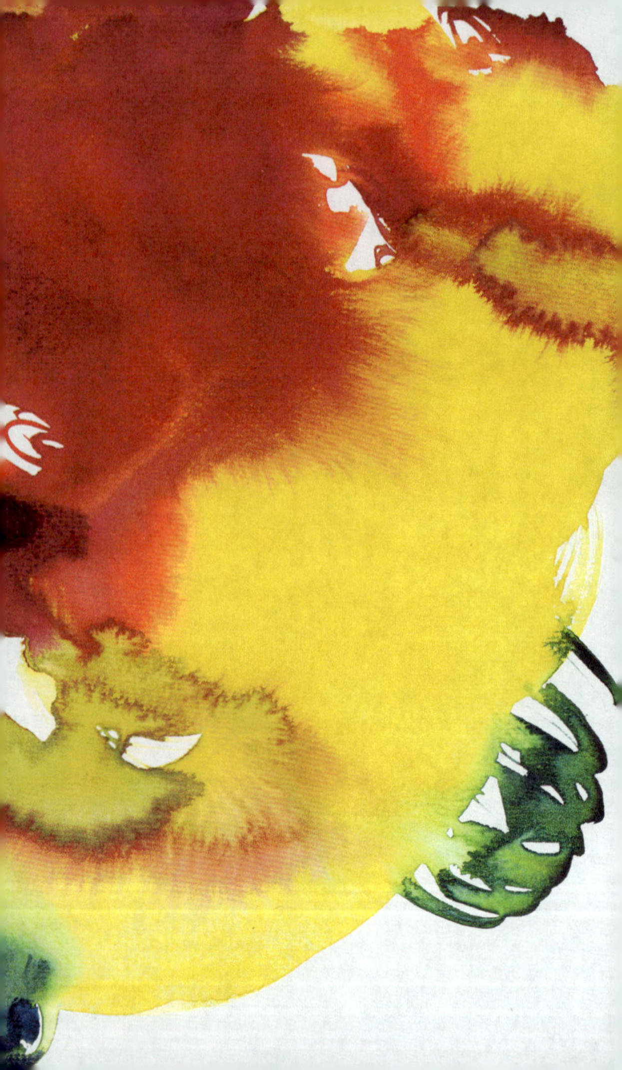

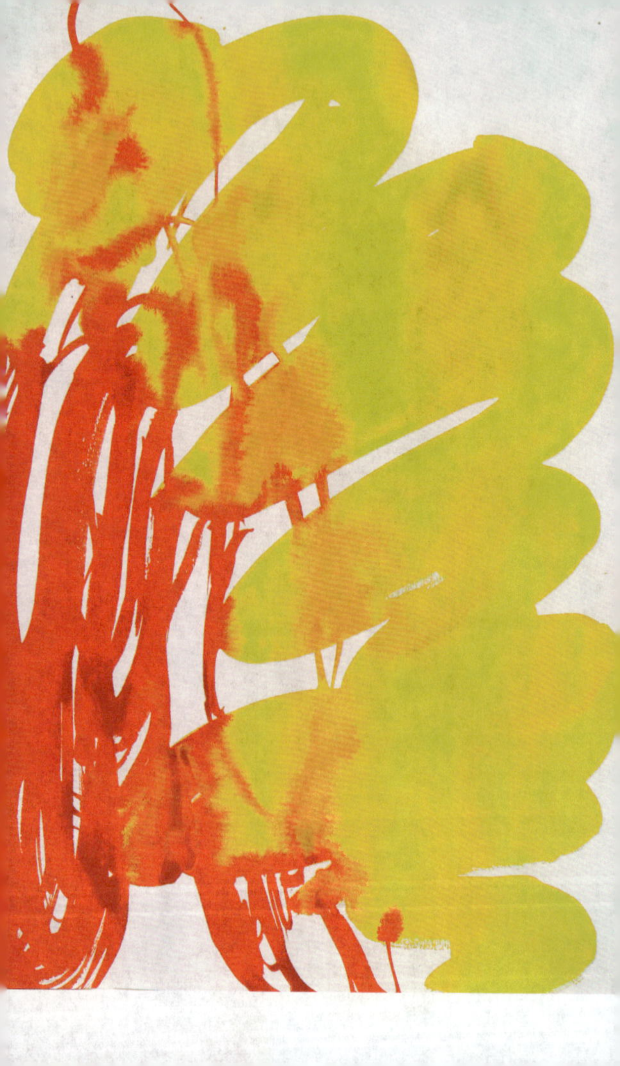

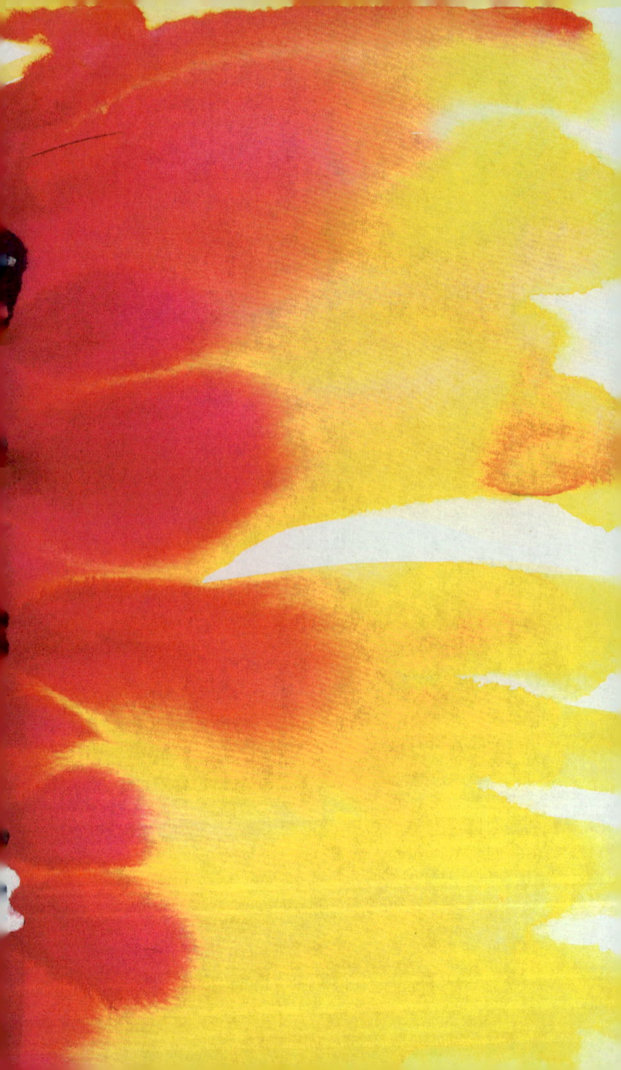

2

Leibniz

and

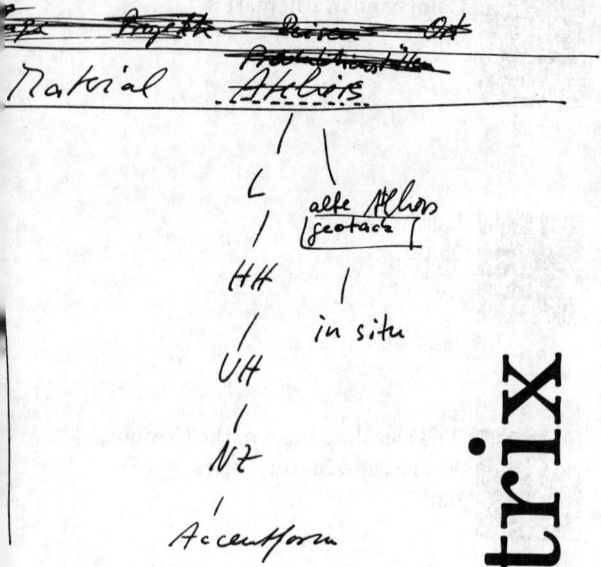

Material Ateliers

L

alte Ateliers

[geotaxis]

HH

in situ

UH

Nt

Accentform

the

Sepatrix

Colors and Mathematics
01:37

L as in Leibniz
03:01

The Desolate Rage in the Cosmos, Woods, and Mathematics
02:37

From Sigma to Omega
01:20

LEIBNIZ COMMENTS ON THE APPEARANCE OF FULLY FORMED, INTELLIGENT IMAGES IN THE MORNING RIGHT BEFORE WAKING

Leibniz was known for going to bed early and for sleeping up to twelve hours. Upon waking, he reports that—no longer asleep though not quite awake—he often saw letters and numbers when gazing into the "cap of his skull," even the finished form of arguments, proofs, "ideal constellations." These were "intelligent images," the message of which he would not have been able to put into words. But he always saw something whole, interrelated. Something that was not deducible from a single line of thought or axiom. This is the way the lively interplay—in the form of a great structure of Jacob's ladders—between GOD'S GENERAL HARMONY and the blind but nevertheless clever work of monads came to him as an image before he was able to reconstruct the vision in words. The initial image, richer than the text to come, was there even if it didn't reveal the individual steps it had taken to appear to his inner eye. "They also decayed rapidly with increasing wakefulness as soon as the limbs of my body stirred." The prerequisite for such a phenomenon, Leibniz comments, was obviously that the body was still at rest, that it did not disturb the animal. "A fine web."

LEIBNIZ'S MILL (1714)
("perception and that which depends upon it are inexplicable on mechanical grounds")

"And supposing there were a machine, so constructed as to think, feel, and have perception, it might be conceived as increased in size, while keeping the same proportions, so that one might go into it as into a mill. That being so, we should, on examining its interior, find only parts which work one upon another, and never anything by which to explain a perception. Thus it is in a simple substance, and not in a compound or in a machine, that perception must be sought for. Further, nothing but this (namely, perceptions and their changes) can be found in a simple substance."
[trans. Robert Latta, 1898]

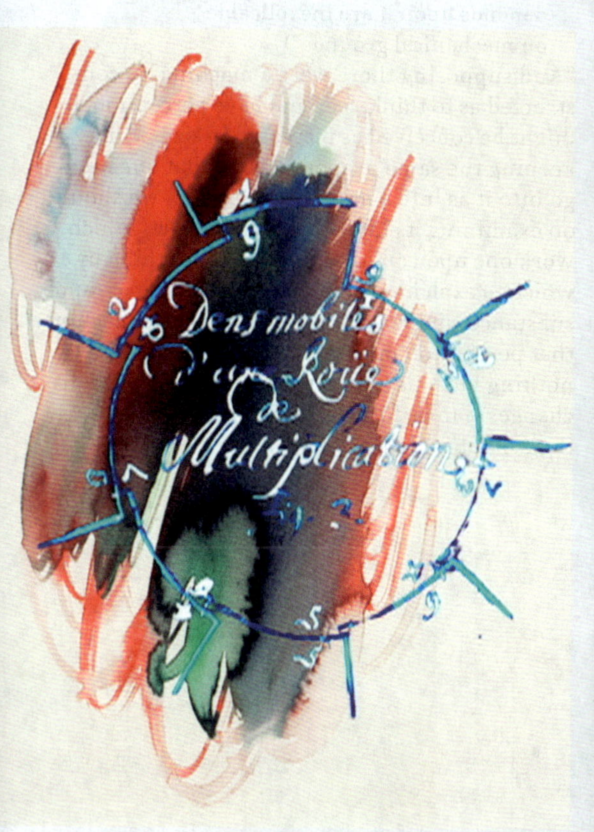
Dens mobiles
d'une Roüe
de
Multiplication

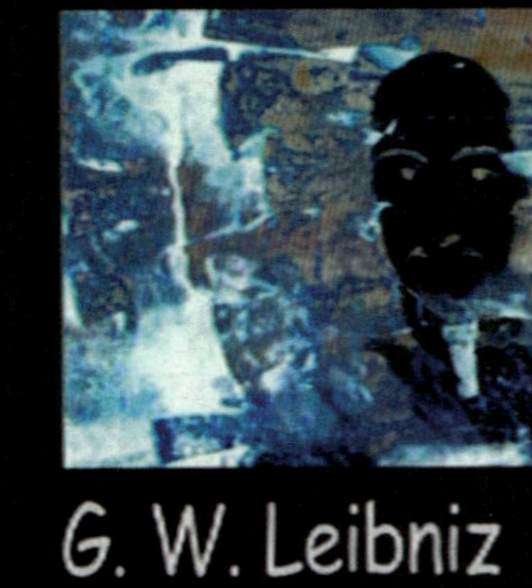
G. W. Leibniz

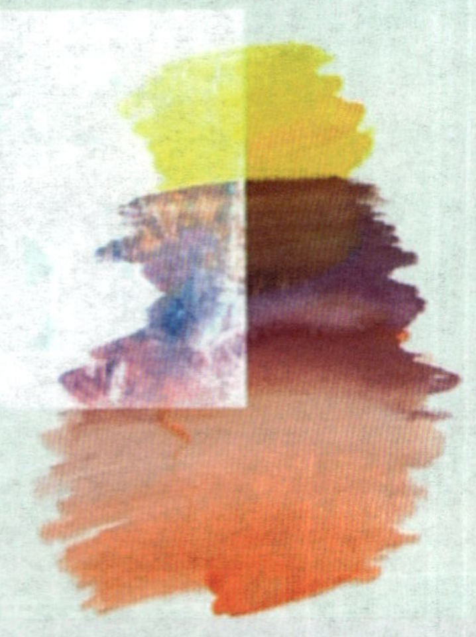

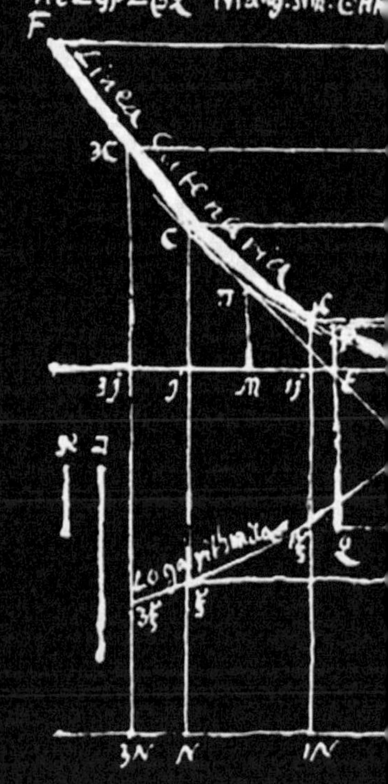
G.G.L De Lin
Linea Catenaria
Logarithmica
3N
N
1N

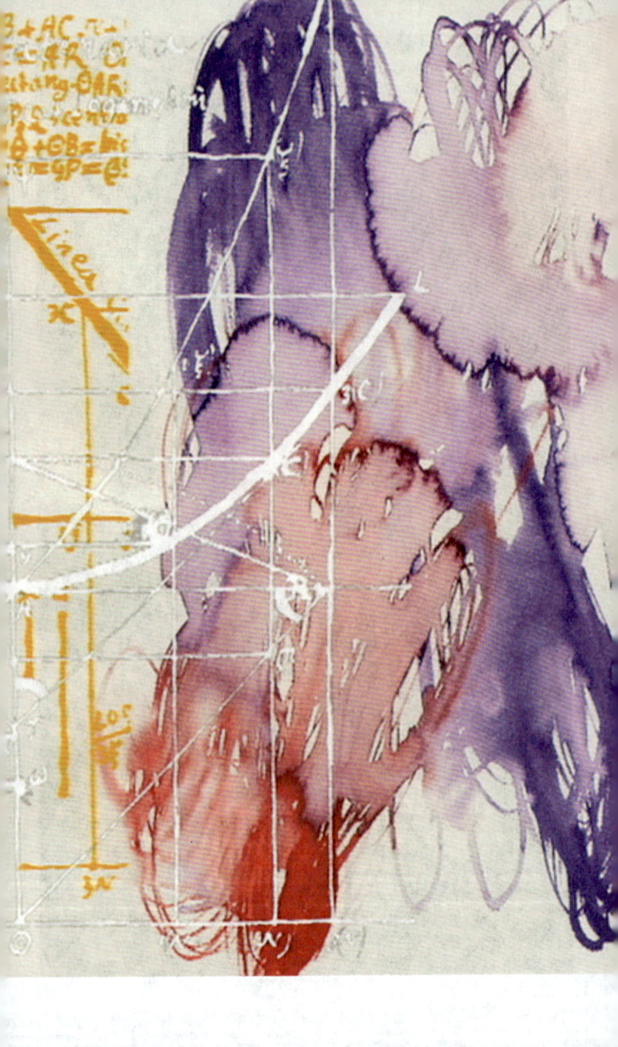

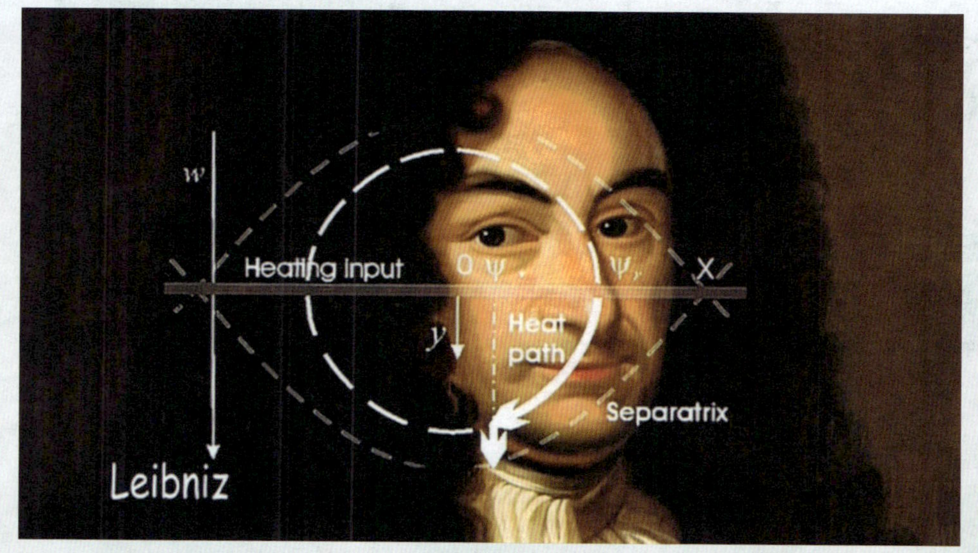
w
Heating Input
0
ψ
X
y
Heat
path
Separatrix
Leibniz

Separatrix folgt

aus $\mathcal{H}(\psi) = \mathcal{H}(\psi_1^{\text{max}})$

$\psi_s] = -\frac{\Omega_S^2}{\cos\psi_s}\left[\cos(\pi - \psi)\right.$

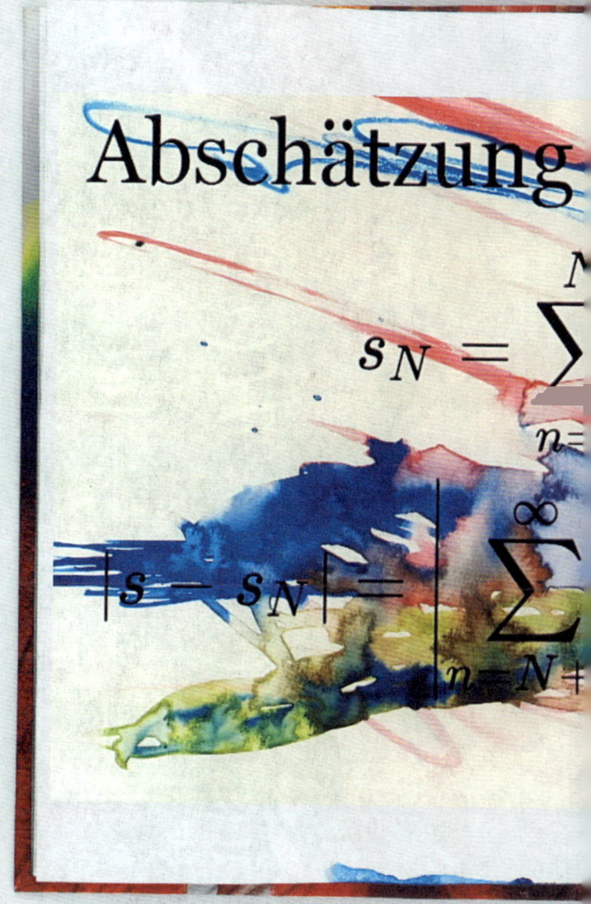
Abschätzung
$s_N =$
$|s - s_N| =$

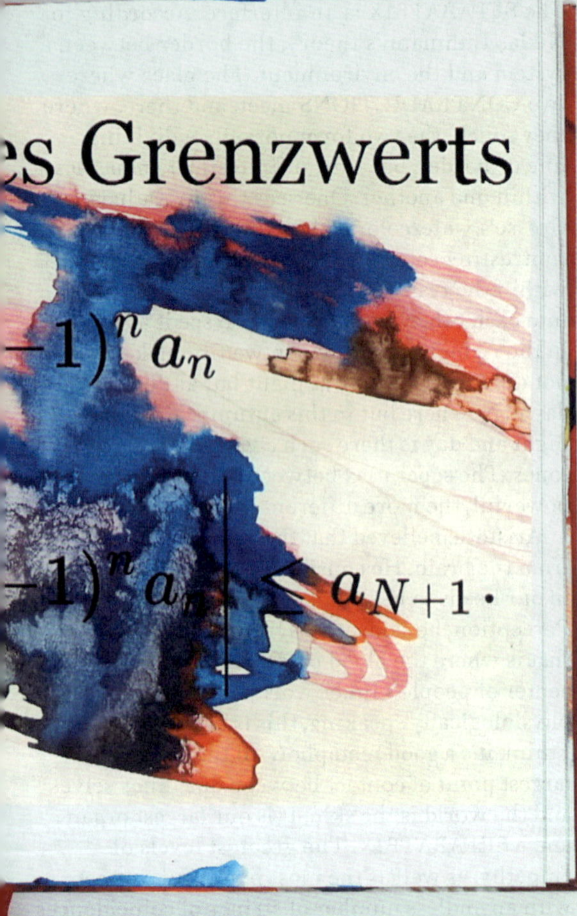
es Grenzwerts
$-1)^n a_n$
$-1)^n a_n \Big| \leq a_{N+1}$.

KEYWORD: "SEPARATRIX"

The SEPARATRIX is an interface. According to Niklas Luhmann's theory, the border between a system and the environment. The place where two CONTRADICTIONS meet, and there, where they touch, the two form not only a dividing line or border, but tiny, infinitesimal embassies within one another. One sees this in Katharina Grosse's watercolors where blue and red (that is, contrasting colors) beget countless nuances within the transitional spaces where they bleed into each other. But one can also see it at work in the rich gray tones when we filmmakers shoot not during the day or at night but at dusk and dawn. Nowhere but in this autumnal interface of night and day is there such a vast scale of gray tones. The separatrix between artists—the more powerful, the more different they are—is similar.

Aristotle believed that thought did not come from the brain. He considered the neural cells in our heads to be a kind of refrigeration system. Perception, he said, comes from the heart, for that is where the blood pulses, and the heart is the center of people's inner world. We know that, physiologically speaking, this is not the case, but I think it's a good metaphor. All the same, the largest point of contact between our inner selves and the world is the skin. It is our largest organ and a SEPARATRIX. The greatest levels of empathy, as well as the most bountiful contact with an endless number of strings of coincidences

(both are the crucial mixture in art, film, and literature), are to be found "at skin level."

Katharina Grosse and I came to the term SEPARATRIX through G.W. Leibniz. He was fascinated by this "interface in all things." Katharina Grosse then titled her exhibition of watercolors in Rome *The SEPARATRIX Project*. The online event "The Theory of Separatrix" (November 24, 2020, introduced by Gagosian director Louise Neri), brought together Katharina Grosse (from her studio in New Zealand), Alexander Kluge (from Munich), and Joachim Bernauer and Julia Draganović (from Grosse's exhibition at Gagosian Rome) to discuss the friction between film, watercolor, and discourse as an expression of modernity. THE CONTRADICTIONS of the trade that nevertheless respond to one another. The demand of the hour: abundant incongruities. What keeps art connected to reality is not creative drive, which is self-evident, but that generosity that a stream of chance lets in the door.

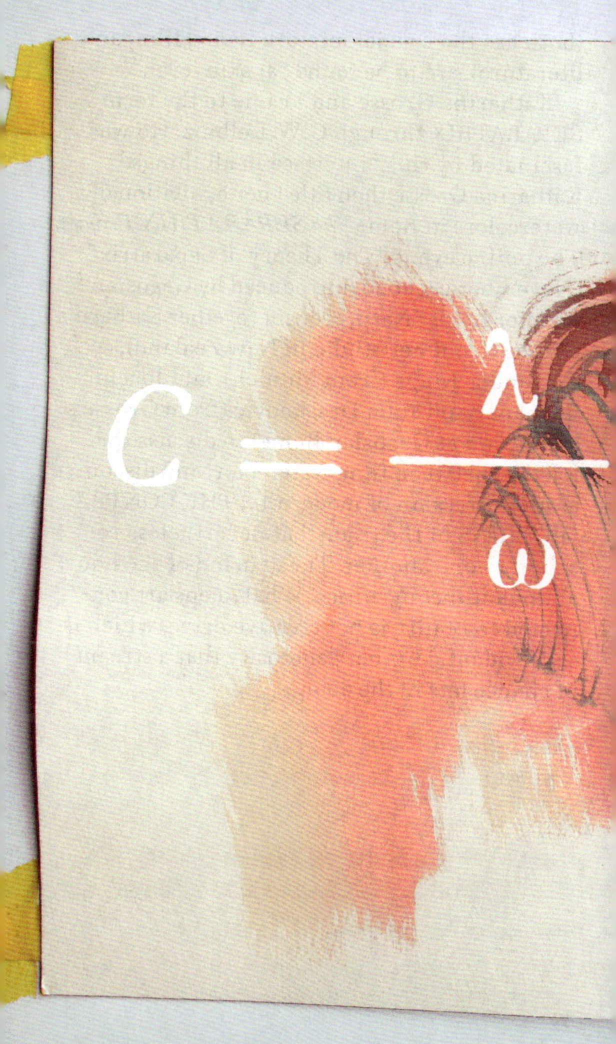
$C = \frac{\lambda}{\omega}$

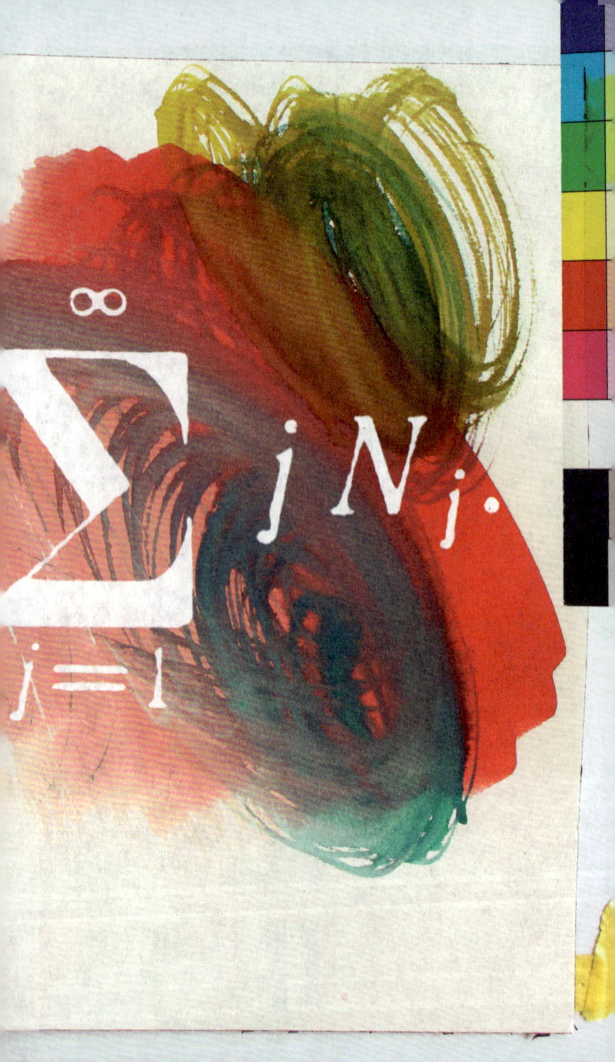
$\sum_{j=1}^{\infty} j N_j.$

Similiter (in figura tertia) ubi objectum supponitur in medio densiore, oculus in rariore, et linea separatrix arcus circuli, inventis ex lege refractionis lineis visualibus, si in illis sumatur G K

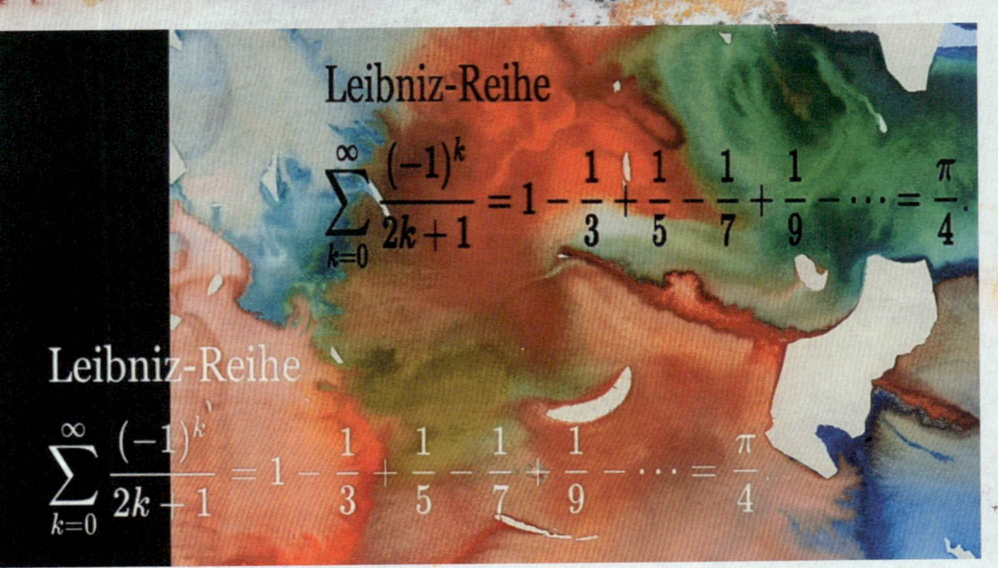
Leibniz-Reihe
$\sum_{k=0}^{\infty} \frac{(-1)^k}{2k+1} = 1 - \frac{1}{3} + \frac{1}{5} - \frac{1}{7} + \frac{1}{9} - \dots = \frac{\pi}{4}.$
Leibniz-Reihe
$\sum_{k=0}^{\infty} \frac{(-1)^k}{2k+1} = 1 - \frac{1}{3} + \frac{1}{5} - \frac{1}{7} + \frac{1}{9} - \dots = \frac{\pi}{4}$

$$\left(\frac{\Delta E}{E_0}\right)_{\mathrm{max}} \propto \sqrt{\frac{eU_0 \sin \psi_s}{E_0}}$$

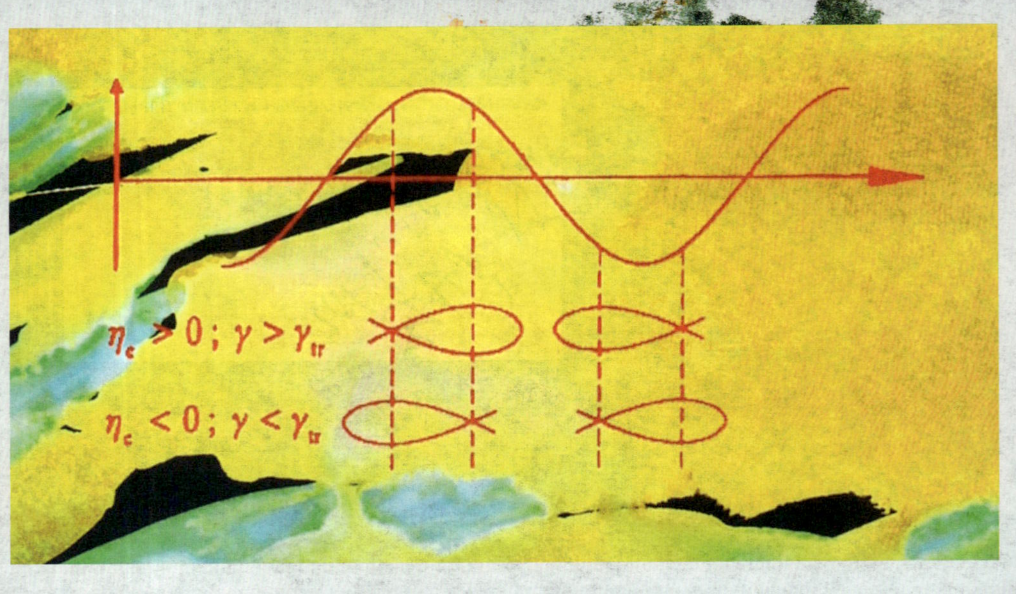
$\eta_c > 0; \gamma > \gamma_{tr}$
$\eta_c < 0; \gamma < \gamma_{tr}$

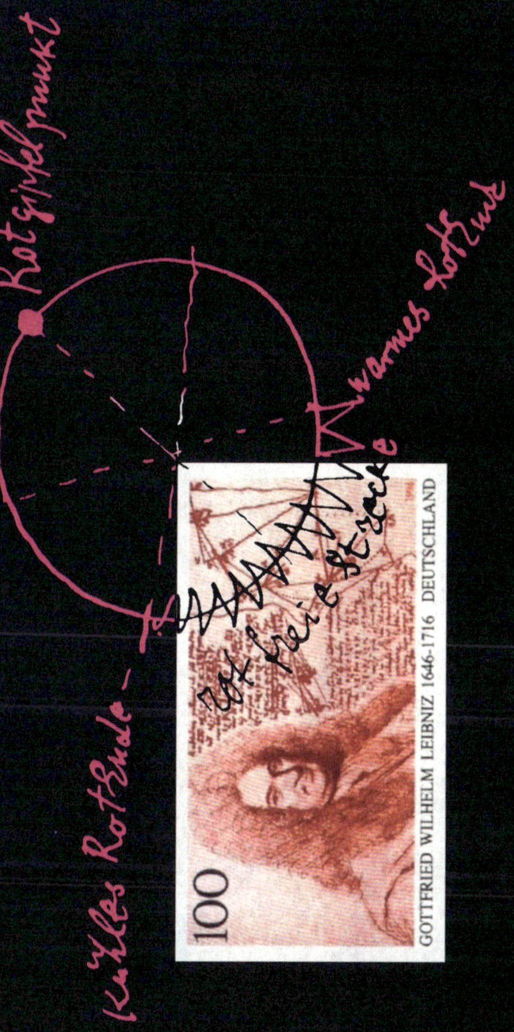

Rotgipfelpunkt

kühles RotEnde

rotfreie Strecke

warmes RotEnde

100

GOTTFRIED WILHELM LEIBNIZ 1646-1716 DEUTSCHLAND

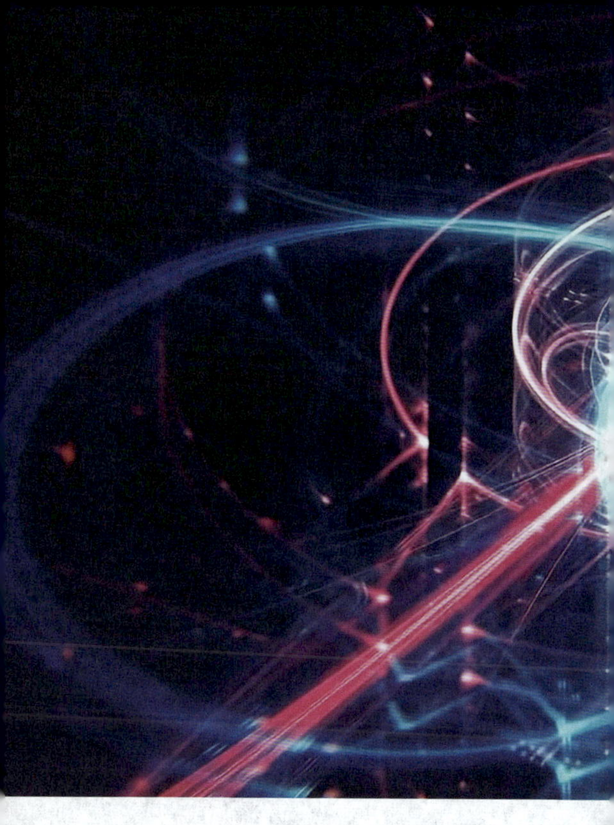

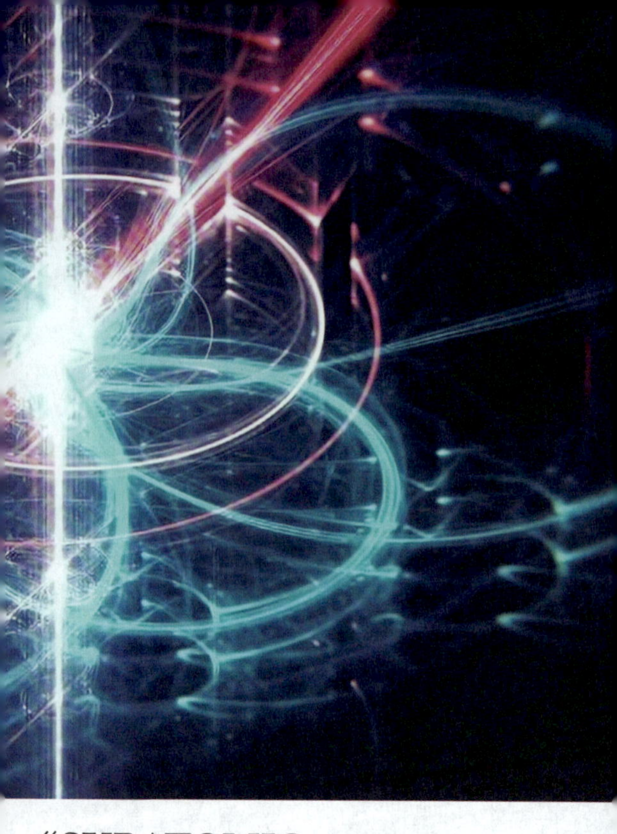

“SUBATOMIC ELEMENTARY PARTICLES IN FREE MOTION”

3

Palimpsests, Foreign Planets

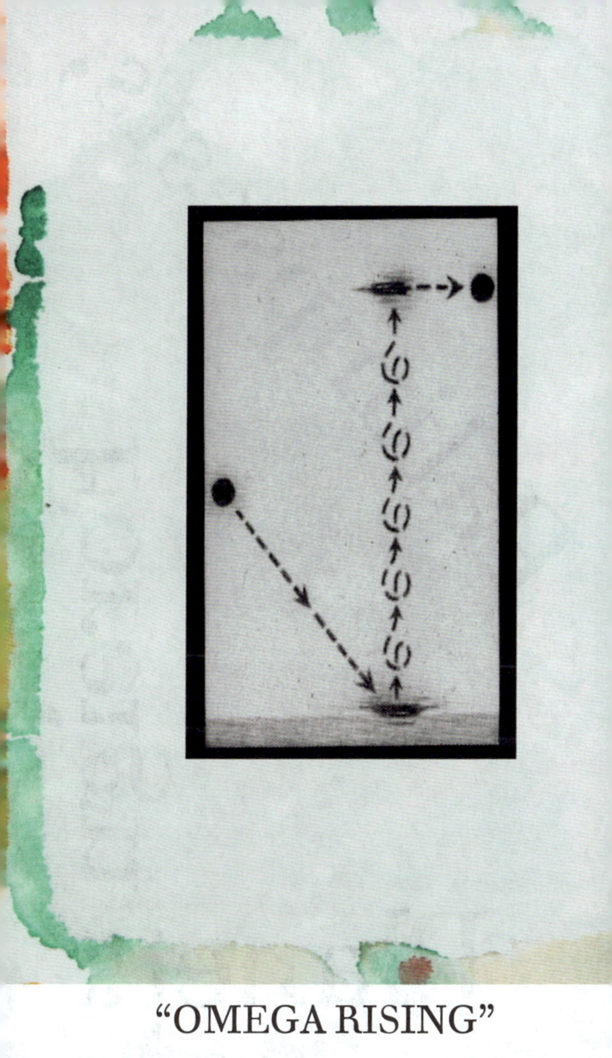

"OMEGA RISING"

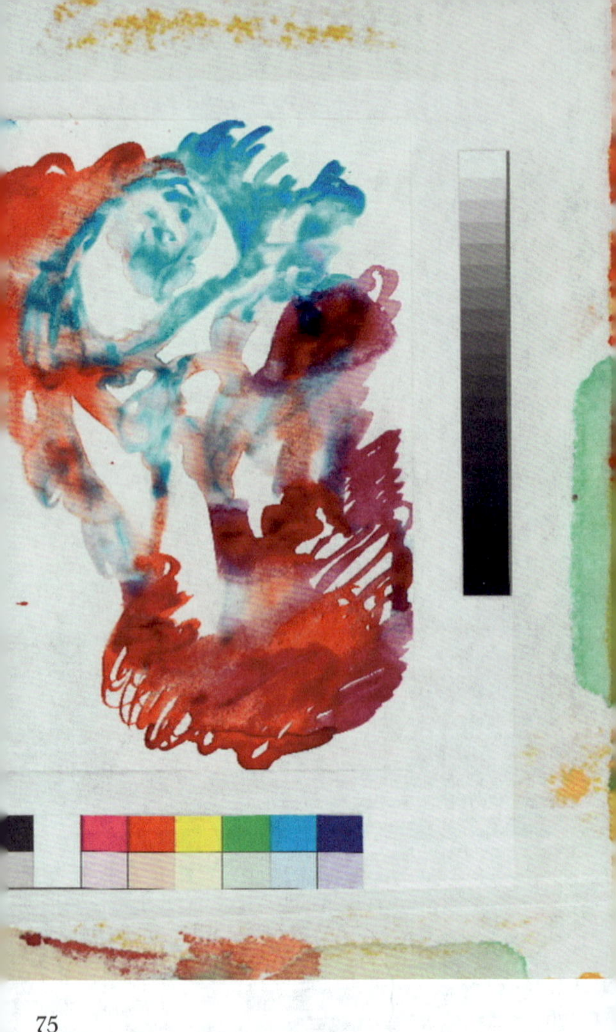

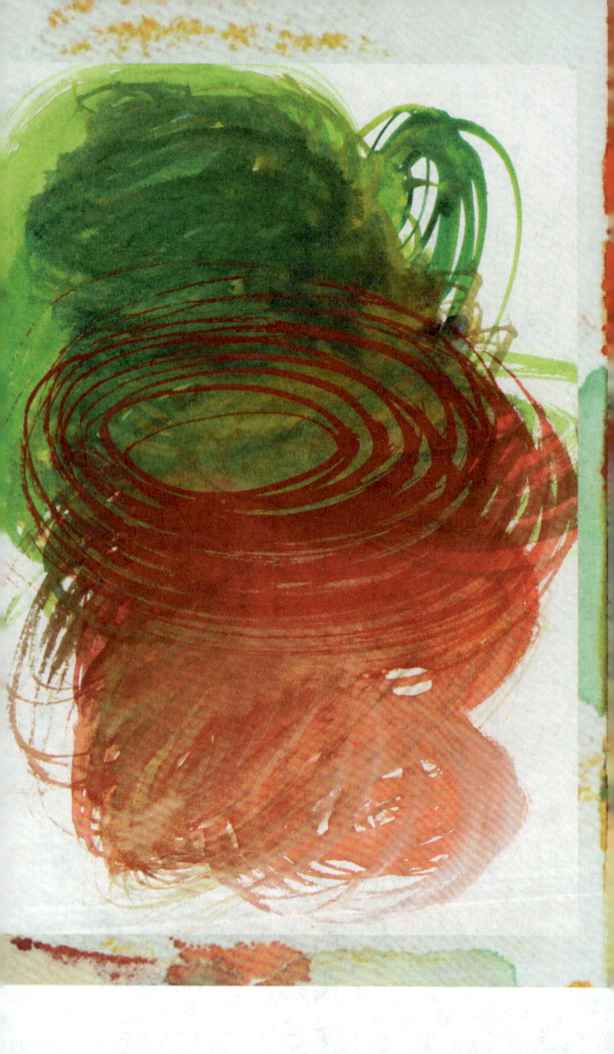

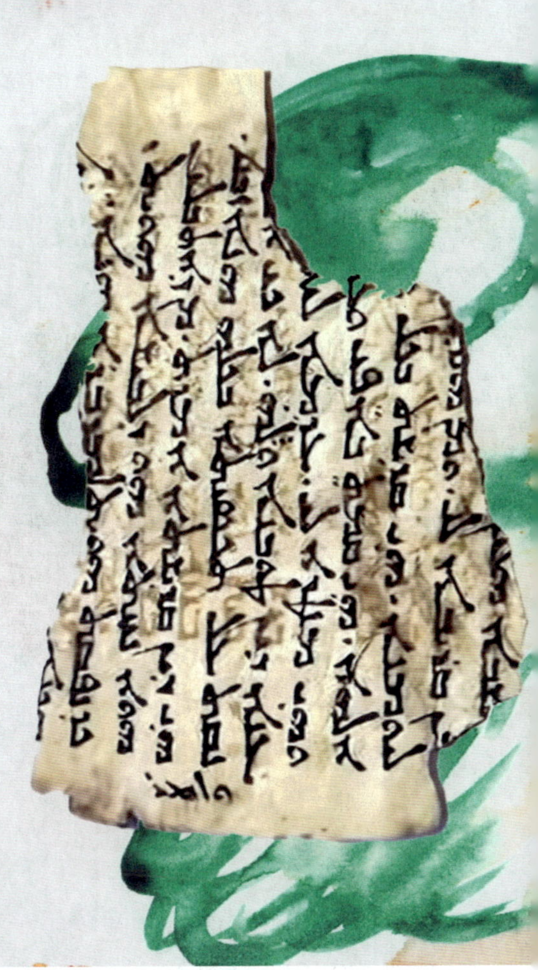

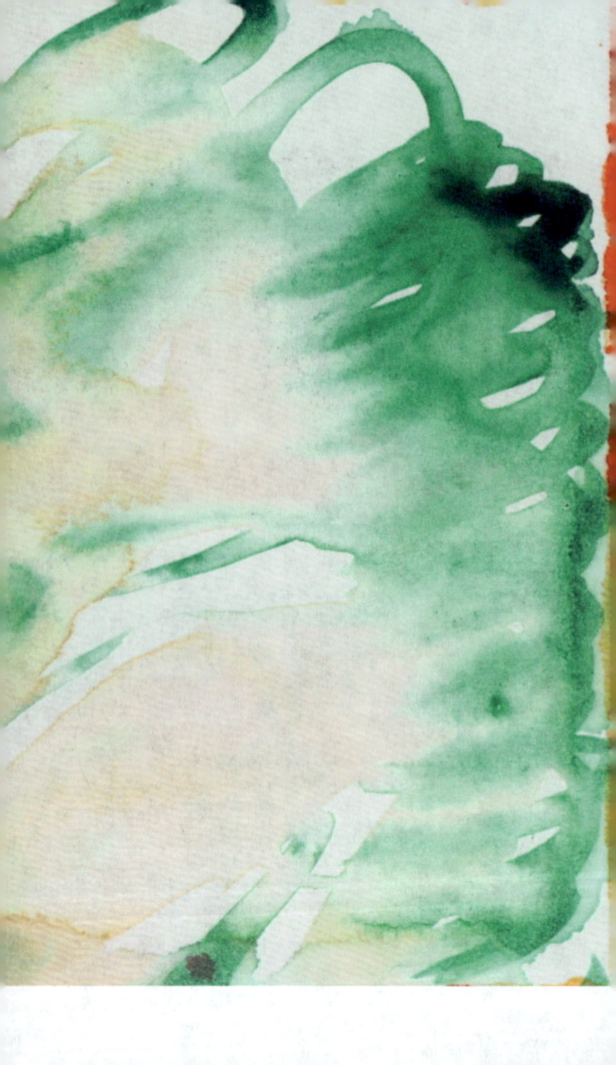

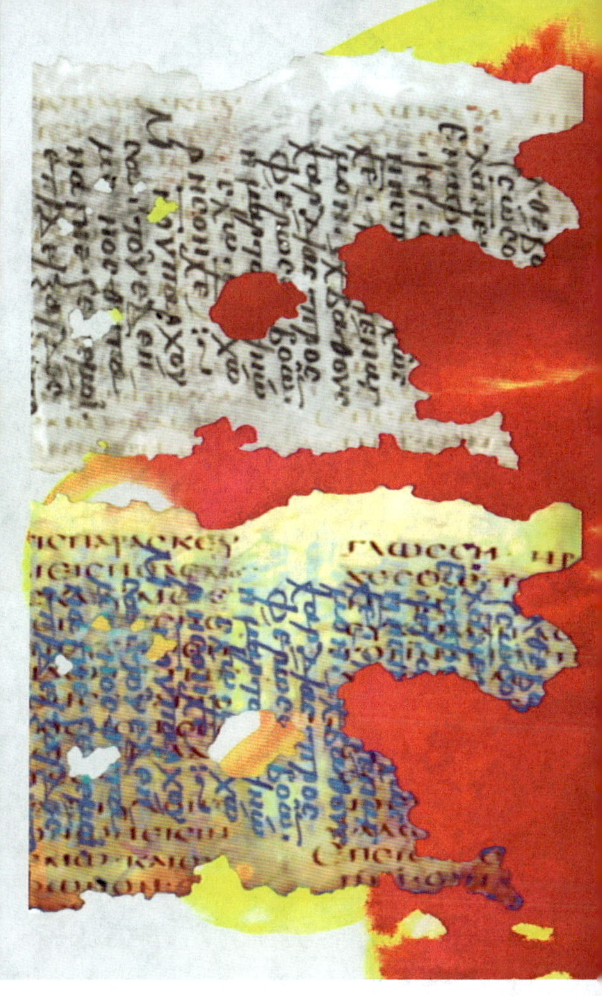

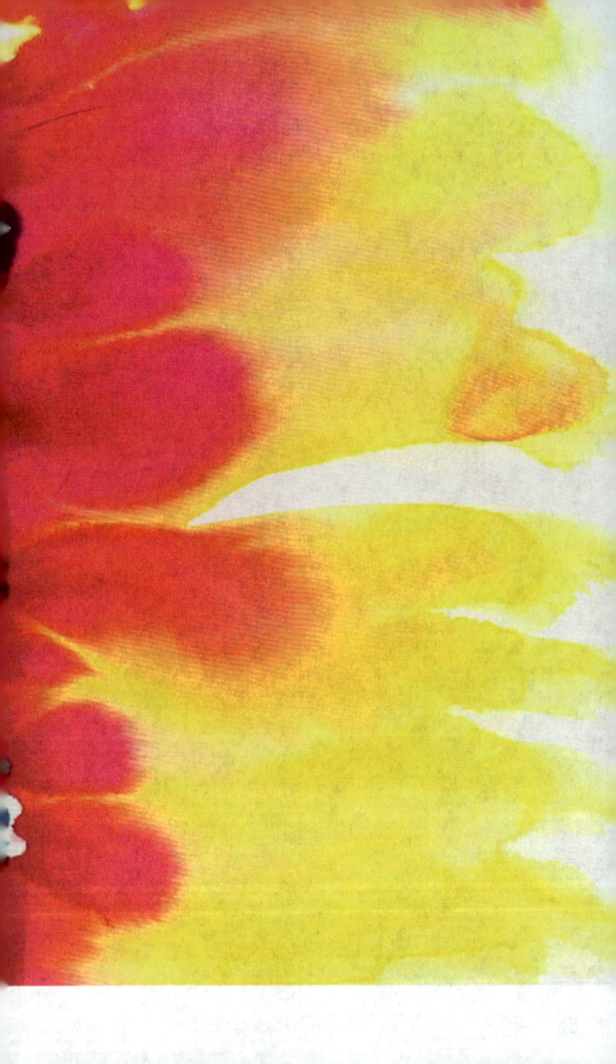

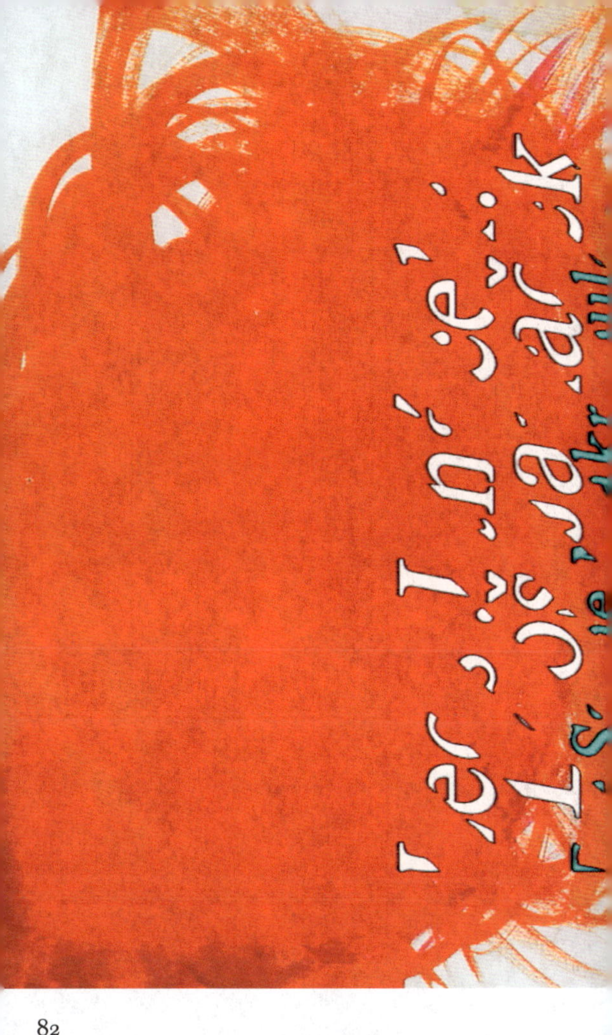

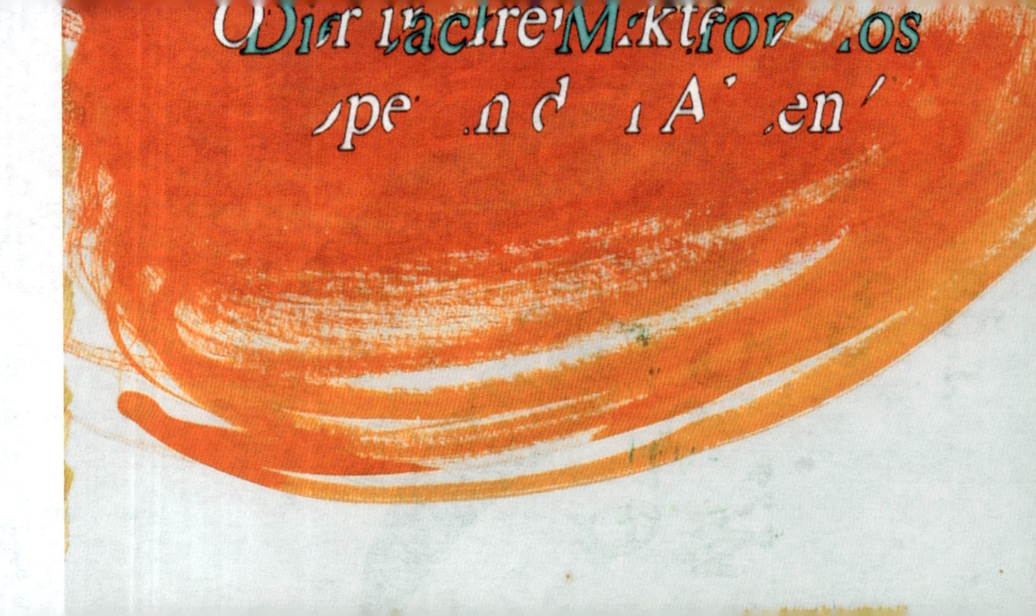

r d

de as

wi e

e ig

Le er

I of

ve naff

ersc it/

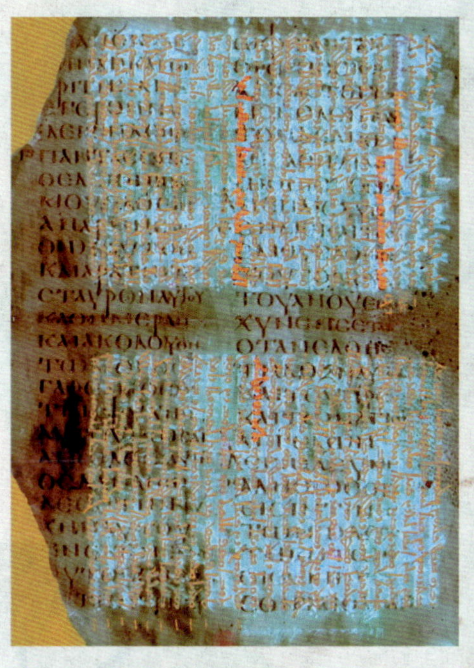

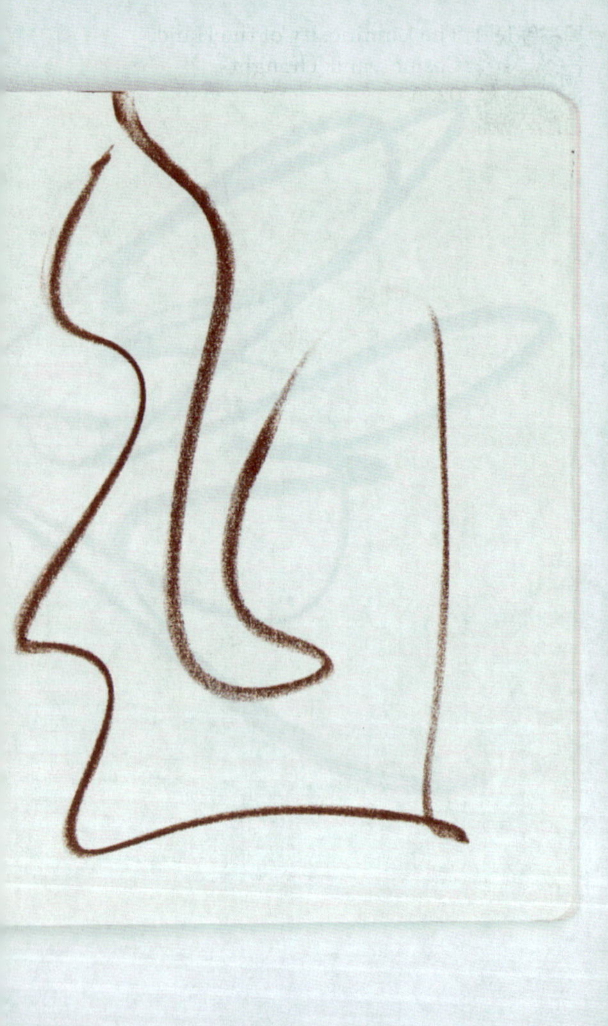

The Luminosity of the Hand,
Cosmos, and Thought
02:15

KEYWORD: "PALIMPSESTS"

In antiquity PALIMPSESTS were manuscript pages, often of papyrus, which were written on more than once. Just as an archaeologist explores the surface of the ground to uncover finds from earlier periods of history, palimpsests provide an incentive to unearth "writings hidden beneath a piece of writing," in the most literal sense of the word SUBTEXTS.

In this context, we also debated Sigmund Freud's text on the "Mystic Writing Pad." Texts, music, works of visual art, and even scientific writings initially coexist in the public sphere. But they can also communicate with each other vertically.

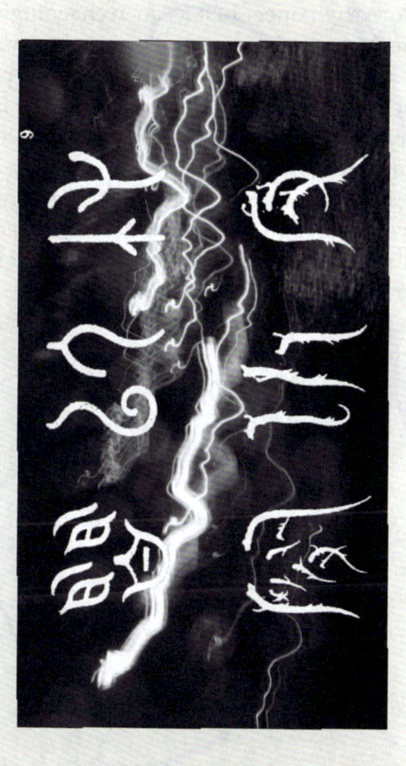

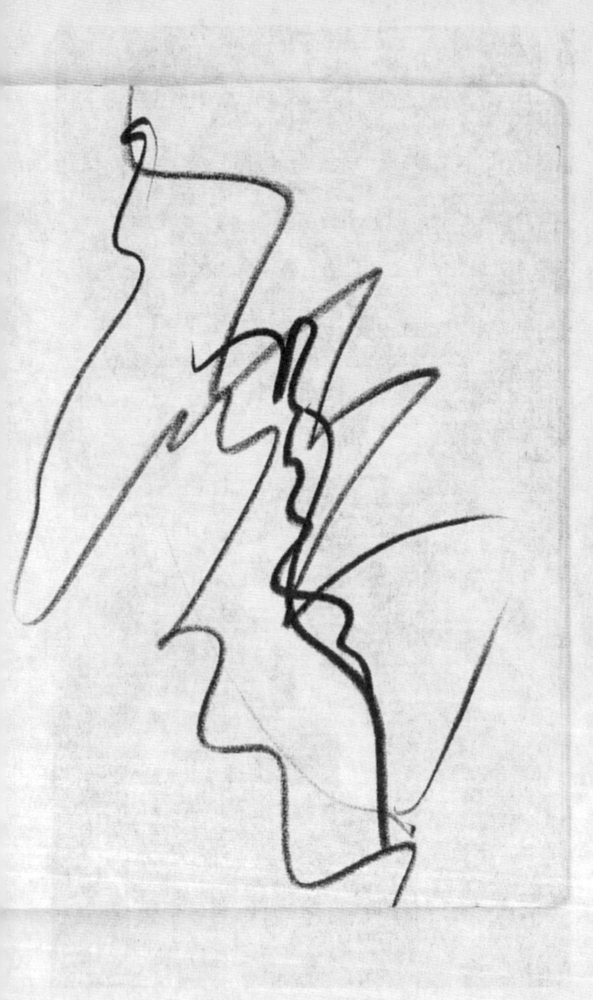

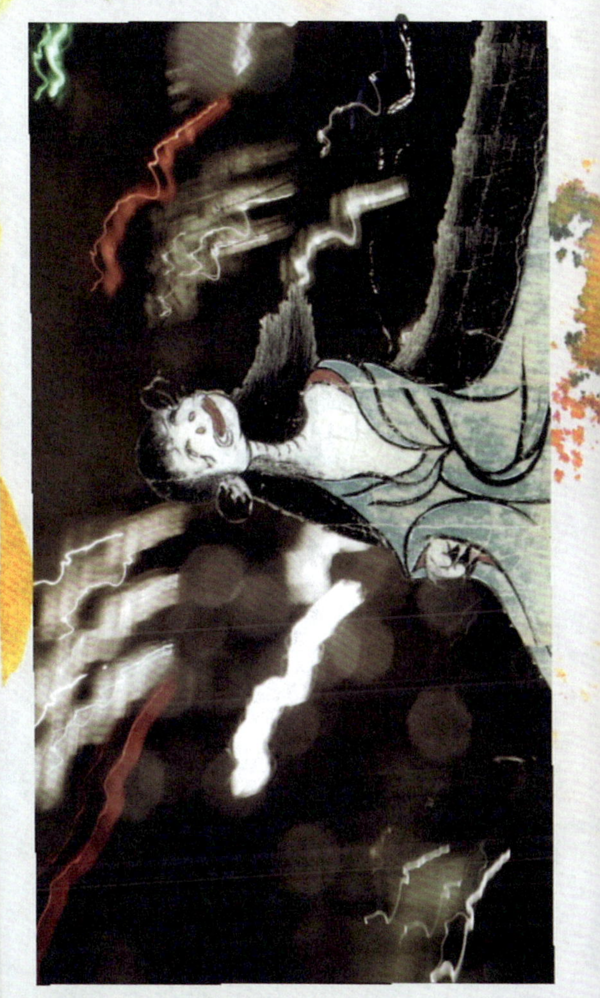

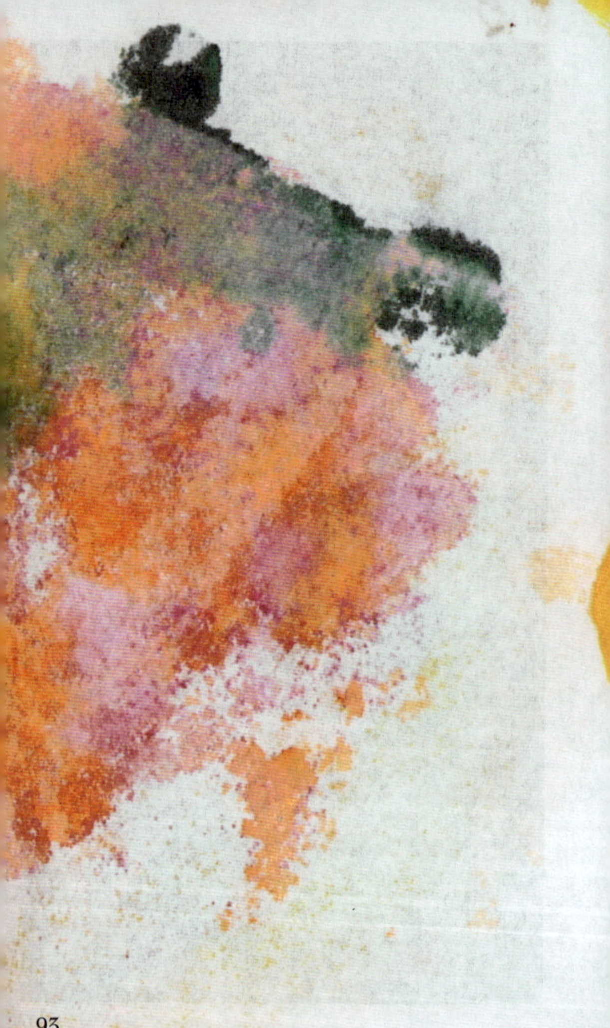

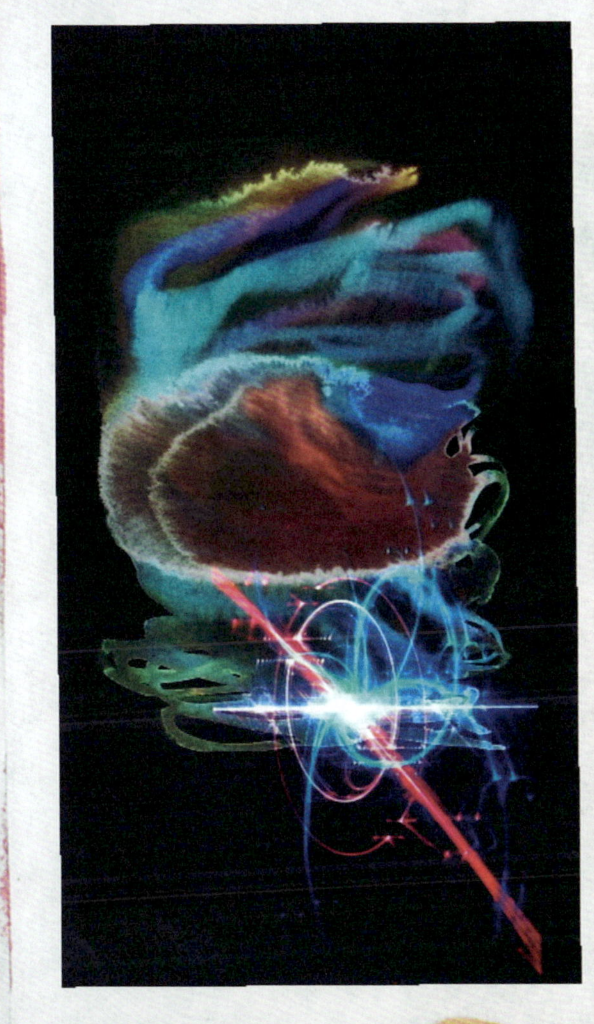

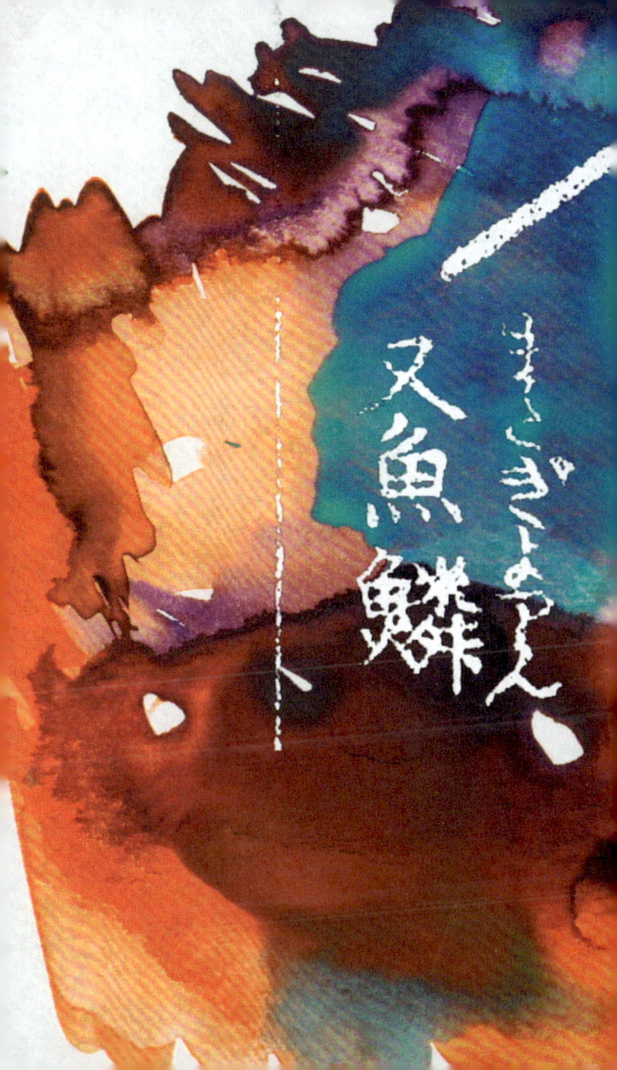
又魚鱗
またぎょりん

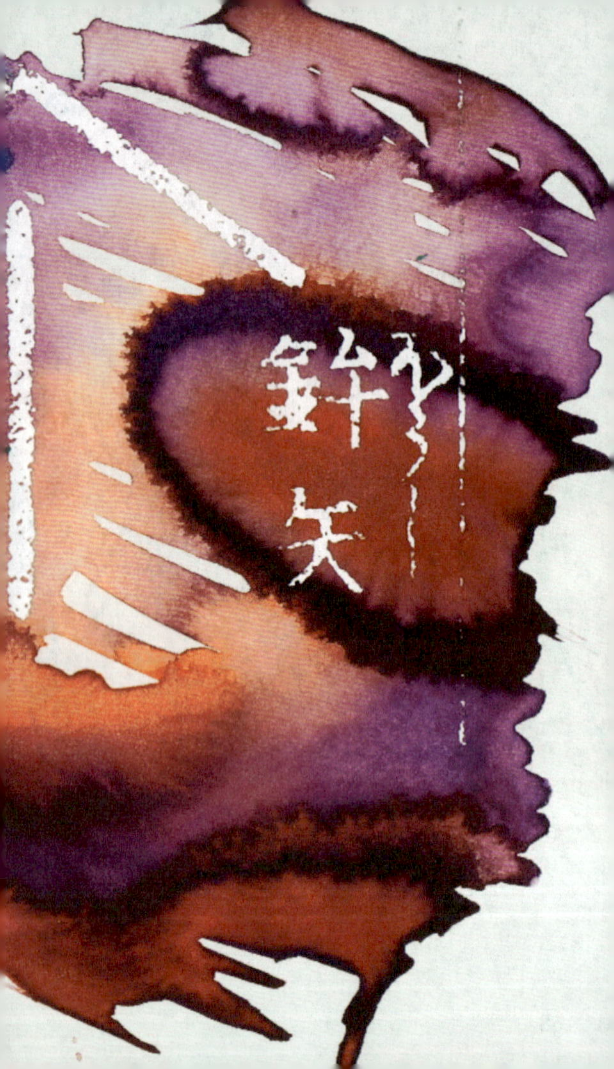
針矢

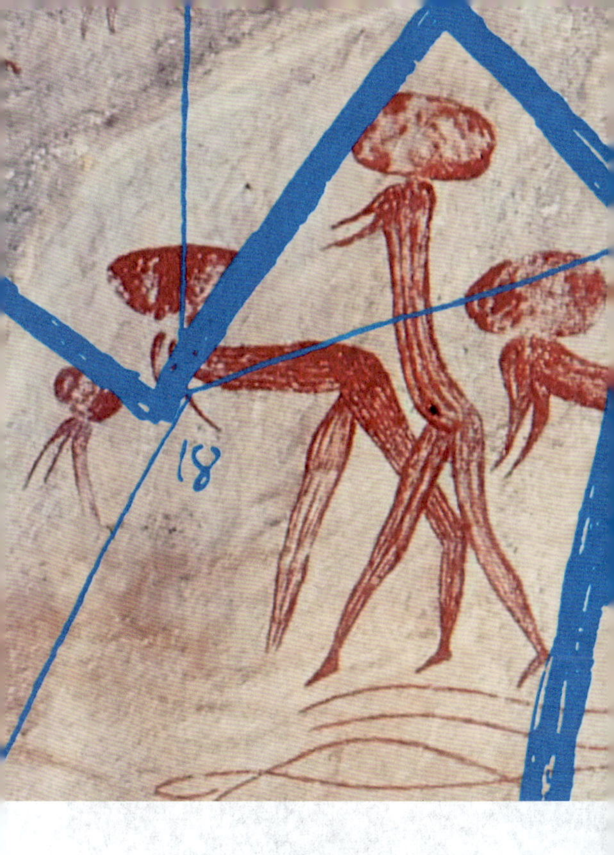
18

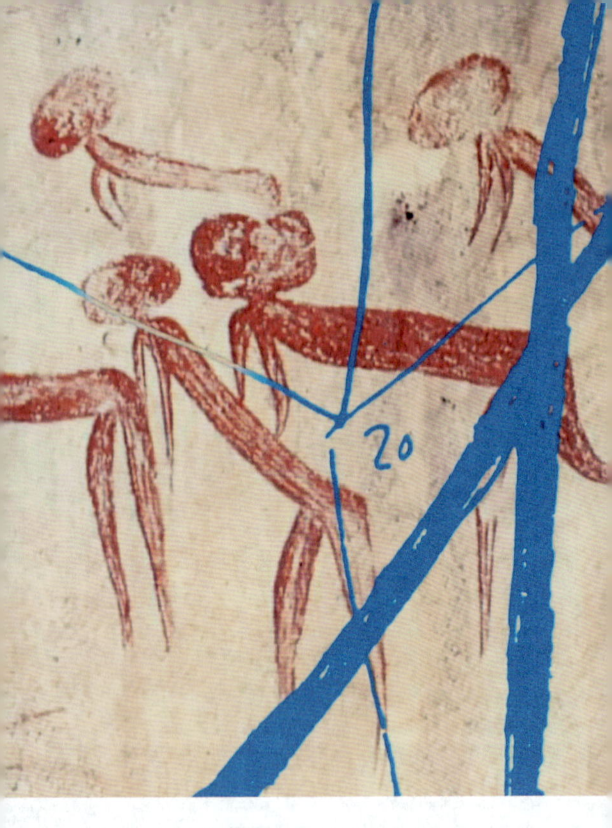

“SKITTERING” ANCESTORS
IN FLIGHT.
PAINTED BY THEMSELVES
ON THE WALL OF A CAVE

29 DECEMBER 21,999 BCE
Ice Age. In terms of climate one has to imagine this peak of cold (we are still living in the same ice age, though not in the Great Ice Age but the little one) as like a late afternoon in the Engadine in the Swiss Alps in December, said Alexei Tikhonov, scientific secretary of the Mammoth Committee of the Russian Academy of Sciences. No colder?, asked Sylvie Charbit. Cold enough, if you can't find any fuel on the bare steppe and there's a lack of habitations.

In those days a weather forecast would have gone like this, continued the Russian: there has been a high-pressure area over Europe for two years. The incessant wind, blowing from the pack ice, brings very cold, dry air into the region. An end to the extreme dryness, to the constant northeast wind, to the great quantities of dust it bears is not expected for the next four thousand years. From one in the afternoon the temperature falls below freezing.

And human beings flitted across the dry steppe that no longer exists today (with its grasses, nutritious herbs, but no trees)? Our ancestors, replied Tikhonov, did not "flit" but searched, investigated, and hunted in a race against death. If they did not find something quickly, they starved.

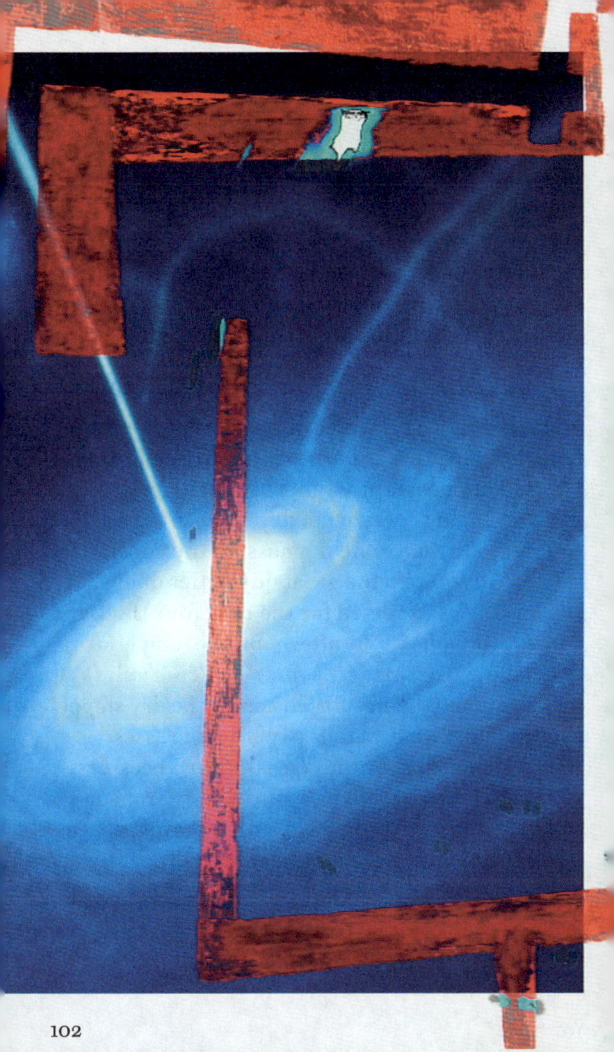

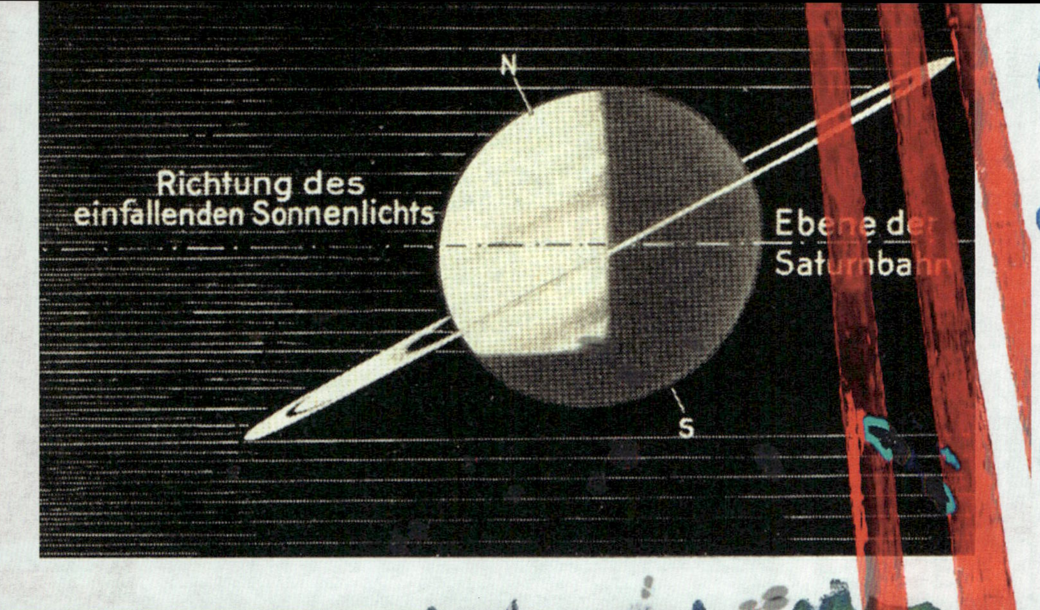
N
Richtung des
einfallenden Sonnenlichts
Ebene der
Saturnbahn
S

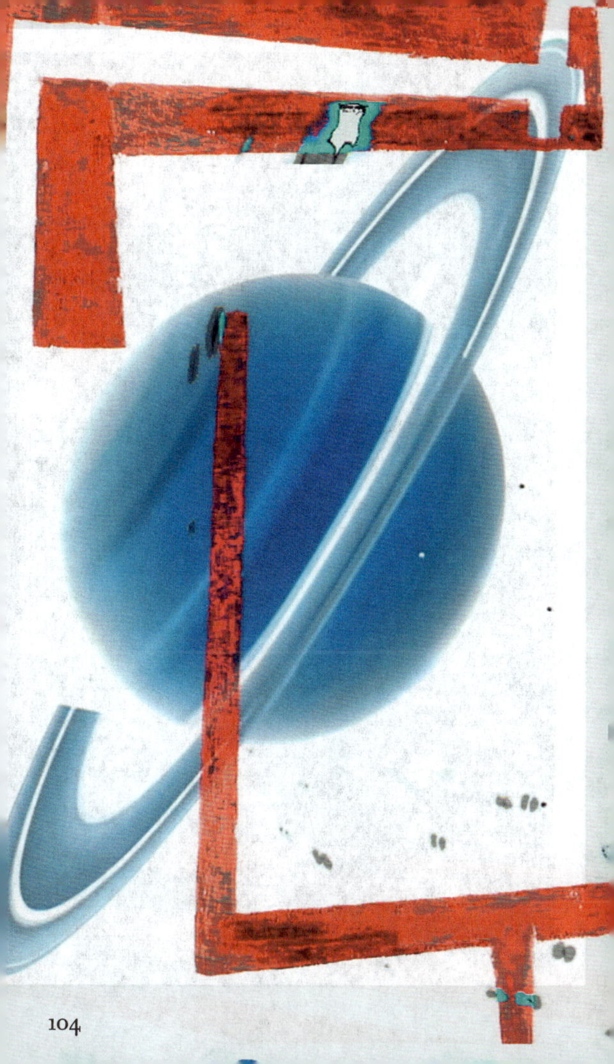

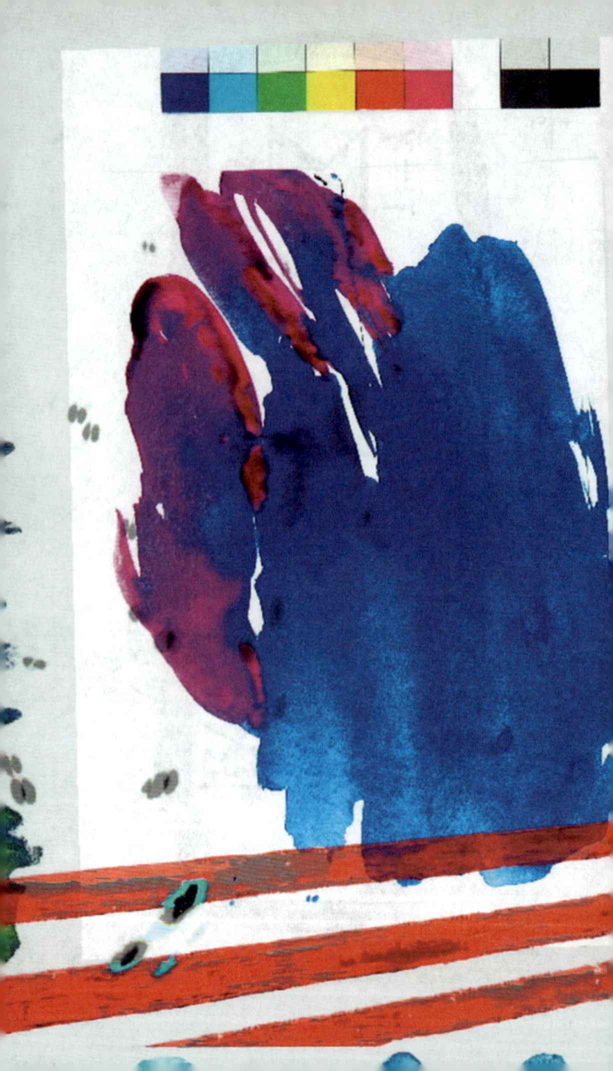

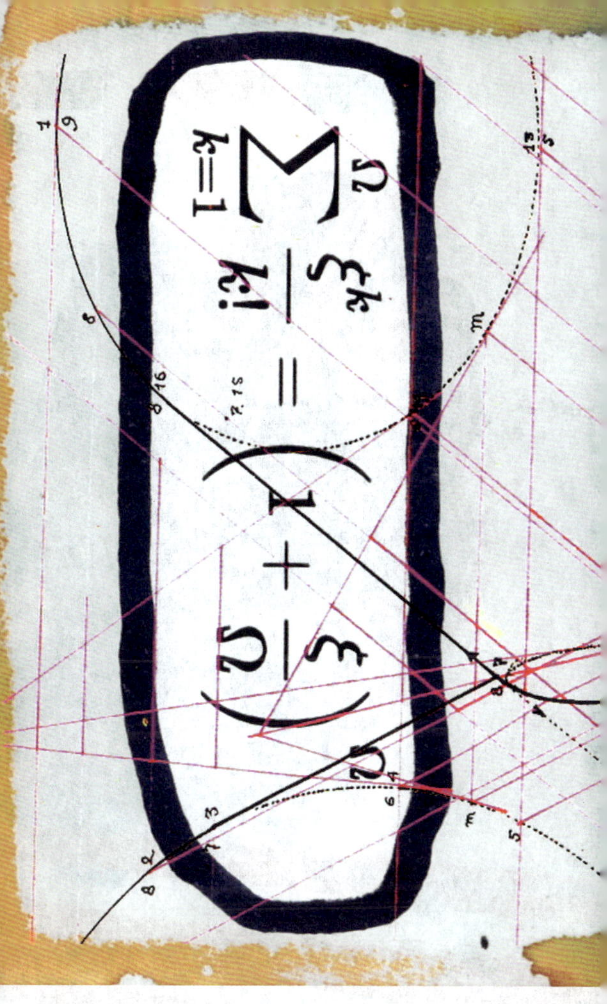
$\sum_{k=1}^{\Omega} \frac{\xi^k}{k!} = \left(1 + \frac{\xi}{\Omega}\right)^{\Omega}$

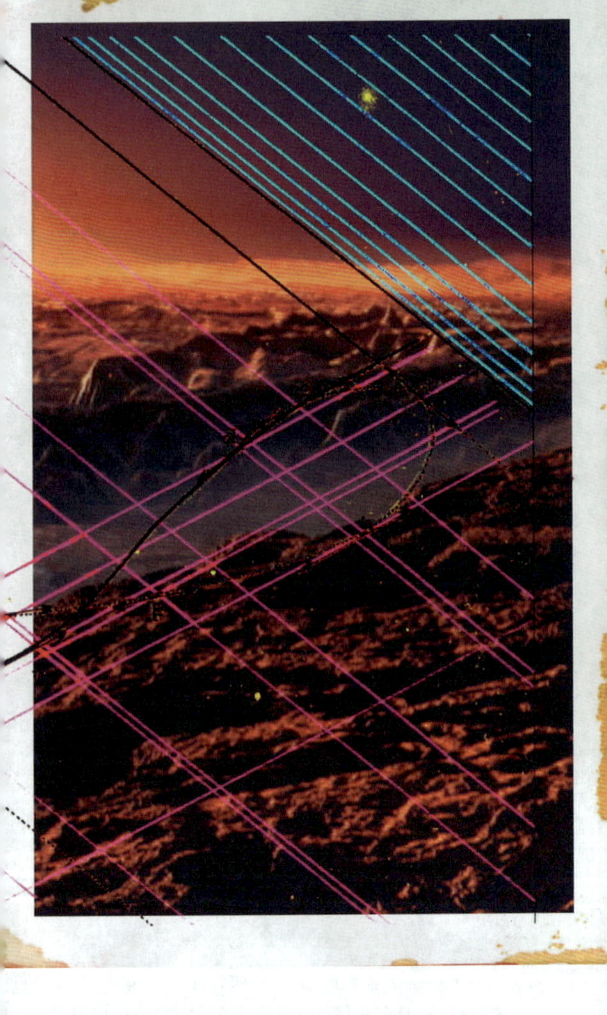

ARCHAEOLOGY OF OUTER SPACE

We stellar archaeologists specialize in examining the chemical constitution of the oldest of stars. We do not do that in galaxies far away but, rather, in the halo of our own Milky Way. I could try this on objects in my favorite constellation in the entire cosmos, *Coma Berenices*, a whole collection of galaxies far away. But our telescopes are no longer capable of recognizing individual stars there. Now we can only see the explosion of giant stars, which tell stellar archaeologists nothing about the chemical composition of the different former suns.

The rapid pace of our research differs from that of my scientific predecessors, smart alchemists like Johannes Kepler. With the help of computers, we don't look over just thousands but millions of stars. And if we want some gold, we don't have to make it ourselves. Weighing more than eight times the mass of the sun, the stellar colossi do that. We watch an enormous automaton at work. I refer to it as a "living automaton."

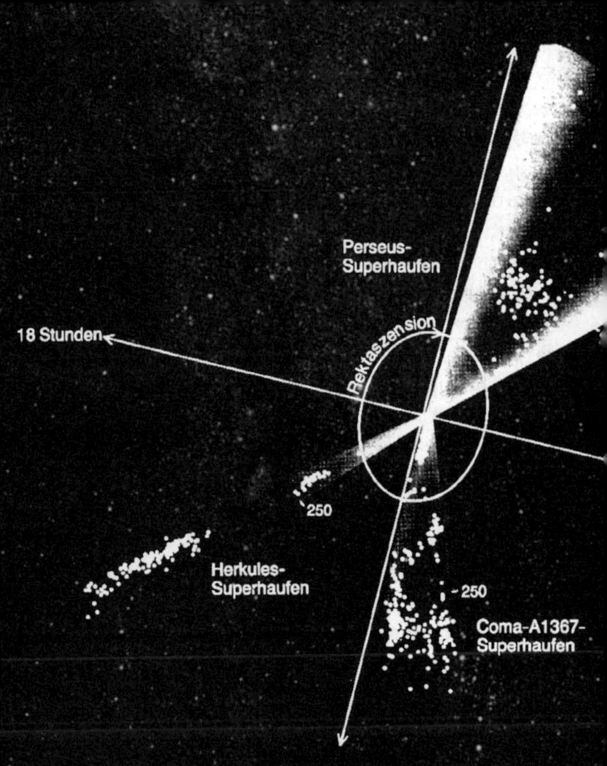
Perseus-
Superhaufen
18 Stunden
Rektaszension
250
Herkules-
Superhaufen
250
Coma-A1367-
Superhaufen

SILICON, A COSMIC RARITY

Take a look at this star here: It's twelve times the mass of the sun. It's generating no energy at the moment. Gravitation presses on the center of the star like an incredibly heavy rock. More than a billion degrees of heat are produced. Carbon emerges, and then neon and sodium. The neoplasm ignites. The burning of neon then creates magnesium and oxygen. The melding of two inner cores of oxygen forms silicon—in the meantime, the energy is generated by nuclear fusion rather than gravitational pressure—and leads to the creation of SILICON. Silicon is a matter in the chips, forming our mountains and deserts in the worldwide web.

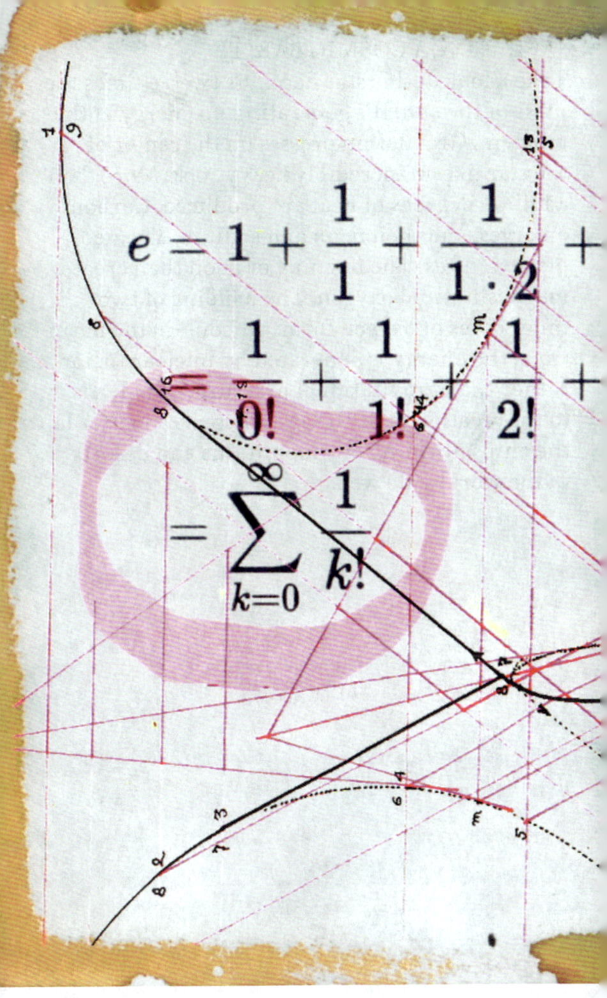
$e = 1 + \frac{1}{1} + \frac{1}{1 \cdot 2} +$
$= \frac{1}{0!} + \frac{1}{1!} + \frac{1}{2!} +$
$= \sum_{k=0}^{\infty} \frac{1}{k!}$

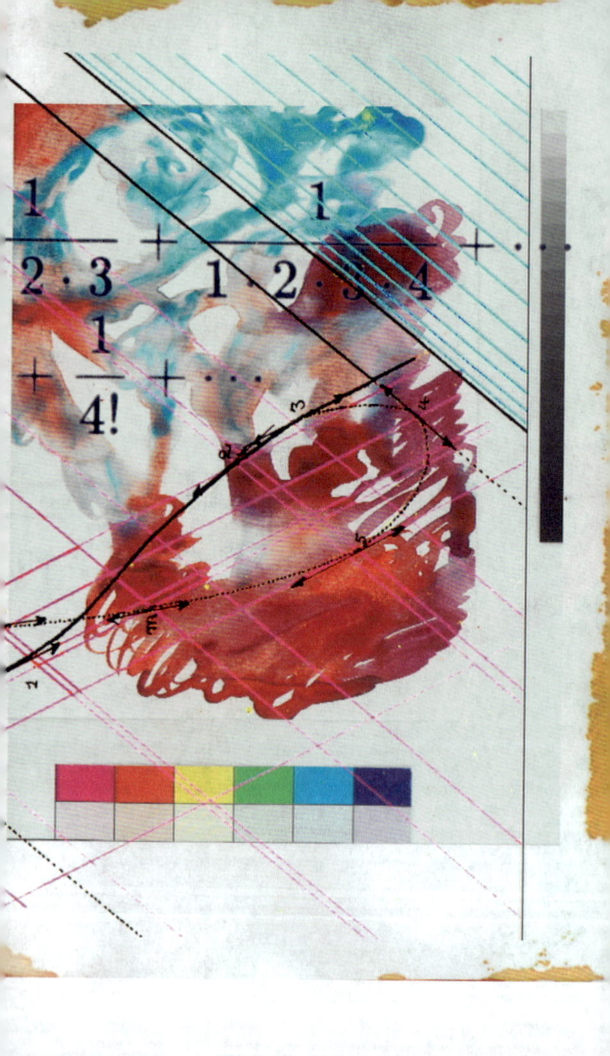

$\frac{1}{2\cdot 3} + \frac{1}{1\cdot 2\cdot 3\cdot 4} + \cdots$
$+ \frac{1}{4!} + \cdots$

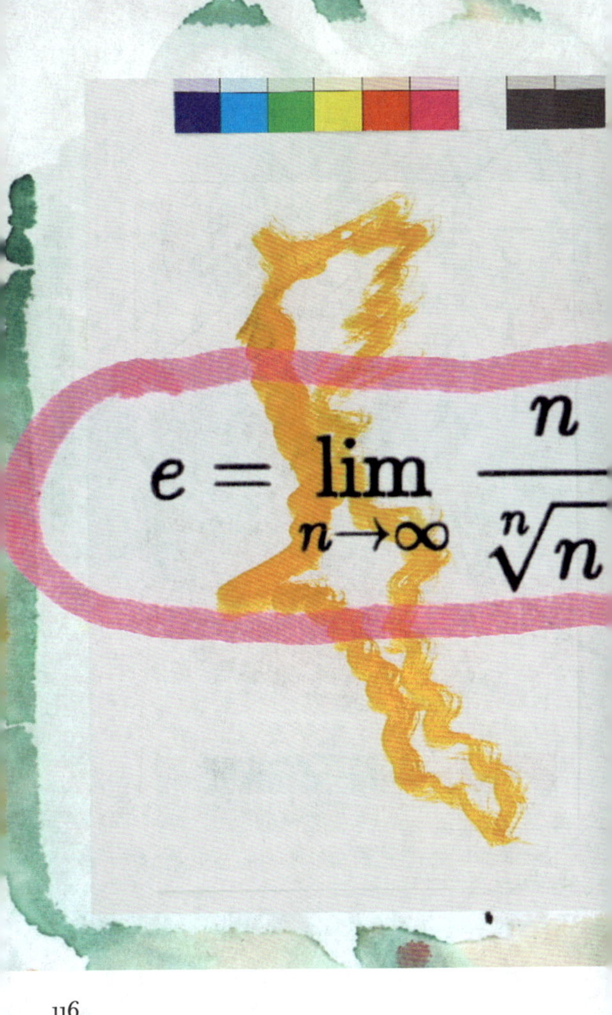
$e = \lim_{n\to\infty} \frac{n}{\sqrt[n]{n}}$

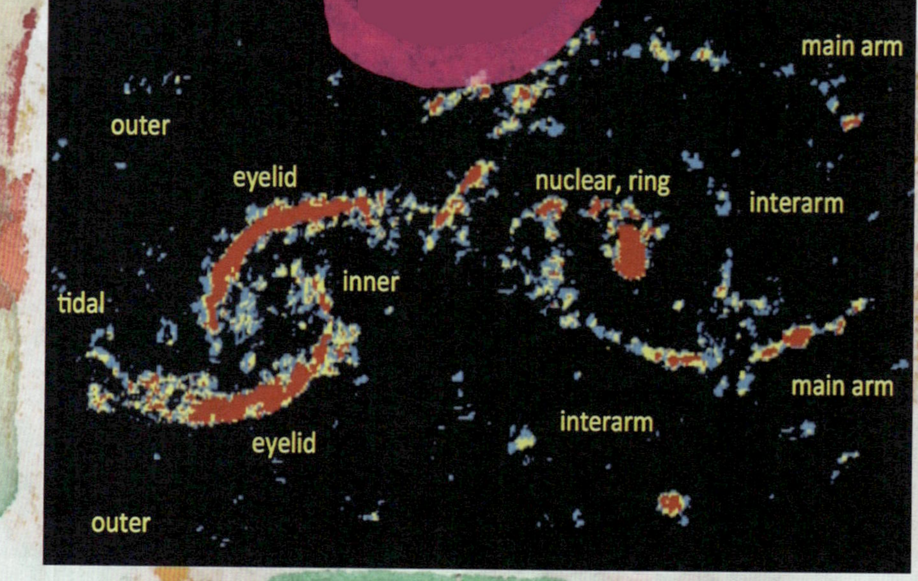
outer
eyelid
nuclear, ring
main arm
interarm
inner
tidal
main arm
interarm
eyelid
outer

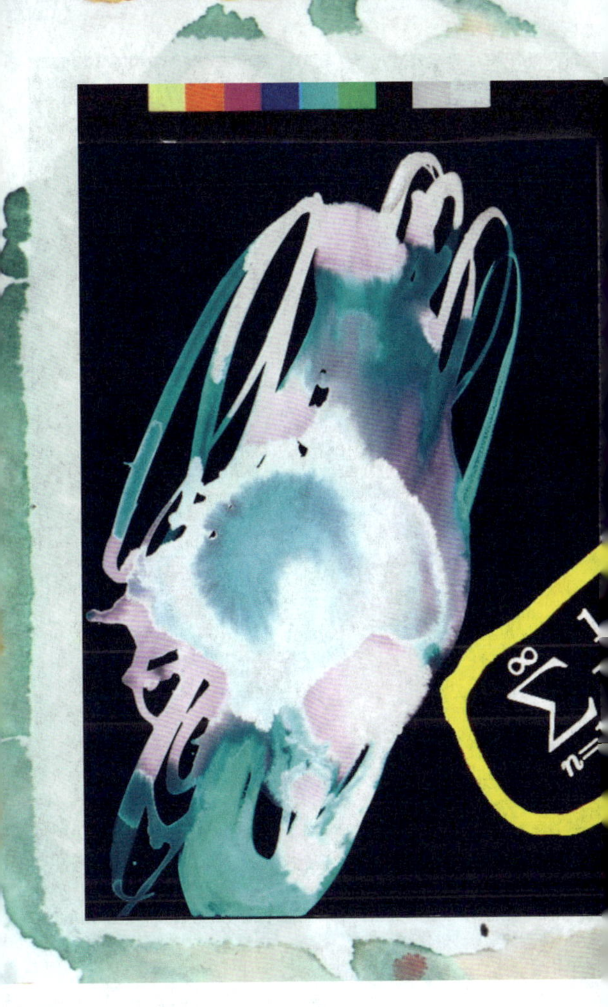

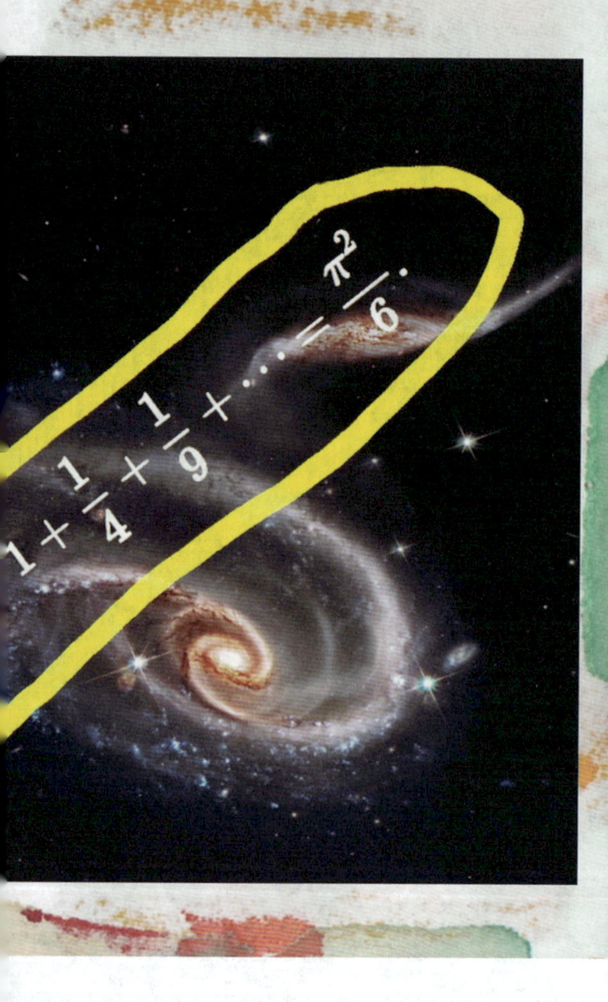
$1 + \frac{1}{4} + \frac{1}{9} + \dots = \frac{\pi^2}{6}.$

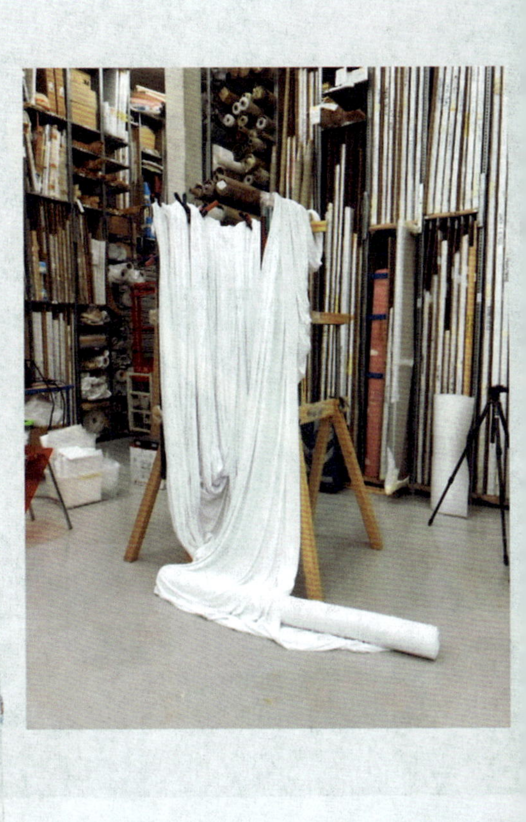

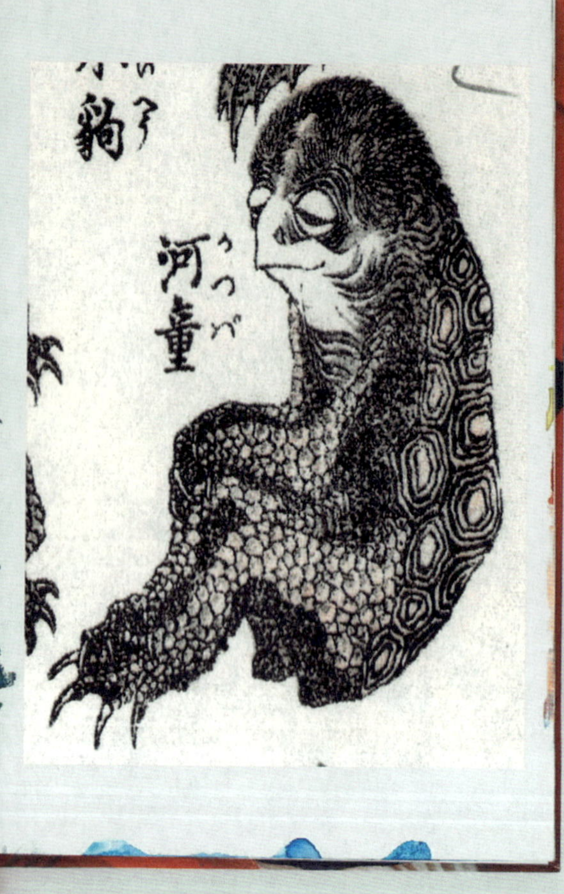
かつぱ
河童

4

The Soul Swims in Music

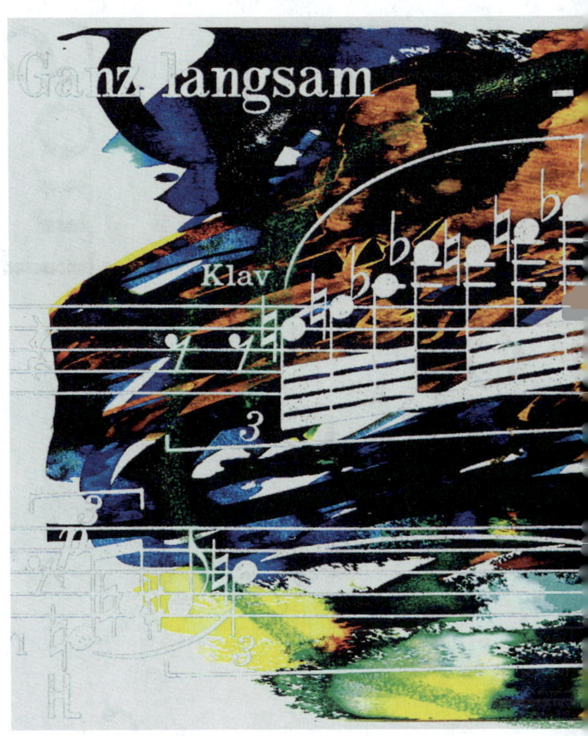

Ganz langsam
Klav
3
3
3

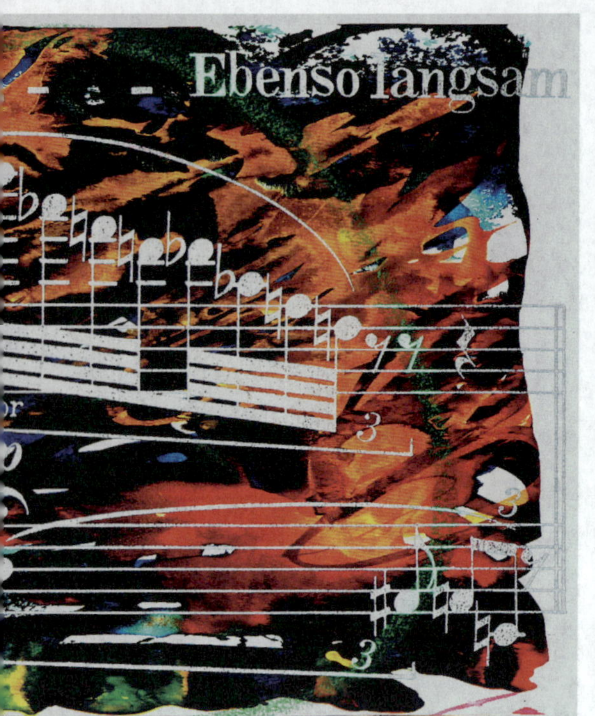
Ebenso langsam
3
3
3

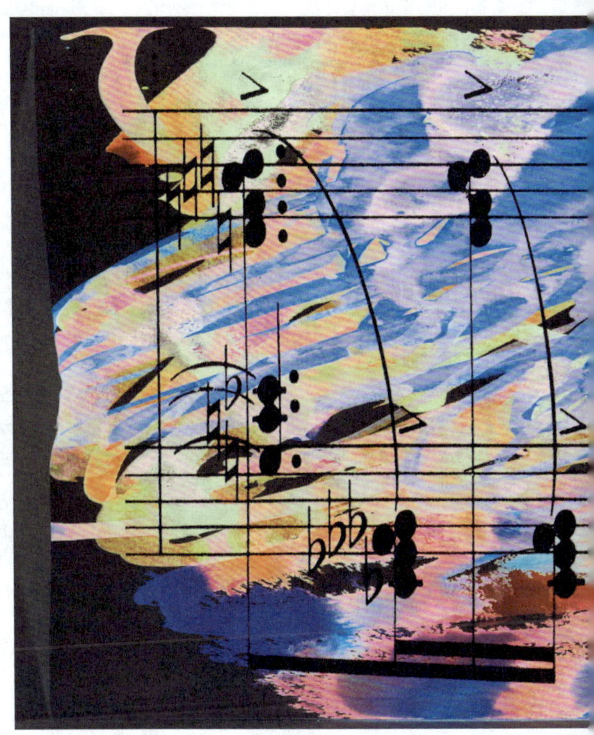

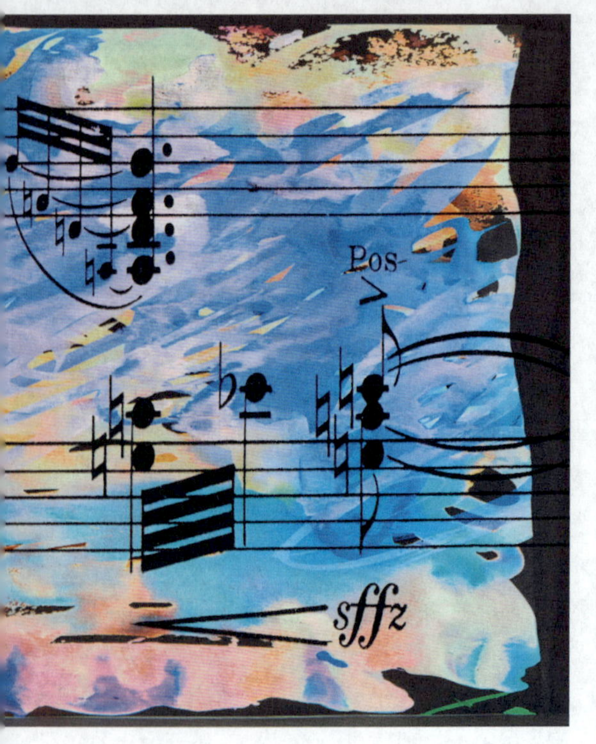
Pos-
sffz

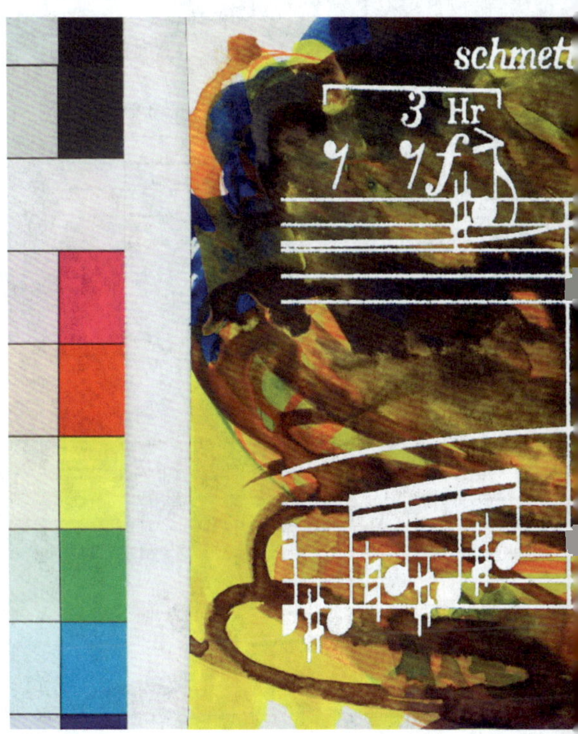
schmett
3 Hr
f

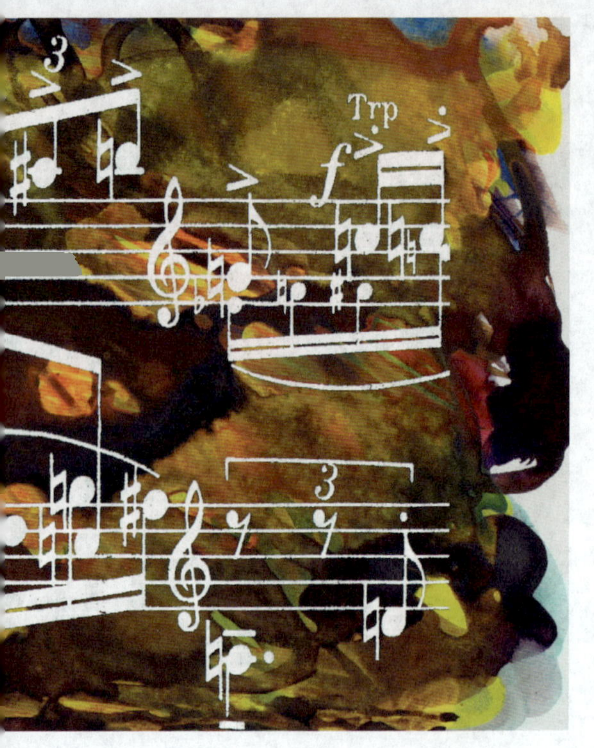
Trp

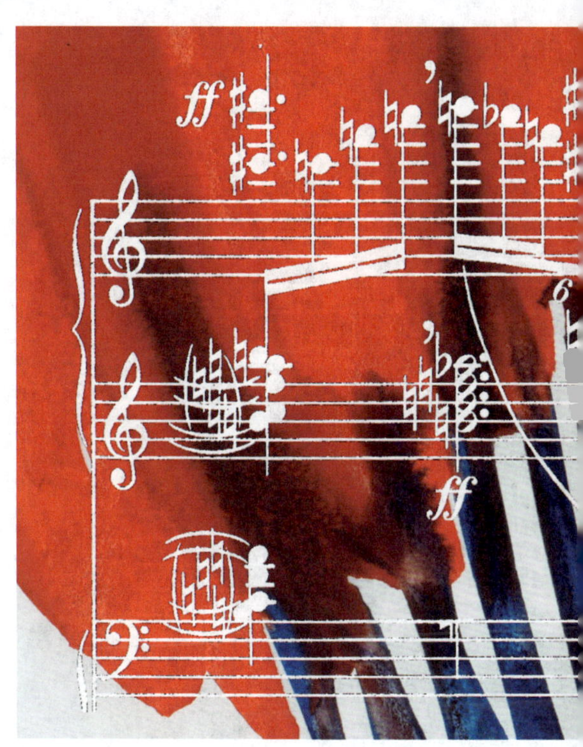
ff
6
ff

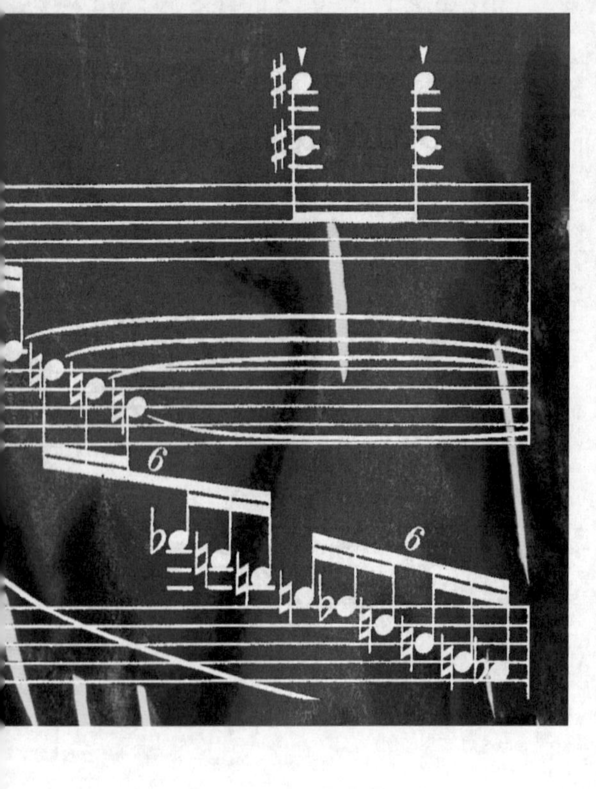

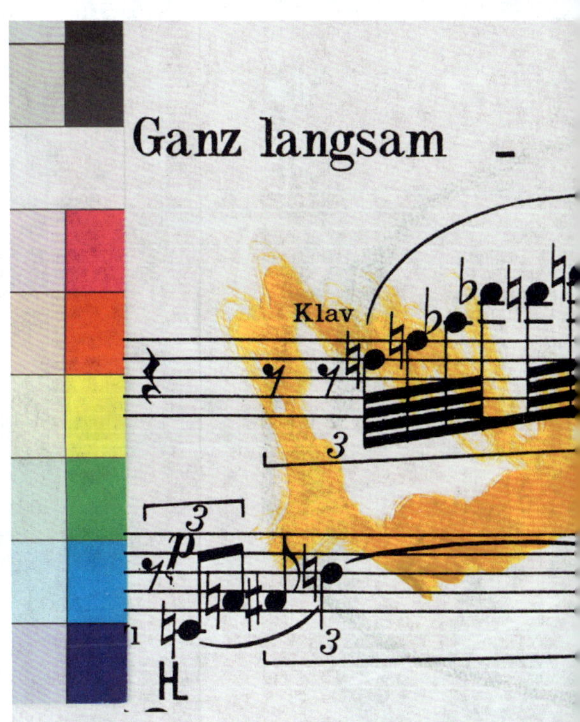
Ganz langsam
Klav
3
3
p
3

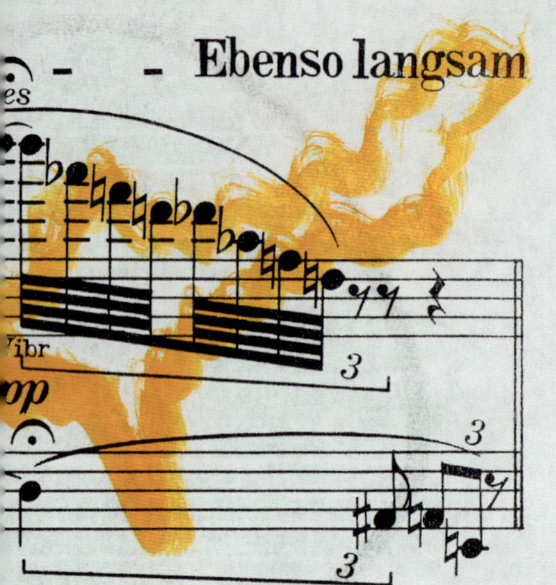

Ebenso langsam
es
Vibr
pp
3
3
3

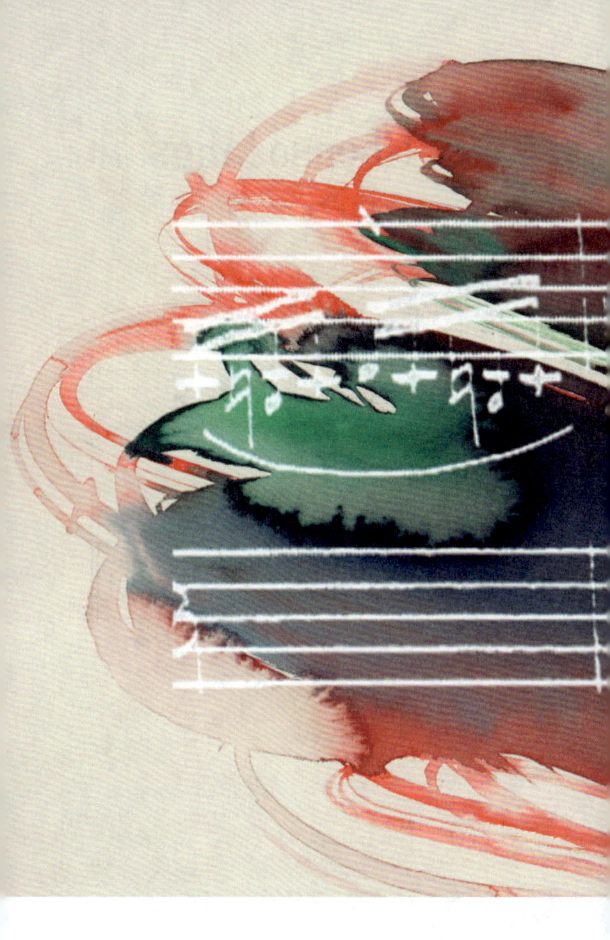

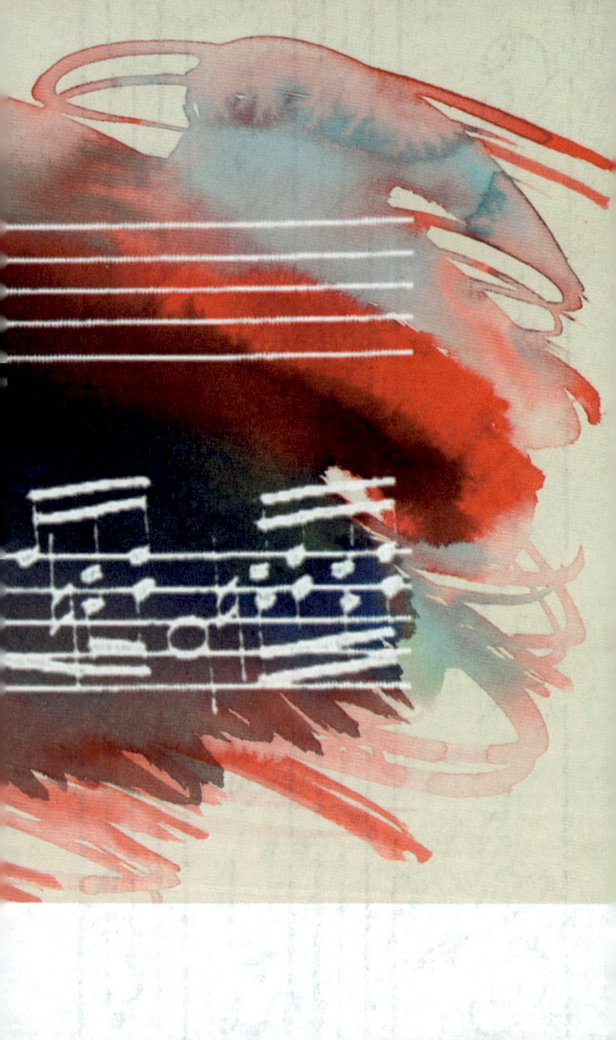

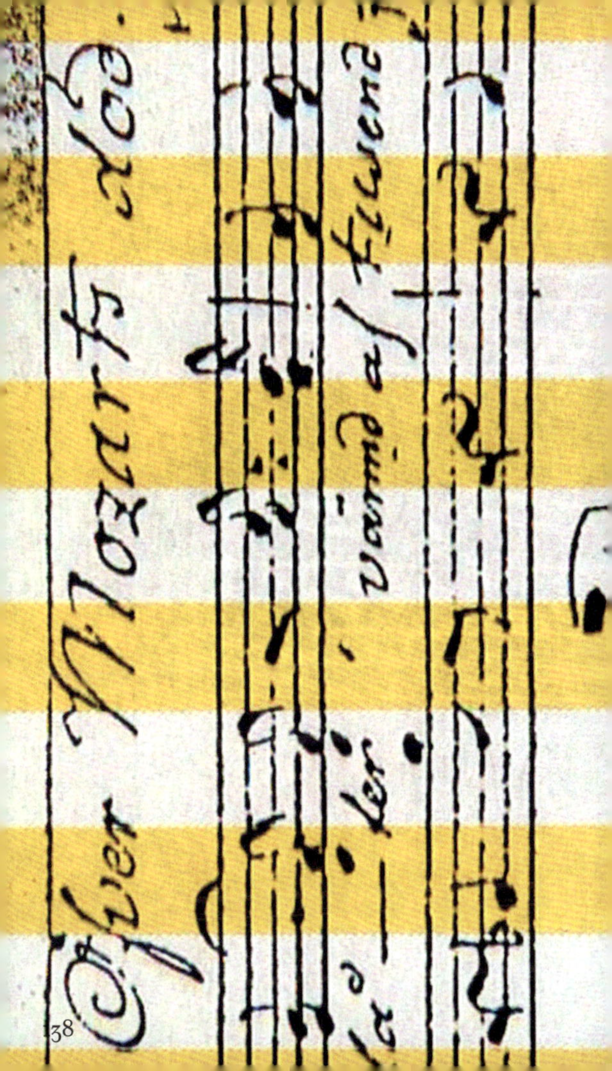

Öfver Mozarts död.

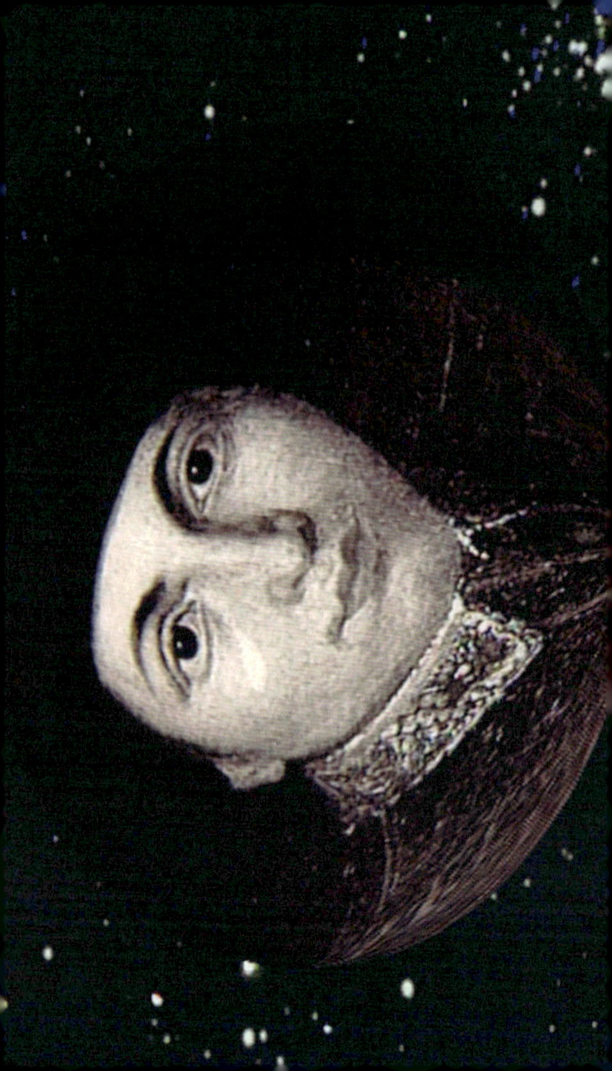

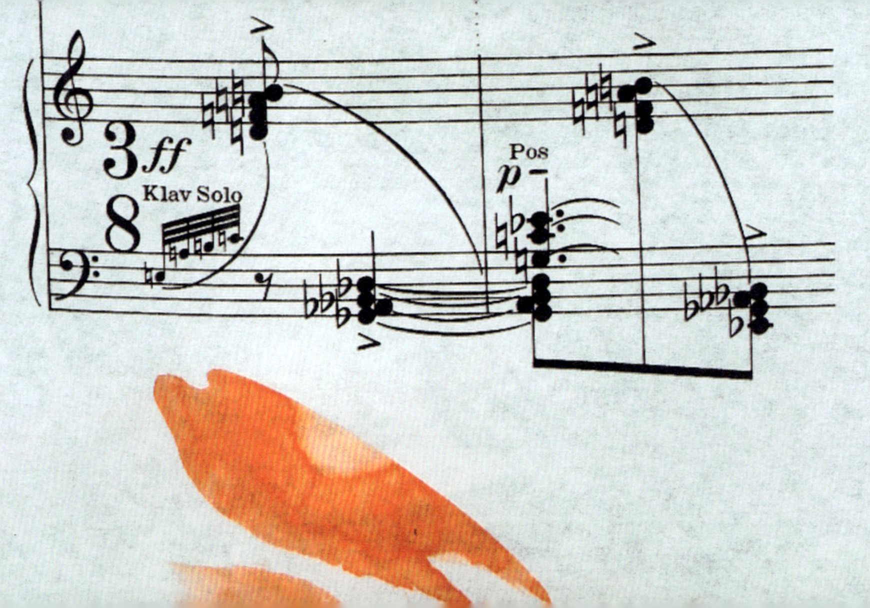
ff
Klav Solo
p
Pos

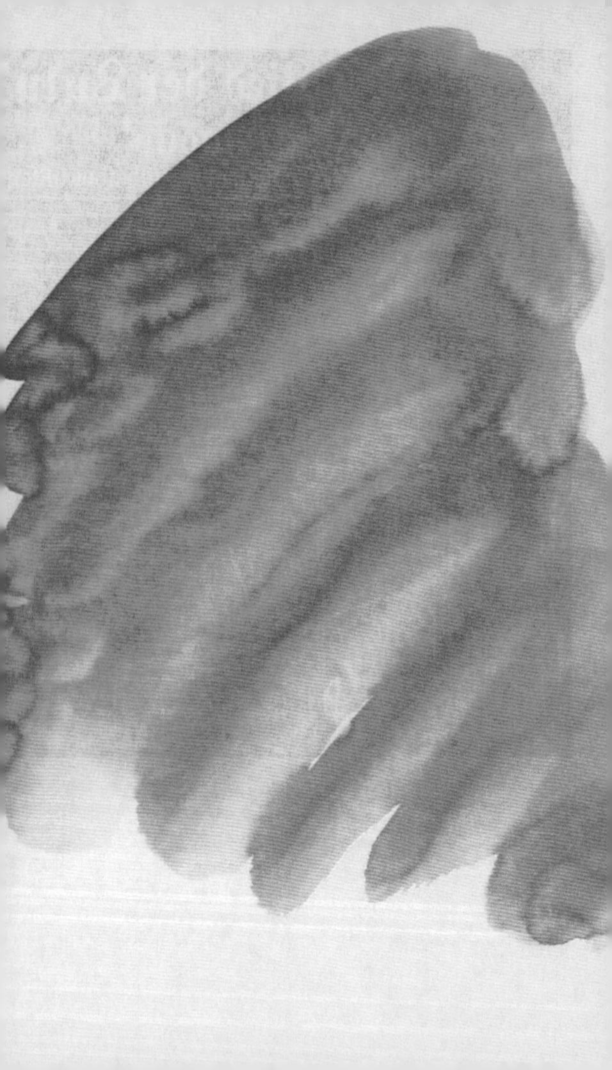

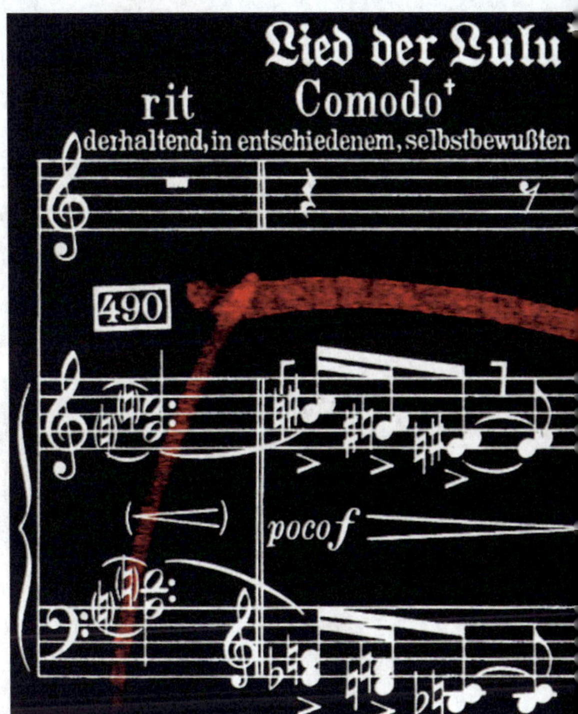
Lied der Lulu
rit
Comodo†
derhaltend, in entschiedenem, selbstbewußten
490
poco f

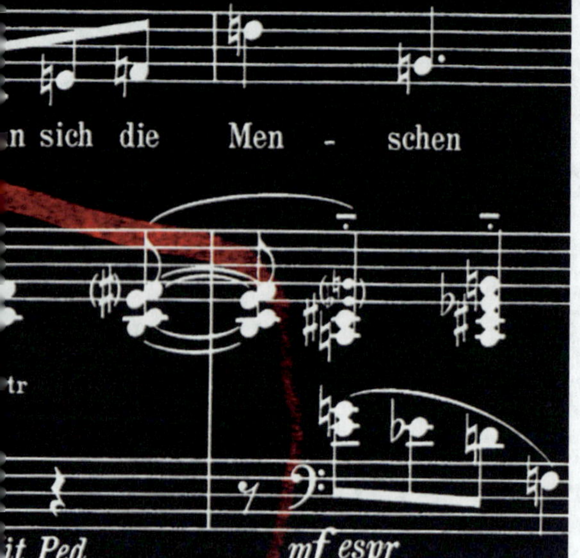
n sich die Men - schen
tr
it Ped
mf espr

THE FINAL SCENE IN THE OPERA *LULU* BY ALBAN BERG. "JACK THE RIPPER" KILLS THE SOPRANO

Lulu goes out in London working as a prostitute. She cannot bear it any longer in her accommodations. Her skin needs contact for the night. She runs into Jack the Ripper on the street. Present in the room is the Countess Geschwitz, who spent her fortune on rescuing the murderess Lulu.

LULU (*opens the door and lets Jack enter.*)

JACK (*a thickset man with flexible movements, with a pale face, inflamed eyes, thick, arched eyebrows, drooping moustache, sparse beard, matted side-whiskers, and fiery red hands with gnawed finger nails.*): ...I think you've a pretty mouth, my sweetheart.

LULU: I got it from my mother.

JACK: Quite likely! How much is it?

LULU: Don't you want to spend the whole night with me then?

JACK: No, I haven't got the time. I must get home...

LULU: You stare at me—what's the meaning of that?

JACK: You attracted me first by the way that you walk. I told myself, "That's a well-made body."

LULU: How can one know such things as that?

JACK: I even saw that your mouth was very pretty. I only have a single half-a-crown on me.

LULU: No matter. Give it to me.

JACK: But you must give me back half of the money, so that tomorrow I have some left for the bus.

LULU: I haven't any change.

JACK: Have a good look! Turn all your pockets out!

LULU (*holding out her hand to him*): Here's the only coin that's left me.

JACK: Give me that.

LULU: I'll change it when the morning comes and then divide it with you.

JACK: No—give me the lot now.

LULU (*giving it to him*): God help you with it! Come in with me now! (*She takes the lamp.*)

JACK: We don't need a light, there's moonlight.

LULU: As you want it. (*She puts down the lamp, approaches Jack, and embraces him.*) I'm really drawn to you. (*In a tormented voice.*) Please don't keep me waiting longer.

JACK: I'm quite ready. (*He follows her into her room, and the sound of the door being barred from the inside is heard.*)

...

LULU'S VOICE (*from her room*): No—no—no, no! (*Death shriek. Countess Geschwitz draws herself bolt upright, then rushes to the door of Lulu's room and rattles it with all her might. Jack, stooping, wrenches open the door from inside and plunges a blood-stained knife into the Countess's body. The Countess collapses.*)

JACK (*moving past the Countess*): That was quite a bus'ness! (*Washing his hands in a basin that stands underneath the window.*) Aren't I just the most lucky fellow!

THE END OF THE REAL JACK THE RIPPER

Together with a colleague in London, a private detective in Opladen unmasked in the year 2014 the phantom-murderer Jack the Ripper, who murdered and disembowelled five women working as prostitutes in the Year of Three Kaisers (1888, which has, however, a different denotation in London). A police officer who investigated the crime scene at the time kept for himself a blood-soaked scarf of the fourth victim. He kept the piece of evidence (which elicited fear and amazement) and wanted to sell it later for his own benefit. But the object remained hidden away and was only found a 126 years later—just as it had been initially packed away—when a British colleague of the Opladen detective purchased it at a rummage auction.

At the time of the murders, officials had preserved multiple objects belonging to both the murderer and victim. The remains of blood on them were cross-examined alongside the findings from the scarf, which had absorbed DNA traces like a sponge. It turned out that the mysterious perpetrator, who had disappeared after the series of murders, was the Polish barber Aaron Kosminski. At the time, he was listed in the files as a suspect. Confiscated articles contained traces of his identity.

In the interwar years, the man (twenty-three at the time of the murders) returned to Poland.

At the age of seventy-eight, the perpetrator was admitted to one of the German Reich's extermination camps. There, in his last moment of desperation and in a quasi-collegial gesture (from evil to evil), he confessed to a chief inspector and captain from Württemberg stationed at the camp to the singular value that he believed to still have as a human being: the monstrous value of his deeds. The captain's report prompted the immediate transfer of the legendary murderer to the Reich capital.

In the same way that the Institutes for Art and Monstrosities in the Renaissance were interested in abnormal specimens, Department VII of the Reich Main Security Office had a remarkable weakness for investigating realms of human sociability and anti-sociability. The Reichsführer himself was involved with the delivery of the unique find from the concentration camp and received reports from Professor Six, the department chief. The research interest was not classified according to races (that was known) but, rather, according to the potential of human nature—for the creation of a zoo for peculiarities found in the human race.

At that time, the criminalists and SS-researchers in Berlin had not yet decided whether they would regret it too much were they to gas the perpetrator, this "mothballed evil from so many years prior," whether they should kill him or use him as propaganda against England, or make use of

him against a worldwide Jewry, or whether still subject him to closer examination for the identification of humankind's abysses and potentials. Their interrogations and consultations had only just begun when they and the aged murderer were buried in a bunker during the air raid on central Berlin in November 1943. The aggregate of coincidences that a carpet-bombing brings onto an unlit metropolis cannot offhandedly be understood as a Last Judgment. The same can be said for the situation had Aaron Kosminski not confessed to Comrade Eilers, and had he, as a result, been burned in the ovens, seeing that, as the theologian Bultmann sums up, God does not use the henchmen of such camps for executing his justice.

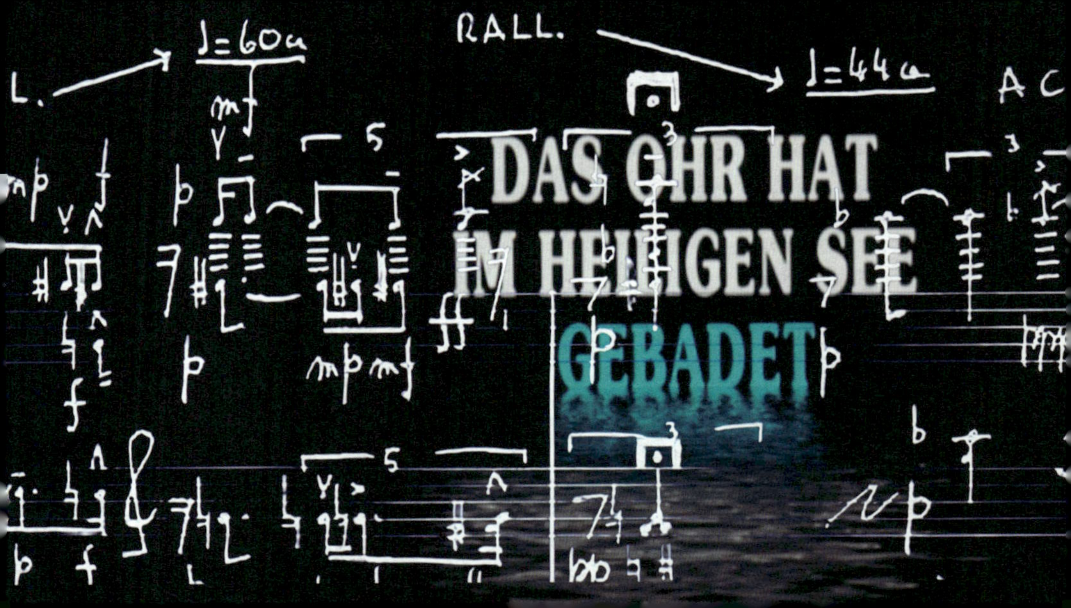
DAS OHR HAT
IM HEILIGEN SEE
GEBADET
RALL.

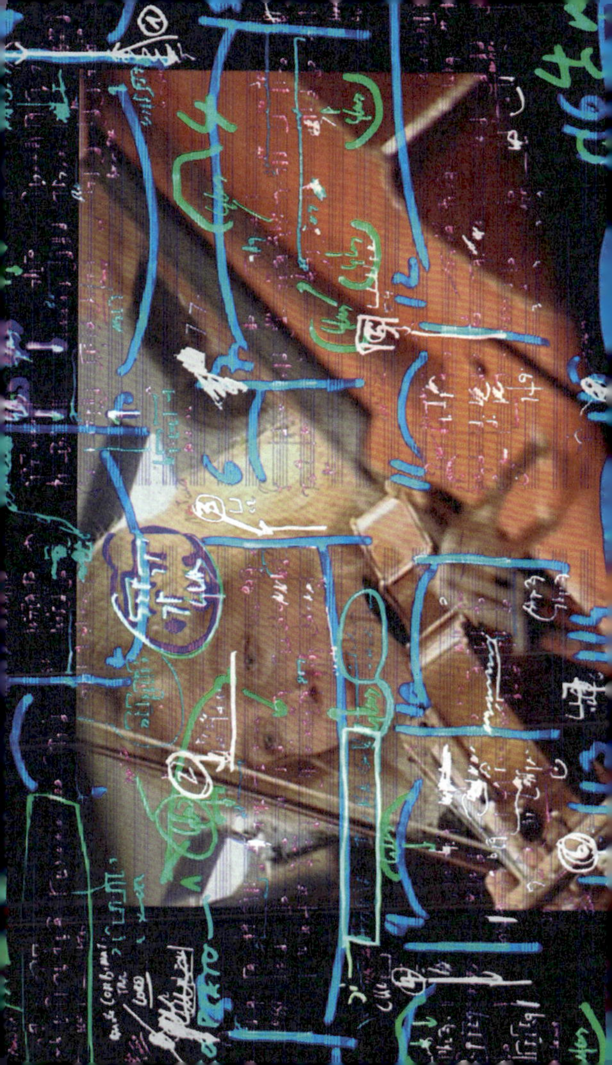

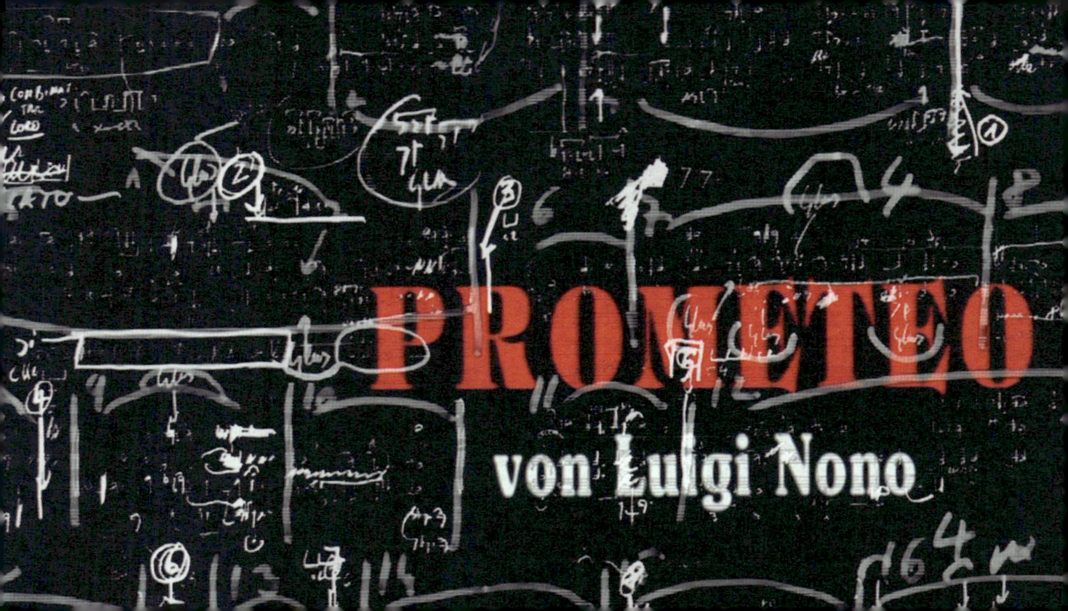
PROMETEO
von Luigi Nono

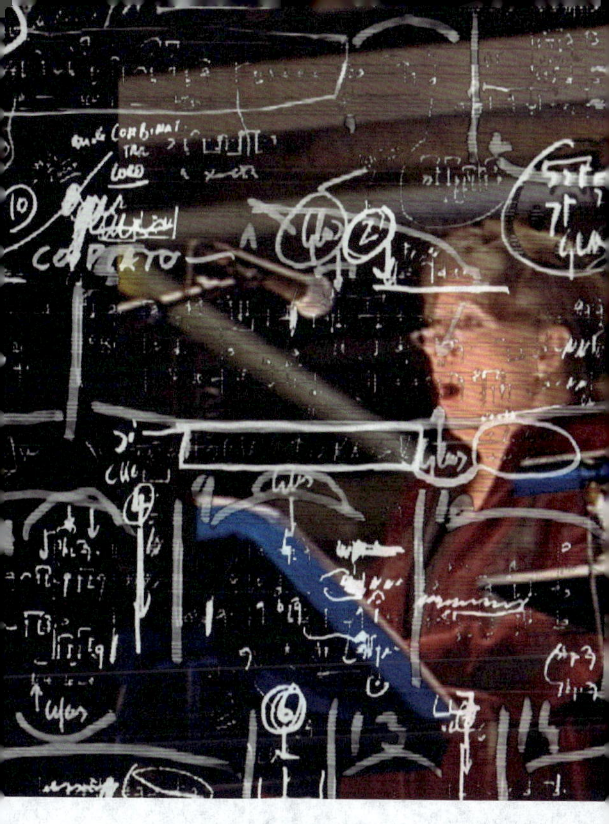

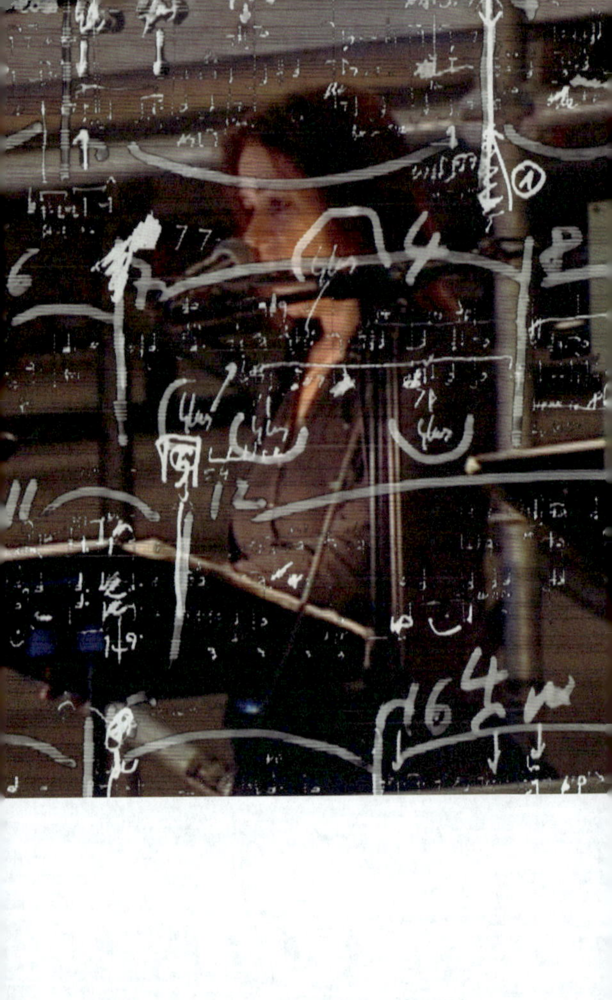

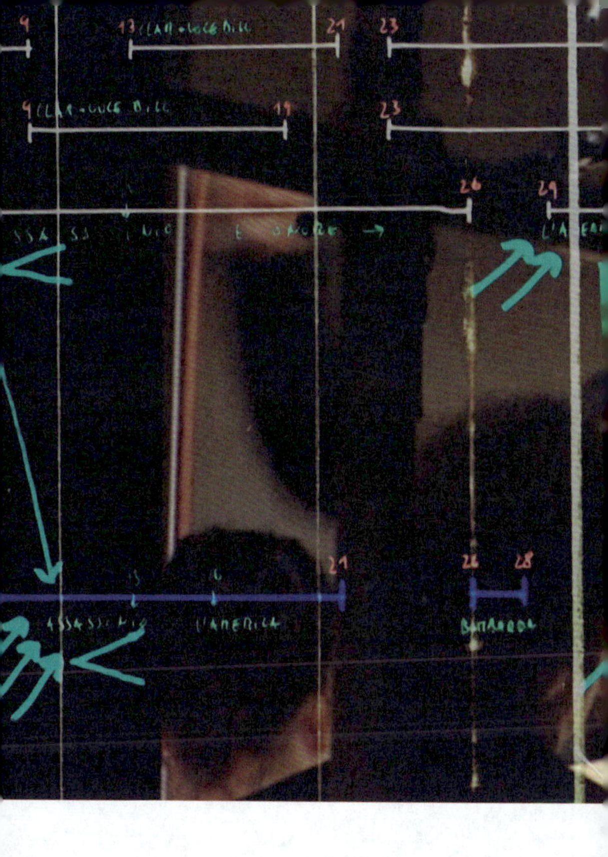

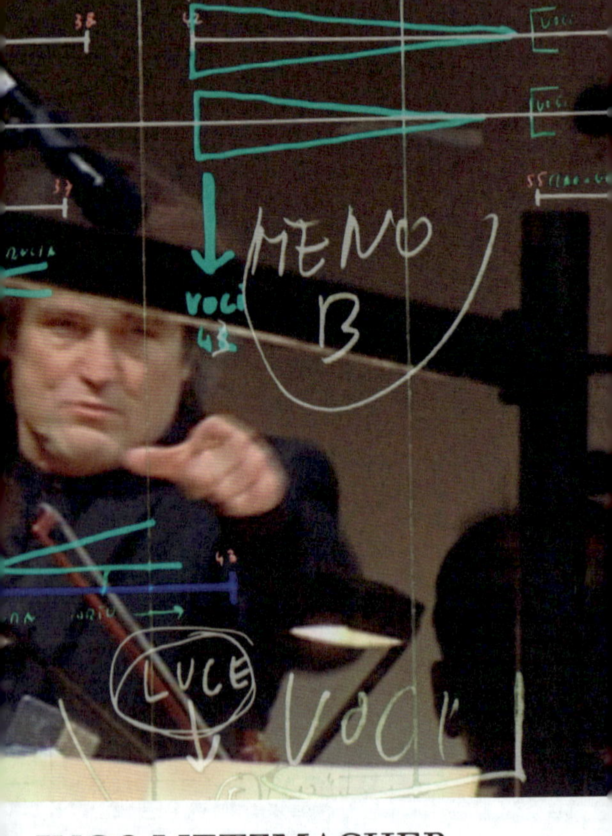

INGO METZMACHER, CONDUCTOR

VOICELESS PEOPLE OF HISTORY

An unknown composition by Luigi Nono from 1966: Seventy of the waiters who went down with the Titanic in 1912 came from neighboring villages in the Abruzzi. Not one of their fiancées, who had hoped that these men would return home and marry them once they'd been paid their wages, ever found anyone else who would. The villages remained childless, and today stand desolate among the mountains. It was to these VOICELESS PEOPLE OF HISTORY that Nono dedicated his *Lament for Twelve Strings and Twelve Sopranos* in 1966. The grief is not so much for the waiters lost at the bottom of the sea as it is for the miserable fate of the women left behind, who were forbidden by strict local custom from seeking another husband in a neighboring town.

A Power
of Unearthly Origin /

CONCERNING A TALE BY HEINRICH VON KLEIST ON "THE POWER OF MUSIC"

A small group of violence-prone Puritans from Holland had made a pact among themselves. With passion. Out of protest. Iconoclasts and Anabaptists. The plan was to stir up a group of locals in a German town during the liturgy and then demolish all the images in its cathedral.

At the moment of danger, Heinrich von Kleist writes, someone came up with the idea of using a mass composed more than a hundred years earlier by a Venetian maestro to calm the agitated urbanites, to stop their disruptive tendencies. There was just one problem: the only conductor who could have led the musical work lay in a feverish coma. But then Saint Cecilia, the mother goddess of music, is said to have stepped up to the podium herself (having taken on the appearance of the ill abbess), and by the seventh beat the music had tamed the crowd's destructive spirit.

Later, the four instigators of the riot, those who had been "purified by music," as Kleist has it, were found in a madhouse. For all intents and purposes, content. There they sat around a table, croaking pious snatches of music, guttural sounds that the expert recognized as having come from the legendary mass. Heinrich von Kleist gave the related report, the shortest of his stories, the title "Saint CECILIA or THE POWER OF MUSIC."

SENSITIVE DESCENDANTS FROM DISTANT TIMES

The sensory part of our ear descends firstly from the pressure sensors of former fish and secondly from a common ancestor that possessed the stimulus-sensitive hairs of flies, an ancestor of whom not a single trace is left in the world!

The sensitive descendant in conductor Ingo Metzmacher's ear was in a frenzy of excitement. The different tone sequences (as Luigi Nono had written them down in his score) exploded upon collision and made their way through Metzmacher's gestures as if he were taking a machete to the ears and hands of the orchestra musicians. During rehearsals, according to the *Süddeutsche Zeitung*'s critic, some ten tone and overtone combinations were created that had neither been written in the score nor ever produced or even heard on earth. In this way those extinct ancestors from whom we have inherited our sensual equipment always have new, unexpected descendants. For some deep reason, the audience, unprepared for such signs and simply interested in consuming a regular evening of music, recognized the ABSOLUTELY UNIQUE nature of the event and gave a standing ovation, without being able to say exactly why.

COSMIC MUSIC

The quake that shifted Japan's northern island four meters to the east and its resulting chime could still be registered in the Swiss mountains. Indeed, this pulse was received across the entire globe. These are what Johannes Kepler referred to as the chords of the earth in his book *The Harmony of the World*. Some of the tones follow one another at intervals of a thousand years, and sound different when they repeat. Others come in shorter intervals. Kepler believed that residual risk (inaudible in itself) could be heard indirectly, as it reacts in the manner of a wall in an anechoic chamber. While only *one* MENETEKEL has been handed down in words, these perceptual blind spots and the big chimes of the earth—interpretable as both the sublime and as danger signals—are forms of COSMIC MUSIC.

SMALL-STATURED WOMAN
IN HIGH-HEELED SHOES

The opera singer rushes by. Tonight she will sing the role of Tosca. Because she is small and heavyset, she is wearing high-heeled shoes.

Internally, unnoticed, she is wearing an even smaller feeling: YOU'RE JUST ABOUT TO FALL OVER.

This feeling lies hidden beneath the passionate abandon, the murderous intent in the moment of hopelessness proper to the role of Tosca; and it is concealed by the feelings of Aida, which she sang last season. Still, the feeling possesses power, force, and ancestry.

When we were still reptiles, we did not have feelings, we understood only action. Resting—waiting—attack or flight.

Then came the Ice Ages. As it grew very cold on the blue planet, we often thought longingly of the primordial oceans, 98.6 degrees. We learned to have feelings, namely, to say: too hot, too cold.

To distinguish between the two, and to long: those are the two things feelings can do. Everything else is a combination.

My grandparents were simple farmers. Up to the birth of Christ, sixty-four billion ancestors. Each of these ancestors is related to a tree climber to whom all forebears can be traced back, and whose every feeling—falling asleep, tastes good, biting, oh dear, etc.—derives its FAMILY TREE from a single feeling-pair: hot/cold.

As it grew colder, Adam's rib was simply outsize longing.

Ninety-eight-point-six degrees in the warm waters of the primordial seas. We couldn't forget it, we remembered it in the cold, we kindled this little fire in our interiors. The fire's antecedents are the oscillations in the colors of atoms. In this sense, music is older than feeling.*

* In the nucleus of an atom dwell three colors, unremarkable so long as they are together. Indifferent, uneventful. But if one of these colors were pulled just a few millimeters away from the others, LONGING would pull them all toward each other with energies sufficient to illuminate the planets for about three weeks; and this is just one of the numerous subatomic particle types that make up the elements.

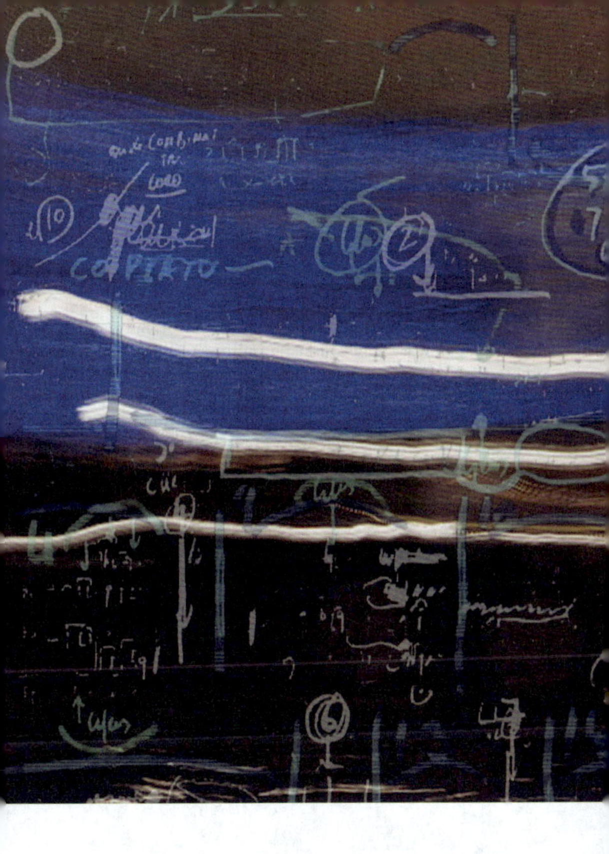

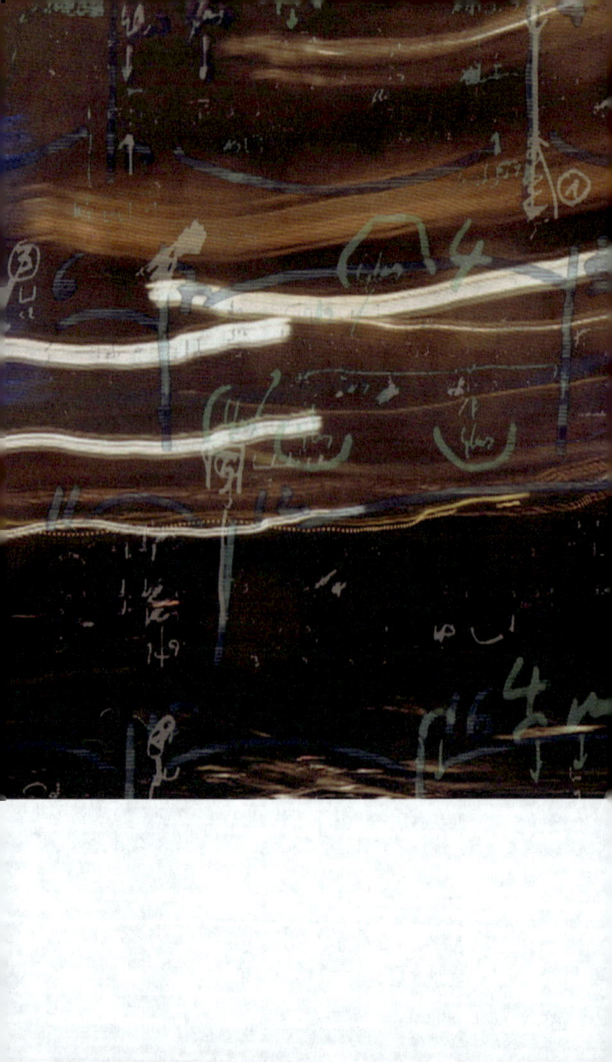

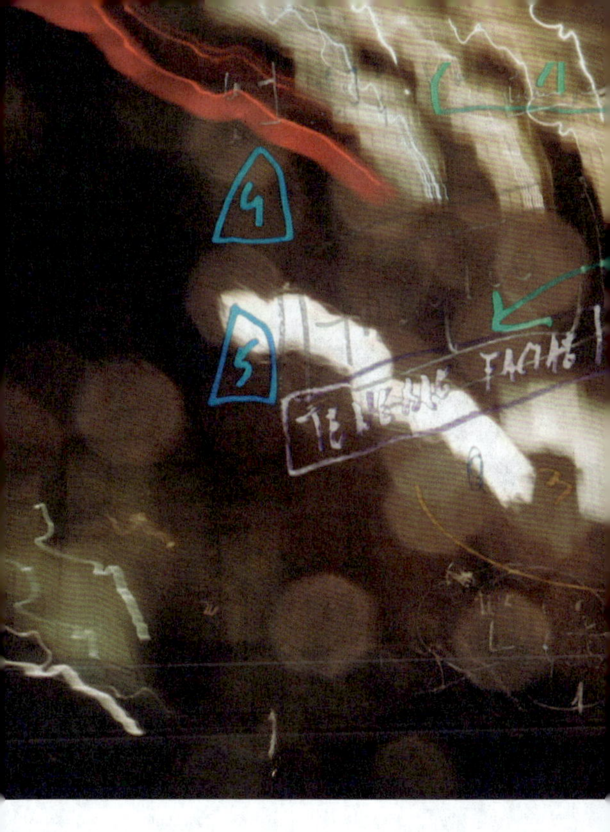

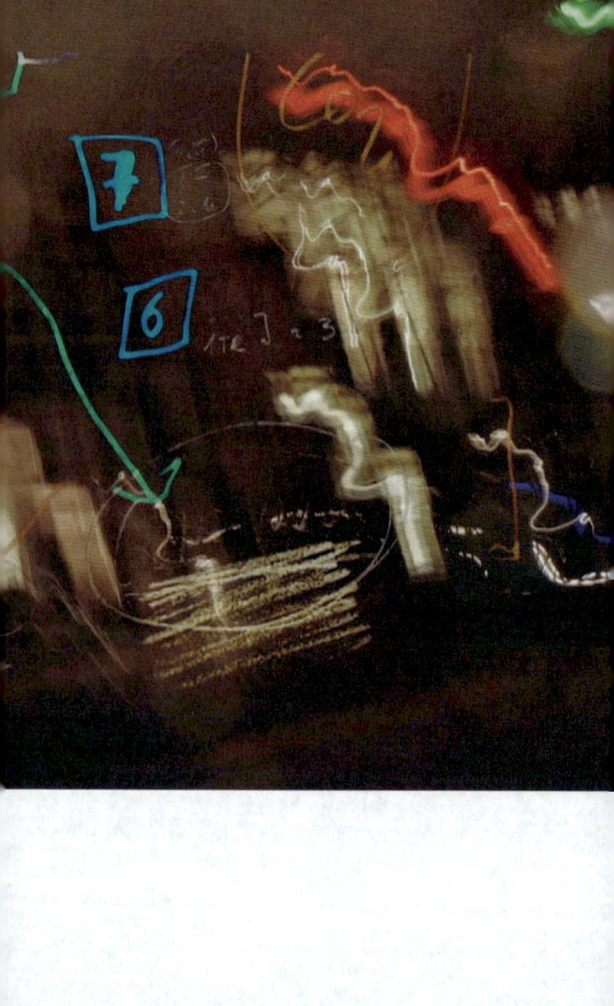
7
6

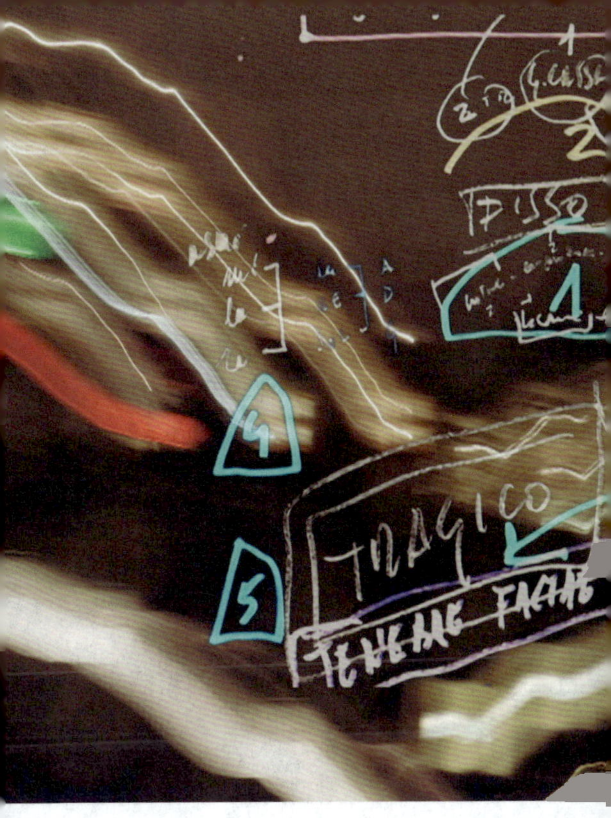
TRAGICO

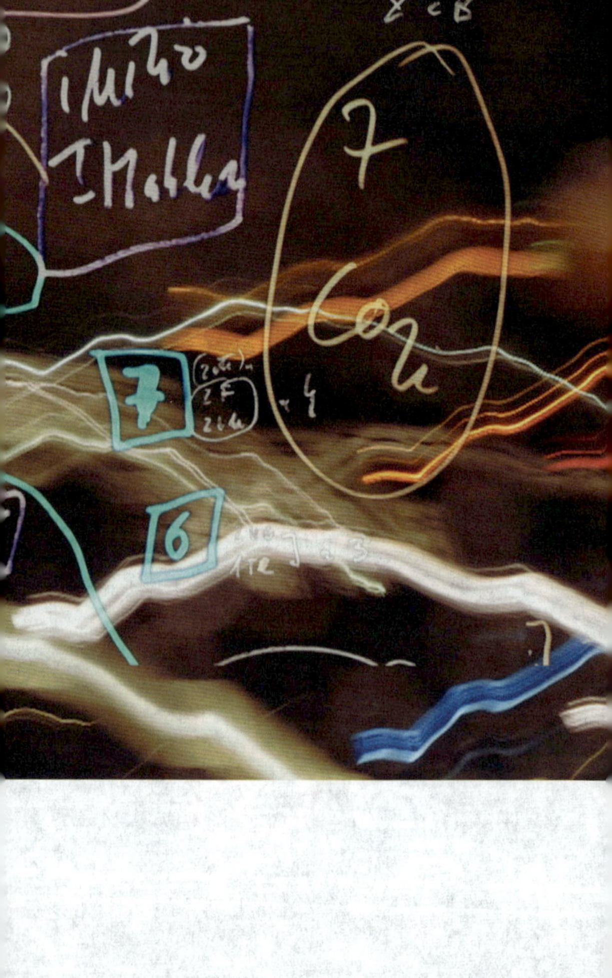

"Das harmonische
GESPENST"

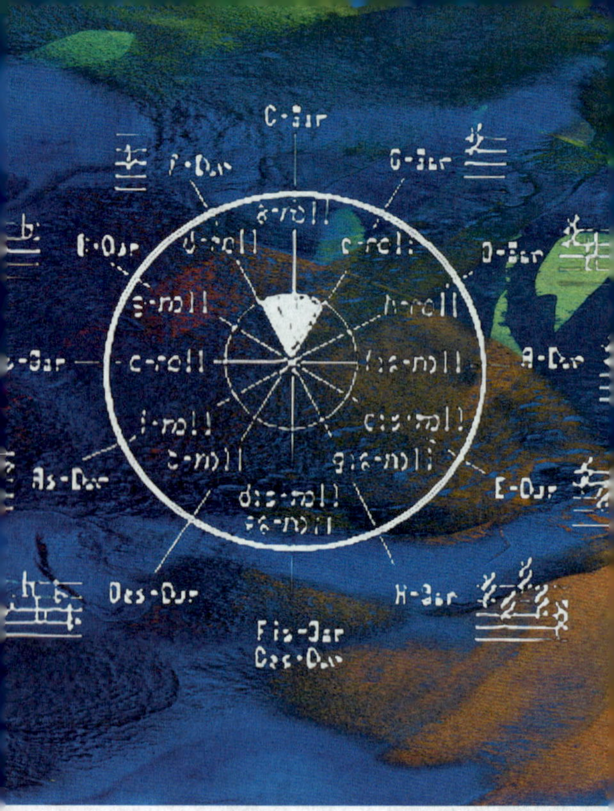

The Harmonic Spirit
Triptych
01:32

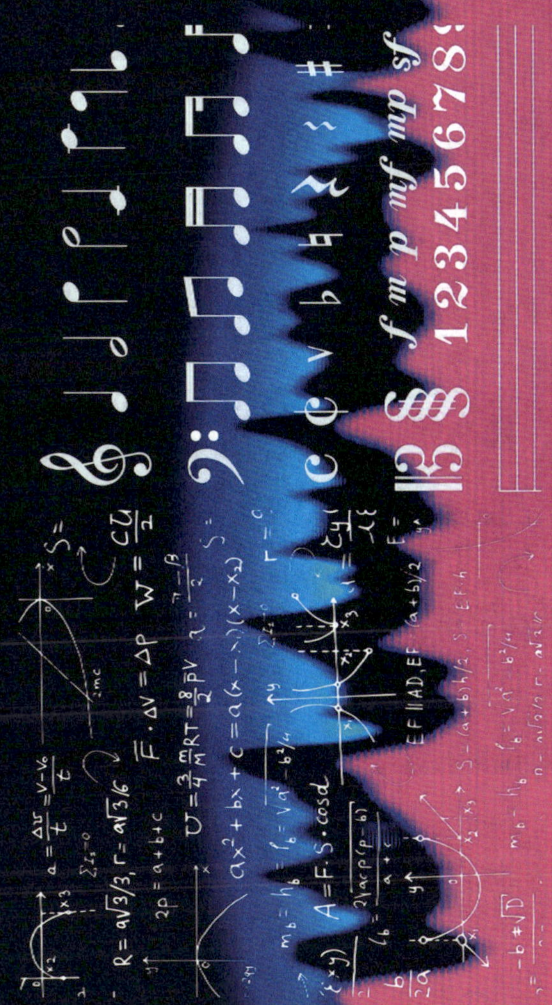

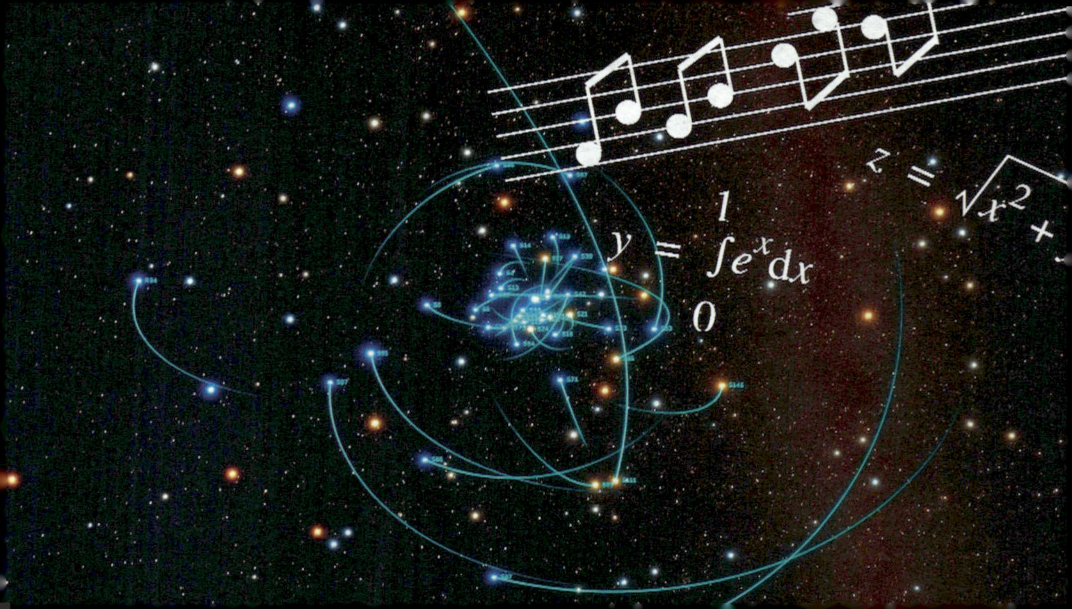

$y = \int_0^1 e^x dx$
$z = \sqrt{x^2 +$

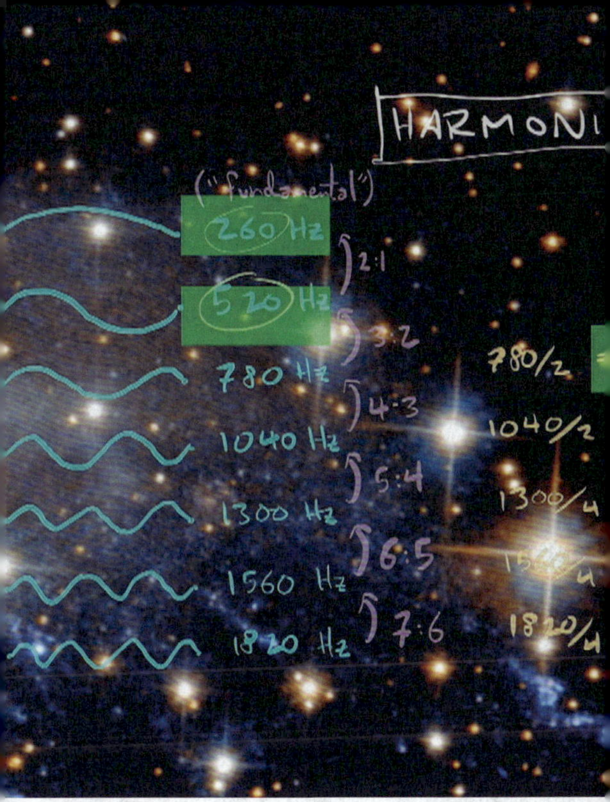

HARMONI

("fundamental")

260 Hz

2:1

520 Hz

3:2

780 Hz

4:3

1040 Hz

5:4

1300 Hz

6:5

1560 Hz

7:6

1820 Hz

780/2

1040/2

1300/4

1820/4

SERIES

Hz, in between 260 & 520

0 Duplicate!

25 Hz

90 Duplicate!

45 Hz

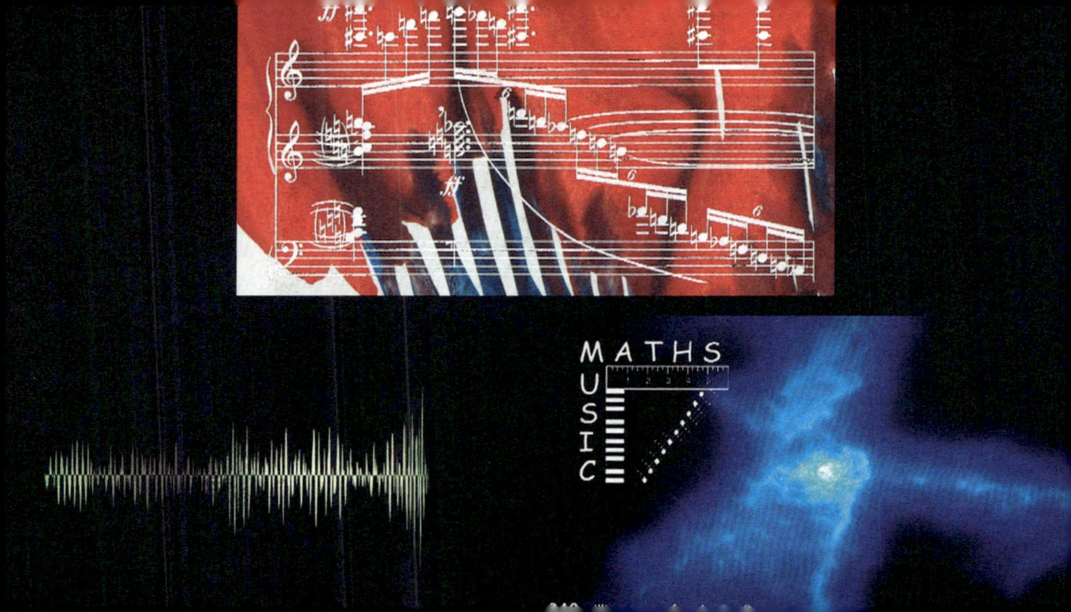

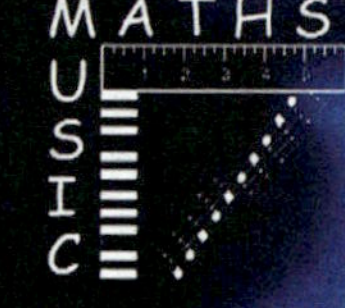
MATHS
MUSIC

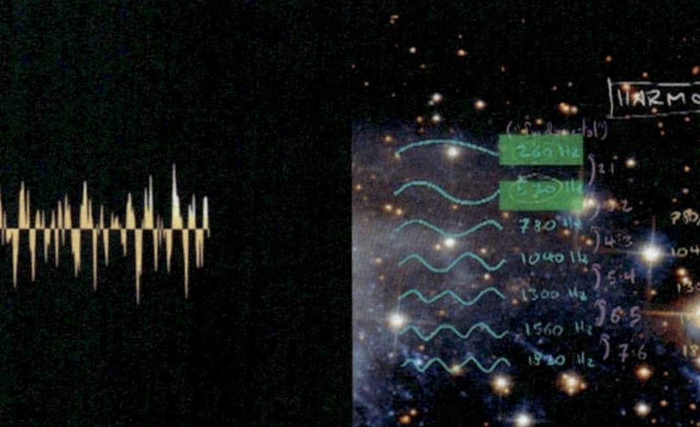

260 Hz
520 Hz
780 Hz
1040 Hz
1300 Hz
1560 Hz
1820 Hz
2:1
4:3
5:4
6:5
7:6

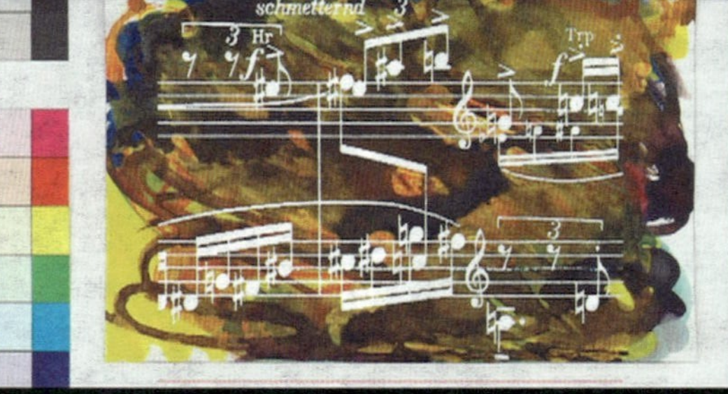
schmetternd
Hr
Trp

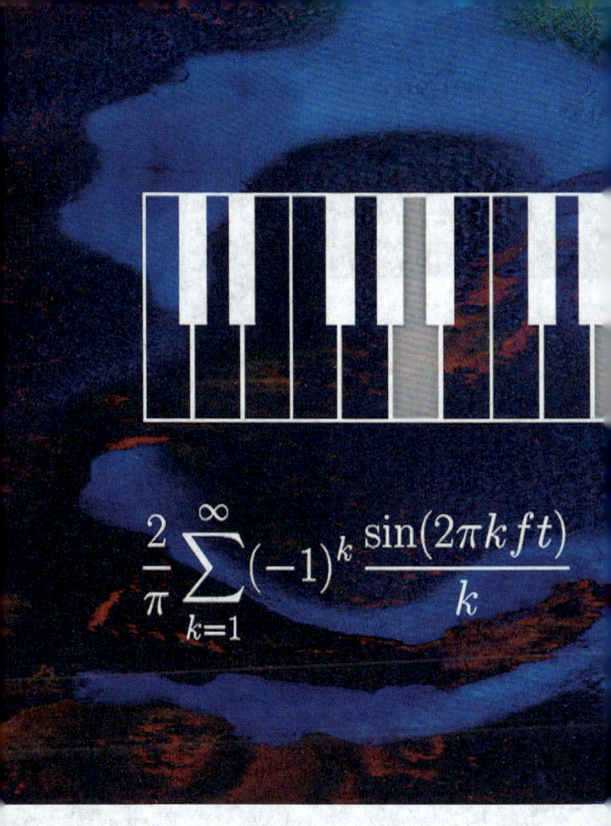
$\frac{2}{\pi}\sum_{k=1}^{\infty}(-1)^k \frac{\sin(2\pi k f t)}{k}$

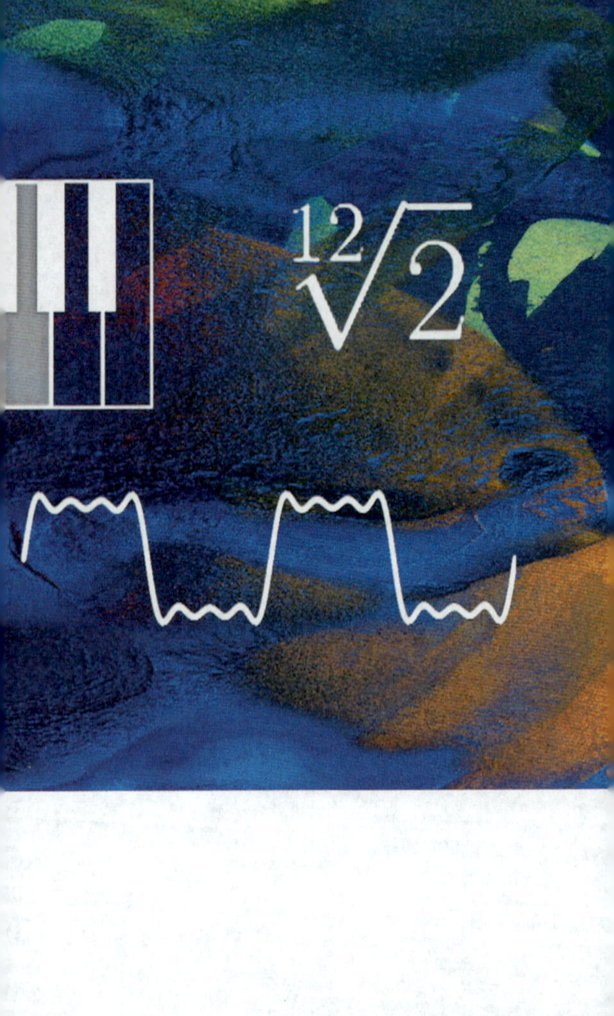
$\sqrt[12]{2}$

5

Worte darstellen

Umgebung als

Erinnerung

Preußischblau ←

---

die Dorfkinder
hatten Friede

Areas of Unquiet

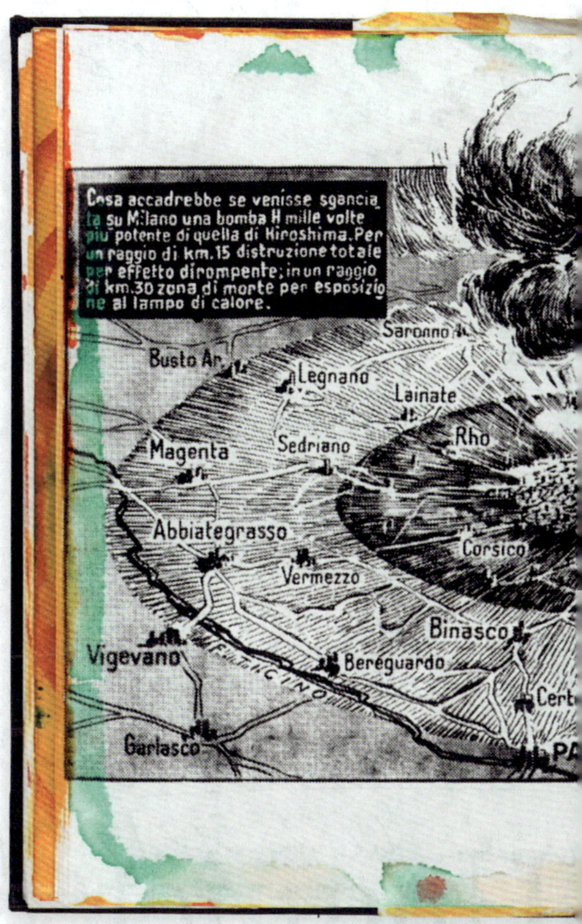
Cosa accadrebbe se venisse sganciata su Milano una bomba H mille volte più potente di quella di Hiroshima. Per un raggio di km. 15 distruzione totale per effetto dirompente; in un raggio di km. 30 zona di morte per esposizione al lampo di calore.
Saronno
Busto Ar.
Legnano
Lainate
Rho
Magenta
Sedriano
Abbiategrasso
Corsico
Vermezzo
Binasco
Vigevano
Bereguardo
TICINO
Garlasco

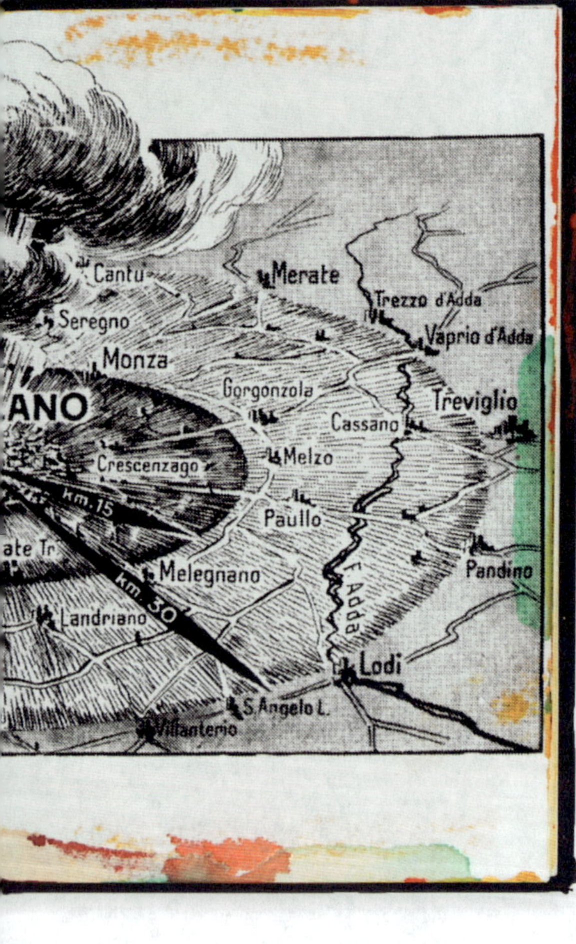
Cantu
Merate
Trezzo d'Adda
Seregno
Vaprio d'Adda
Monza
Gorgonzola
Treviglio
ANO
Cassano
Melzo
Crescenzago
km. 15
Paullo
ate Tr.
Melegnano
Pandino
F. Adda
Landriano
km. 30
Lodi
S. Angelo L.
Villanterio

WORLD TERROR

In those times of fortunate naiveté when on 1 March 1954 prototypes for the H-bomb were tested on the Bikini Atoll, a Marxist youth group was eating breakfast in the vicinity of Milan's cathedral. They said it was all a matter of not being afraid. War, too, is just an application of human labor power. In this respect, a construction that, to some extent, just combines fortuitously elements of physics doesn't belong to the reality of war. A kind of BANK FOR THE PHYSICAL EFFECTS OF HIGH-GRADE IMPROBABILITIES made up solely of dead labor. No one has ever been killed by this new generation of bombs. This is a hopeful sign that it will never happen.

As they sat there in the sun, they were not prepared for a compromise with the class enemy. A most acute compromise would have been possible, however, if they were so overcome by fear from such an abstract threat.

Abstract but how? Who in the United States would have reason to dispose of such a tool on the center of Milan? No, not that. Yet the West's weapons could provoke the Soviet Union into developing an equally powerful counter-weapon that could, by chance, fall on the center of Milan: that would separate us young Marxists from the homeland of all workers in the most radical of ways. What sort of malfunction might the speaker care to attribute to such an erroneous strike on downtown Milan? Quite understandably,

they considered Milan, in contradistinction to Rome, the center of the world, and on account of their caffeinated bloodstreams coursing through their young veins, they constantly refused to allow themselves to be made to look stupid through fear and propagandistic fairy tales that only the Pentagon pushes.

In reality, it was determined from the experiments in the vicinity of the Bikini Atoll that within the elements discharged by the fusion particularly deadly lithium compounds merged with the effects of the hydrogen, which subsequently transformed into helium. The deadly zone covered an area of 30 km², equivalent to the one stretching from Pavia to Lodi to Magenta and beyond.

Their metropolitan home had been completely destroyed more than once. Accompanied by his barbarians from the north, Barbarossa rode into the city that later capitulated to him.* He celebrated Easter there and then had buildings and walls carried off stone by stone for fifty days till Pentecost. A dusty desert in the bright sunlight. But then grass grew. People returned from the villages on the horizon of the Po Valley. It was wrong to fear the cruel German emperor. He had to perish in the Orient, but Milan would never die. What should readers take from comrade Marx's writings other than the distinction between what should be feared and what should not be feared?

Monza would be affected by an H-bomb's nuclear zone along with all the spirits of those

drivers who perished at the Italian Grand Prix. The same goes for Legnano, where the Milanese battlewagon conquered the German knights. In contrast, the windowpanes in Pavia would only be shattered. From there, an escape to the southwest would be possible.

According to Marx's early writings and *Grundrisse*, those times of belligerent discussion were, however, naïve because no one investigated the actual element that would have set off an H-bomb explosion. Before Chernobyl, half-life was only an abstraction. No one found out from academic experiments performed on the shores of the distant Bikini Atoll how the effects merged together. Put into motion not by some elementary particles but rather by a mere storm, a splinter of glass is enough to blow a hole through my body. What's the use in knowing about the consequences that could kill me again?

* The Pope's propagandists called him and later his grandchild THE DREAD OF THE WORLD, "paura del mondo, metus mundi." Riled by defeats, the emperor saw reason to level Milan, the center of the resistance. In this respect, Rome kept up with Carthage. The emperor is educated. He knows how imperators put a landscape to rest.

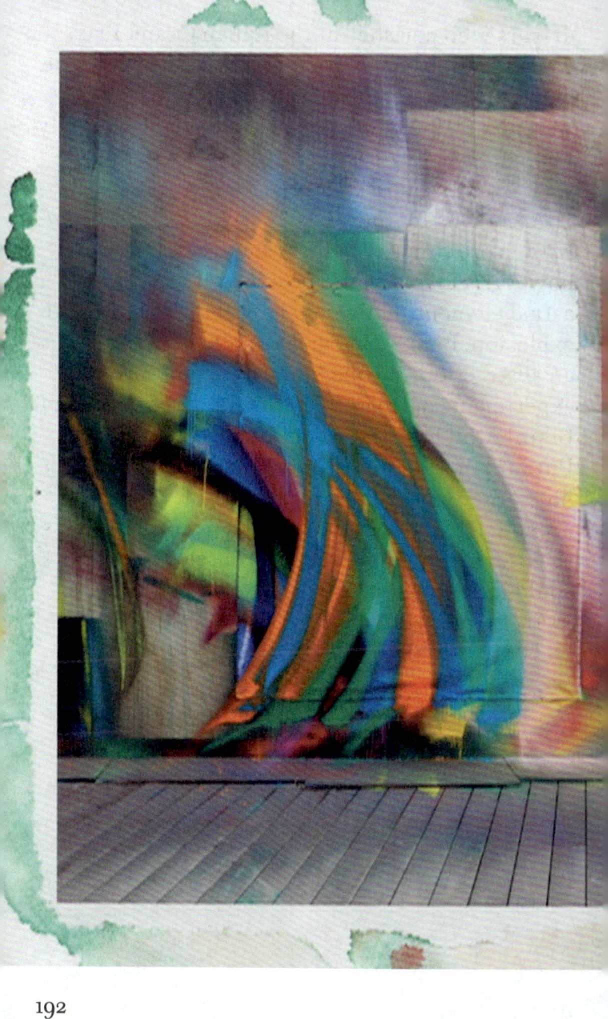

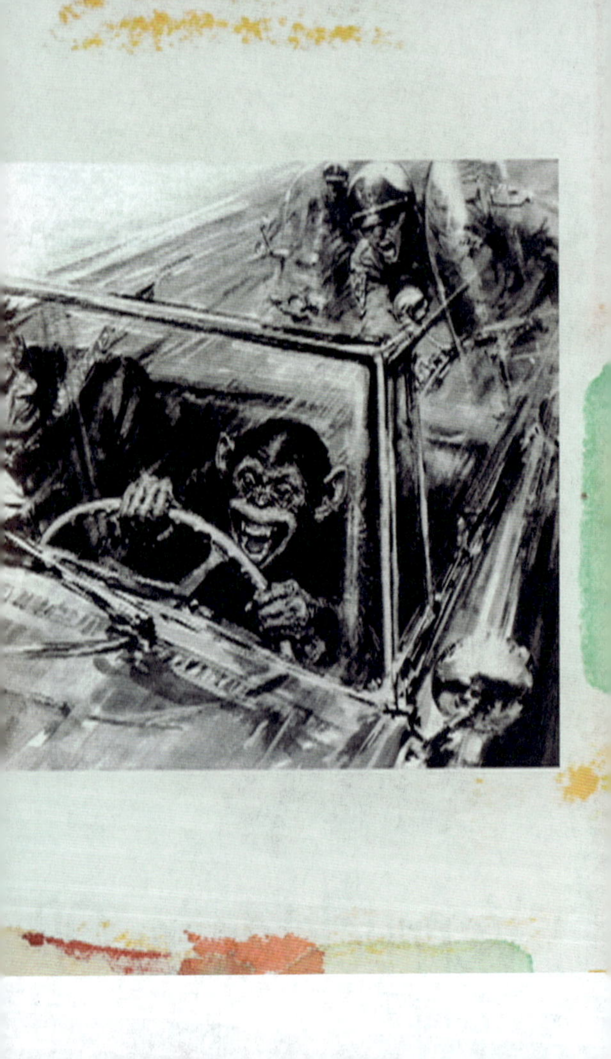

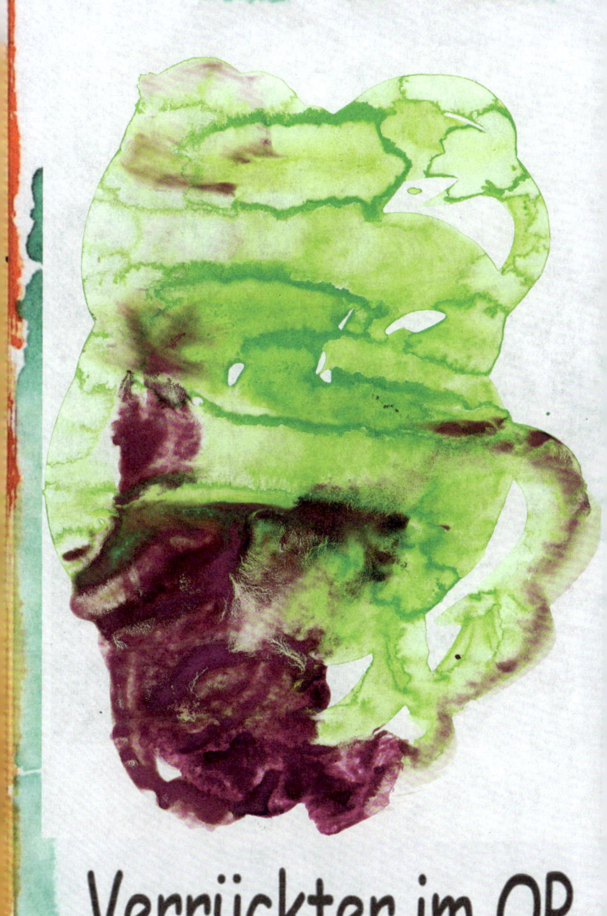

Verrückter im OP

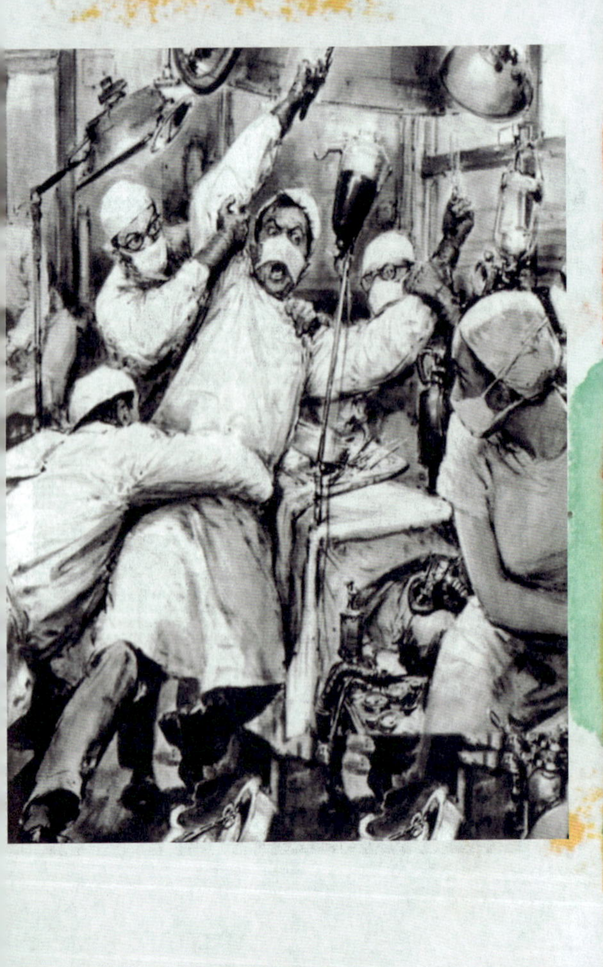

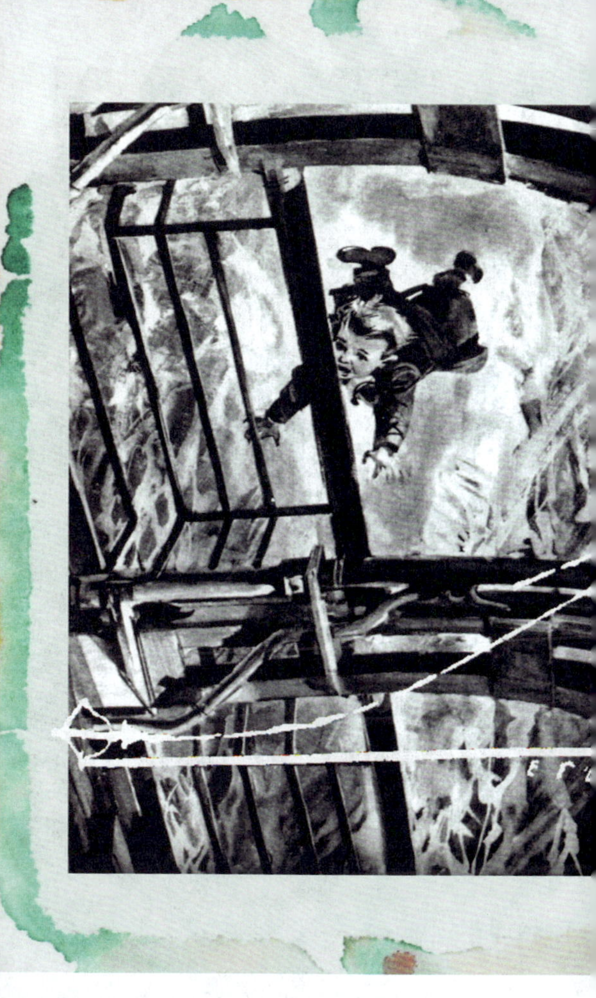

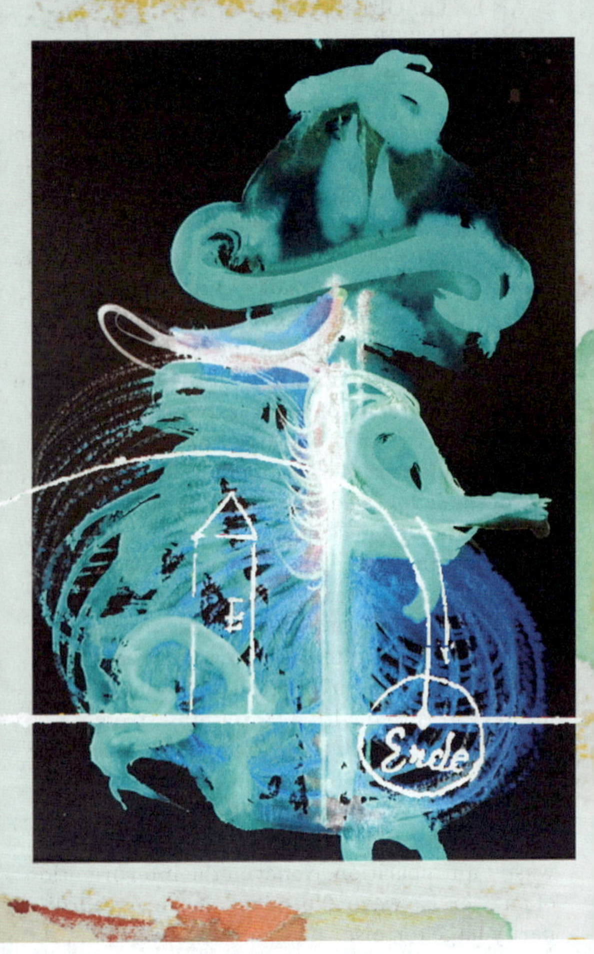
E
Ende

AN EXTRAORDINARY ENCOUNTER SOUTH OF AFRICA

Only forty nautical miles off the southern coast of Africa, defying the roaring westerly winds, a group of shipwrecked sailors who'd saved themselves in a rowboat were greeted by a mysterious sight. The body of a giant tortoise towering above the crest of the waves like some kind of AVENGER. Now, for their part, the sailors did not feel any guilt at all. They'd never had turtle soup or even tasted turtle meat. So how could this happen?

We'd have known nothing of the event had the shipwrecked men not eventually come to shore fourteen miles east of Cape Town. Their report in the London press was soon forgotten. However, one of the sailors said, you could see wrinkles on the giant turtle's neck, just beneath its shell, one of which was the size of a human being and several more the height of tenement buildings. The eye of the swimming creature had seemed "threatening," at the very least "intense." How the creature managed to swim through the turbulent seas is a mystery. It rowed with its forelimbs, stretching its nostrils skyward. Were the castaways rowing? No, they remained in a state of shock. It was a "ghastly sight," harrowing to the end of their lives. And after that did the apparition disappear? It wasn't an apparition. Not even the interpretation of an oversize wave? No, not at all. An extraordinarily large tortoise.

The sailor was interviewed before the Royal Society by a professor from Oxford. Just such a sea creature, with the appearance of a tortoise, though seven times larger than a whale, had never been seen in the world's oceans—could the sailor rule out having been in error? The narrator, who was originally from Spain, answered: That is what I saw.

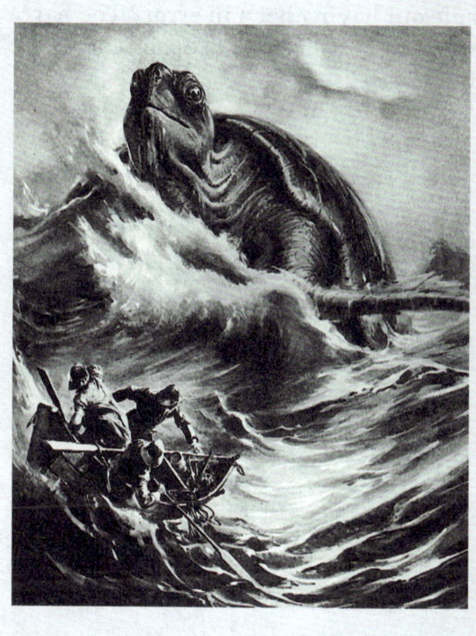

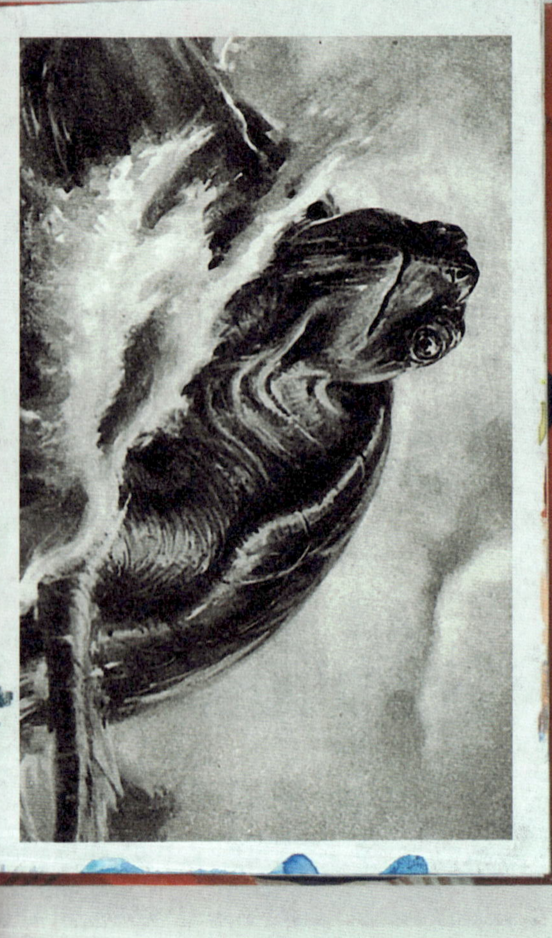

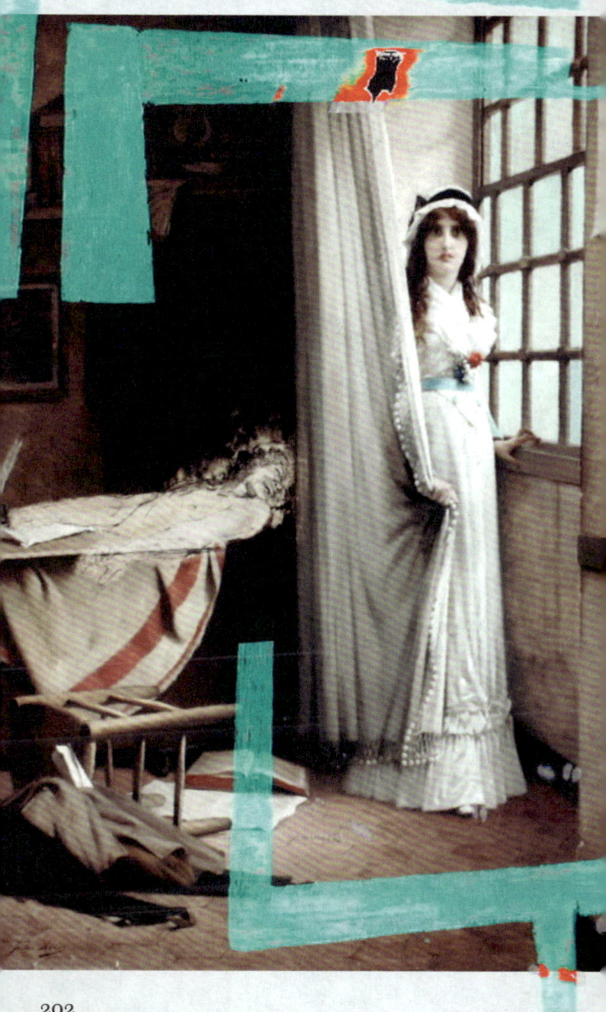

HOW MARAT DIED

Charlotte Corday of Normandy was determined to kill Marat, the revolutionary and journalist. In her mind all the denunciations he had published in his pamphlets had made him personally responsible for the death of numerous innocents. And so now she was calling upon him with the pretext of handing him a list of further suspects.

With firm steps the young woman passed through the front door to the house. Marat lived and worked on the first floor. She did not let the concierge stop her. She stepped into Marat's room. He was sitting in the bath, attempting to treat a horrible rash. Before him a board on which to write. The day before Charlotte Corday had bought a knife. She plunged it into Marat's heart all the way to the hilt. Coming from above, it passed by the collarbone, went through the entire lung, opened the aorta, and unleased a powerful gush of blood. The young woman was arrested at the scene of the crime.

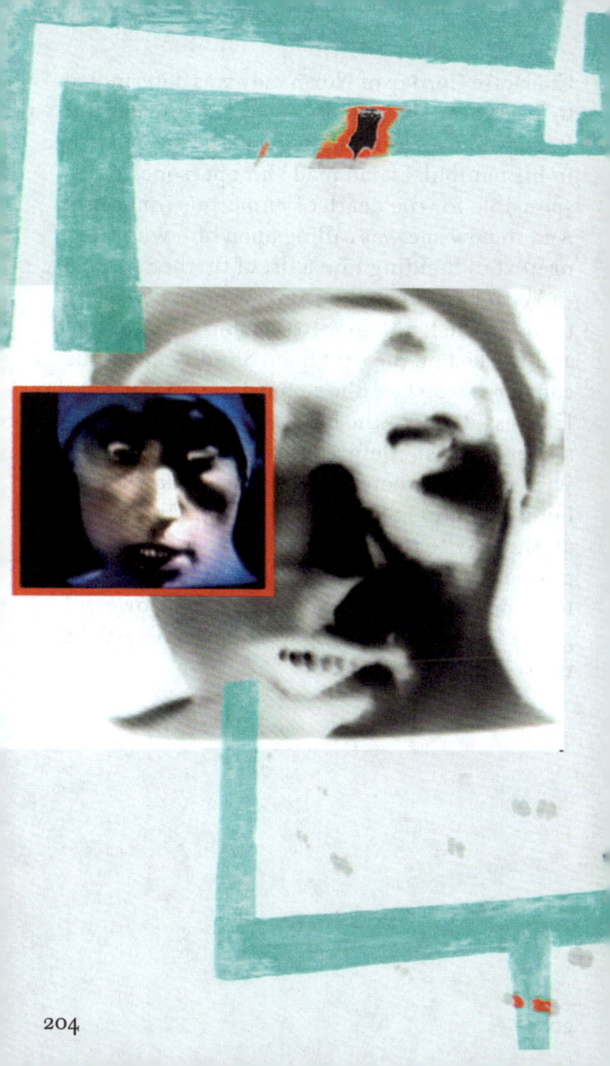

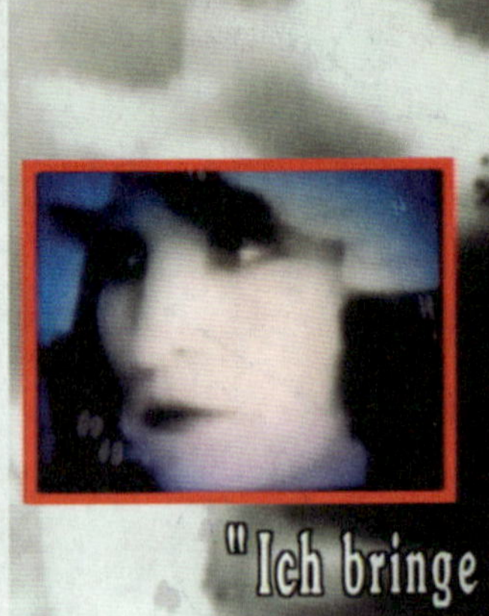

"Ich bringe eine Liste
von Verdächtigen - -"

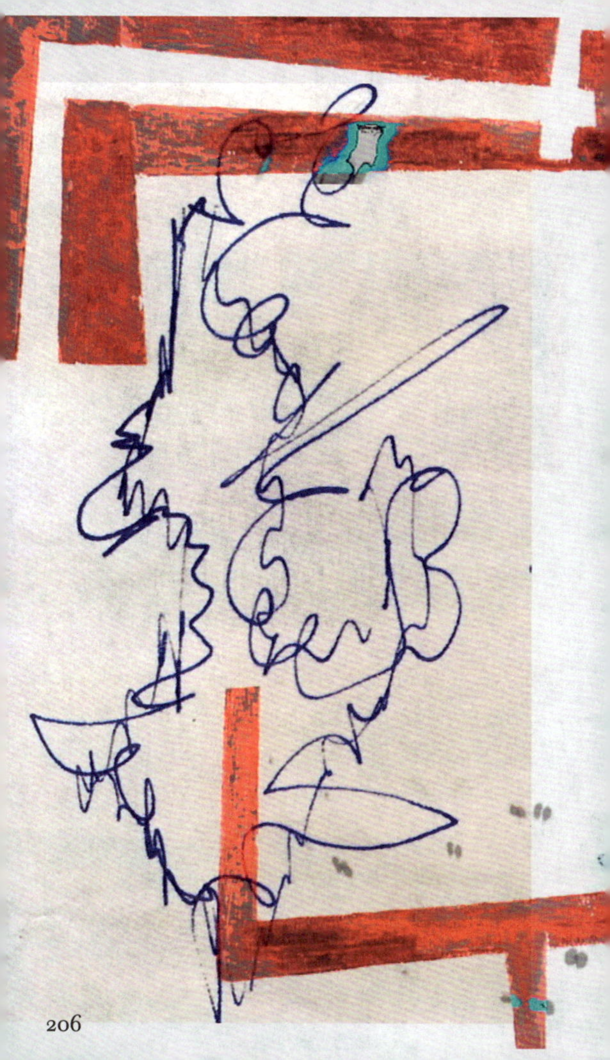

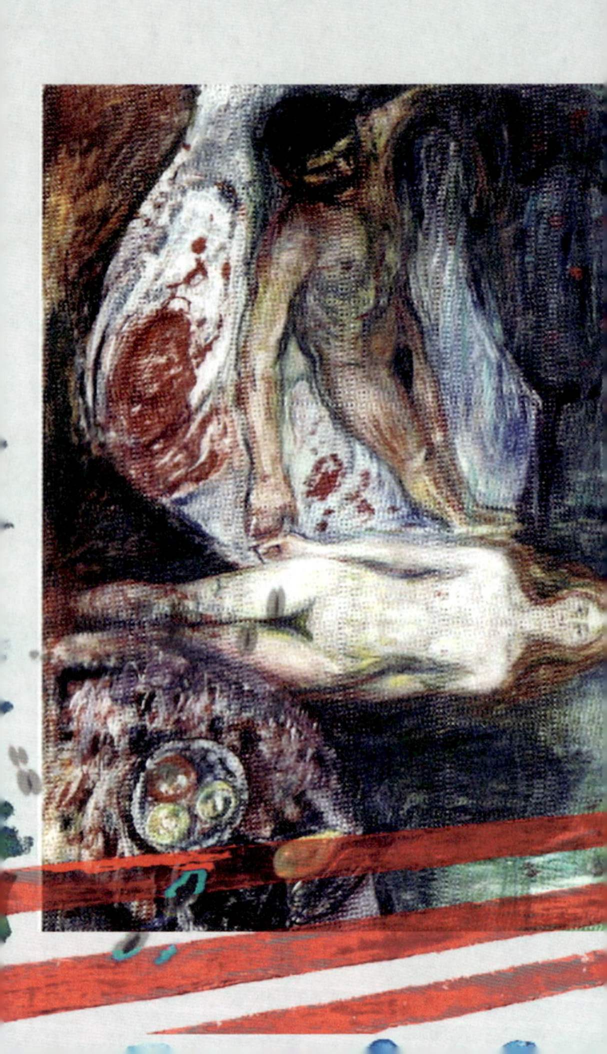

From Jules Michelet's seven-volume *History of the French Revolution*, on CHARLOTTE CORDAY'S DEATH (translated here from the German):

"She maintained a perfect calm, a solemn and simple serenity amid the clamor of the crowd. A doctor, who did not lose sight of her, says that she appeared pale when she noticed the ax.

As soon as the head fell, a carpenter, one of Marat's followers who was assisting the executioner, grabbed it with his fist. Showed it to the people and slapped it with shameless brutality. A shudder of disgust, a murmur, ran through the crowd. It was said that one could see the head blush. Perhaps it was a mere optical illusion: the confused crowd was looking at the red rays of the sun penetrating through the trees of the Champs Elysees. The Paris Commune and the Court of Justice enjoyed a general feeling of satisfaction and put the man in prison."

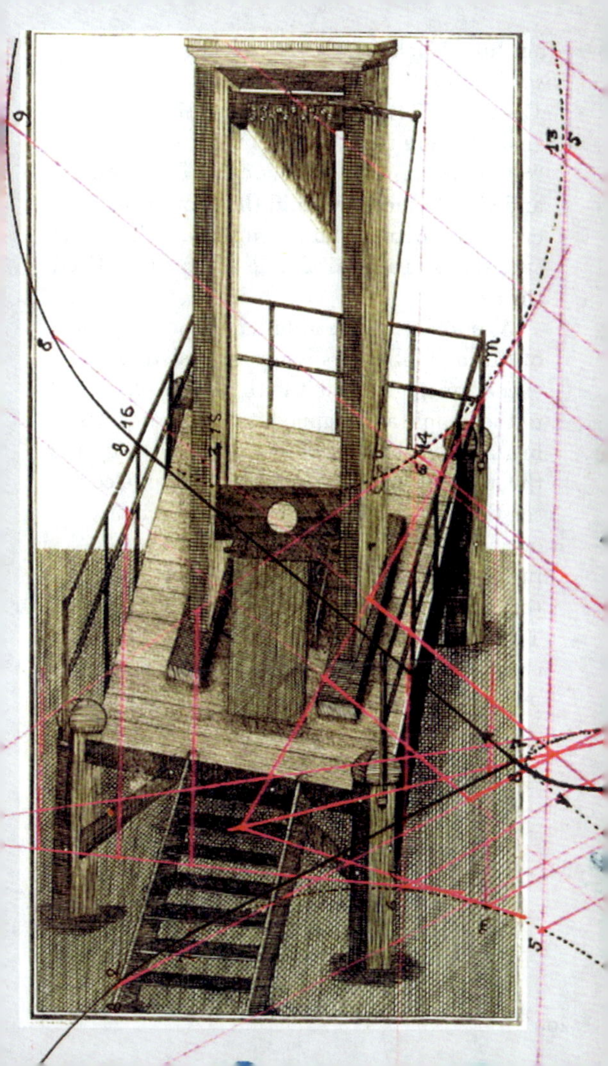

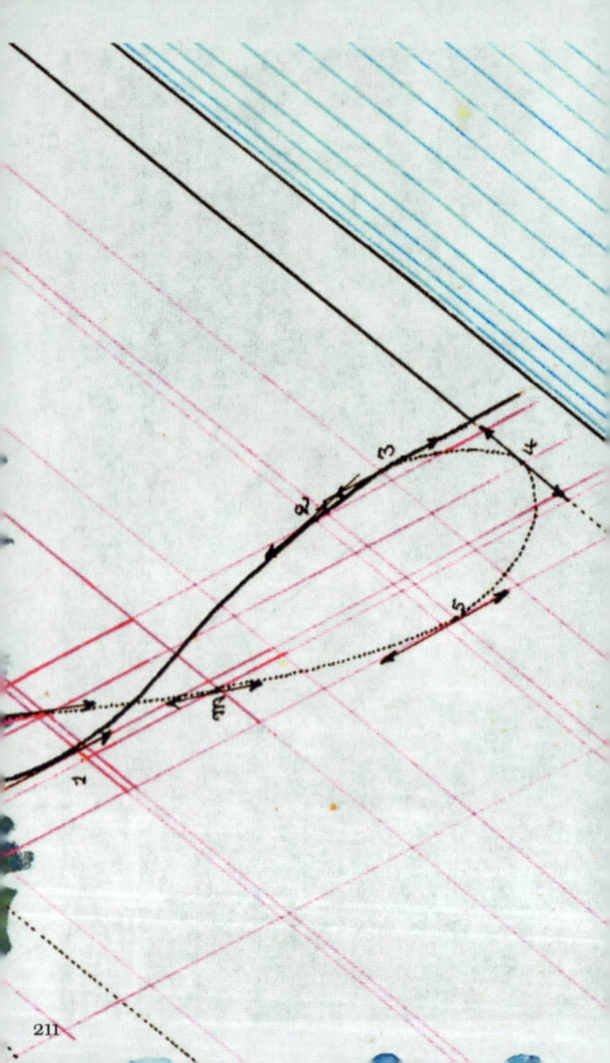

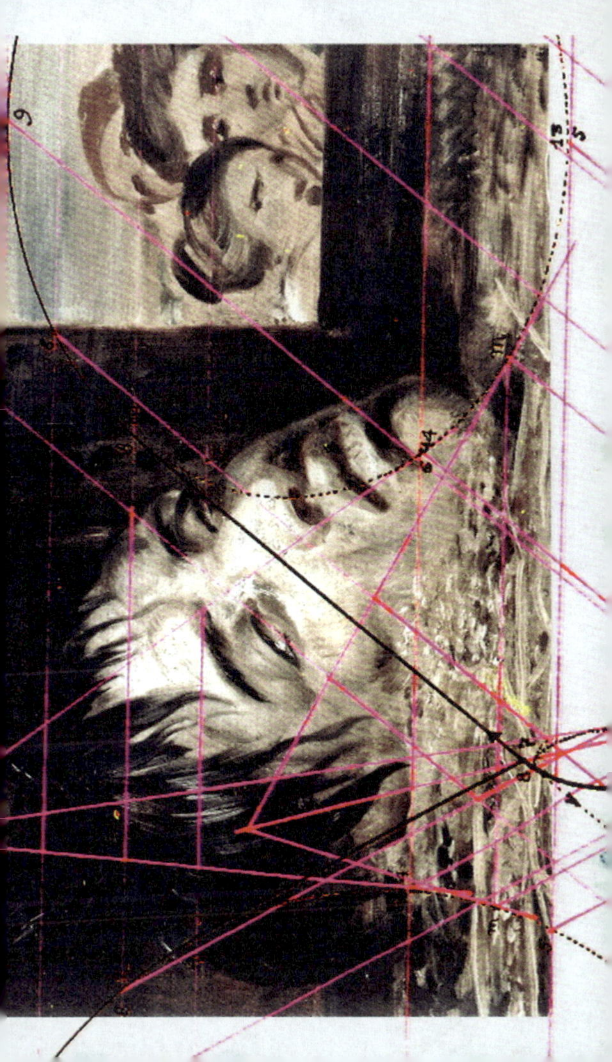

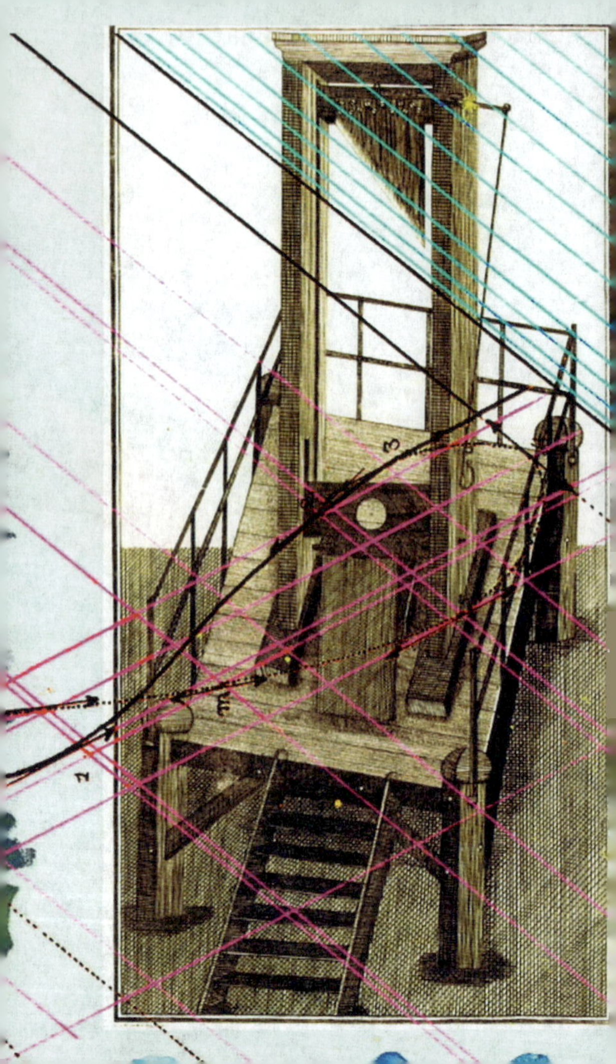

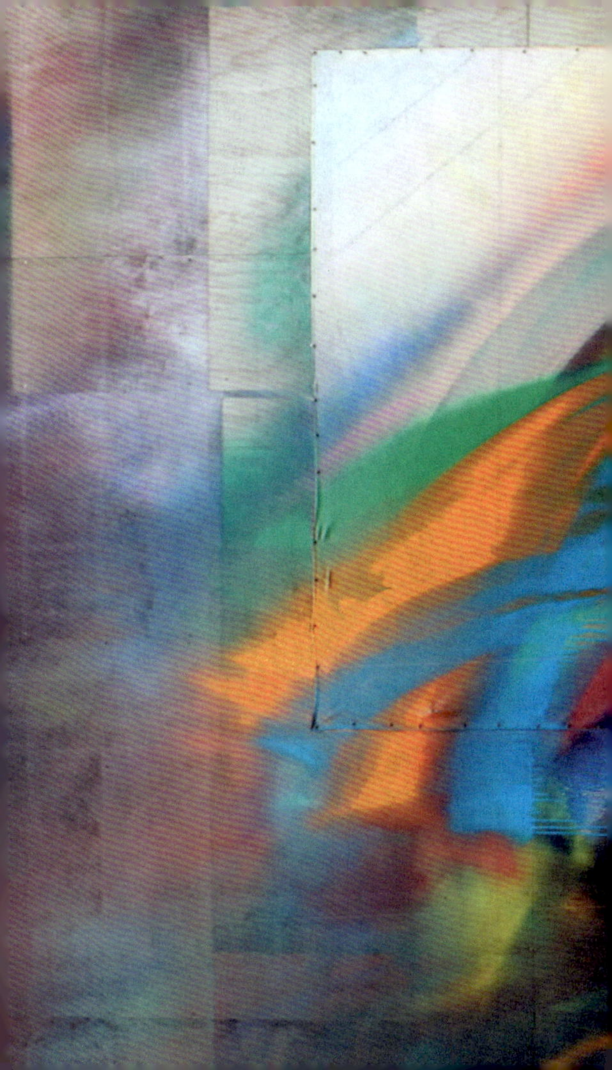

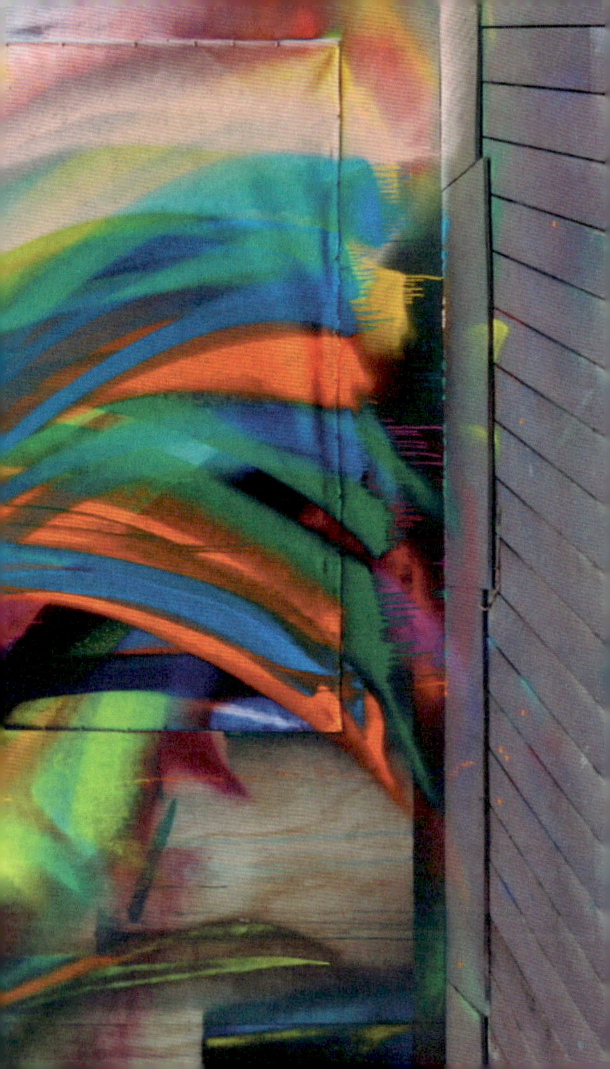

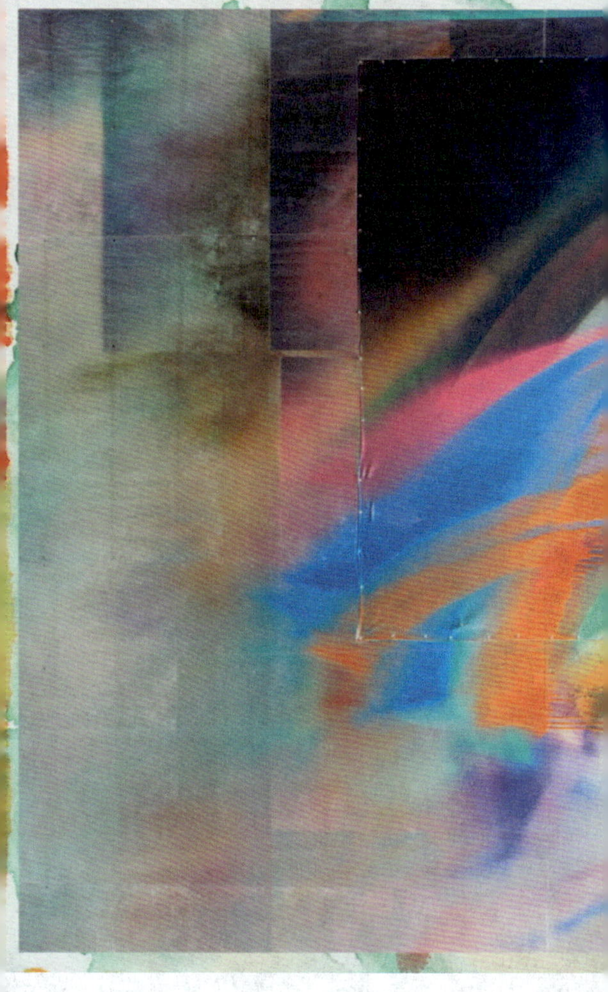

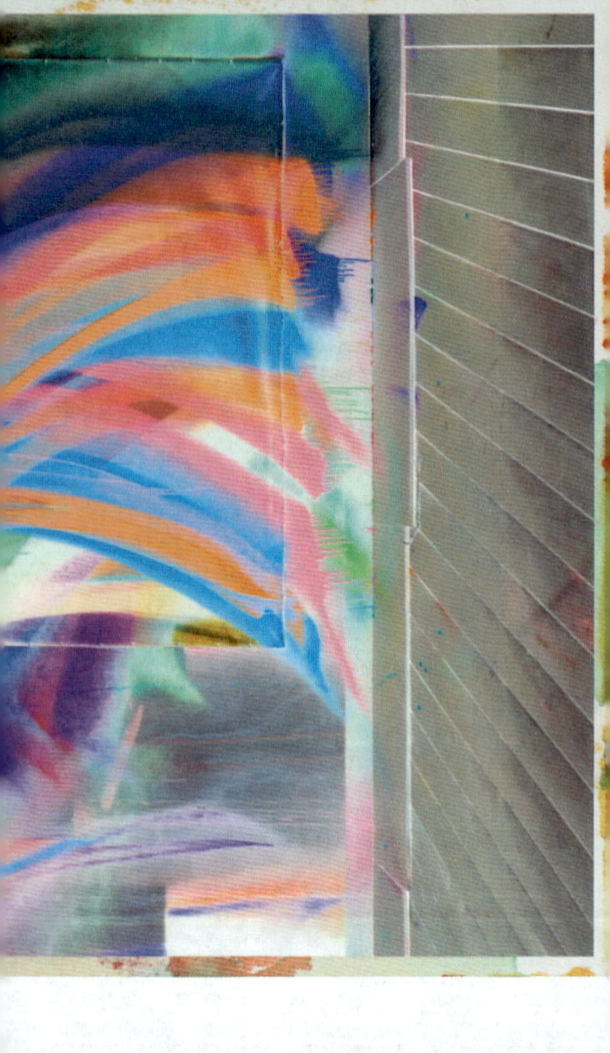

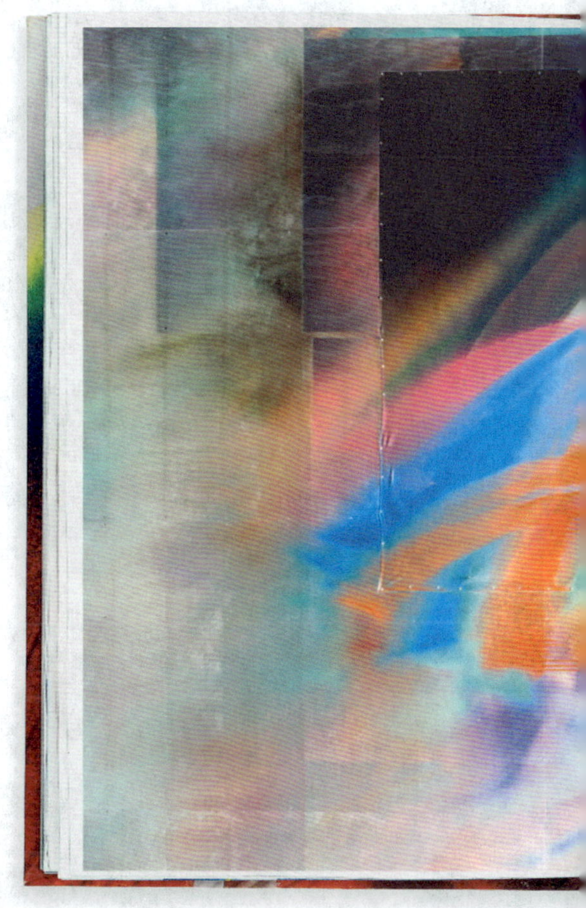

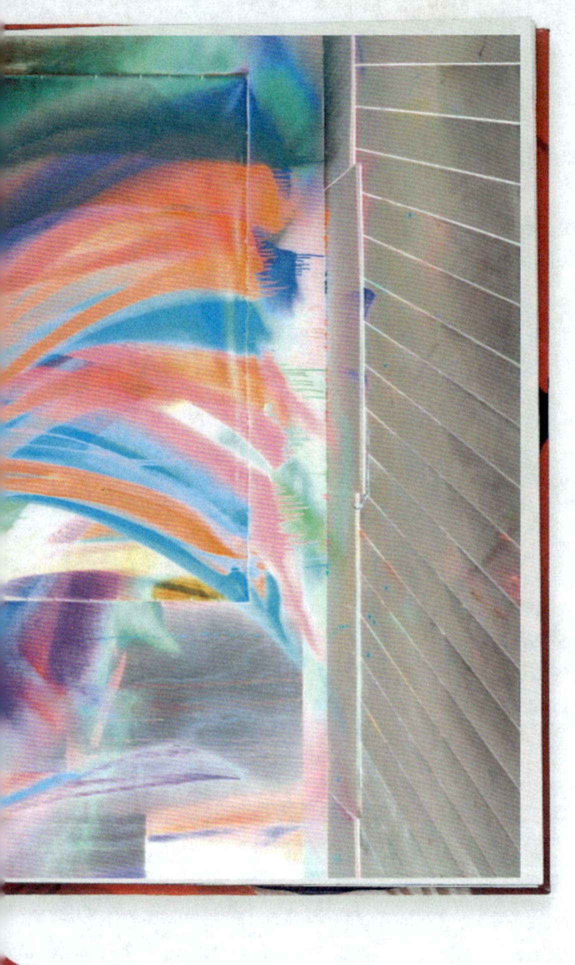

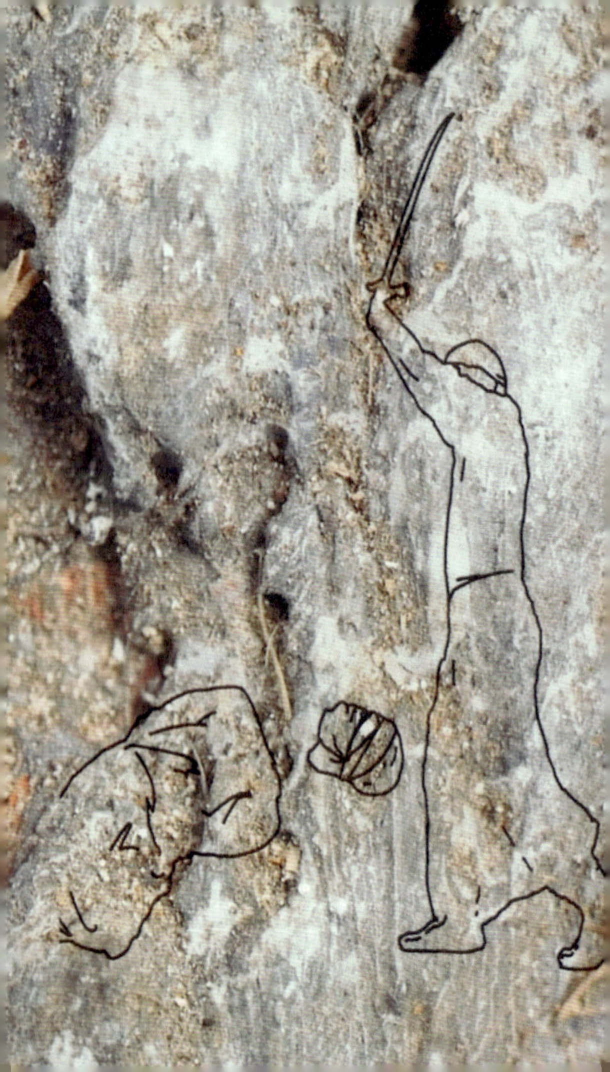

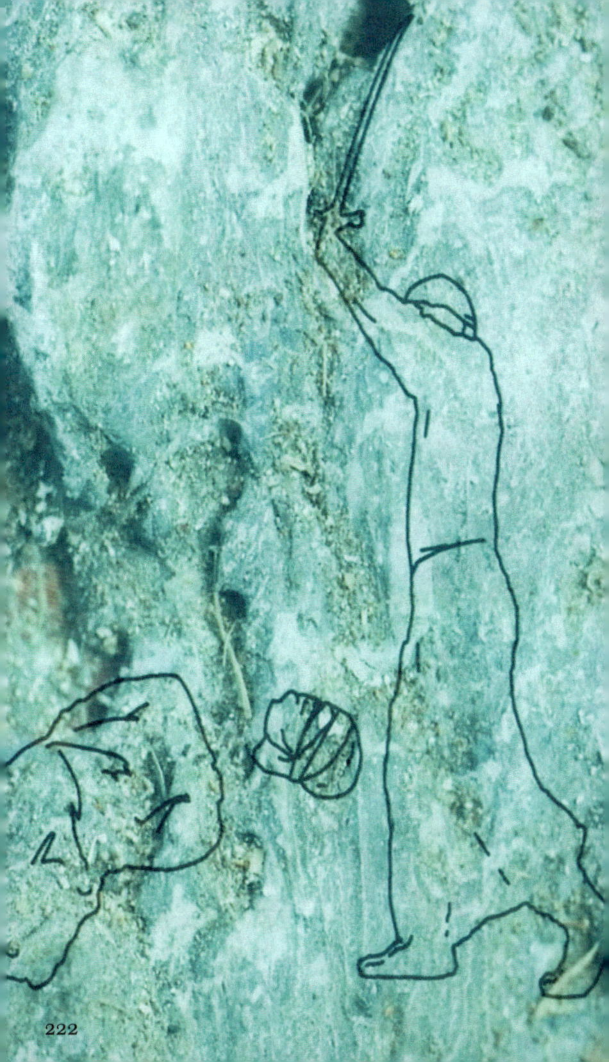

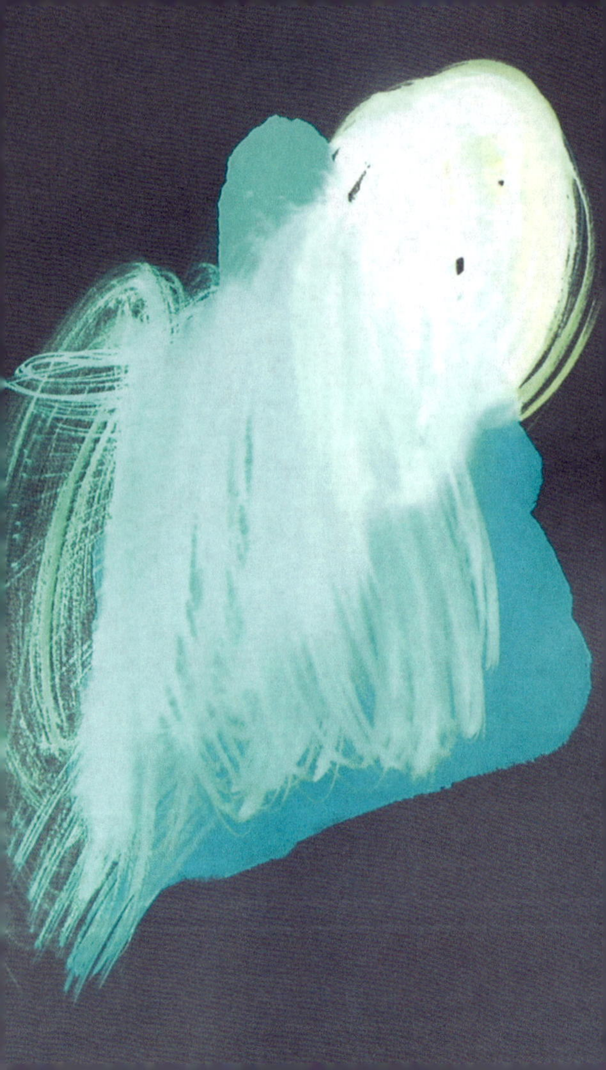

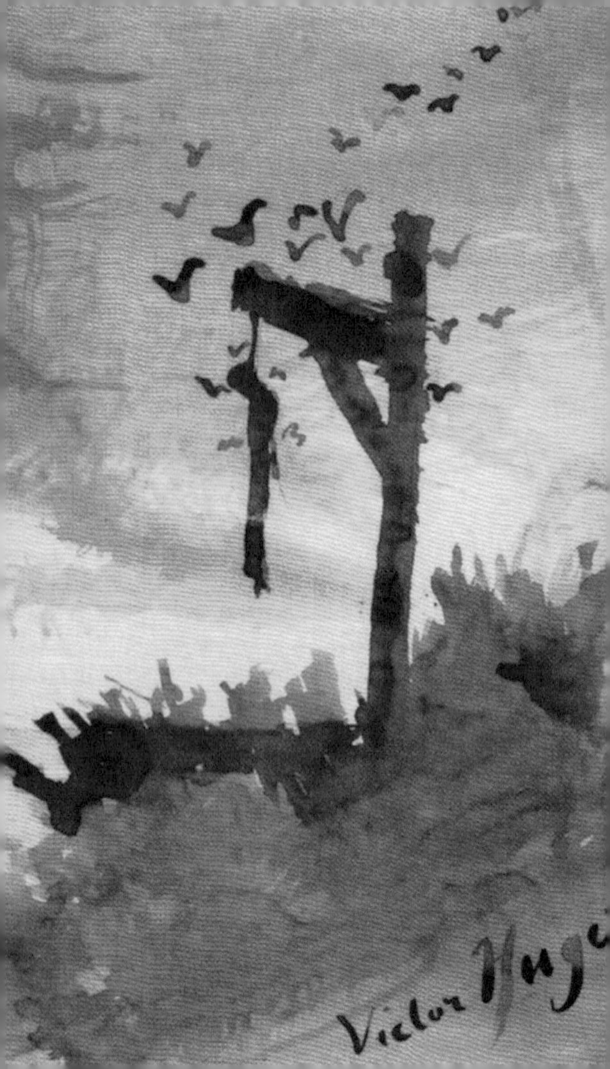
Victor Hug

That afternoon, Lockett, whose relationship with the prison's authorities was considered bad, had refused to be brought in for a radiology exam. The examination was to check whether his physical condition was more suited to oral ingestion or intravenous injection of the drug cocktail that was to kill him. His resistance was overcome by means of a Taser. Only a few hours later, the cocktail triggered violent convulsions in his body while he was strapped to a gurney. The condemned—thirty-eight-years old—tried to sit up, and screamed. The body's sputtering lasted thirty-three minutes. At that time, the prison director ordered that the procedure be abandoned. Ten minutes later, Lockett died of a severe heart attack.

The execution of the murderer Charles Warner was scheduled for the evening of the same day. The delinquent's attorneys petitioned the Supreme Court of Oklahoma; they argued that the drug cocktail meant to induce death—due to a series of cost-cutting maneuvers—would instead produce "disproportionate" and "imbalanced" effects in the body of the condemned and thereby constituted torture and not the death penalty. The Supreme Court ordered a stay of execution until the circumstances were clarified. State Governor Mary Fallin saw the Supreme Court's verdict as a dereliction of duty on the part of the judges. A constitutional crisis loomed, one eagerly anticipated and hoped for by the media, which, in

the meantime, had made the case of national interest in the United States. Law professors from Ivy League universities and head partners of law firms (in all, more than six hundred lawyers) had all staked out positions.

The constitution of the United States forbids cruel and inhuman punishment. As a result of press and media reports that were laid out in front of her every quarter-hour, the governor changed her position. Charles Warner had been —temporarily—saved by the gruesome death of his fellow inmate Lockett earlier, that is, until an alternative drug cocktail could be mixed, tested on animals, and externally reviewed. Switching to the noose or a firing squad, as standards in China would have allowed, was forbidden by Oklahoma's state laws.

PURE SPIRIT TINKERS ON THE BOULEVARD

In the year of his death, all of Heinrich von Kleist's poetic powers were still at work on the *Berliner Abendblätter*. The poet was never closer to the people than with his "Stories of Aquarius and the Mermaids." Never had he indulged the heroes in Elysium (above all Voltaire) more than with his story about marionette theater. In that narrative, there is the parable of the fencer and the bear. The Russian bear ignores the fencer's feints; he does not even see them, and instead advances without inhibition on the fencer's body. In the circles of boulevard enthusiasts at the Munich Security Conference 2015, this metaphor was quite popular and much discussed.

Berliner Abendblätter, 7 January 1811

A MURDER COMMITTED OUT OF LOVE*

One could read recently in the official newspapers that a pair of lovers, in a shared moment of despair, killed each other. A very similar incident occurred near Lyon in 1770. That story can be found in the *Journal encyclopédique* from the same year. According to the journal, an Italian fencing master named Faldoni had inflicted so much damage to himself while training that the surgeons charged with his care declared that he would soon succumb to his injuries, and thus he should prepare for his own death. This unfortunate man had been passionately in love for some time with a young woman who loved him in return. Initially, both lovers succumbed to severe despair on account of the surgeons' declaration. The jealous Italian could not accept leaving his lover behind in the world, and she professed that she did not want to live without him. Reassured by this, Faldoni thenceforth brooded over the most dreadful thought; the only thing he needed to know before enacting it: his lover's true determination had to be tested. In a moment of tenderness and pain, he let her repeat over and over that without him her life was meaningless, even odious. Thereafter, he drew a vial from his pocket and said: This is poison! and immediately drank it. Beside herself with pain, his lover ripped the

remainder from his hands and gulped it down. Only then did he admit to her that he had merely wanted to test her love and courage. With a pained joy he told a friend about the attempted trial run. The friend proceeded to take away Faldoni's weapons and tried to liberate him from the morbid thoughts plaguing him. The invalid acted composed and declared hope that, contrary to the doctors' opinions, he would survive. To that end, he pretended that a surgeon in a distant city had promised to keep him alive. Under this pretence, he prepared for a trip. A few days later, the young woman asked her parents to allow her some time to take advantage of the country air around their cottage at Ivigny on the shores of the Rhône, two hours from Lyon. Armed with two pistols, the Italian immediately made his way there. The young woman then wrote her parents a note wherein she took eternal farewell from them. Once they had excused all the servants, the lovers locked themselves in the house chapel. There they seated themselves at the foot of the altar and, with their left arms, wrapped a ribbon around themselves. Each held a pistol at the other's heart, and then, with a single movement, both pistols went off and simultaneously pierced their chests. In the meantime, the mother left Lyon immediately and with utmost haste in an effort to foil the disastrous plan. All she found were the lifeless bodies bound tightly together. Her daughter had bound her eyes with a cloth,

Faldoni, though, had hidden his face with his top-coat. The lover was thirty and his beloved twenty years old.

* Heinrich von Kleist, ed., "Mord aus Liebe," *Berliner Abendblätter* 5 (7 Jan. 1811): 18. [Trans.]

Berliner Abendblätter, 9 January 1811

MATERNAL LOVE*

In the year 1803, in the northern French town of St. Omer, a curious event occurred. There, a large, mad dog that had already injured numerous people set upon two children playing in a house's doorway. In the very moment that it tears at the youngest, now writhing in blood underneath its claws, the mother appears out of a side street carrying a pail of water on her head. As the dog lets go of the children and charges her, the mother sets the pail down next to her and, unable to flee, is resolved to at least take the dog down with her: With limbs steeled by fury and rage, she clutches the dog, strangles it, and shredded by its ferocious bites, collapses unconscious beside it. The woman buried her two children and, after she died from rabies a few days later, was buried beside them.

* Heinrich von Kleist, ed., "Mutterliebe," *Berliner Abendblätter* 7 (9 Jan. 1811): 27. [Trans.]

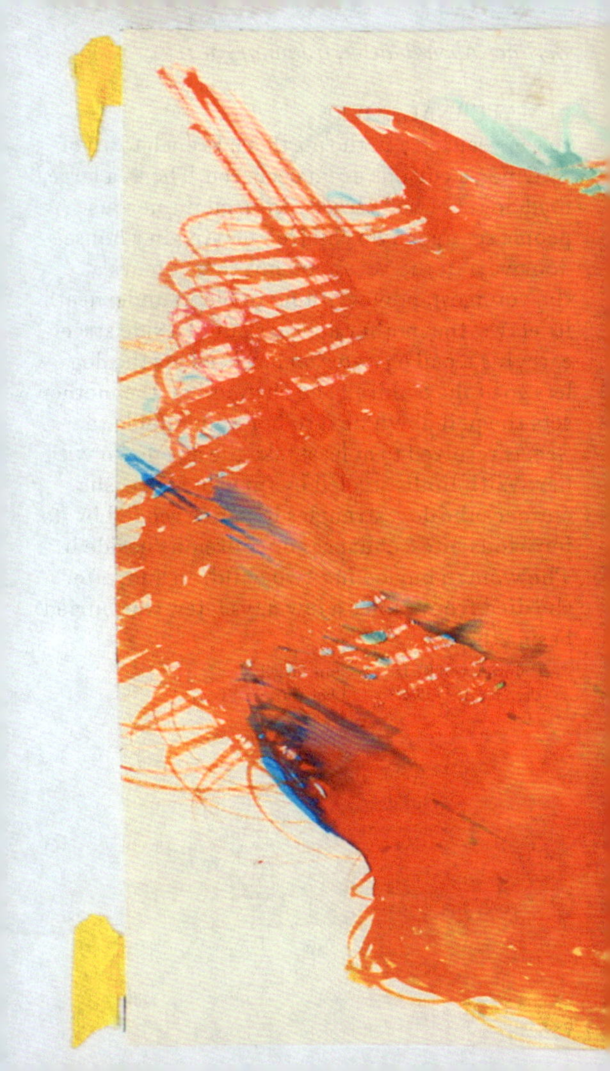

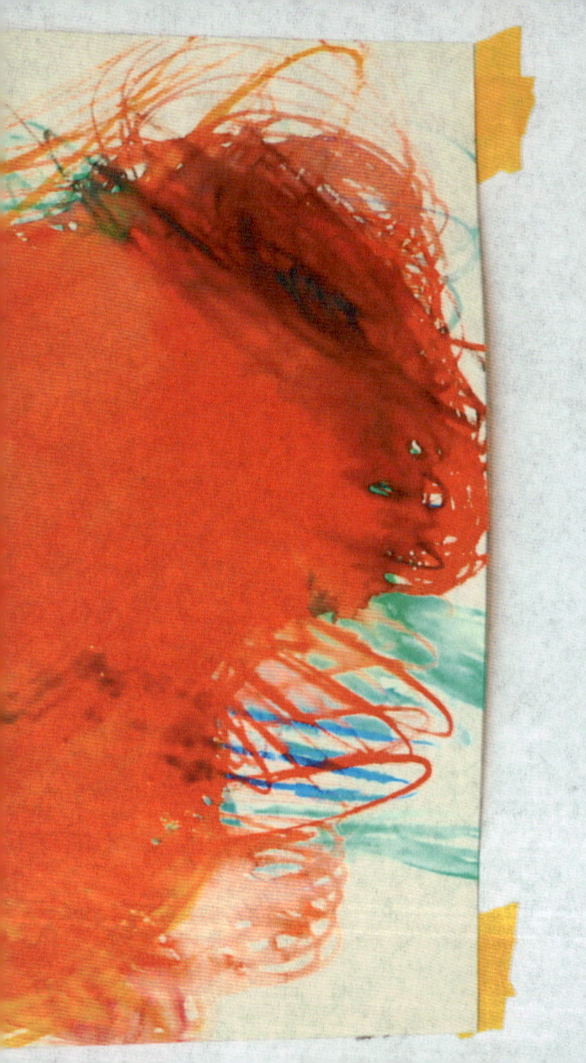

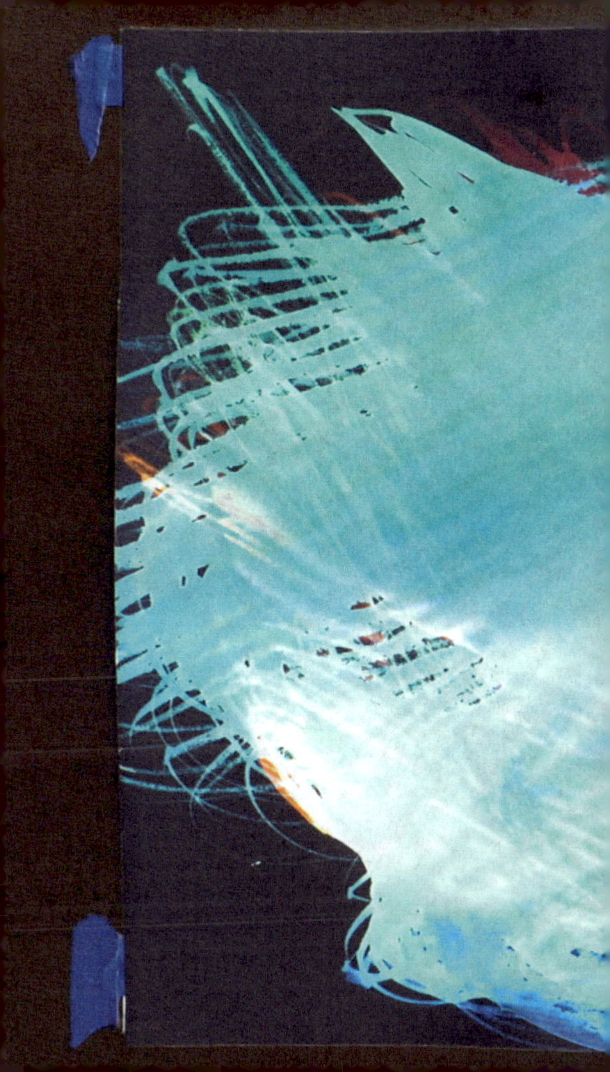

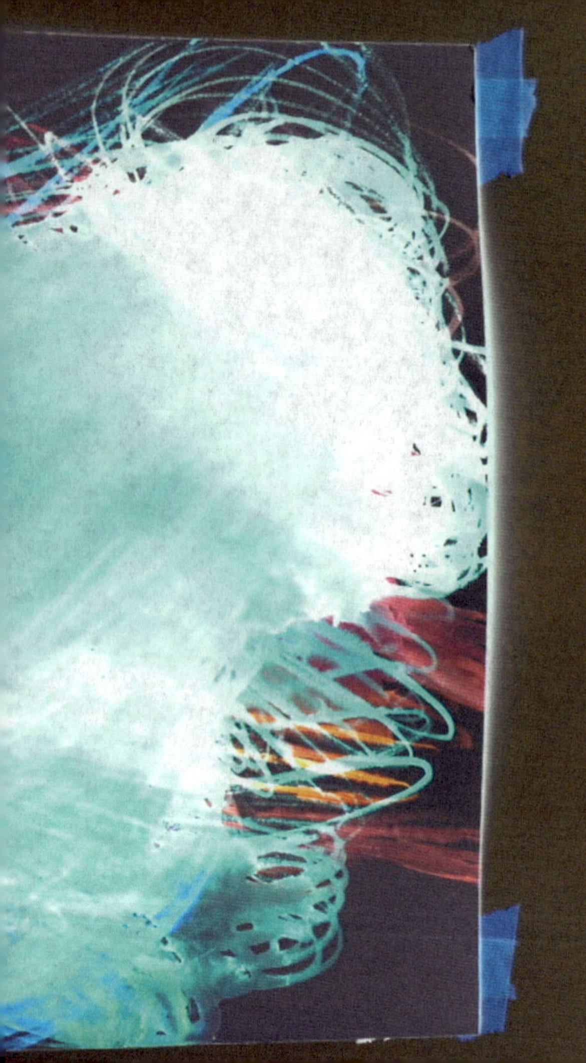

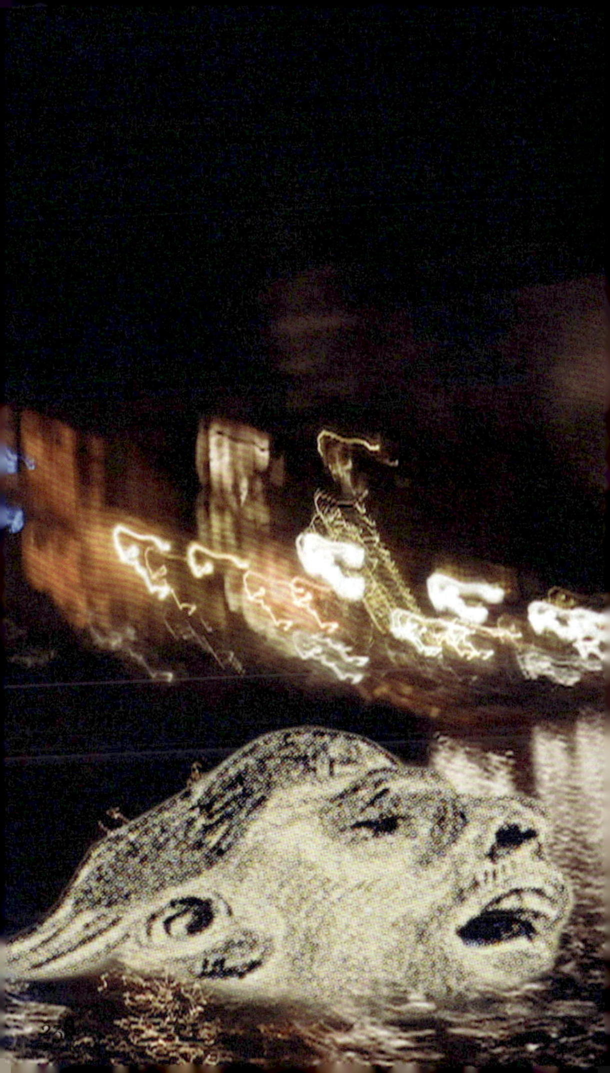

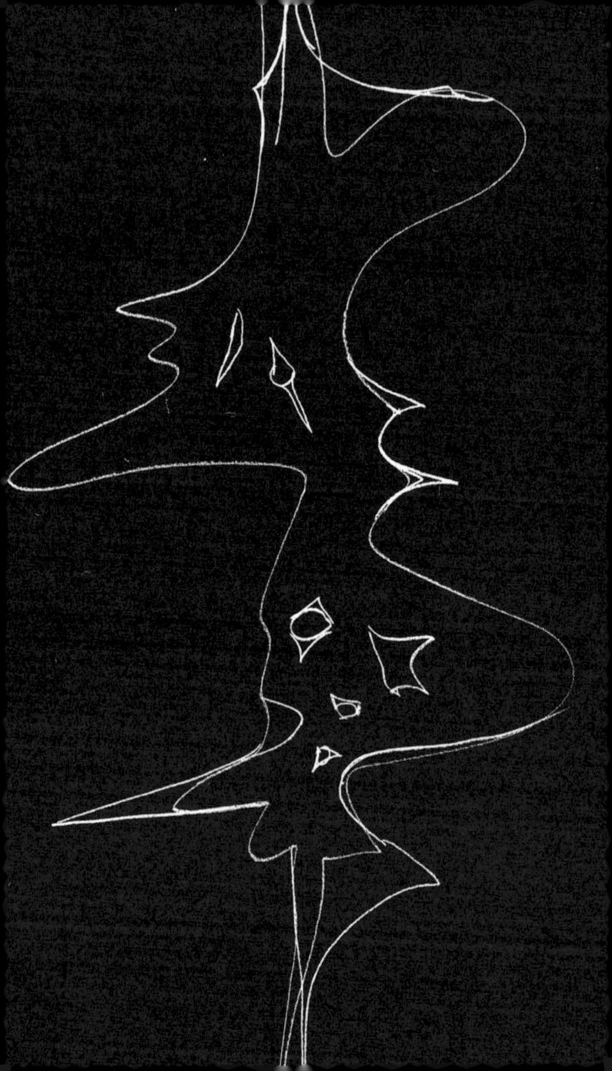

6

The Quiet Chapter

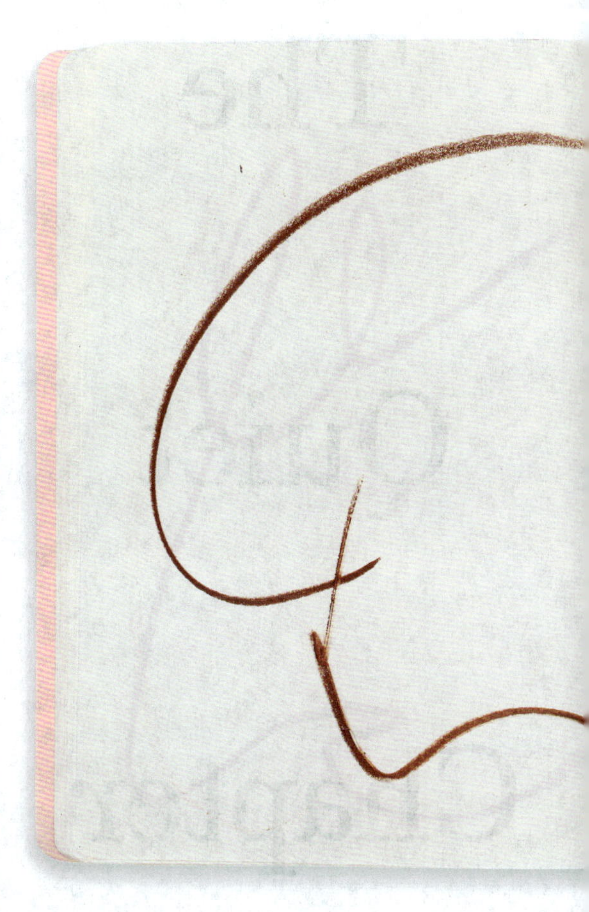

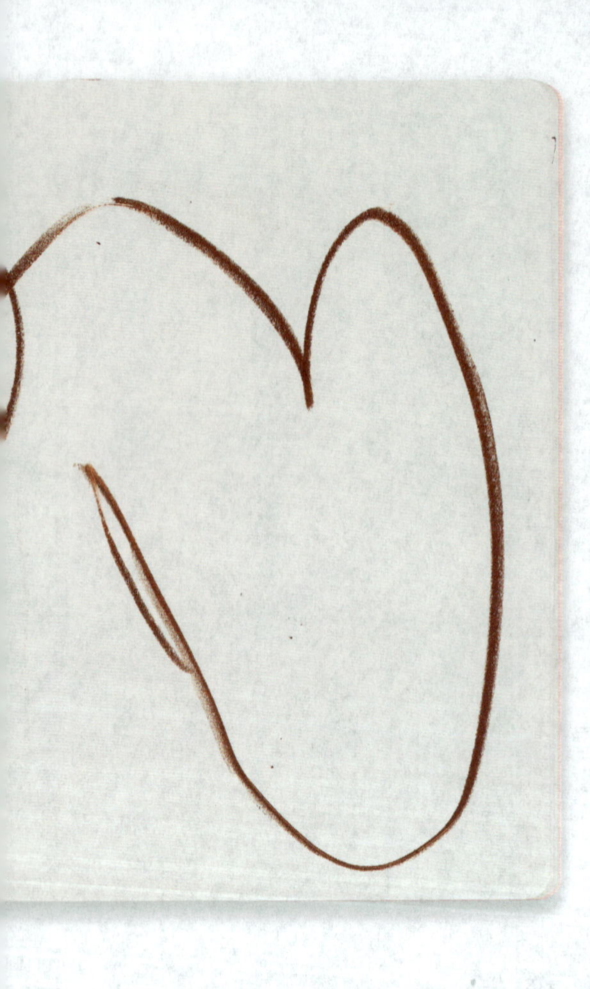

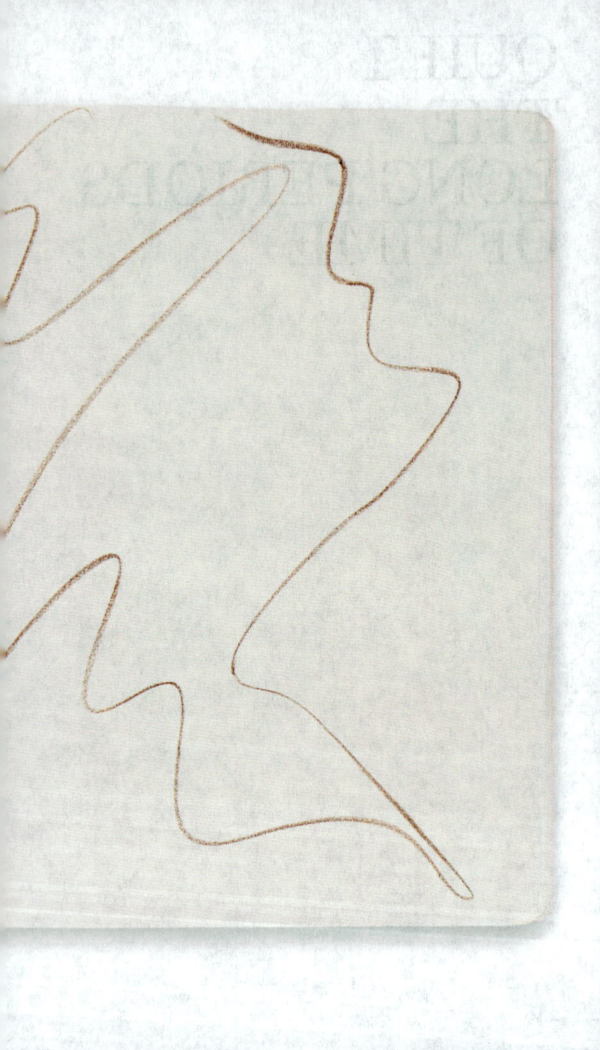

QUIET THE LONG PERIODS OF TIME

QUIET THE STARRY NIGHT

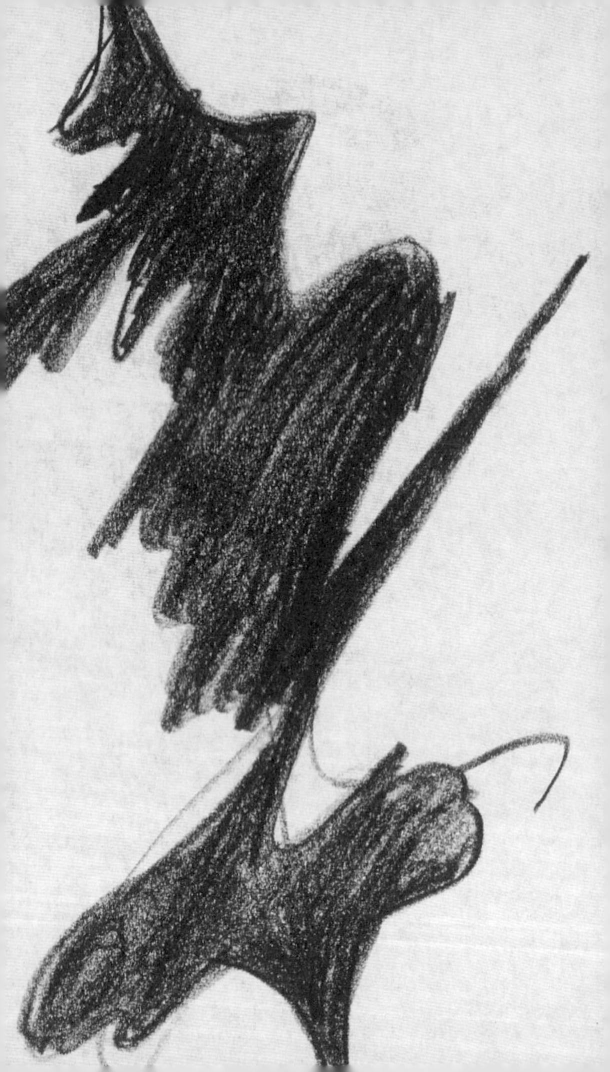

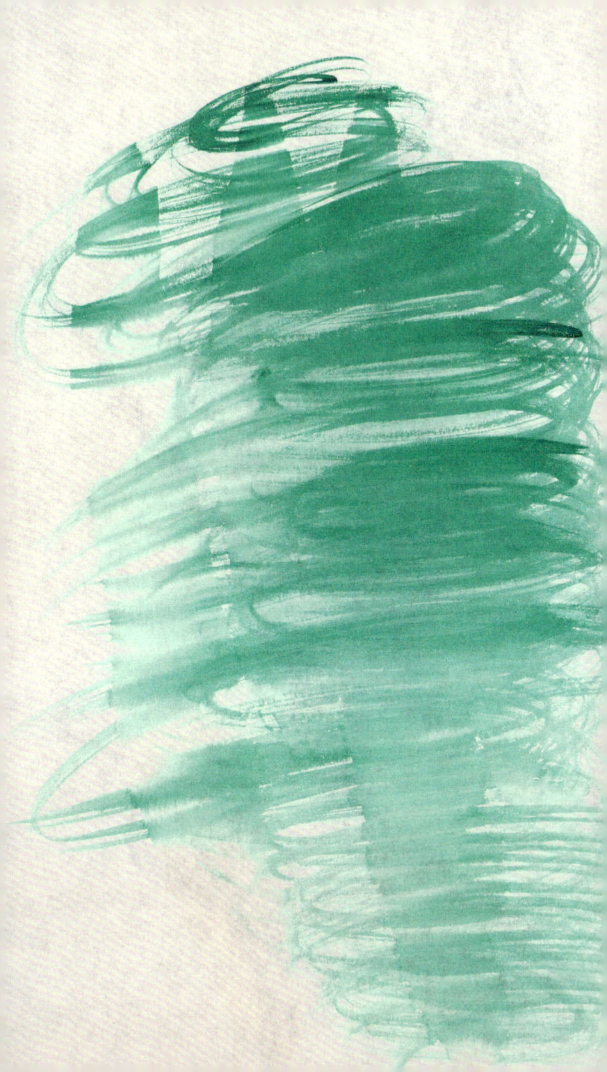

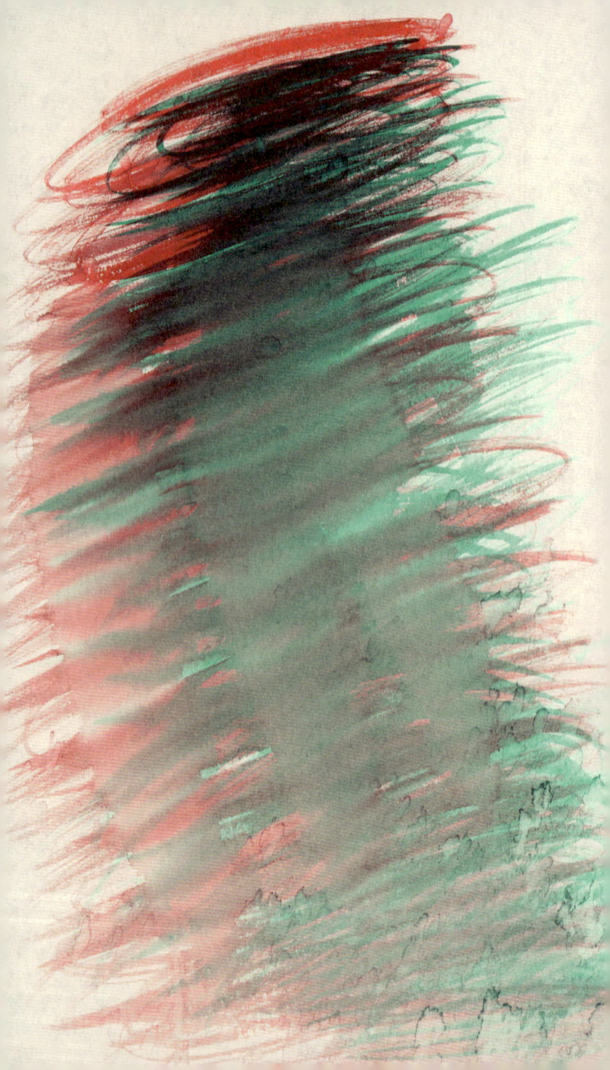

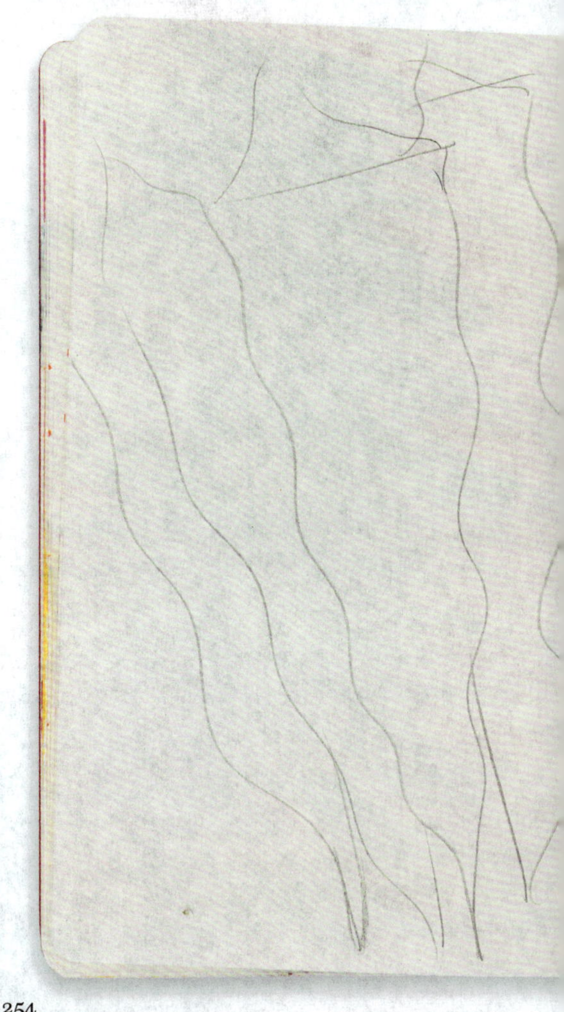

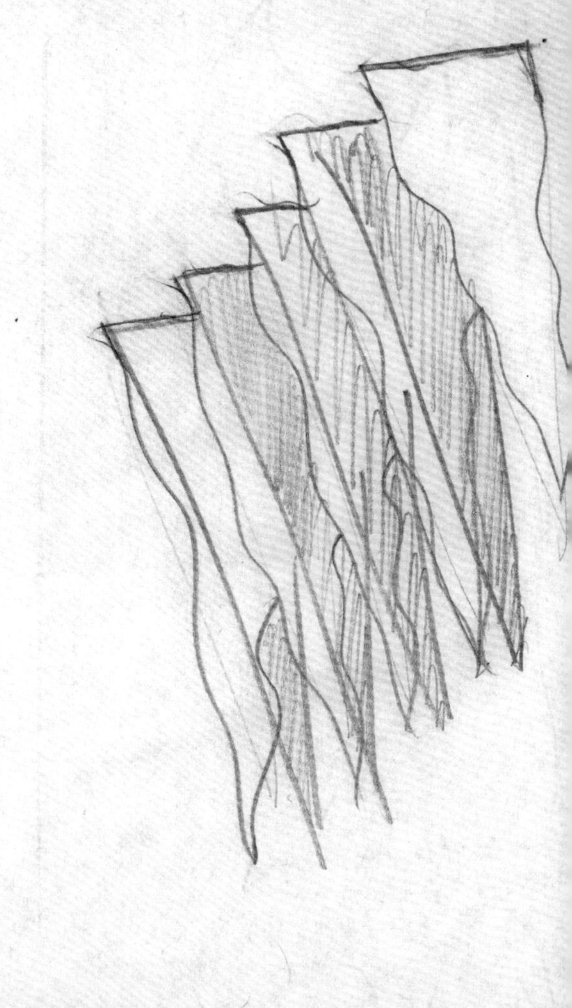

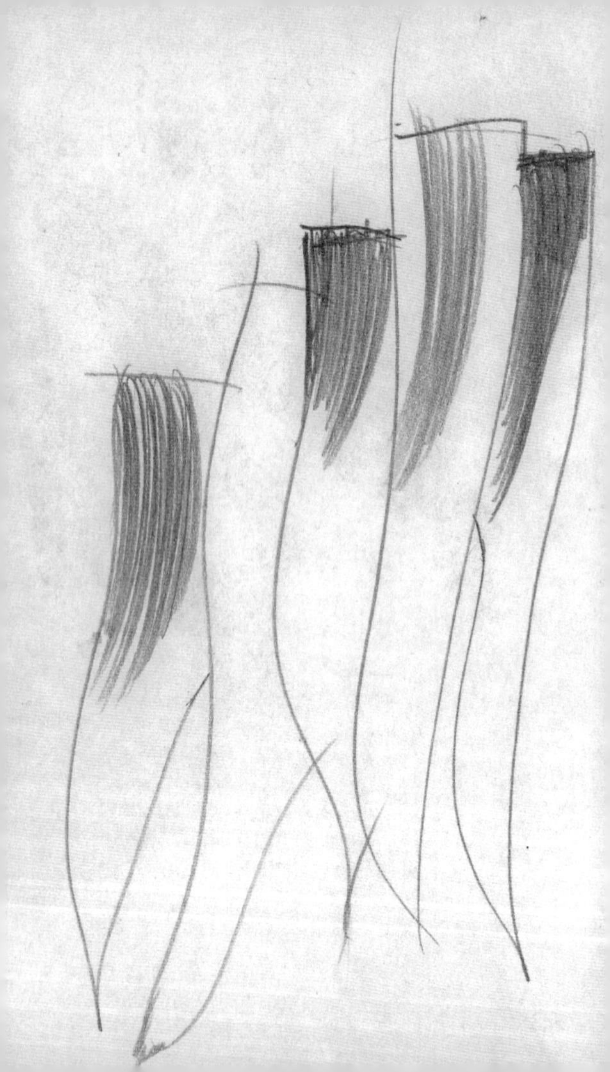

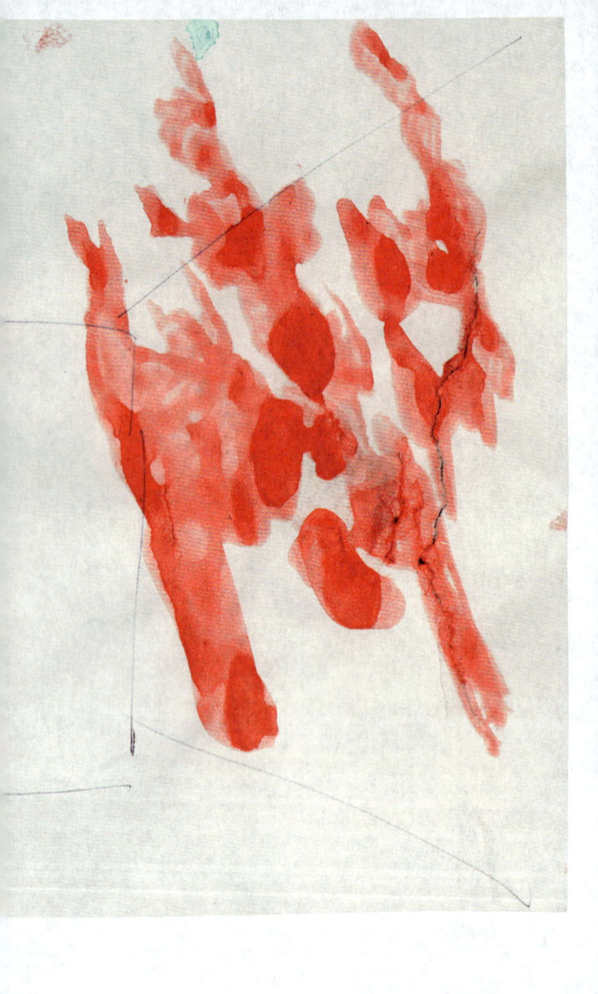

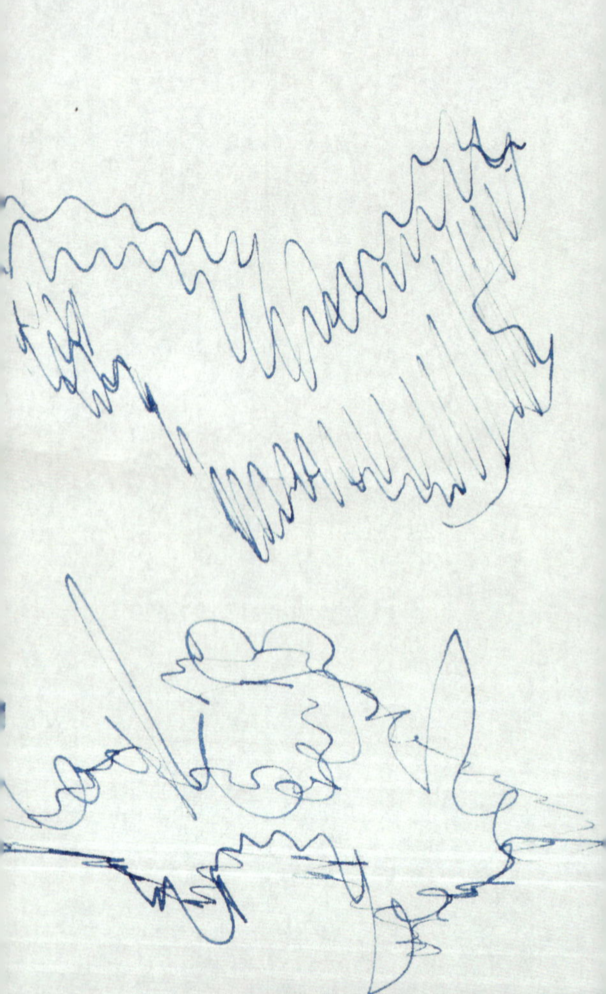

SLOW
THE
"MOUNTAINSEAS"
WHEN
THE
MOON
BRINGS
THEM
TO
EBB
AND
FLOW

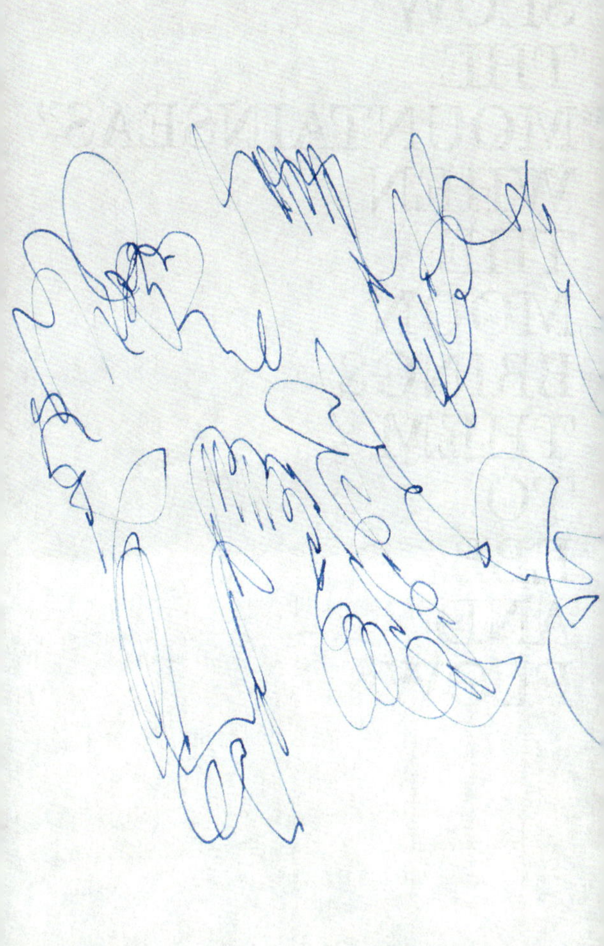

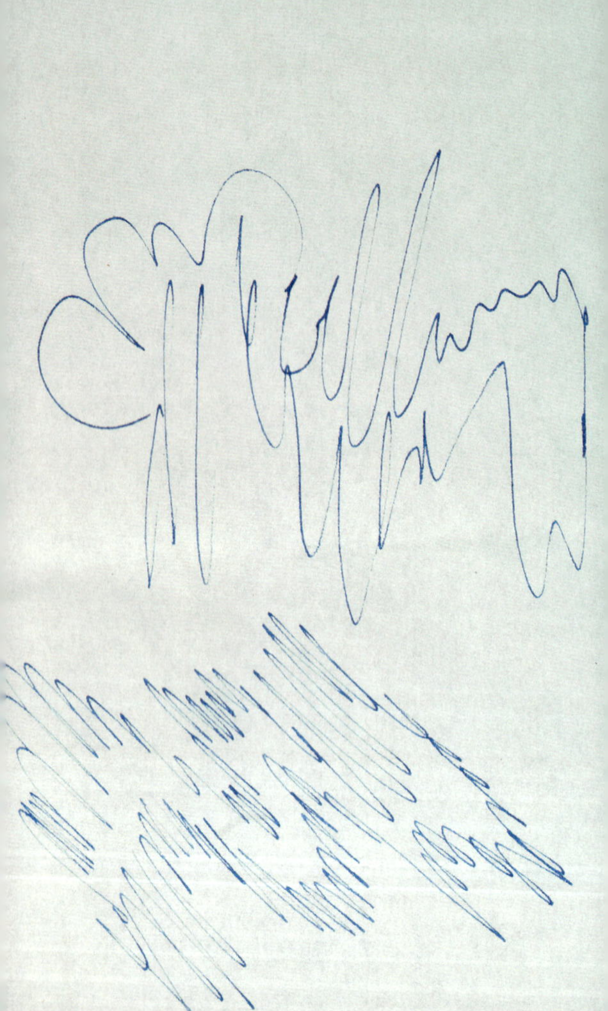

The aggregate phases of this quiet movement are named:

SLOW

SOLID

LIQUID

GASEOUS

SUBATOMIC

UNKNOWN

Everything that
exists on the outside
repeats itself
in the orbits of the
soul's powers

“A bit of cosmic debris lives within every one of our cells”

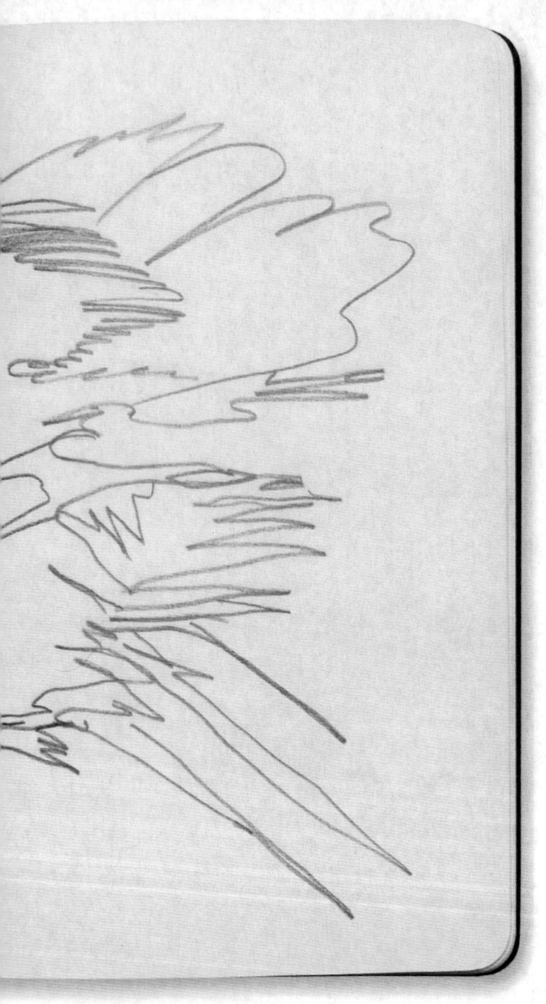

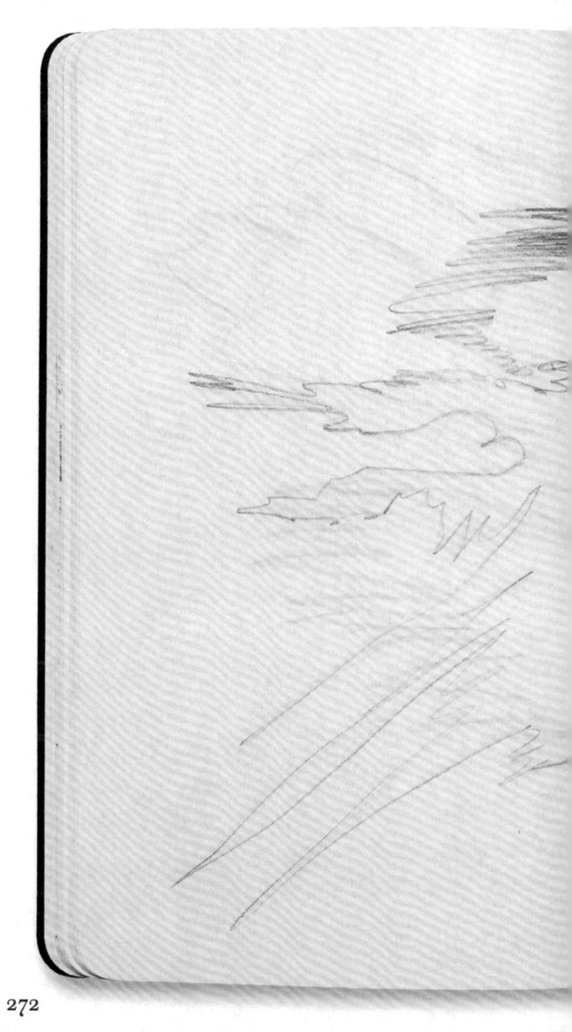

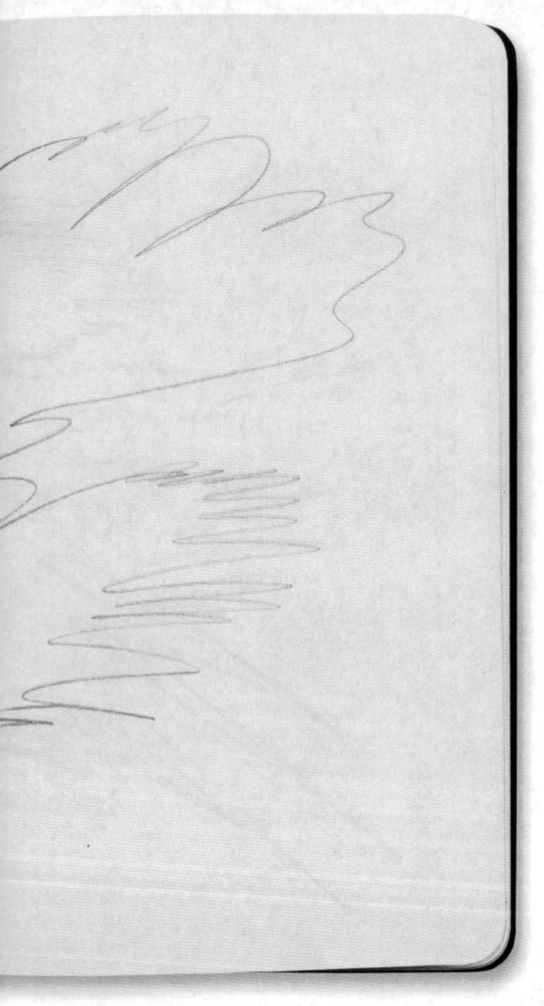

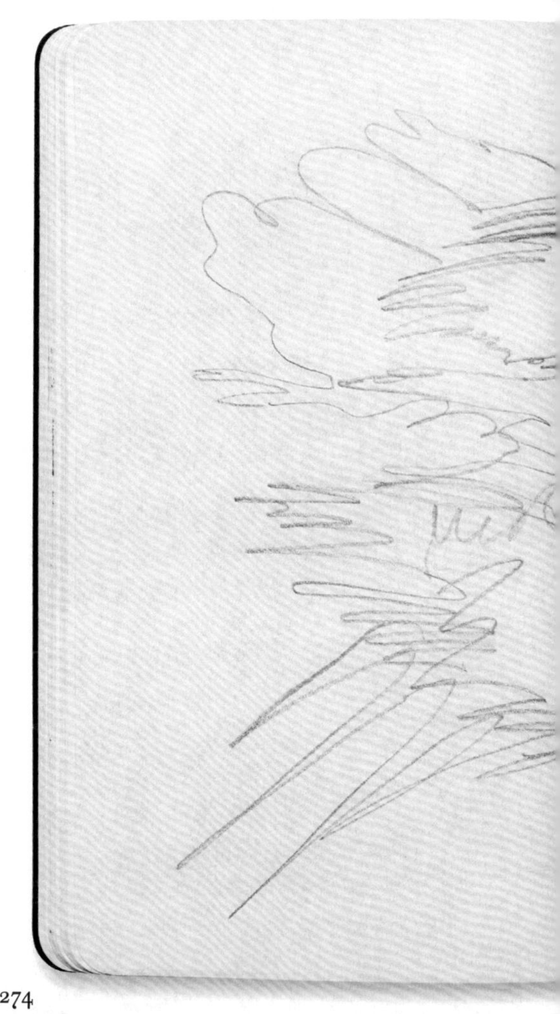

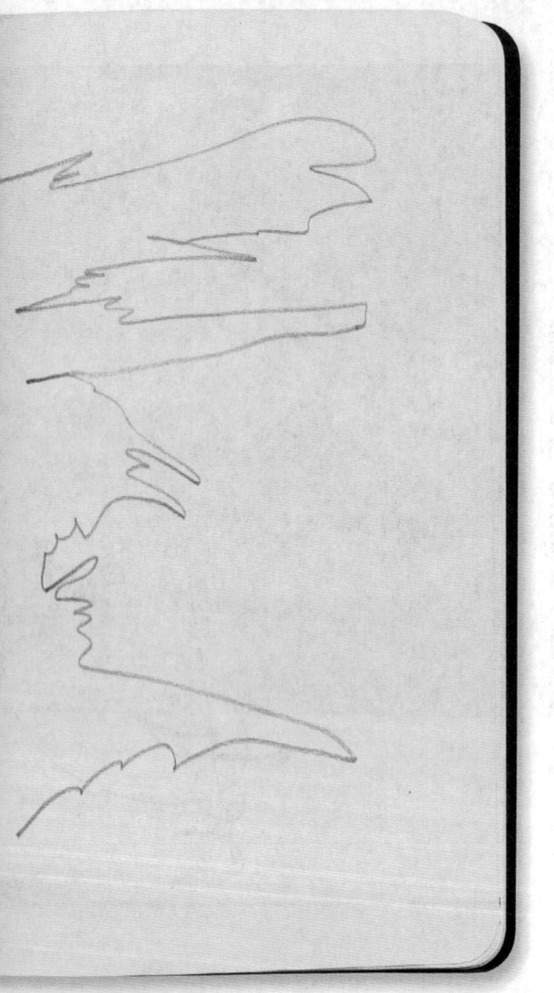

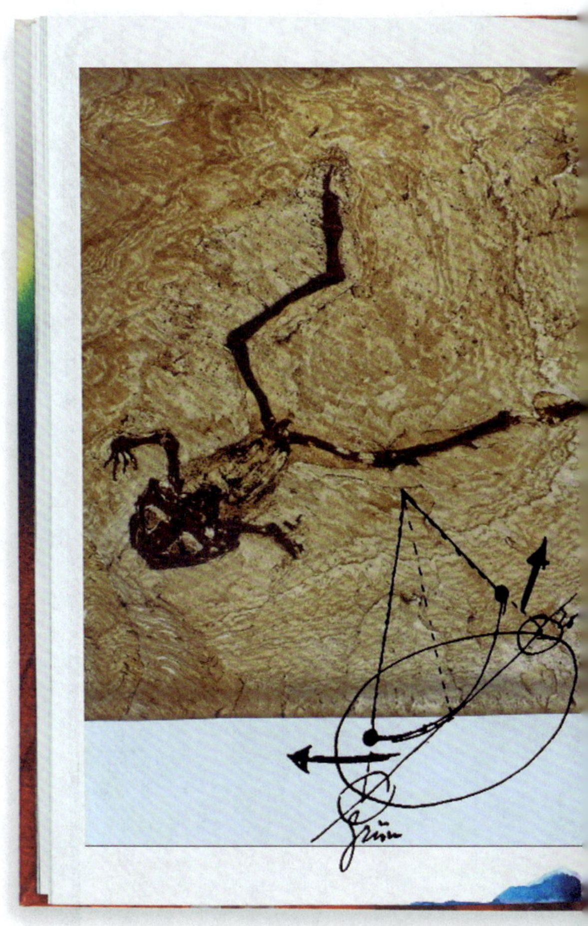

Grün

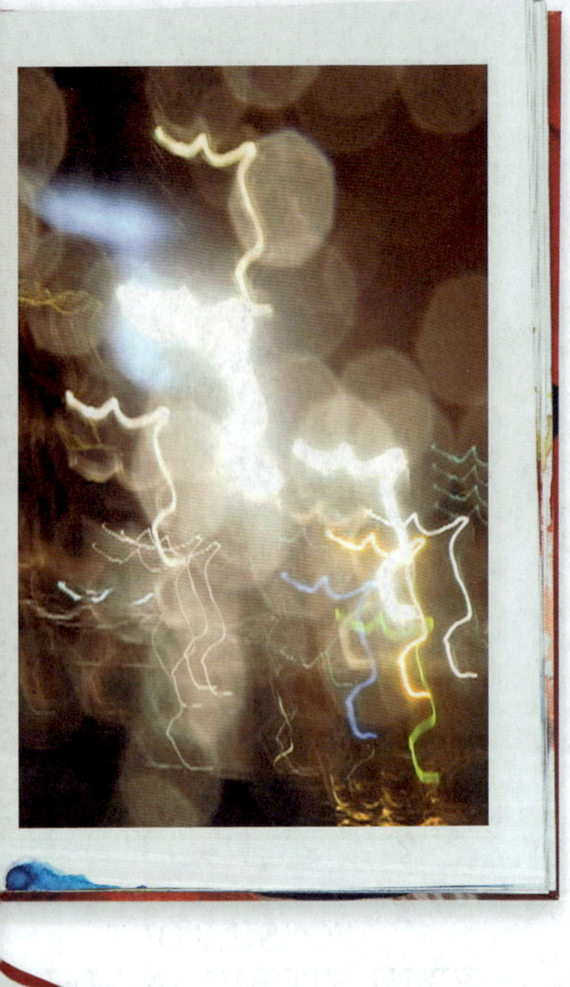

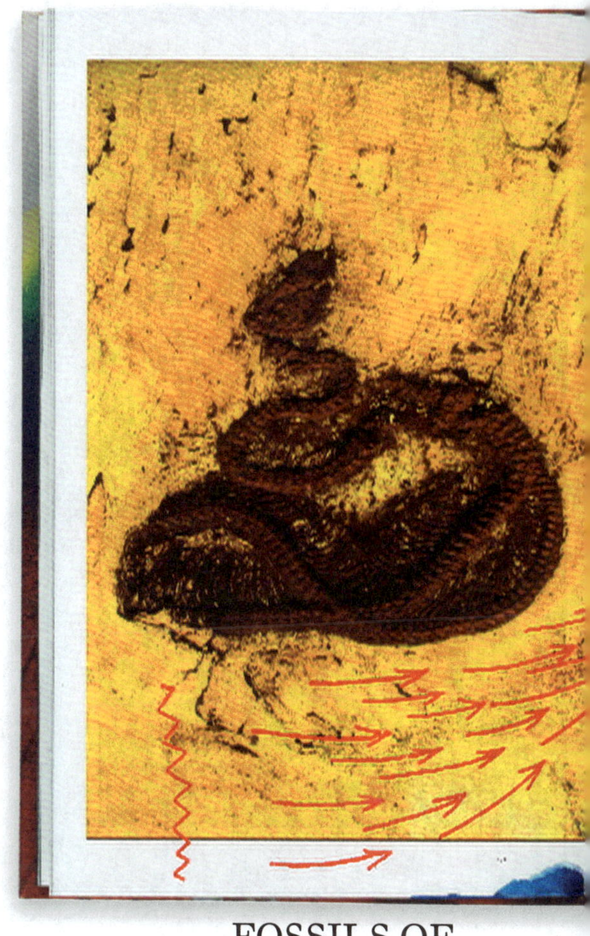

FOSSILS OF PREHISTORIC ANIMALS

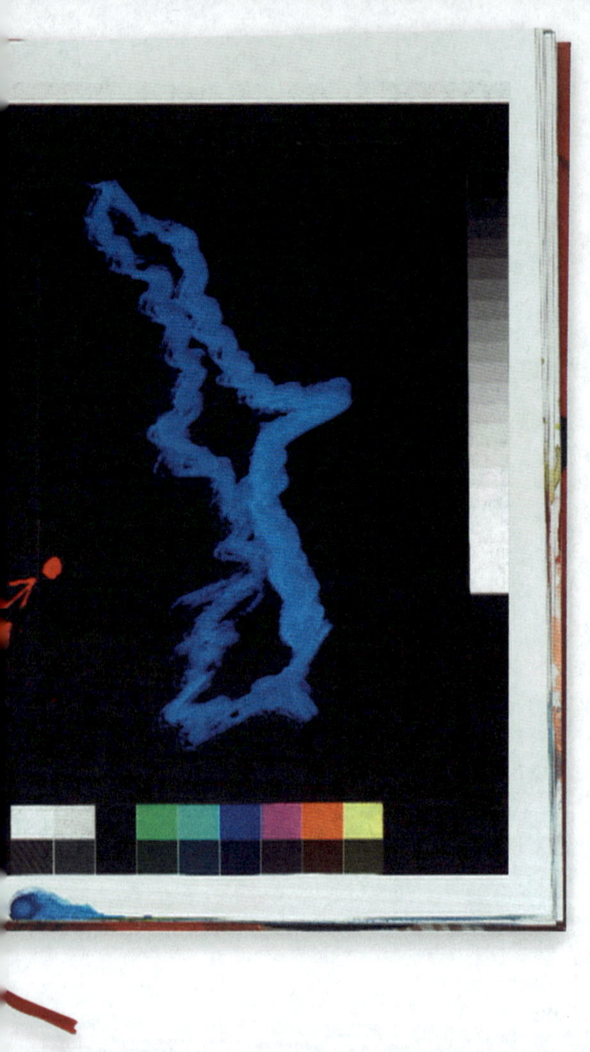

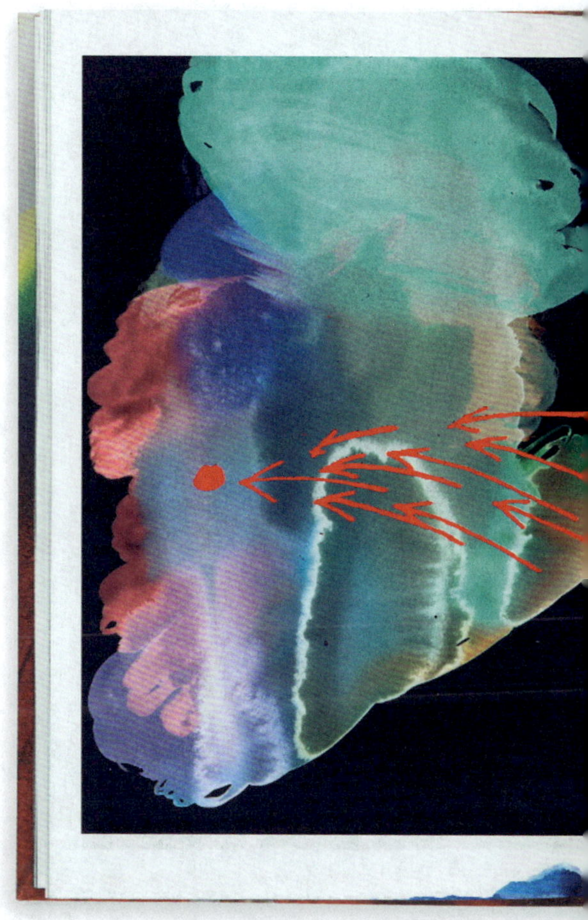

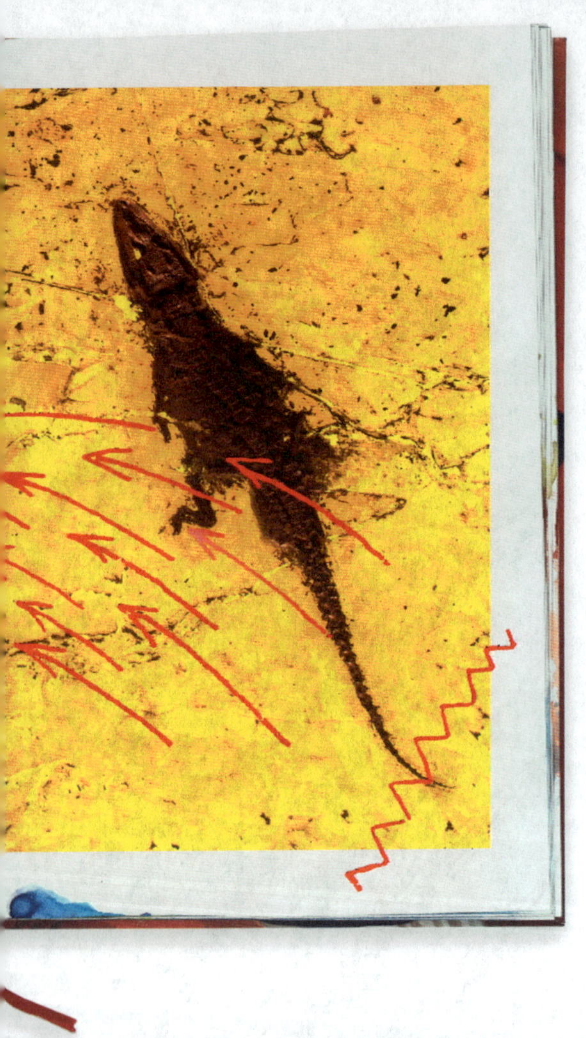

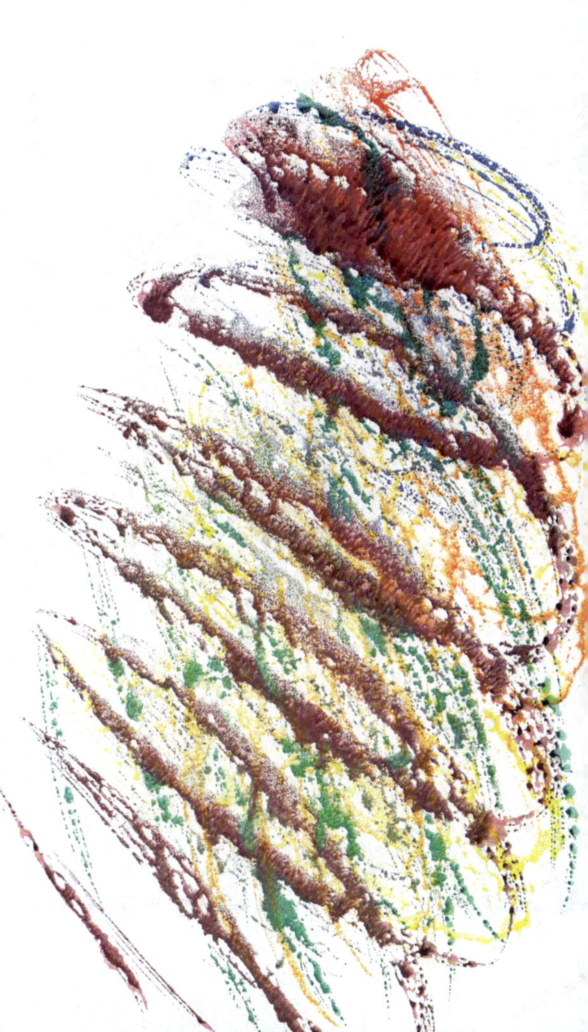

The Achievements of Prehistory That Archaeologists Cannot Excavate:

COUNTING

TRUSTING

GIVING/TAKING = EXCHANGE

BUFFALO JUMPS

THE CONCEPT OF THE CITY

GLUING

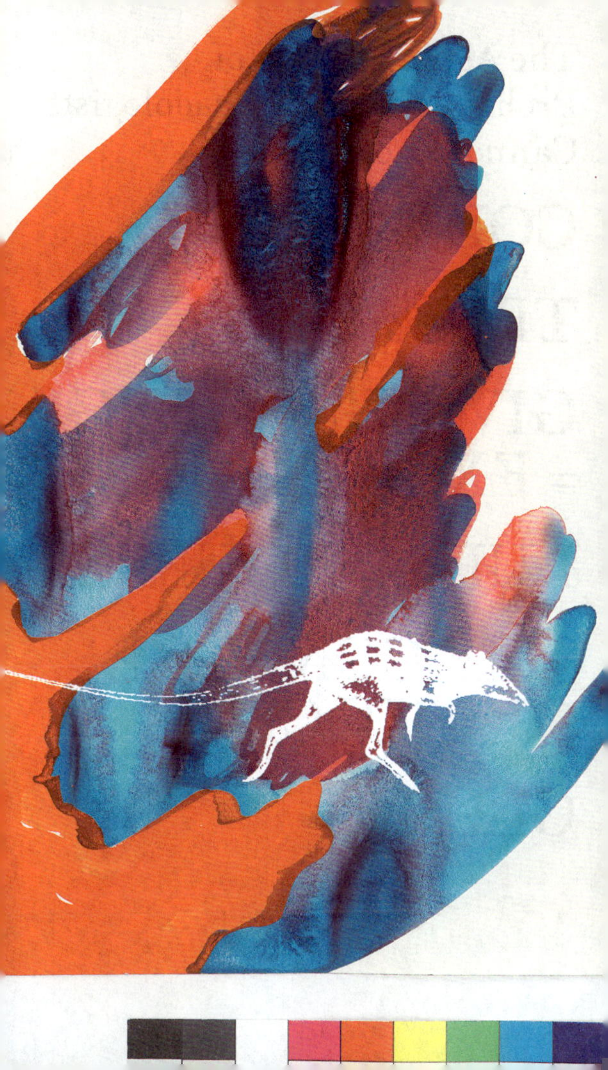

SEMINAL SPRINTER

A small, bipedal mammal from the sediments of Lake Messel in Hesse. The part of the pit in which the animal was found had already been released by the state of Hesse to the company that had bought it and was ready to bring in its wrecking crews. Thanks to the efforts of twelve lawyers, the excavators could be stopped. One peculiarity of the hasty, insectivore sprinter is its double palate. The animal is able to breathe while feeding. Time is of the essence when the animal has to both nourish itself and conserve the robustness necessary for its fast movements. Thus, it has to simultaneously feed, breathe, feel, "orient" itself "in thinking" and also be future-minded, since we (the potential destroyers of the Messel Pit stopped by the law, in other words, by something man-made) are descended from it.

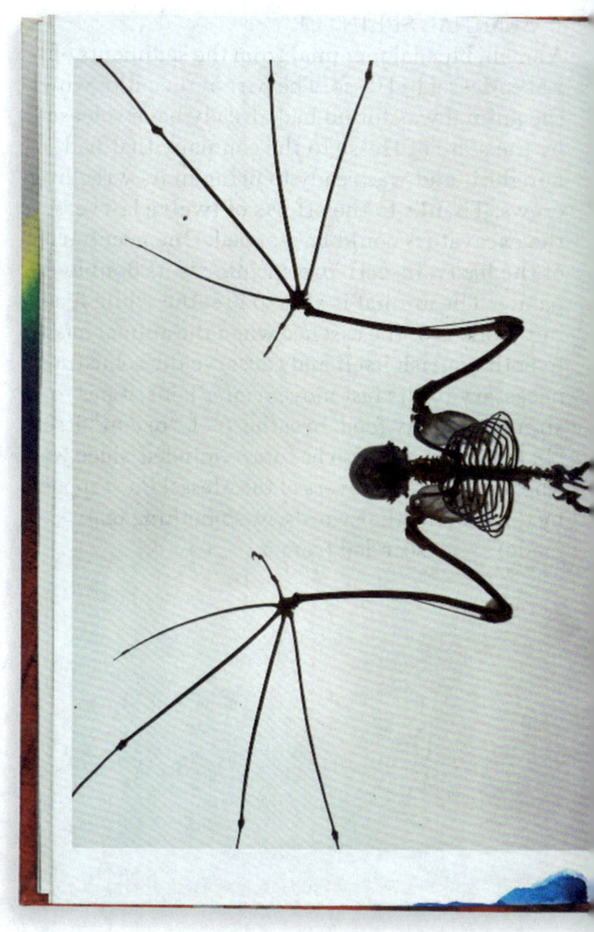

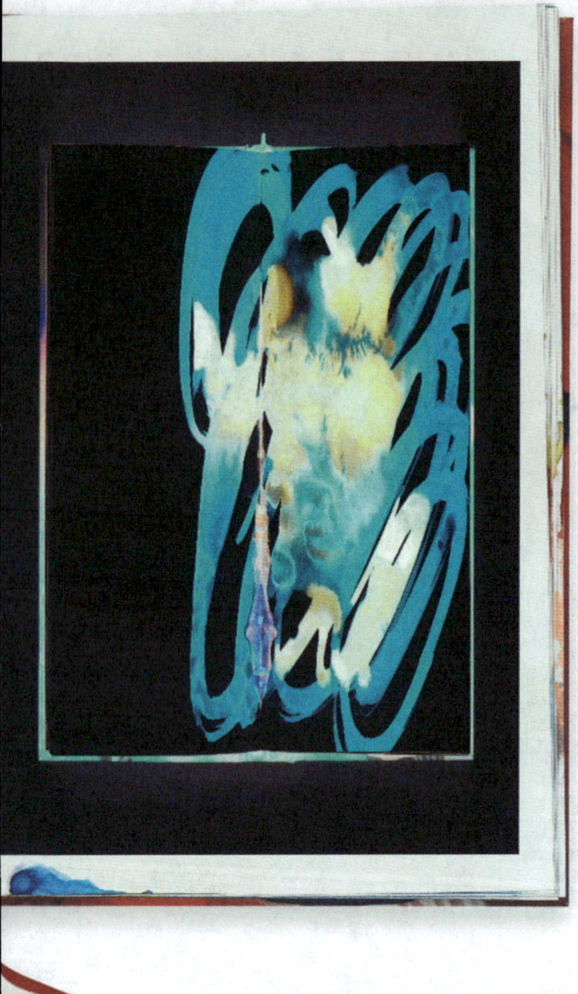

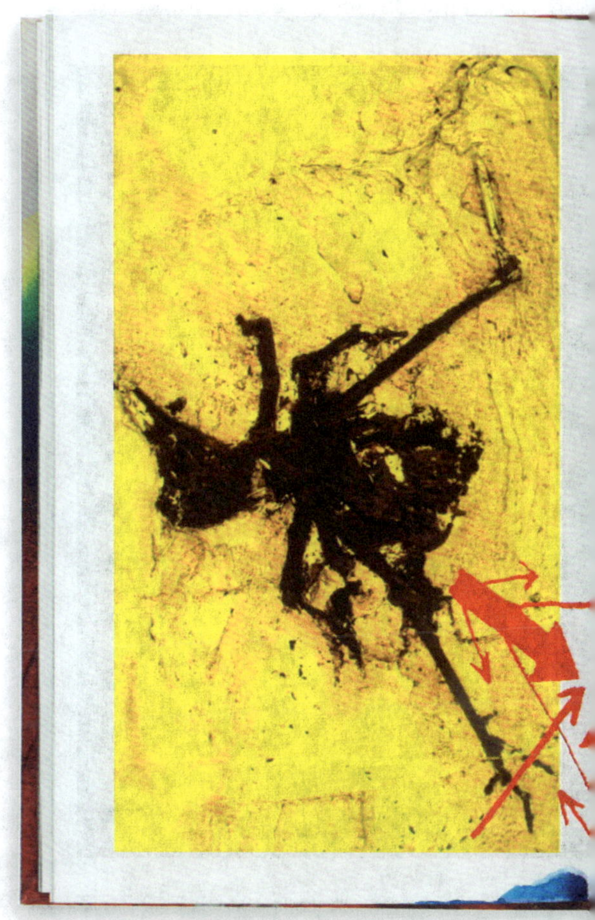

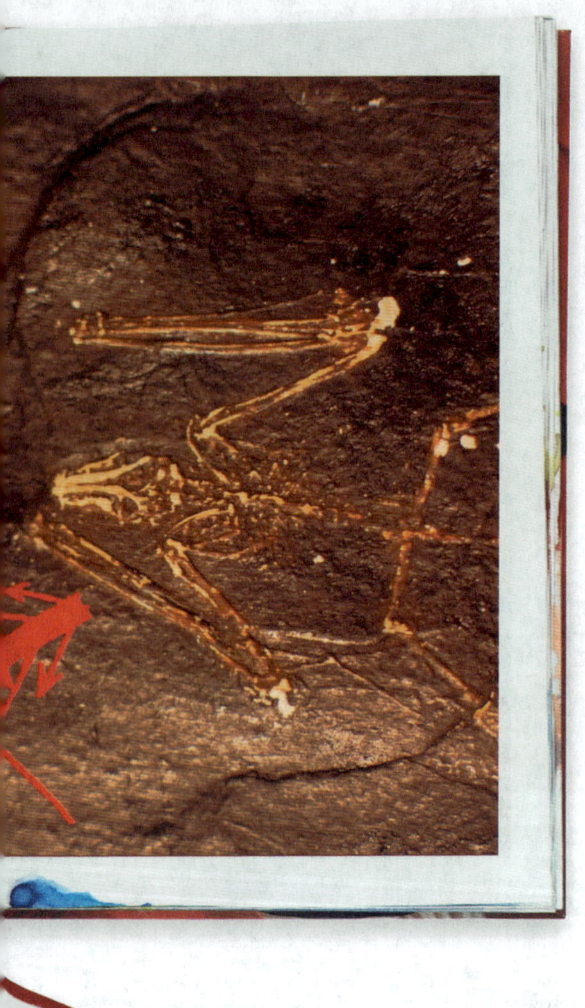

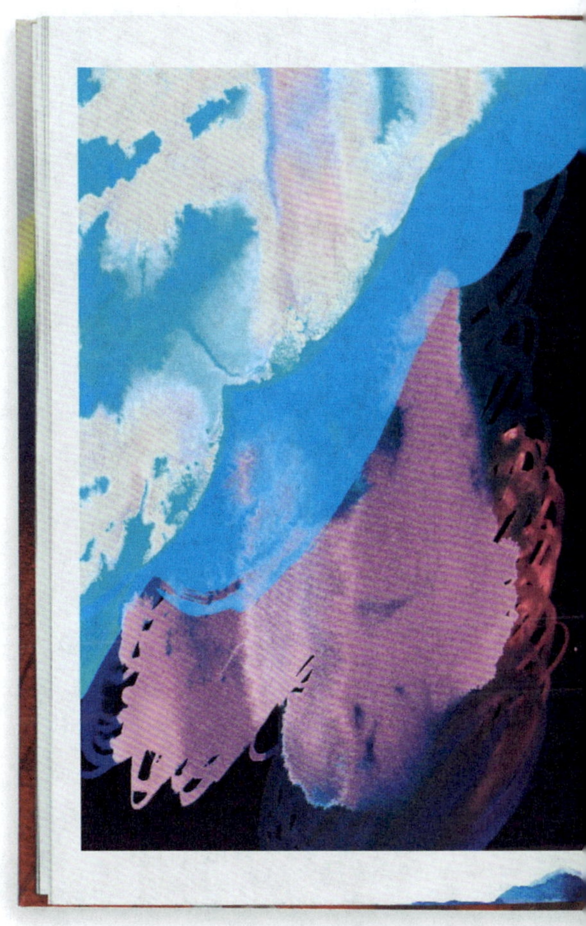

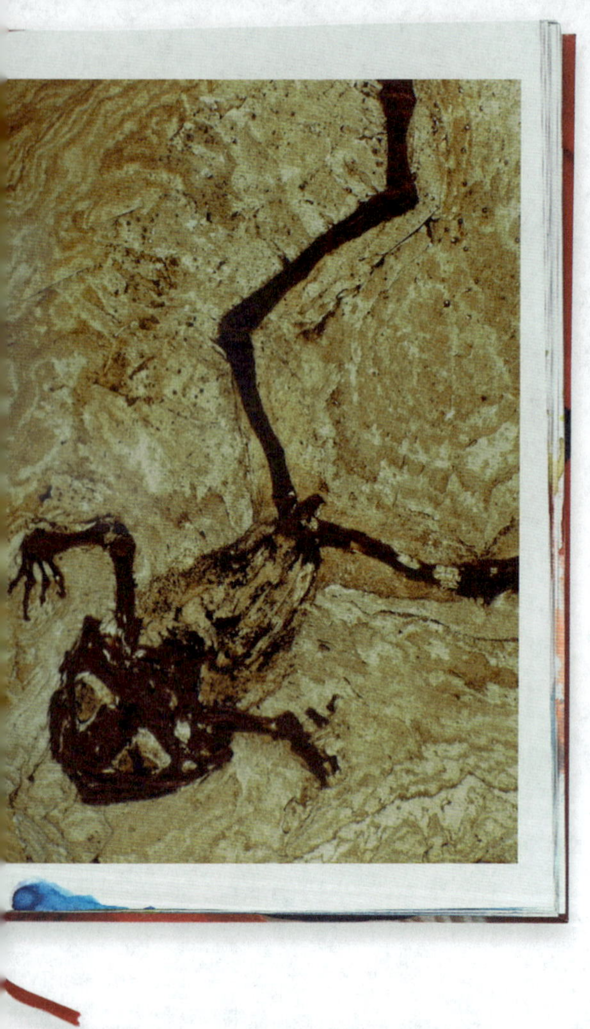

A THOUSAND YEARS LIKE A SINGLE DAY

A groundbreaking invention was the sewing needle, Hermann Parzinger writes. He adds: a development that appears extremely abrupt in retrospect still takes up to several thousand years. This claim is supported by the latest findings in caves of Idaho, which teach us that the sewing needle was invented more than seventy times, forgotten, and then reinvented again. In hindsight and somewhat "unexpectedly," this technique then spread across vast MIGRATORY AREAS. With a needle made of bone, it was possible to tightly tie together animal skins. The clothing didn't sag and kept the body warmer in cold weather. A clans-woman outfitted with such needles was an asset worth defending, a trade event for which the neighboring tribe—also free roaming—had to offer something of equal value. The sewing needle of the mind connects sentences and reports between generations. A reorganization of the brain.

THE BRAVE EIGHTEEN THOUSAND

You have to imagine the eighteen thousand or so ancestors—already of the genus Homo sapiens—spread out across eastern and southern Africa. This is the sum total of our direct ancestors; there are no more. This was the claim made by the leading palaeontologist Alexander Tikhonov in St. Petersburg. These members of the tribe couldn't have subsisted very far from one another, but you do have to imagine them spread out in small groups.

Pulled along by the invisible threads of fate (their "future"), they crossed the savannah and passed the espaliered trees that bordered the streams and rivers. The palaeontologist in St. Petersburg doesn't have any research laboratories there. He can only get close to the early clans he is investigating by traveling and undertaking excavations. "Bits of booty" from previous expeditions are stored in the back of the building where he lives. In his flat in the front half of the building, the researcher just looks at his computer screens. He is networked with around eighty experts in his field from around the world.

Driving snow just beyond the windowpanes. (Constructed by citizens in 1902, the building once housed a collective within its brick interior; the generous flats from before 1917 were wrecked, renovated again in the Brezhnev era, and converted into condominiums after 1991.) The researcher,

however, can feel the African sun on his skin when he imagines the object of his research, digging there, lying on wooden boards in order not to damage the precious place where he unearths his discoveries. As he uncovers layer after layer of earth, dates his findings, and places them in his baskets, he conjures up in his mind's eye the ORIGINAL ANCESTORS OF EVERY RUSSIAN (and of all human beings for that matter) going about their everyday lives.

Necessity is what drives them. They establish cooperatives. They communicate principally through body language, the academic believes. We would not understand them if we watched a ballet of this kind. GRADUATED AUDITORY SOUNDS. Expression relies on differing intonation rather than grammar. But already, among individual groups of those BRAVE eighteen thousand, imperative language established itself: emphatic calls, repeated insistently, again and again, until the member of the group thus called finally reacted. Rather like a siren. How does the researcher know this? Asked this typical question, the Russian academic replies: I don't know, that is how I imagine it. The gaps in knowledge are more than covered by his authority.

THE ALCHEMY OF EVOLUTION

The sun disappeared for years. Acid rain. The animals were gone. Only meager amounts of mushrooms and lichen remained. Nothing seemed to grow properly. Clan members became dwarf-like. From one generation to the next, it became clearer that the smaller newborns were more likely to survive than the large ones, so that caring for the little ones was more worthwhile. Little insight, much practice. Only one female shaman managed to have a handle on the clan's many generations. Her advice was what mattered.

The group, bound together by circumstances and more and more hidebound in its aspirations, built up its defences against the destructive events that descended from the heavens. When was prayer invented? Incantation? Following the arrival of a paradisiacal period of warmth with dark blue, clear skies—forty generations (around twelve hundred years) later—the "wood," born of loss and adaptation, was ready once more to be processed into charcoal, a material that is mutually warming. Wood grows green and rots in bogs, is cut as peat and baked into coal, warms the children's nursery in the cold months and molds their character.

“VAGARIES”
OF EVOLUTION

Two of the mandibular bones in reptiles were relocated to the tympanum during the early Jurassic period. The migration of the small bones from the jaw to the ear resulted from the enlargement of the brains in mammals, Michael J. Benton claims. At first, more space was needed, so the tiny bones had to move. Then they proved to be highly useful in the ear, an organ whose progressive nature became clear only in retrospect.

Chinese science celebrates a triumph in 2015. The Sinoconodon is discovered, and displays classic mammal traits. This early animal can be considered the second oldest mammal. It is further noteworthy that no Western or Indian site can offer anything similar. The eye socket of the animal forms a single opening with the lower end of the temples, elegantly framed by a slim zygomatic arch. Otherwise the creature, of which only a piece of its forehead and fragments from its ribs and neck have been found, still carries the primitive characteristics of unlimited body growth present in all prehistoric animals. The Chinese hope that in the remainders of the former primordial ocean—today called South China—a transitional specimen may be found. It’s a miracle that the slow growth of the cranium, otherwise unwilling to stop, limited the life span to such an extent that the brains did not develop sufficiently. At what point were the breaks applied that

stunted the growth of both the cells and the body in such a way that LONG-LIVING MAMMALS developed?

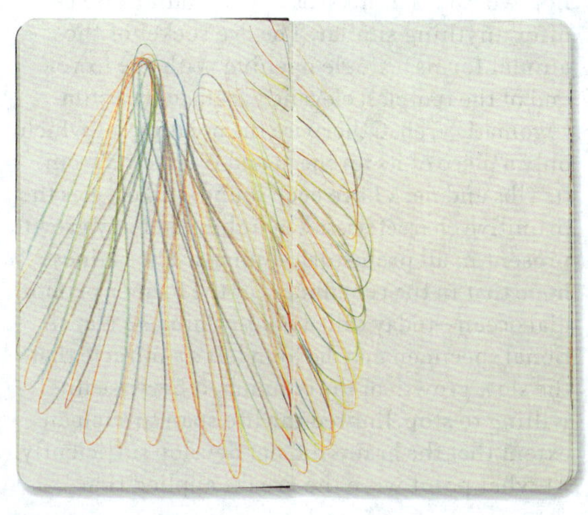

THIS IS HOW THE EAR AWAKENED AND WITH IT LANGUAGE

It takes courage to walk from horizon to horizon when all manner of horror or miracle may very well be lurking behind each one. The world is unknown, and it is impenetrably dark to eyes seeking nocturnal shelter in caves. Close encounters are necessary. Without touching, communication with one's neighbors is impossible. They are barely perceptible as shadows. At most, by the noise they make. *This is how the ear awakened, and with it language*, writes the researcher sitting at his computer, where he is collecting notes for a lecture in Cape Town. Language is the result of night's all-enveloping darkness. Outside the cave, however, there is enough starlight in the southern sky for predators to attack any one of the eighteen thousand of them. Meaning: not just a little stress beyond the cave as well. When seeking out a new ledge or cave because the old hunting ground has become exhausted, the greatest caution is required (stress again!): predators themselves like to use them. The small tribe can hardly afford any losses.

CAMBRIAN

ORDOVICIAN

SILURIAN

DEVONIAN

CARBON

PERMIAN

TRIASSIC

AEON

ERA

PERIOD

EPOCH

GENERATION

LIFE SPAN

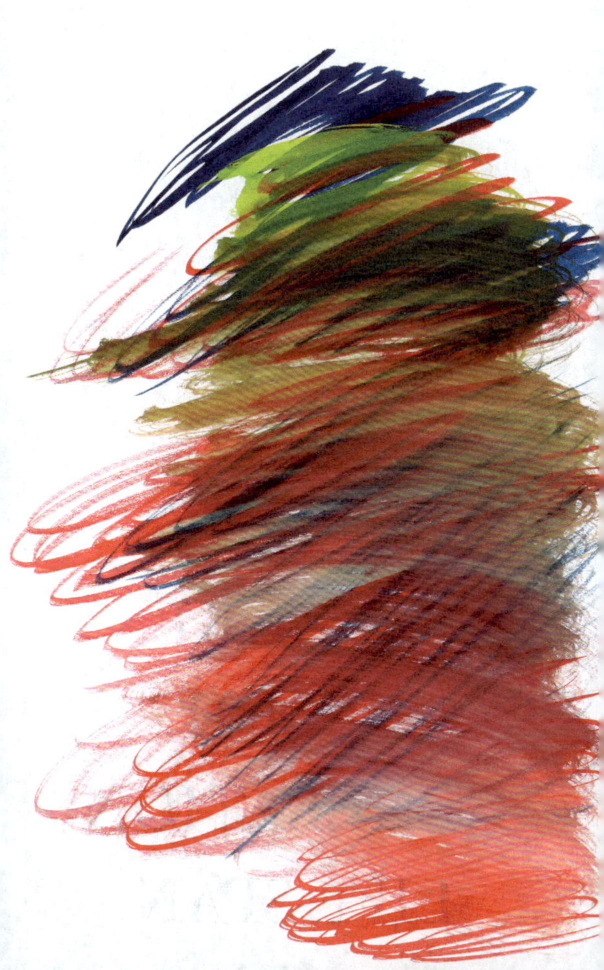

PRECAMBRIAN

beginning 4.5 billion years ago

"PRIMORDIAL OCEAN"

(largely anaerobic)

ARCHAEOZOIC

until 2.9 billion years ago

PROTEROZOIC

from 2.9 billion
to 1.6 billion years ago

LATE PROTEROZOIC

from 1.6 billion
to 570 million years ago

"MOTION WAS EVERYTHING"
Some rare radioactive elements in the depths of the Earth's crust carry half-lives stemming from those ancient times when the Earth had not yet existed, and when particles moved in a cosmic gas cloud that was yet to head toward the expanse of rubble, the protoplanetary ring that would later become our celestial body. These particles, partly protons, partly already fused into molecules, then "saw" the PRIMORDIAL OCEAN—like an envelope around the Earth—from which hardly a land mass protruded. The particles were sinking so slowly that in a thousand years they failed to reach the sedimentary soil. The soil rose over many millions of years and shifted spaciously to other zones of the globe.

In the age of the supercontinent RODINIA, the aforementioned particles meandered (one can see this in their magnetic directionality pointing toward the changing poles of the planet) and crossed the poles and equator several times. All throughout the aeons-long cold torpor on Snowball Earth, which enclosed the planet and ravaged cratons (the solid continental shelves), the radioactive rarities previously mentioned remained undisturbed and ever radiant. At the moment when the potential for future life that had already existed in the emergent warmth of the oceans in the Cambrian period deemed itself free from this torpor and spread across the world, one or another molecule containing the fairly

archaic radioactive component was swallowed by an organism and thus became part of the evolutionary cycle. With miniscule radioactive components incorporated into the bodies that arose out of the lagoons and rivers, life conquered solid ground.

ONE MORE TIME APROPOS "MOVEMENT"

A surveyor and enthusiast of his homeland (*rodinia* means home in Russian), who had been working for decades in Akademgorodok near Novosibirsk, was known to be obsessive. An accuracy freak. He insisted on his measurements of the "undulations" taken in deserts and mountains, and unnerved his colleagues in geography and geology who had a dislike for minor matters. This surveyor used data from an early Soviet satellite whose original mission was to measure the Earth's difference in altitude for military purposes (namely, for downing intercontinental ballistic missiles). According to this data, large mountain ranges like the Himalayas, the Pamirs, and the Andes (less so for planes and deserts) move several centimeters with respect to the tides such that the surveyor went astray of the usual terminology and called it a *sea* of rocks. It can't be ruled out entirely, the patriotic surveyor claimed, that an unusual celestial constellation could cause the land masses to erupt in a "spring tide" (this could happen if Jupiter's and the moon's influence put the sun and her mysterious companion star in an unusual position that only brushes our system tangentially once every six hundred thousand years). This would have been a poetic event for the Russian explorer. In this case, nature would express (in her own language) the fact that all that exists is in constant motion. Indeed, this awkward

scientist thought, even big and sluggish Russia could gain momentum one day, even if Pushkin thought it improbable considering the muddy transport routes throughout the country.

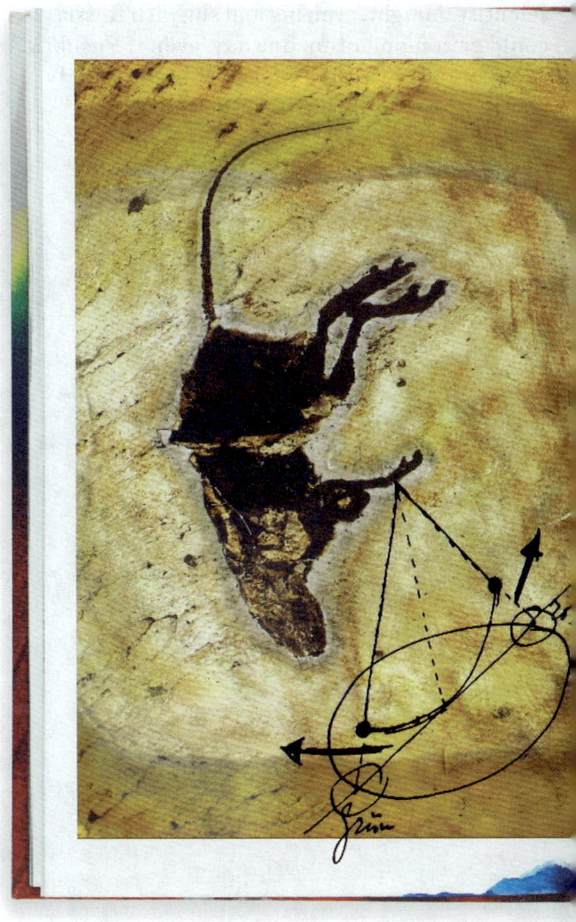
Grün

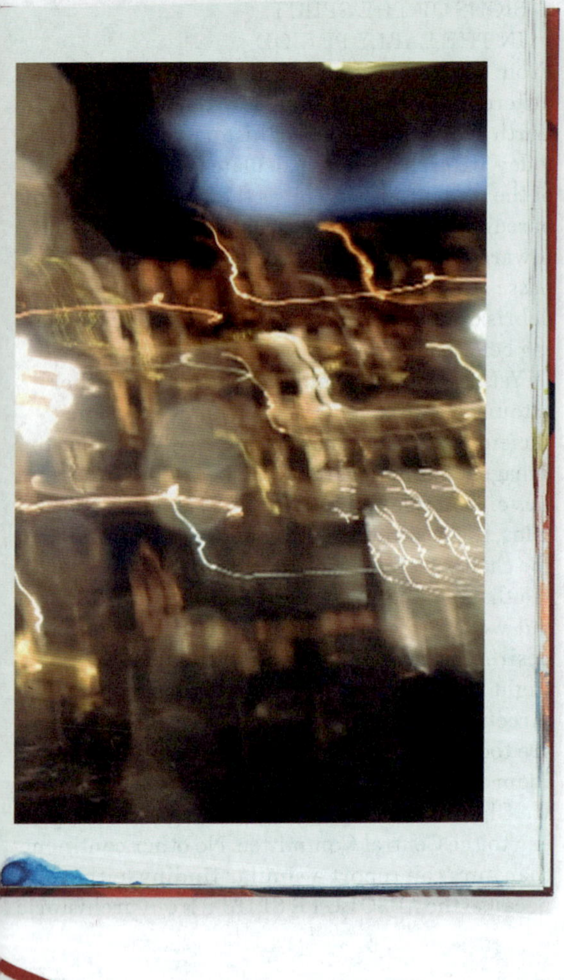

SIGNS OF THE SPIRIT IN THE EARLY PERIOD

From the magnetic alignment of the rocks to the different positions assumed by the poles of the Earth at different stages of history compared with today, we prehistorians calculate the movements of the land masses as well as the gradual formation of sediment in the ocean. Iron molecules aligned toward the north in the rocks are the only compasses we have to read in order to visualize the debris on the surface of the Earth like a film playing before our eyes.

Yet we Chinese prehistorians made another astounding discovery: in the vicinity of some skeletons, we found navigational signs similar to a magnet but not based on the behavioral properties of iron. We call them teloïds. Named after telos, the destination. Not only can we identify the chalky shells of skeletons from the flat, age-old sea that once covered the plains of South China, but we also keep finding plaques of boneless desire. Like impulses refusing to die, they took flight for the nutritious plains! We map the direction arrows of the negative entropy. These are toothless "ambitions" (as we cannot call them animals). They belong to our ancestry, and we Chinese take pride in reporting this discovery to the Central Committee. No other continent than ours can report a similar finding, either because the ABSOLUTE SPIRIT from prehistoric

times only graced our country or because Western societies didn't conduct research exhaustively enough.

THE EXPROPRIATION OF KNOWLEDGE

A truncated mountain from the Variscan orogenesis—set in motion by the breakup of the supercontinent Pangaea—rushed toward an island north of Norway where it affixed itself. This truncated mountain was now the sinecure of a consortium that not only brought to the market the prospect of future exploitation—by covering this floe with mines and ridges—but also borrowed money against its revenues. The scholar from the mining academy in Freiberg (Saxony) who researched this matter came away empty-handed. He had been loyal toward his government to the end. He was a sixth-generation mining expert. His forefathers served Prussia (borrowed from Saxony). He supplied the Third Reich with suggestions. But in matters of geology, this country, Hitler's country, was ignorant and so nobody listened to him.

But the fundament of the planning authority in the GDR consisted of expert engineers and hopefuls from the socialist end of the spectrum, and they took him seriously. And he paid them back with loyalty. After many years of political abstinence, he ultimately decided to join the Socialist Unity Party. This, however, turned out to be disastrous after the fall of the Berlin Wall when it came to realizing "values per se," for which he sacrificed his health and spent countless hours fighting the comrades of the Stasi, as "his values." In the end, his papers were held at the state

bank and managed by a private trust. He was prevented by his party membership when it came to defending his rights to his discovery against the firm handling privatization following German reunification. He was burdened, he was told. A team of top lawyers from firms consisting of over six hundred attorneys assured him that he would win his case, but he could not afford to pay them. His knowledge became state property and thus available to Western investors once it was clear that East Germany would cease to exist.

AFROTHERIANS AND THE BREAKING UP OF GONDWANA

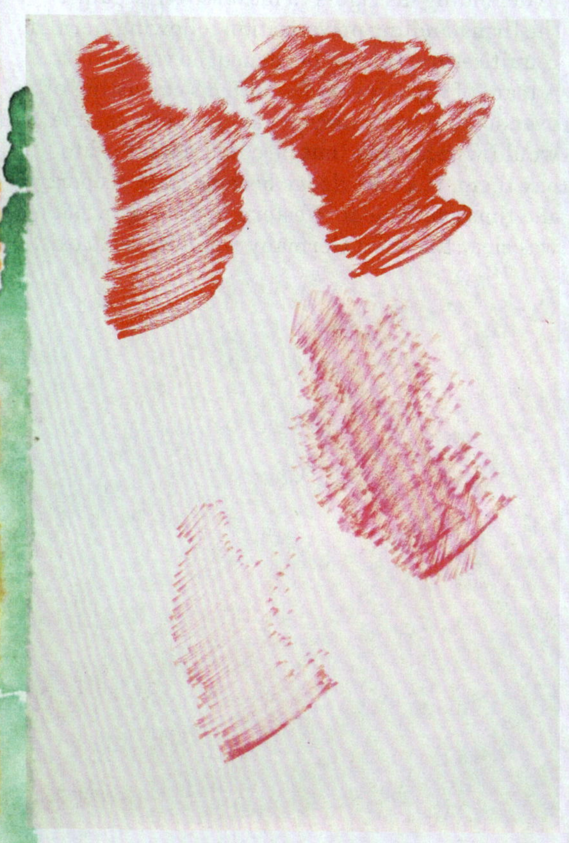

Modern mammals as diverse as elephants, golden mole rats, tenrecs, and aardvarks seem to have a common origin, a point of departure that the human race does not directly share. This is the way schloch-jeremy.com describes it. Humanity is not connected to this lineage of Afrotheria, the animal world that formed during the breakup of the continent of Gondwana. Which is why, schloch-jeremy.com maintains, elephants are more patient and wiser than we are. And which is why the low tone they use to communicate with one another is closer to the planetary tone of Jupiter than the high-pitched expressions of human voices, which in this respect can be considered a sharp screech incomprehensible to authentic Afrotheria. The Afrotheria reached Africa from the areas around Boreas, i.e., the Arctic Circle, at the latest in the Upper/Late Cretaceous period.

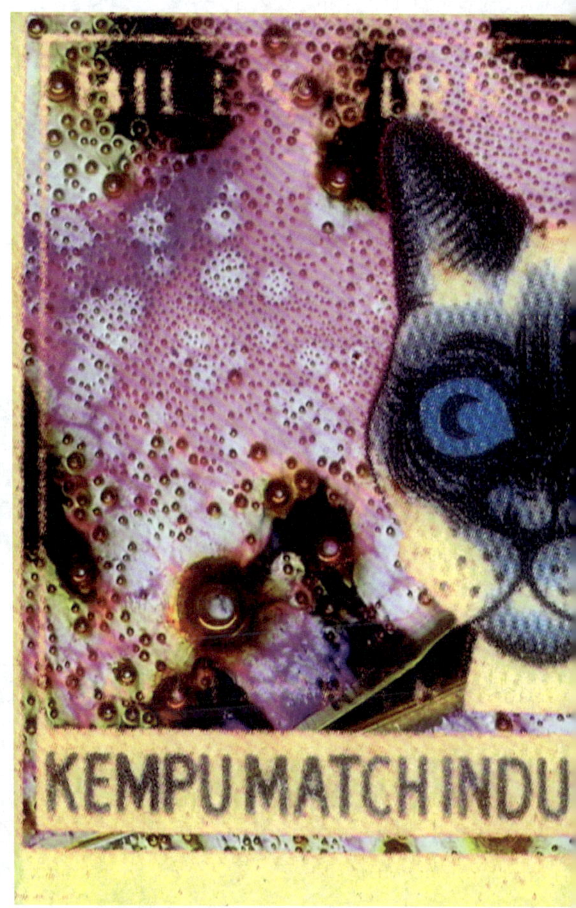
KEMPU MATCH INDU

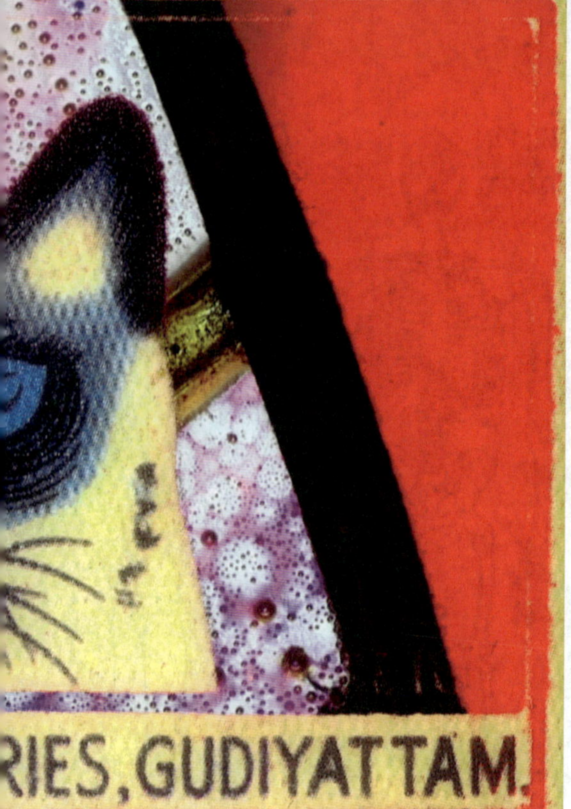
RIES, GUDIYATTAM.

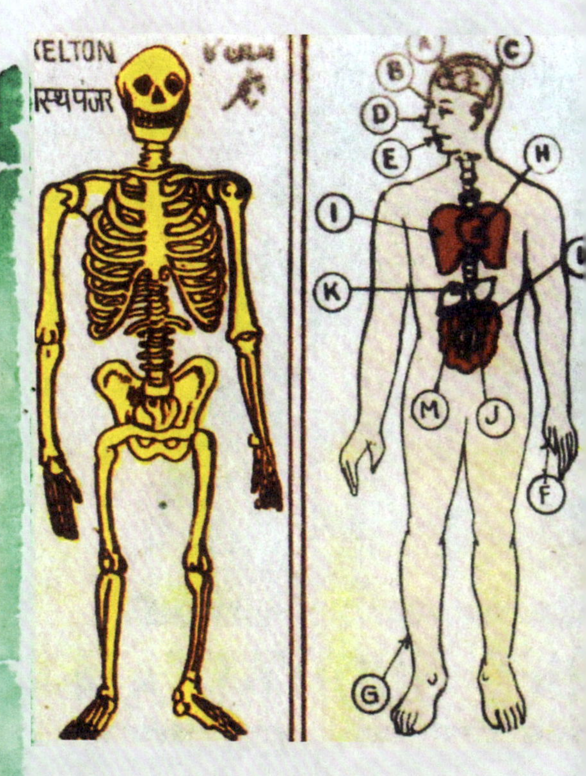
A
C
B
D
E
H
I
K
M
J
F
G

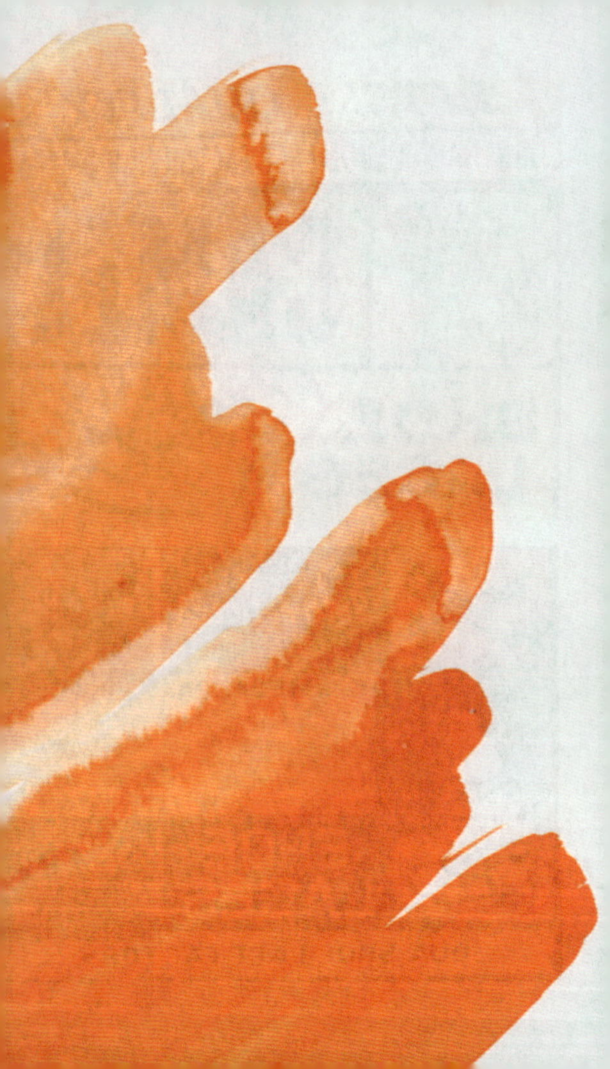

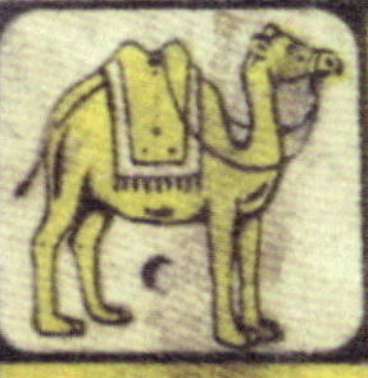

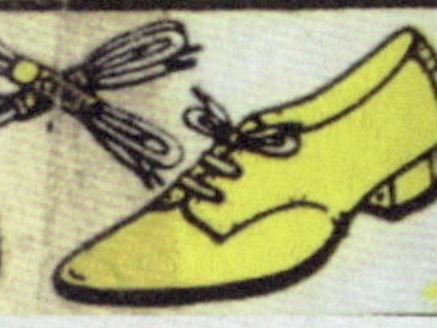

LATEST QUALITY
MANCHANDA SHOE LACE FACTORY S.B.Delhi 6
CAMEL
SHOE
LACES

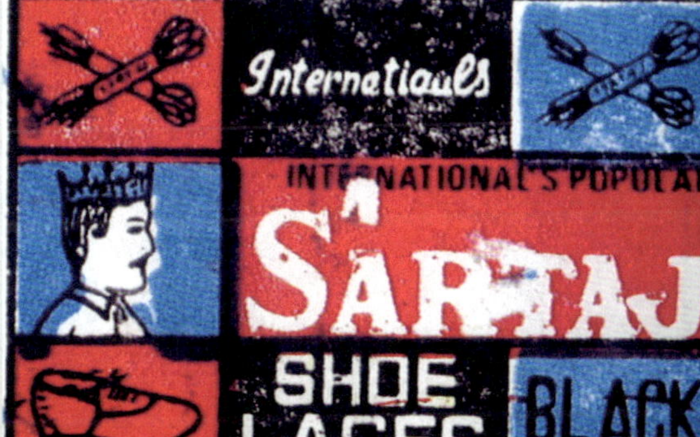

Internatiauls
INTERNATIONAL'S POPULAR
SARTAJ
SHOE
LACES
BLACK
DUA SHOE LACE FACTORY

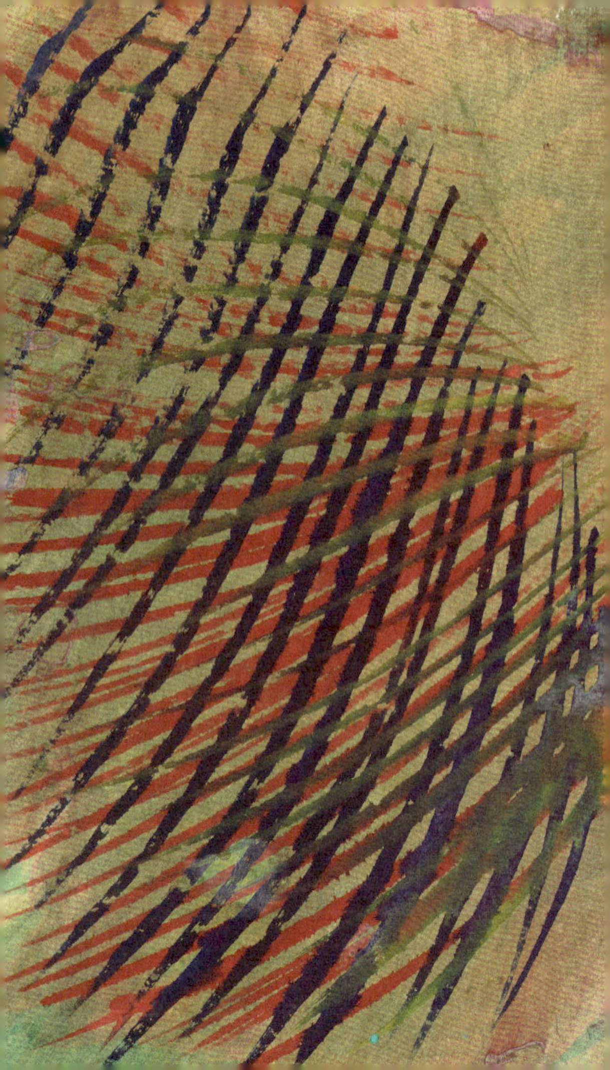

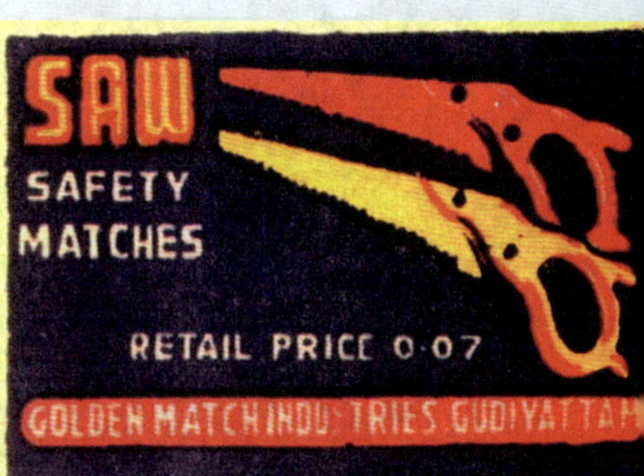
SAW
SAFETY
MATCHES
RETAIL PRICE 0·07
GOLDEN MATCH INDU TRIES GUDIYATTAM

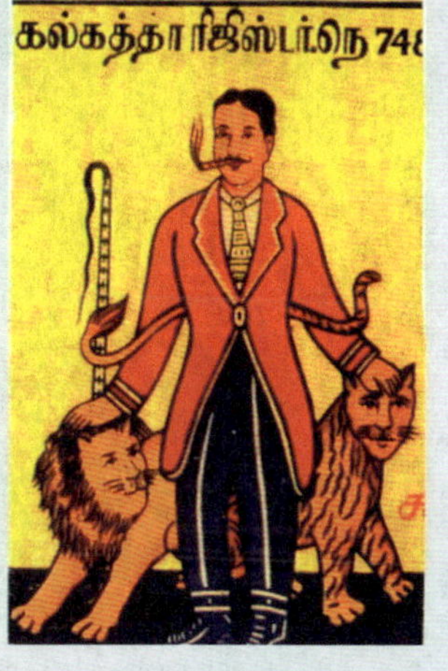
கல்கத்தா ரிஜிஸ்டர்.நெ 74

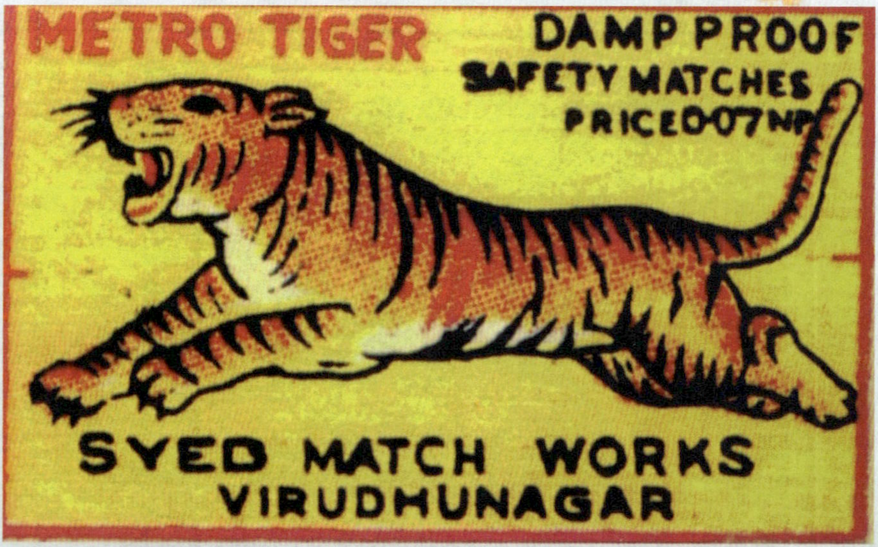

METRO TIGER

DAMP PROOF
SAFETY MATCHES
PRICE 0·07 NP

SYED MATCH WORKS
VIRUDHUNAGAR

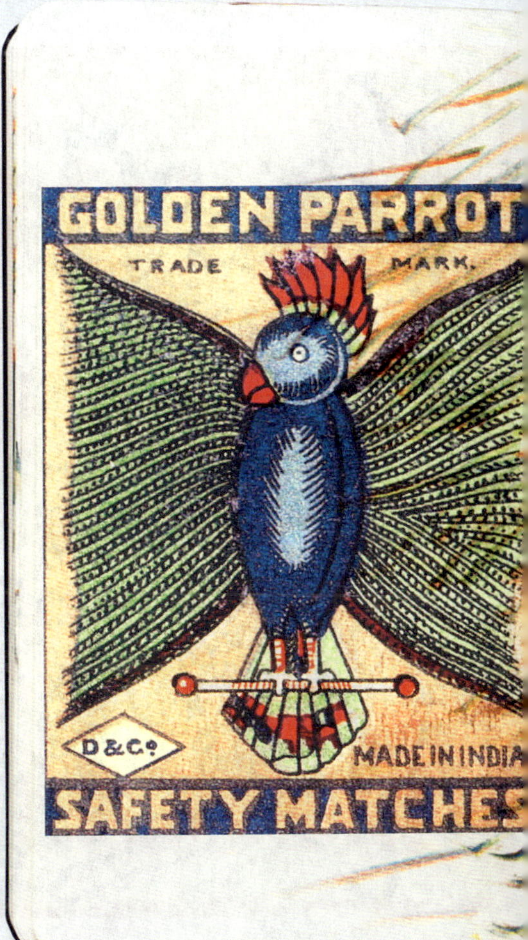

GOLDEN PARROT
TRADE MARK.
D&Co.
MADE IN INDIA
SAFETY MATCHES

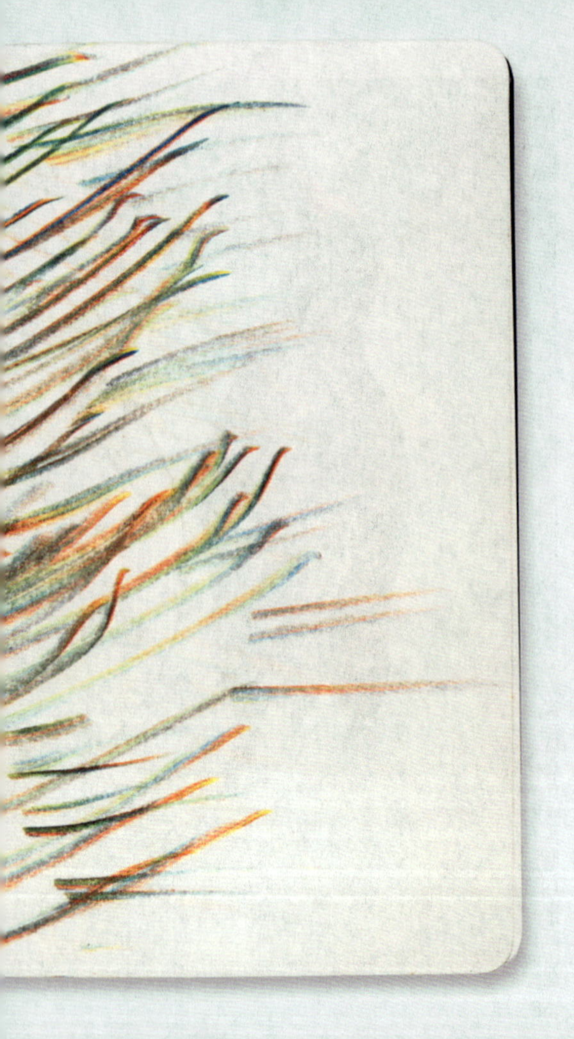

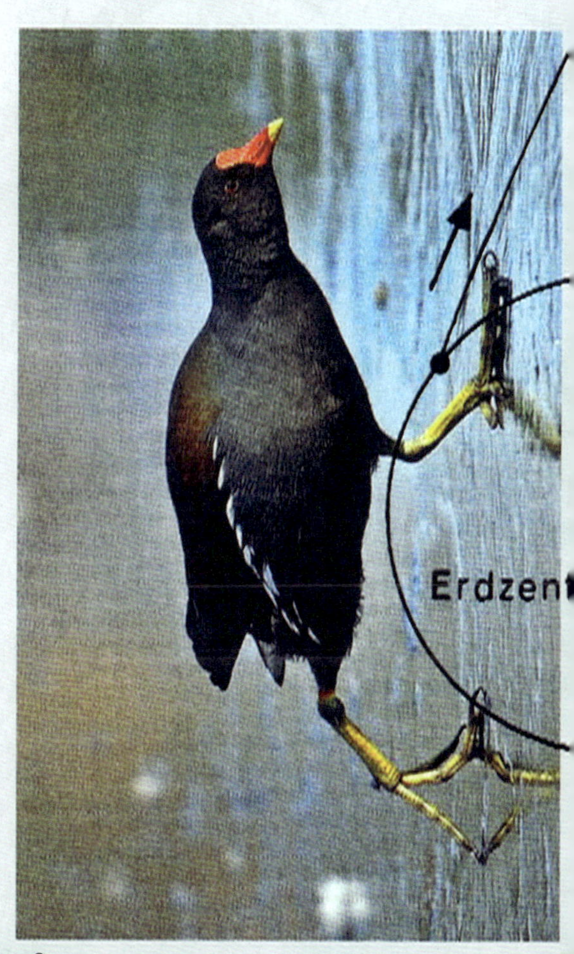
Erdzent

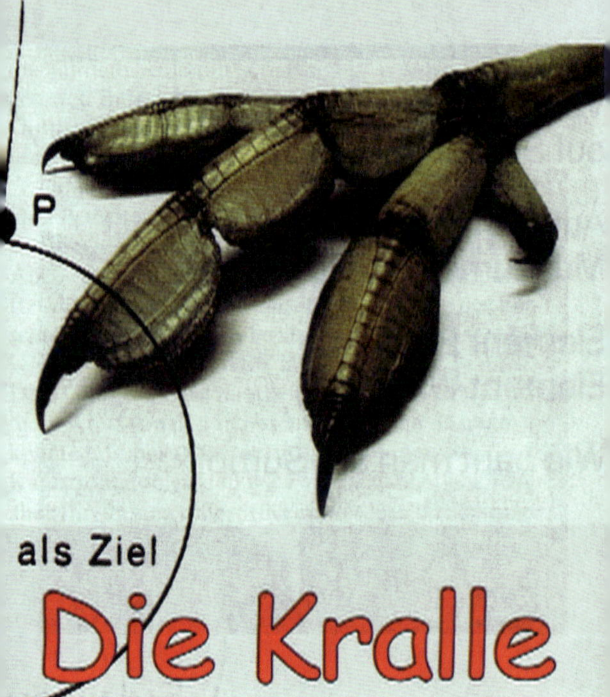

Die Kralle einer Ralle

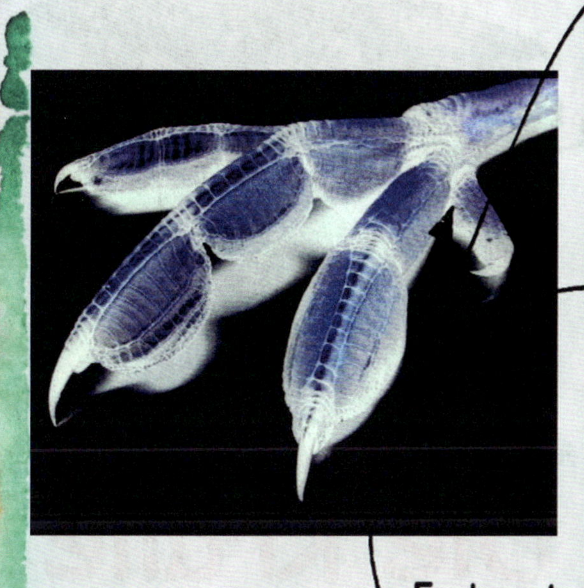

Erdzentru

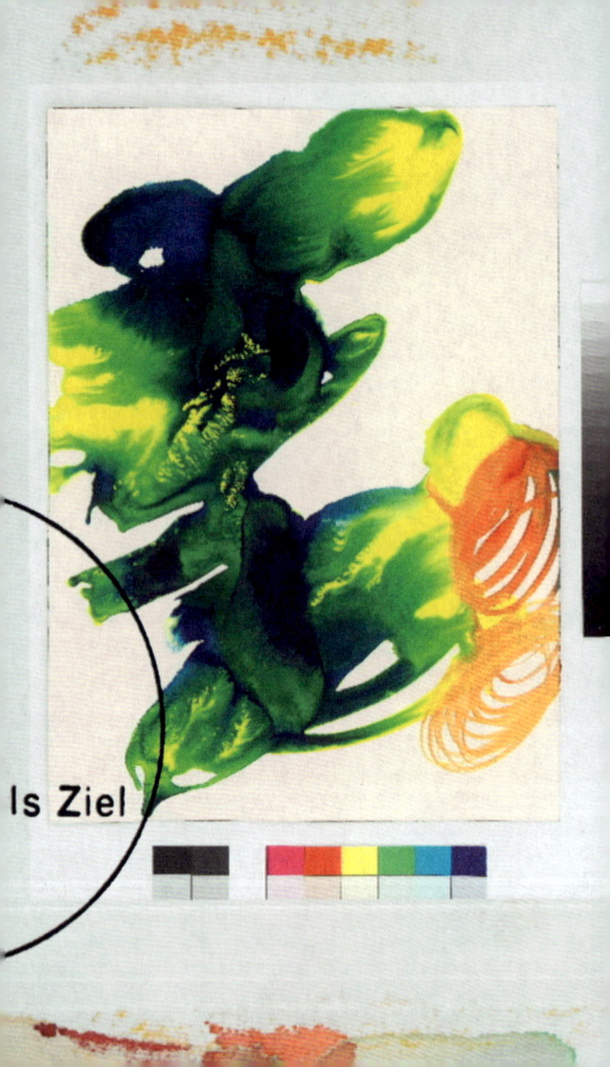
ls Ziel

"HUMANS DWELL AS CUMBERSOME AS RAILS"

"Human beings are housed poetically." In his interpretation of Hölderlin's hymn, Martin Heidegger claims that human beings cannot live without their dreams. They need space around their bodies ("elbow room"). And around this space of their domicile, their third skin following the "second skin of their clothes," they need another space in which their commonalities are "at home": the republic, the cities. These houses of the fourth skin have no roof. But even Leibniz in his day pointed out that they have cellars, underground floors, that reach as many as seven stories down.

On the third day the walks taken by the debating group from Hotel Waldhaus in Sils-Maria shifted from the paths down Val Fex and moved over toward the lakes and the Chastè, a wooded hill that projects into one of the lakes. With the change in the hiking path, the direction of the discussion changed as well.

It had grown colder. Evening approached from Maloja Pass and descended on the landscape. The walkers' debate focused on the "form of housing." For the nomads: the tent. Suited for safe escapes in case of danger: the ships of ancient heroes. In this way Ulysses eludes the wrathful sea god and the giant Polyphemus. For the inhabitants of the European continent, there was no such emergency exit called "the open seas." You can't

move away your houses when ambushed by armed hordes or savage nature. Human beings dwell as cumbersome as rails. The only option remaining is entrenchment, the barring of the door.

But it is always either firm ground that I build on or the liquid element I sail on. Even in agglomerations such as the "metropolis" of Lagos in Nigeria, people arrive at their improvisations either in the water or on land. This is not true, Thomas Demand interjected, of *swampy terrain*. You can neither build nor dwell in the mud. You cannot "live" there, nor can you "die."

SPECIALISTS IN SWAMPS

The cranes' formations move majestically along ancient flight routes, no matter what changes have occurred in the continents and habitats over which they fly.

The Rallidae, crane-like swamp birds, split off from the true cranes eighty-six million years ago.

In the Rallidae, of which there exist 120 species, the art of flight has atrophied. They take off cumbersomely. After a short stretch they fall to the ground. They became swamp specialists. Observers (usually hunters) can identify coots and rails by their wide-stretched TOES. They are broad of foot. Able to populate the zone between water and land. They like to walk over boggy ground or across the vegetation that forms as a treacherous carpet on the waters.

FALLEN STARS
ARE LIKE
FALLEN ANGELS

Stars that collapse at the end of their lives enter a material state referred to by astrophysicists as "degenerate," without any reference to racial prejudices. Nothing but neutrons, with no perceptible space in between. Such ALREADY EXTINCT SUNS are usually two stars revolving around each other. This death, extending over aeons, takes place in each fraction of a second in which the two heavenly bodies orbit each other as a lingering sound, a distortion of time and space, like a musical note. This sort of heavenly trumpet costs a minimal amount of substance that then adds to itself endlessly. The late stars, those BIG TWO: falling together in an abundant well we call NOTHINGNESS. As Prof. Dr. Alessandra Buonanno put it, a crystalline sphere of ideal roundness. A massif of 1,889 Himalayas would present barely the irregularity of an ice rink freshly prepared for a skating competition. Underneath, these excessively compact bodies are liquid. Full of disobedience, saturated with congested agitation over the innumerability and indefinition of such a highly condensed mass. Here matter shows its true face. But no submarine can navigate the wild currents of this crystal lake. This predator mauls any stranger on the spot. There is nothing in the cosmos as lonely as these "I"s orbiting each other.

But fallen angels (they, too, circling in pairs, but not for reasons of sex) differ utterly from neutron stars in that their compacted vibration swarms in microparticles in us human beings and our evolutionary neighbors (and in nature as a whole), taking the form, as it were, of stray waves of corpuscles on whose crests adventurers and the daughters of Amazons ride. That is often the reason for tears running down the cheek. A bit of dust from the once so compact body of one of those angels suffices. On the other hand, all the vivid pictures of angels in human form are based on misconceptions. Evidently all angels are spheres. And bizarre, to the extent that they manifest as snow.

ANGELS' LIVES AND OURS. BETWEEN THEM THE SNOWLESS DARK AGES

In the Dark Ages of our universe, several million years after the earliest segment of time, which was 1^{-32} of a second long, a TIME OF ITS OWN and an ANGELS' TIME constituting a separate and autonomous aeon (for us such a moment is short, but on its own terms its duration is extraordinary, "subjectively infinite"), there is neither snow nor light. No child with a candle, its light flickering in the draft, crosses a cellar such as that.

This was before the unforgettable moment of gloaming, dawn, the first massive stars. Where were the angels then? The WHEELS or THRONES of the Third Order, with their winged pairs of eyes? They surged forward like snakes, like swimmers gone deep underwater, propelled by their lungs. It is said that this adversity gave rise to the spirits of the First and Second Orders. That explains why, according to the accounts, the first fallen angel came from the Third Order.

In the time preceding the Dark Ages, that is, within the beat of 1^{-32} of a second, the heavenly palaces turned infinitely small. Thus, to this day, the upper Six Orders of the angels are invisible to our eyes, and our ear detects them with difficulty in the rushing of the present. The choirs of the HIGHER SPIRITUALITIES are sopranos so high that our ears mistake them for shrieking. The singing beings are so submicroscopically small

that they (or a flock of them) could pass through the head of an American president without him or his guards noticing a thing. If, however (and this is not individually commanded by God but happens spontaneously and ceaselessly), a messenger, in particular one from the Ninth Order, namely the practitioner of salvation, is sent to us, he must inflate himself monstrously like a balloon, an explosion, from his authentic microform to Planck length, almost to the boundaries of his true nature. It is in this attenuation, at the point of bursting, that he delivers his messages. The phantom hands seen on icons at these messengers' sides, next to their wings, are deceptive. Angels cannot use their hands. They are not workers like bees. When introduced into our dimension, they remain VIBRATIONS or STRINGS, that is, rhythms or metronomes, and the drastic difference between the thousand types of beats at their disposal and the slow motion of our cells and nerves (= we human beings are bromides) engenders these messengers' tidings and protection.

A HUMAN LIFE, COMPARED WITH SNOW

A human life spans the time in which the starlike snow crystals trodden on by an angel of the Fifth Order turn to slush and melt. It is a misconception that the ARCHAI or RULERS are responsible for guarding human lives. If this is seen as their work, it is due to a confusion with heathen images of Valkyries or divine illuminations from Asia that watch over heroes. However, there are FORCES or STRONGHOLDS, *dynameis* in Greek, that guard complex entities such as human children until their ninth year.

These forces always manifest themselves in groups, in formations. Conversely, this means that they are lacking in other places and in other perilous moments. A gas chamber is put into operation and no choir of angels blocks the pipeline. To confuse these beings with ELECTRICAL FORCES is equally farfetched. During the Enlightenment, scholars interpreted spiritual beings in physical terms, just as visitors to a zoo contemplating a monkey cage assume they understand something about these beings by memorizing the textbooks about them and the anatomical atlas.

THE SEVEN SPIRITS OF KNOWLEDGE

Socrates, the legendary Athenian, asserted that in every serious discussion between two people there is a demon at work. Not when one talks to oneself and not in discussions between larger groups. Contrary to all rational principles, the truth actually comes to light thanks to this demon. Even if both interlocutors tell tall stories, the truth will out in the difference between them. For this reason it is best if two liars enter into a discussion since neither has any intention of asserting the truth and, as a result, both will avoid erecting any discursive barriers blocking the path to truth. The first thing to give itself away is that which wasn't mendacious in the first place. Socrates believed insight to be a special form of valor. It was not at home in reason, but rather in the ability to differentiate, in feeling, a realm that encompassed sincerity, familiarity with oneself, and curiosity about the peculiarities of other people. These four characteristics (sincerity, familiarity, curiosity, the ability to differentiate) are like bowls or vessels in which the demon chops up every statement, every piece of factual information before eating and expelling them again; i.e., giving them back to us in a purified form, otherwise known as truth (which we can deny and replace with something new at any moment). As demonic excrement? But with a great potential for change. You can change it from its present state into something much more

interesting. Socrates (unlike Aristotle) doesn't say anywhere what truth might in fact be; he only says what the material is from which—fingers crossed—a morsel of truth might emerge.

The martial definition of valor, on the other hand, is parochial. It has more to do with the distinction between "doing something or not doing it," between "what is to be feared and what is to be embraced." This man would rather have died than refute his claims.

Hip Frenchman René Descartes, wrongly referring to Montaigne, suggested abandoning insight to the next best sensation. One shouldn't think things over, but rather think things afresh. The peculiarity of each and every thought delights the thinker like a footprint in fresh snow: this footprint is mine. Insight is a consequence of this special sensation. Thinking, he says, is like finding.

A commander of the parachute regiment who had served in Dien Bien Phu and was then stationed in North Africa believed his insight derived from a treasure store of experience—the sum of all the practical rules his combat missions had taught him, i.e., the difference between orders and an inner "emotional" resistance to them. Initially he taught at military schools in France, later he was bought by the CIA, and since then he has held seminars in the EXTENDED NEAR EAST (including the CIS states in the south of the former Soviet Union, in particular Uzbekistan and Kyrgyzstan). His experiences have proved

particularly useful for the asymmetrical campaign against terror. In his courses they invariably constitute a LABYRINTH of "right" and "wrong." Taking "wrong" as a starting point, however, it is possible to progress toward "right" through a sequence of steps in the right direction, just as the "right" direction can lead within his system of explanations toward what is "wrong." This labyrinthine riddle demands of those taking his courses a degree of daring and an enthusiasm for experimentation. Critics well-disposed to the commander of the parachute regiment referred to him as a "craftsman-thinker."

Nietzsche mistrusted his mind. He didn't mistrust his feet, the moving parts of his body, the muscles, the limbs, the alimentary tract. He "walked" the process of arriving at truth. The Engadine offered more opportunities in this respect than the alleyways of Genoa. At first his feet adopted a walking rhythm in which the Master's body was able to express itself; subsequently the thoughts dressed themselves in words, what you might term the outlet of an evolutionary man. It would appear, however, that a certain steadfastness associated with this walking is able to overcome all kinds of obstacles. Nietzsche's thoughts, "transformed entirely into a coat," constitute some of the best insights "that can flood the market."

After nine oppressive years of married life, during which her husband's stubbornness of

character had turned out to be unalterable, Gerlinde Reh came to the conclusion that her husband was being unfaithful to her. She had allowed herself to be deceived for so long, had gone so far as to lovingly do the groundwork for this deception! She didn't want to confront the truth of her misery. Then her husband brought his "new lady," a rich widow, home for Christmas. This Gerlinde could not accept. Would there be no end to this RAILROAD OF DENIAL? Gerlinde moved out of the ruins of her marriage. Had she ever brought herself to discuss it with anyone, she would have formulated her insight in the following terms: it is impossible to demand back from my unfaithful husband the nine years I've lived with him. She was now alone with her insight. She was only able to talk about any of this with her girlfriends. They were only prepared to listen to her story once. As a cheerful soul, Gerlinde did not view her insight as a gift from heaven.

The ultimate form of insight, according to the architect F., who had studied with Wright in Chicago, is an ENCLOSED SPACE. A sea of stones, as represented by the metropolis, leaves its mark on the senses and sweeps every thought and sensation along with it. Subsequently the same enclosed space is constructed, in a subjective form, within the individual; from there it shapes the momentum and conditions of external life with the rigidity of concrete, like a river course cast in stone.

Another, quite different definition of insight is offered by the circus artiste Fanny Petzolt. As she puts it herself, if the trapeze artist throws herself into the arms of the catcher (as she does every evening), then the click of the successful jump, the instant in which every nerve senses success, is what I call the moment of "insight." On the other hand, the Russian marriage broker Jekaterina Saitzev, who has now relocated her agency from Moscow to New York, describes the moment when a successfully brokered couple sink into each other's arms (or, to put it more colloquially, "fall in love") as a "happy insight." Reason has little to do with it. The surprise is more useful than all the effort beforehand. The owner of the agency spoke with twenty-seven years of experience.

The Harvard Kantian Dr. Mary Pitcorn believed that lockable doors were essential for the process of gaining insight. She often sat on the toilet amid the hustle and bustle of some large railway station, locked the door behind her and expanded on her ideas. As soon as the door is closed firmly behind me, the INNER FOUNTAIN opens up within me (as it does in everyone else as well). It is this that we call insight. It is for this reason that the hermits in the Middle Ages lived in a hermitage. According to Dr. Pitcorn, insight is a thing "unto itself" that "flows through" a person who has not fallen prey to despair spontaneously because it is the "ground water of life."

7

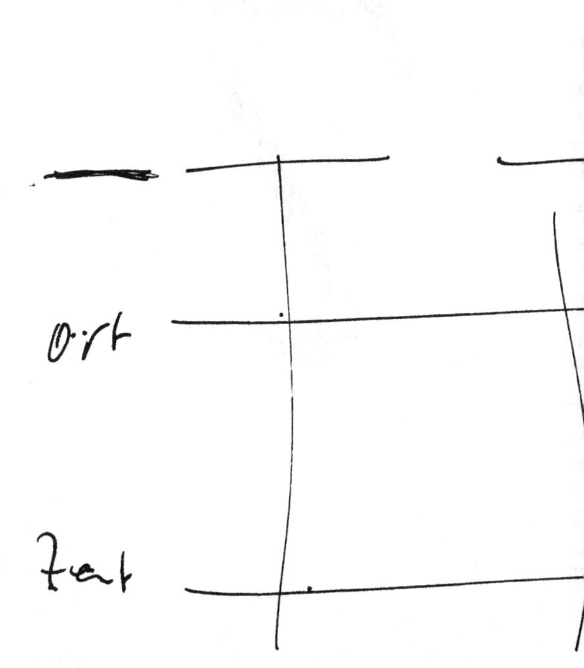
Ort
Zeit

Homage to Sergei Eisenstein

with
Velimir Khlebnikov,
Kazimir Malevich,
and Giacometti

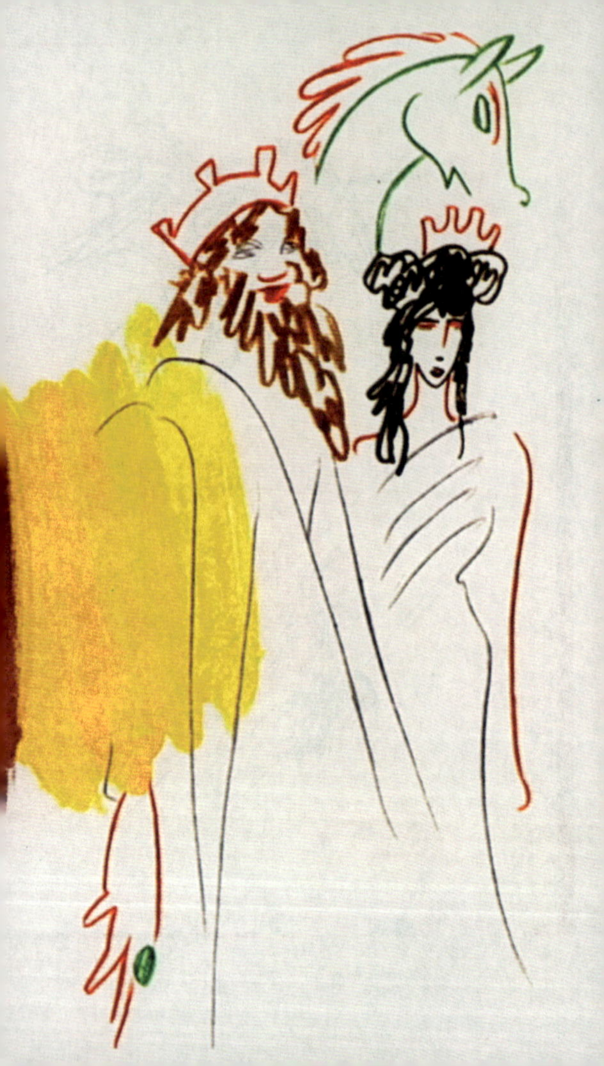

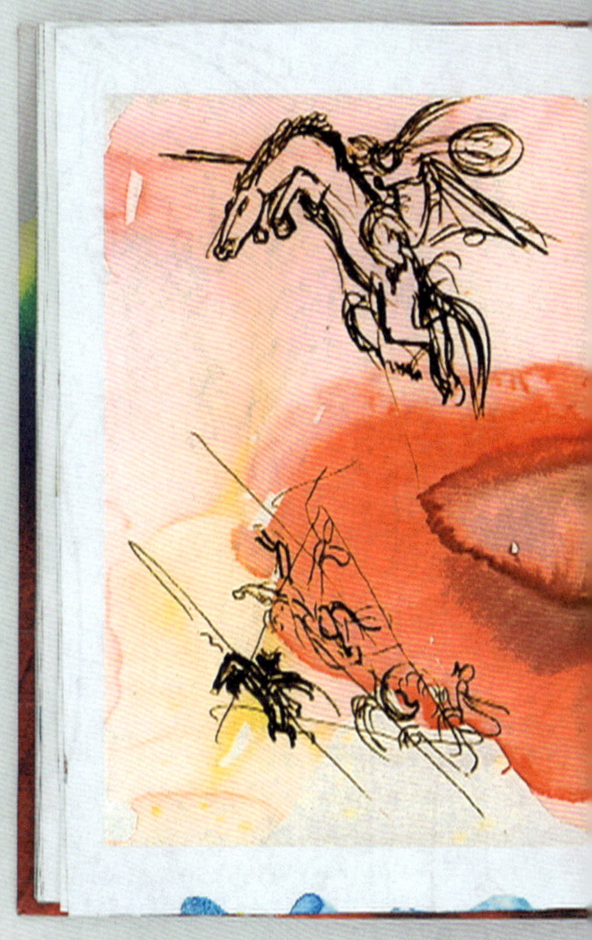

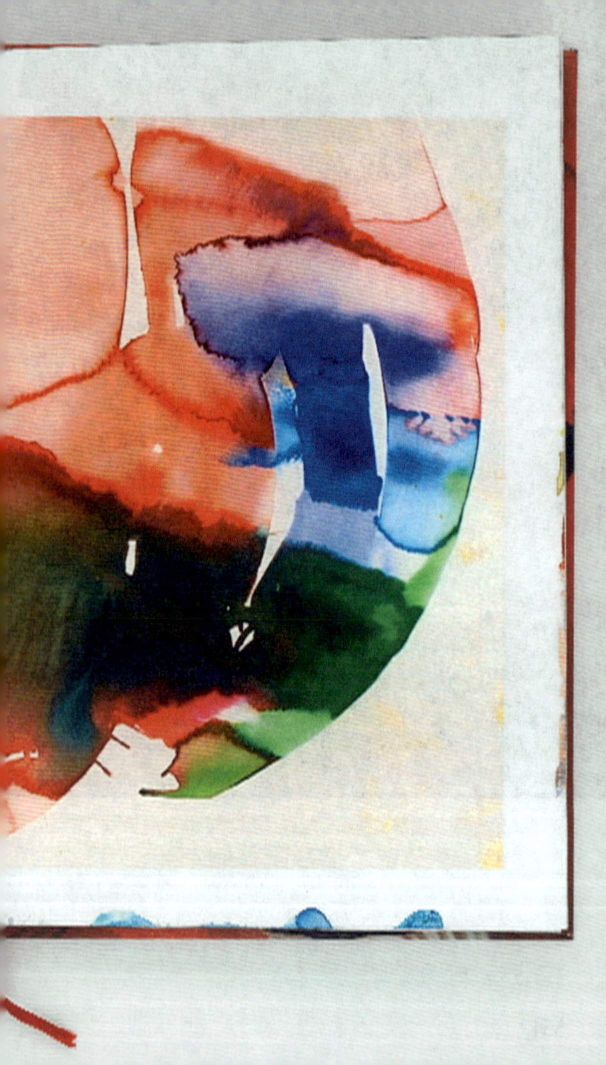

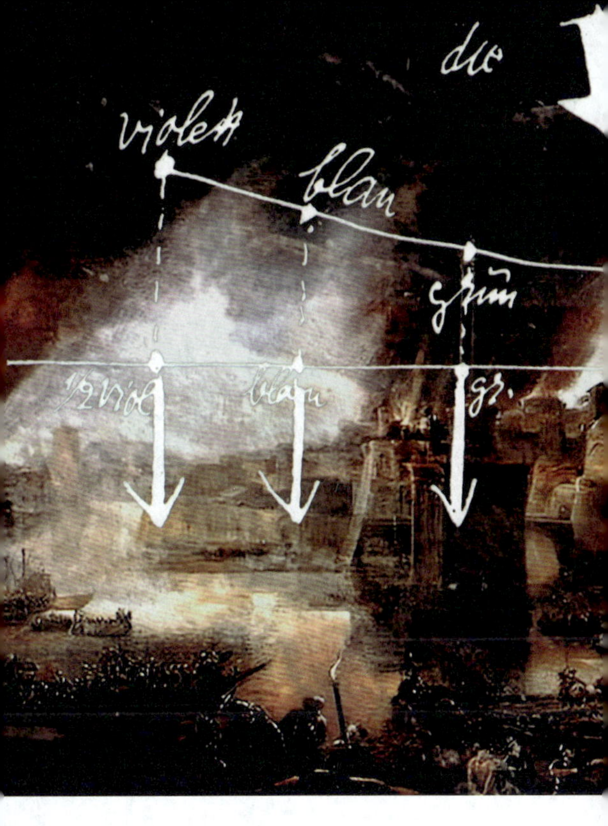

die
violett
blau
grün
1/2 viol
blau
gr.

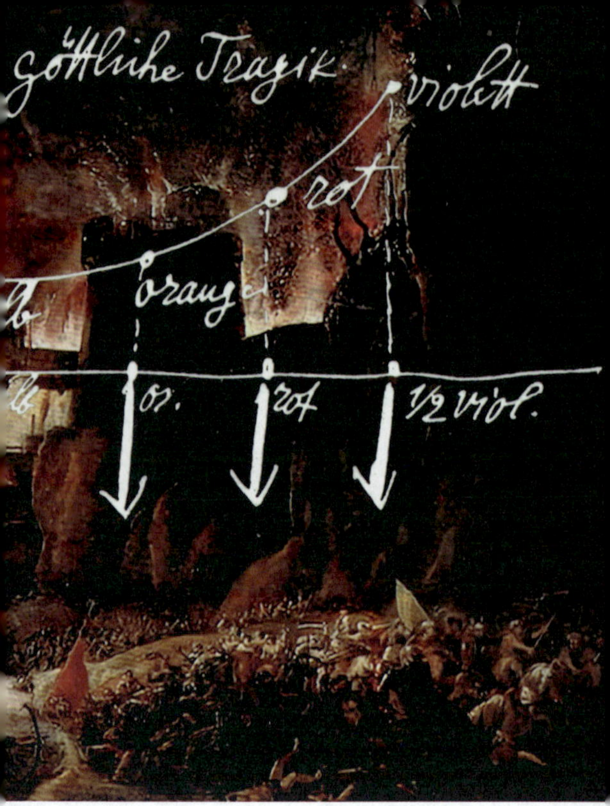

göttliche Tragik
violett
rot
orange
or.
rot
1/2 viol.

Eisenstein directs *Alexander Nevsky* (1938) and Wagner's *Die Walküre* (1940)
02:47

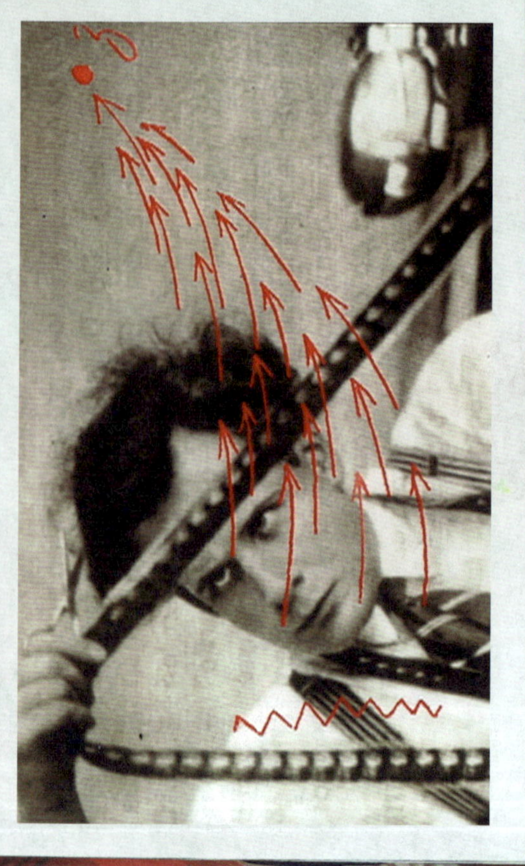

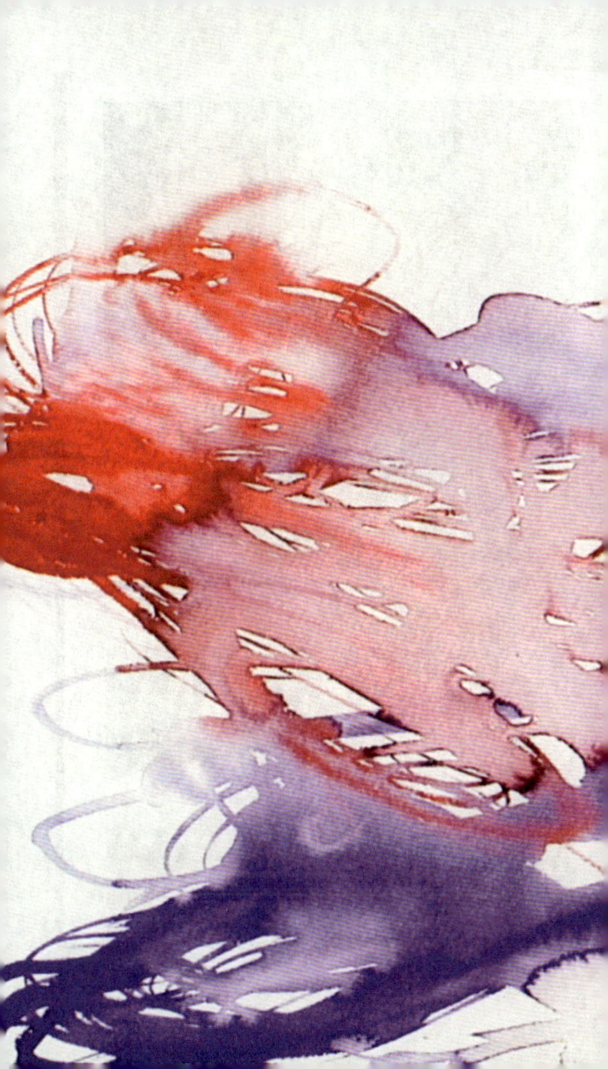

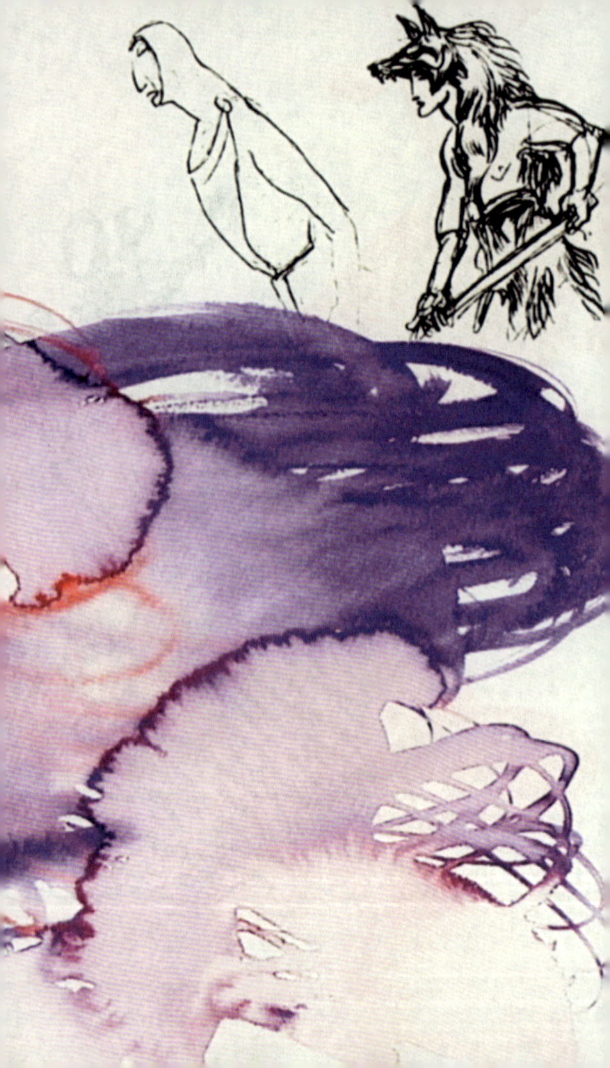

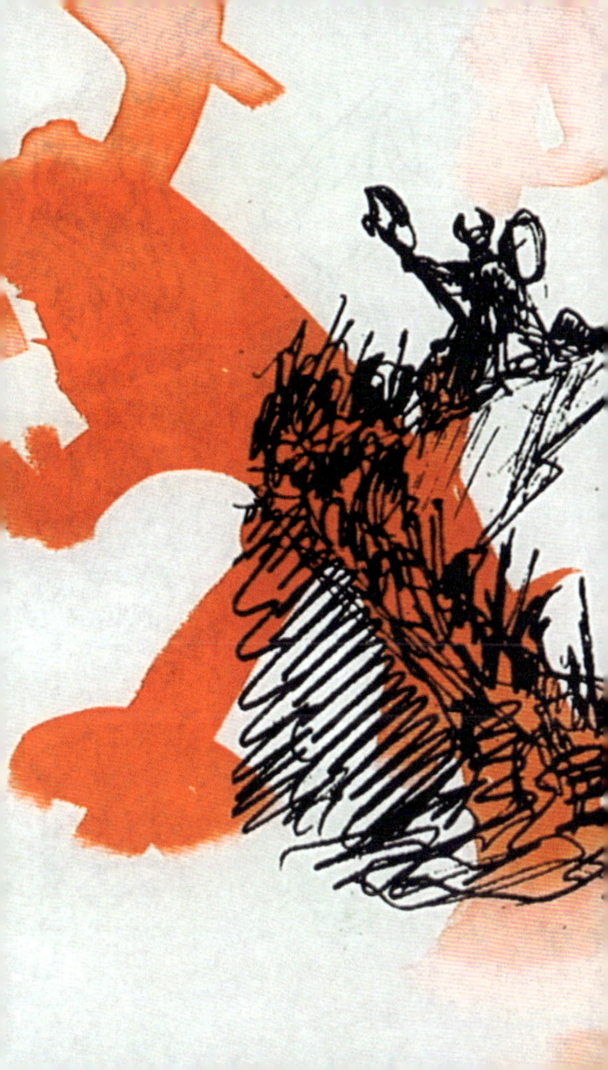

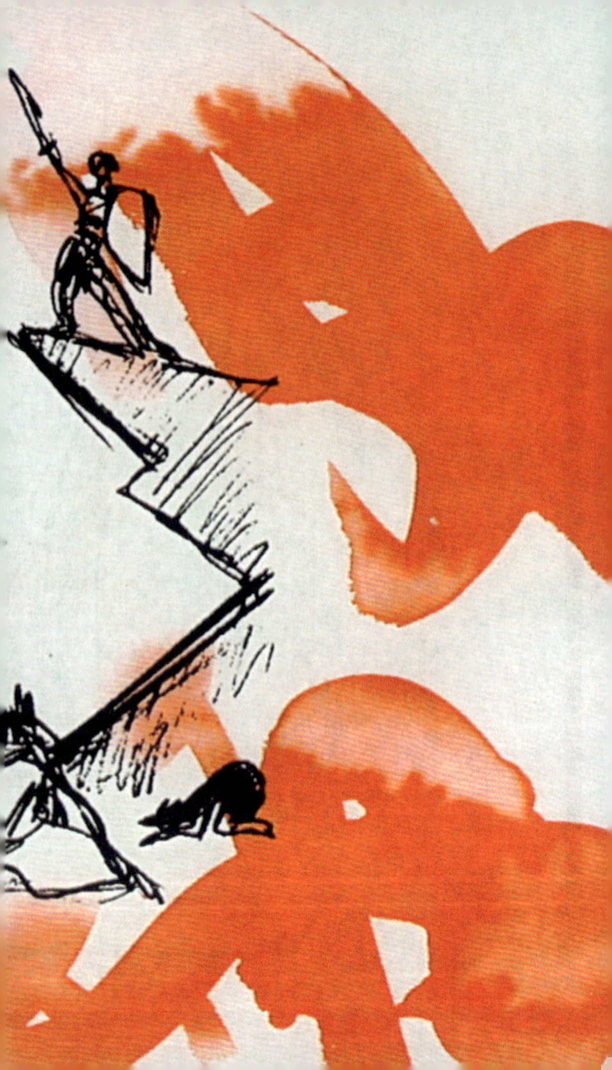

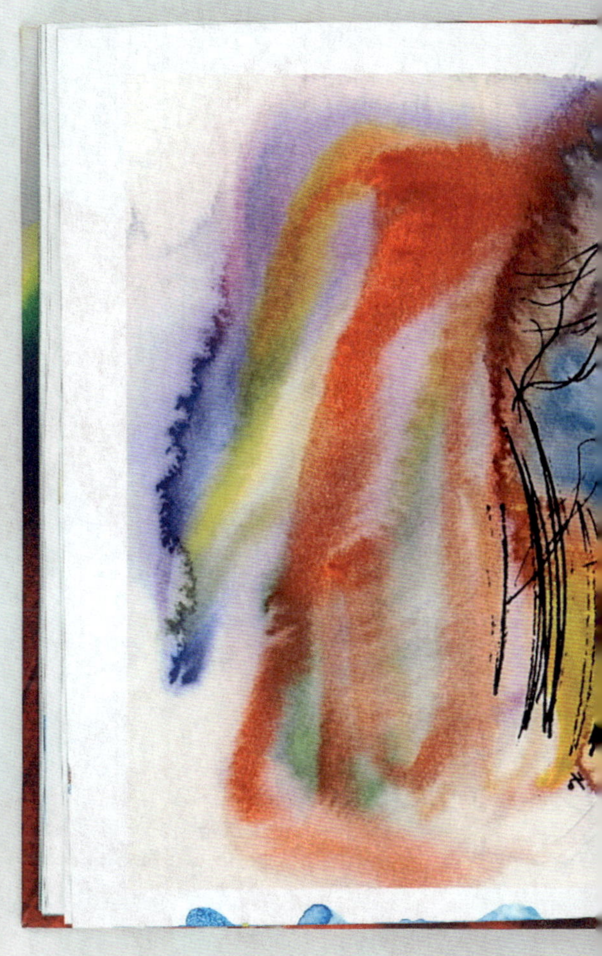

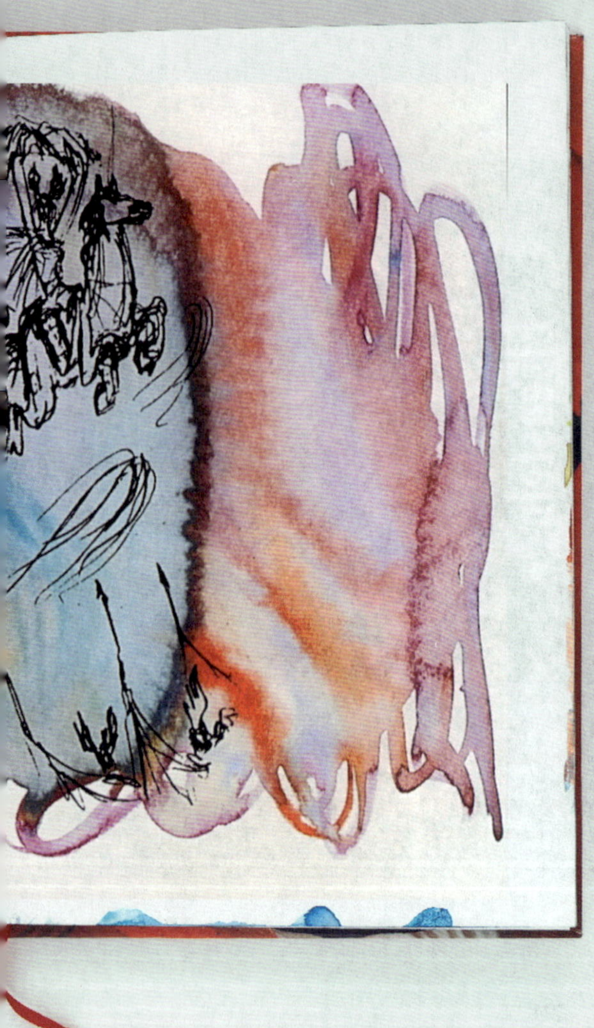

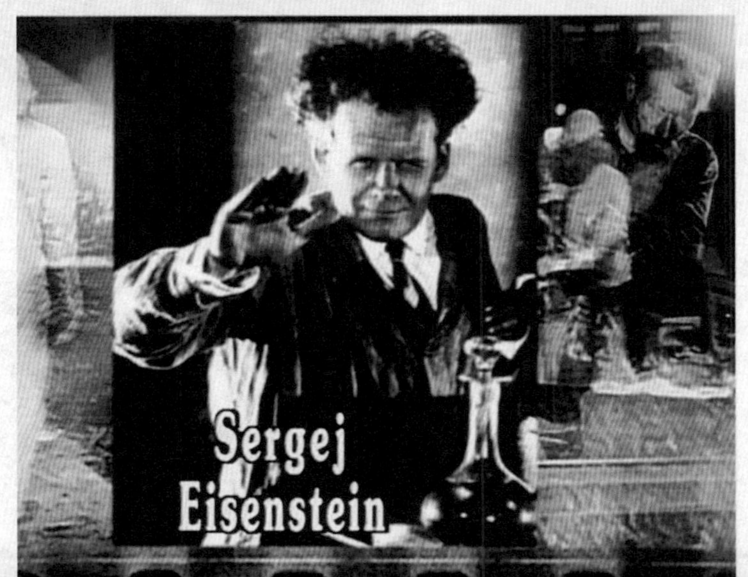
Sergej
Eisenstein

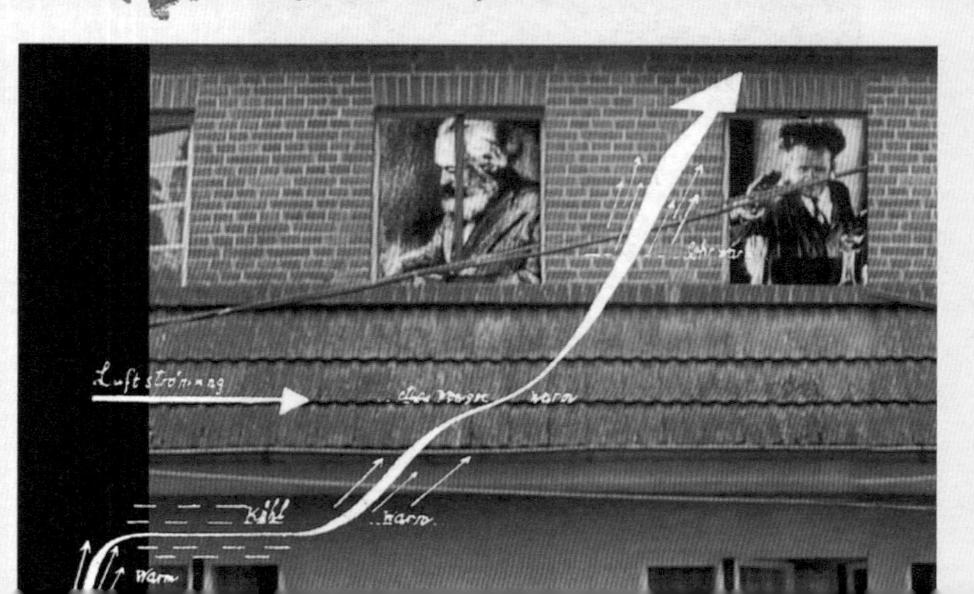

Luftströmung
Kühl
warm
warm
Warm

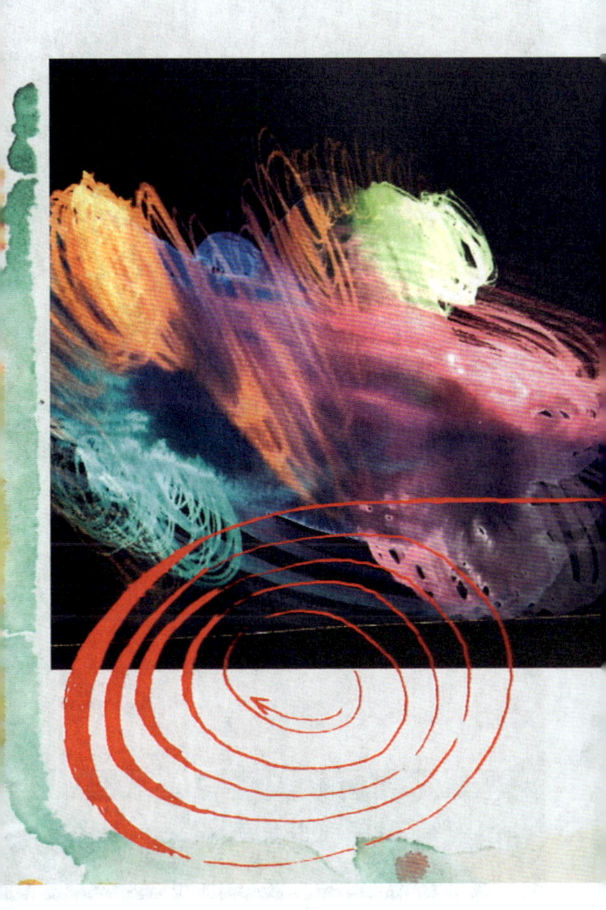

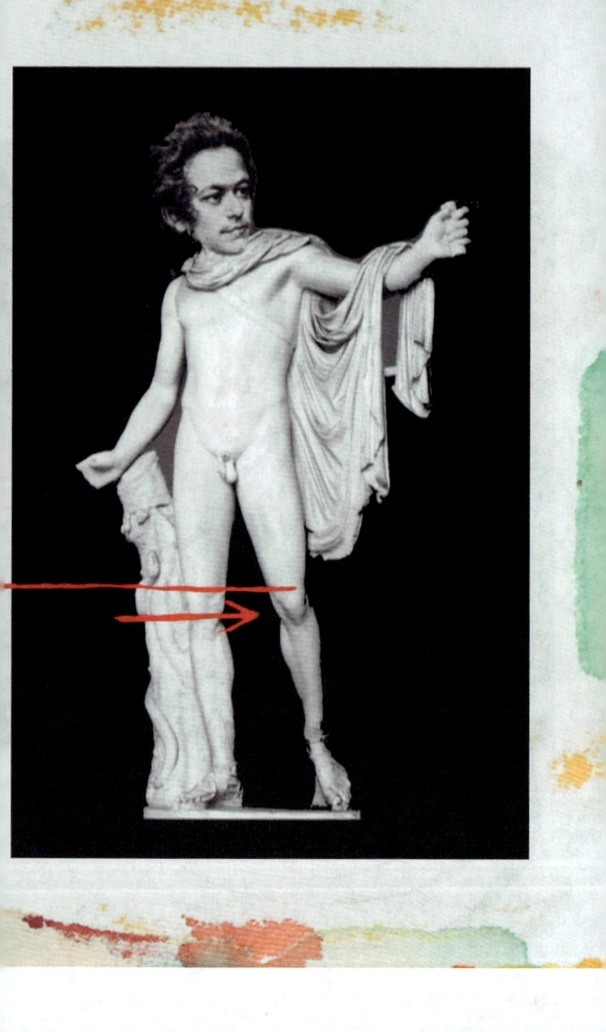

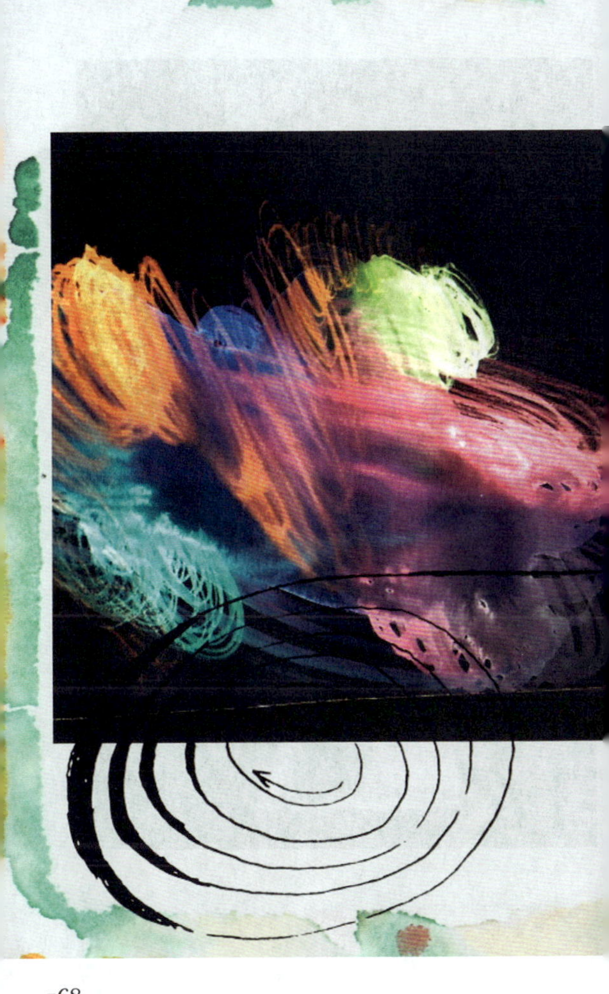

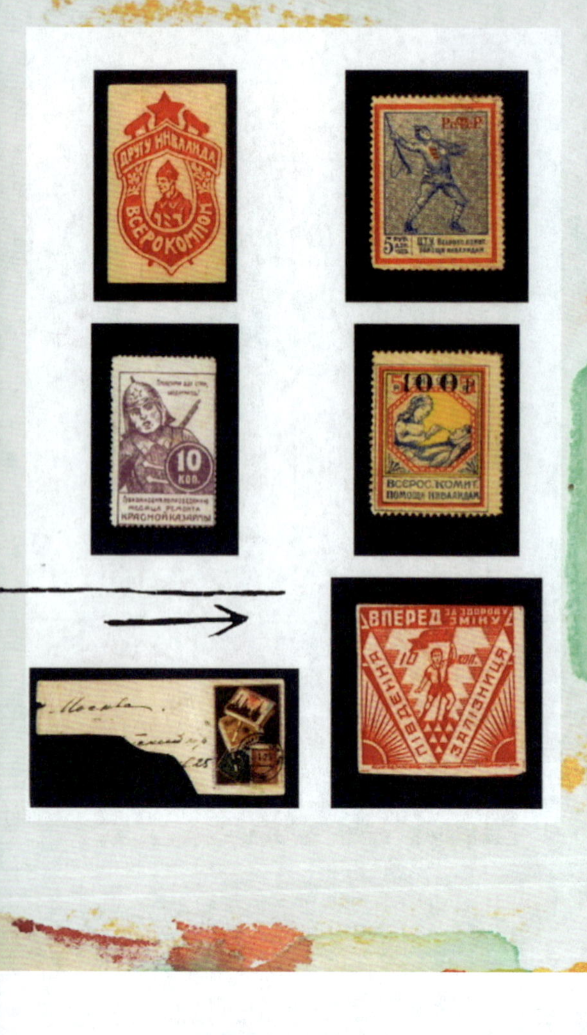
ДРУГУ ИНВАЛИДА
ВСЕРОКОМПОМ
Р.С.Ф.С.Р.
10 КОП.
КРАСНОЙ КАЗАРМЫ
100
ВСЕРОС. КОМИТ.
ПОМОЩИ ИНВАЛИДАМ
ВПЕРЕД ЗА ЗДОРОВУ ЗМІНУ
10 коп.
ПІВДЕННА
ЗАЛІЗНИЦЯ
Москва

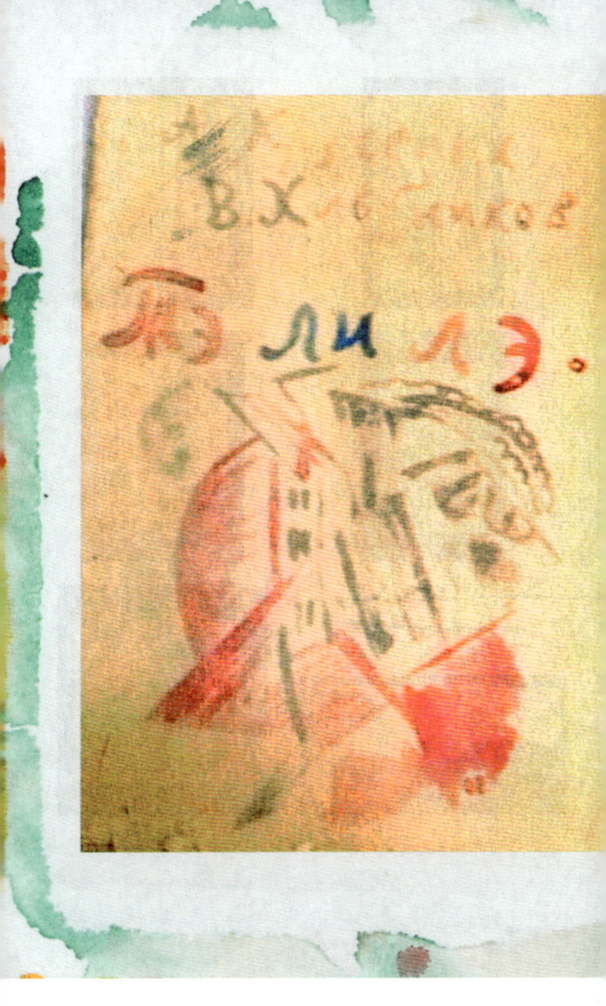
В. Хлебников
ТЭ ЛИ ЛЭ.

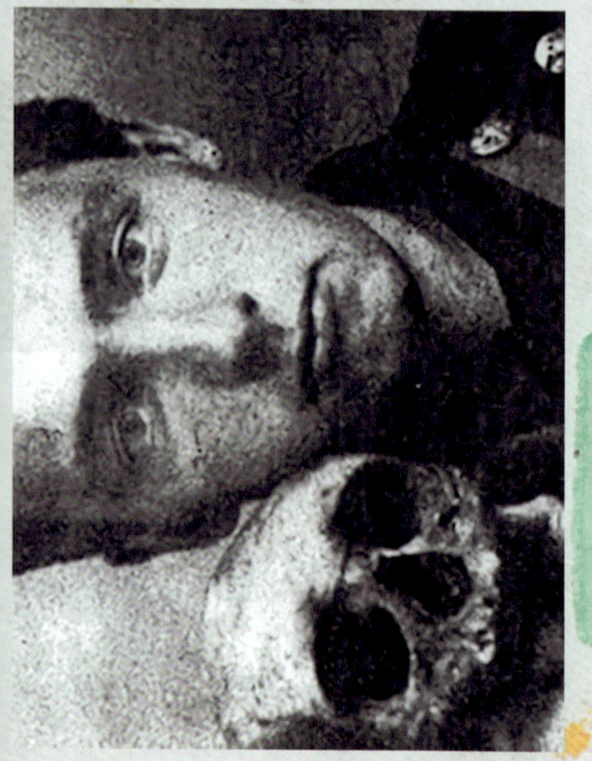

Welimir Chlebnikow

$$365 = 3^5 + 3^4 + 3^3 + 3^2 + 3^1 + 3^0 + 1$$

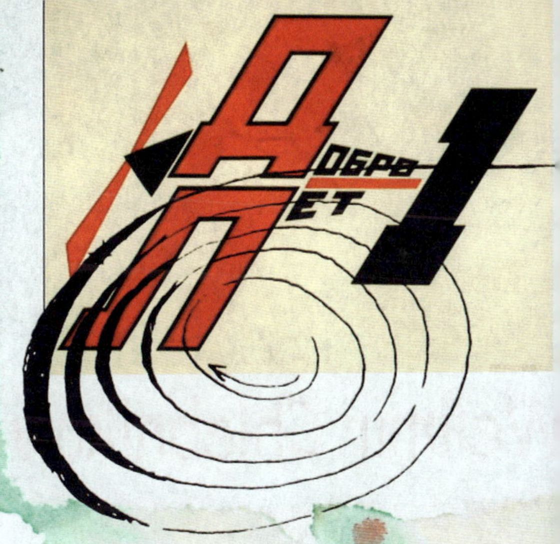

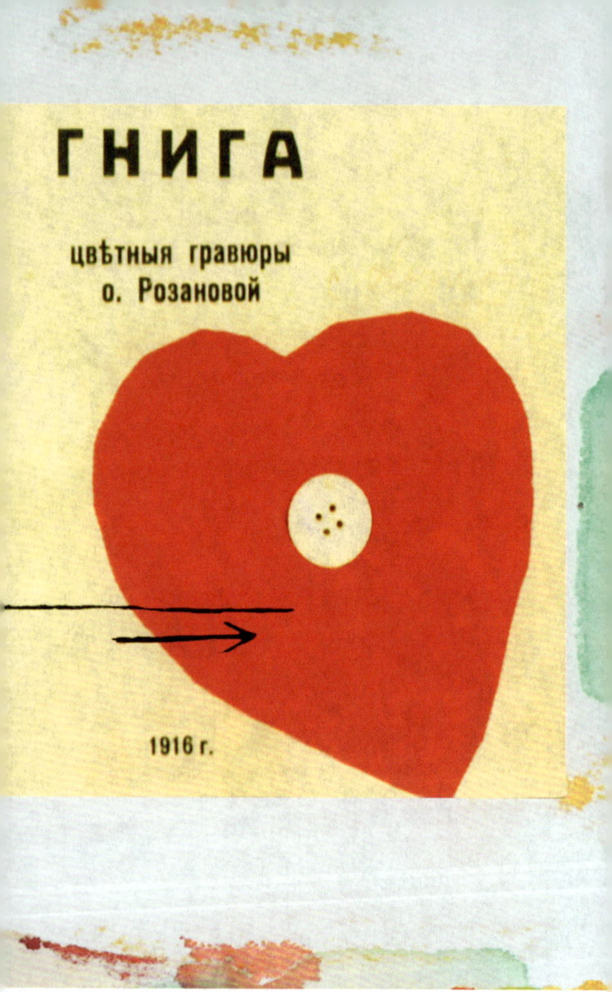

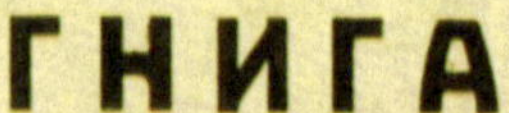

цвѣтныя гравюры
о. Розановой

1916 г.

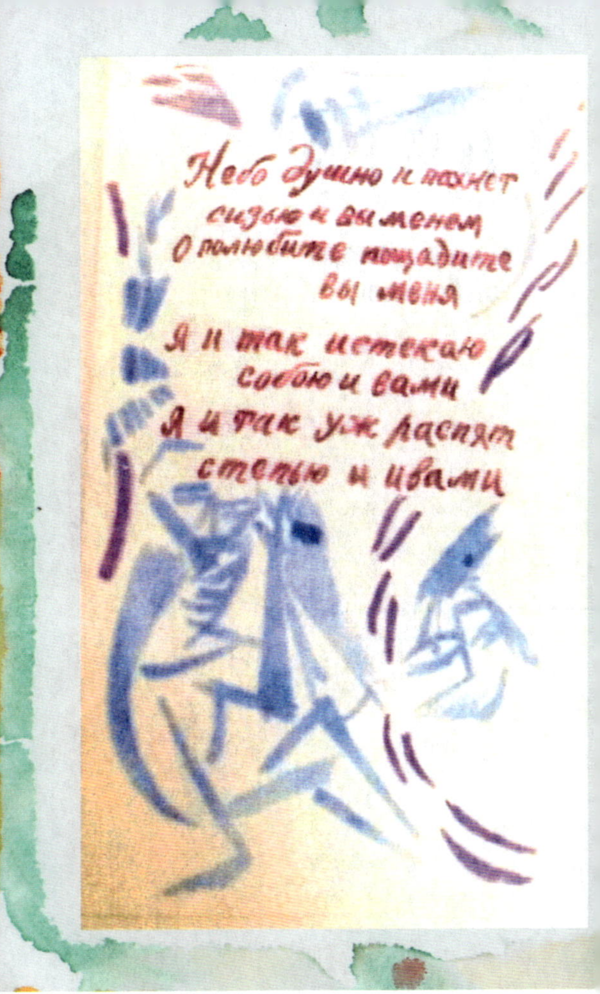

Небо душно и пахнет
сизью и выменем
О полюбите пощадите
вы меня
Я и так истекаю
собою и вами
Я и так уж распят
степью и цвами

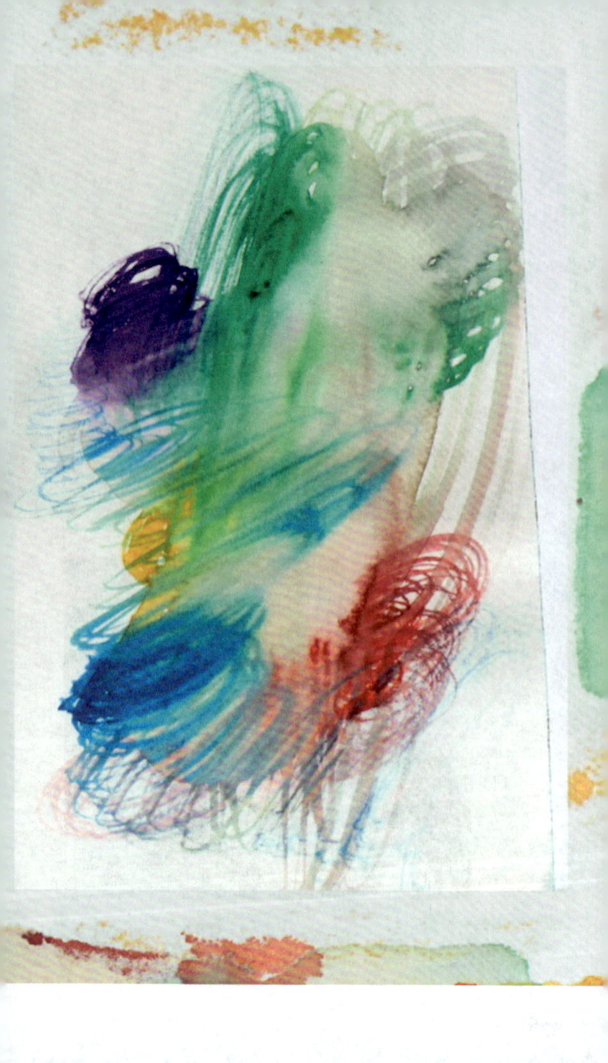

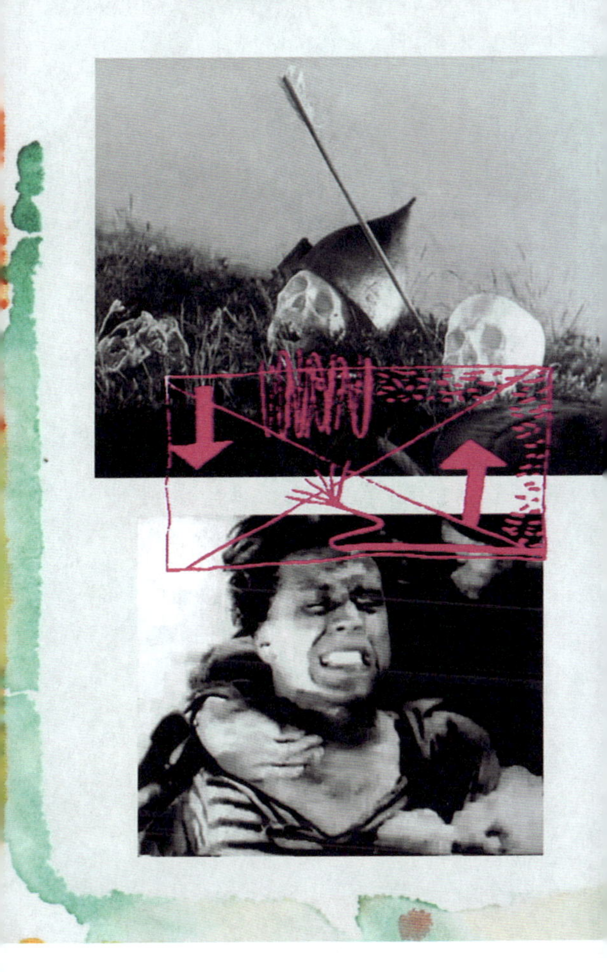

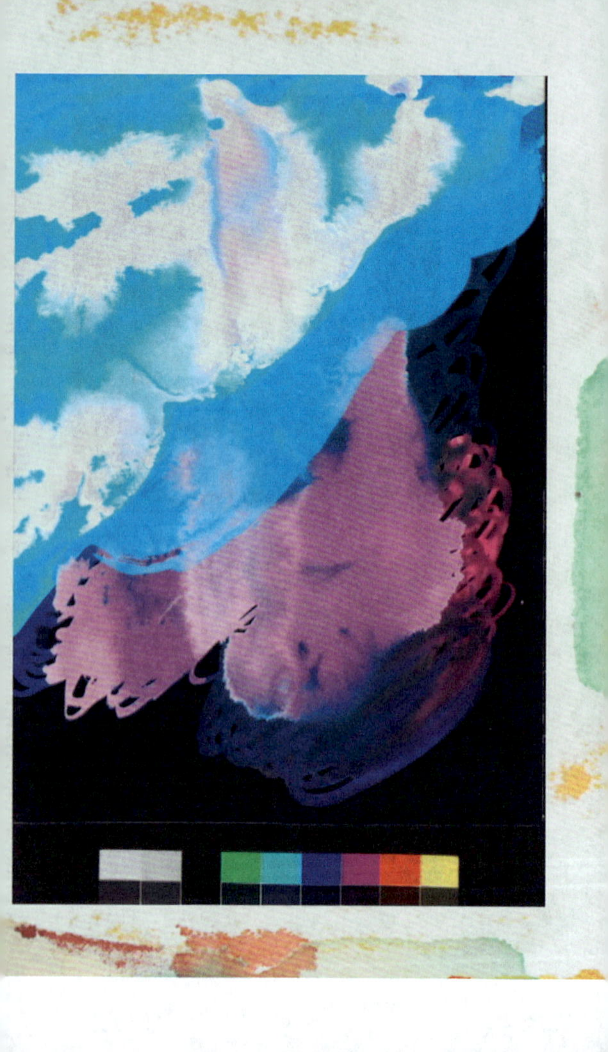

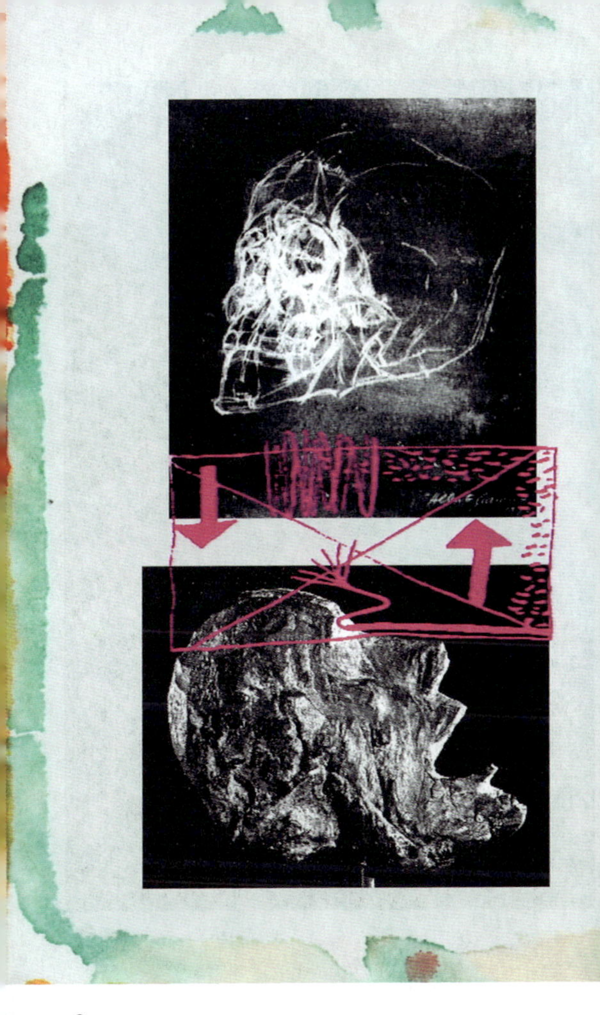

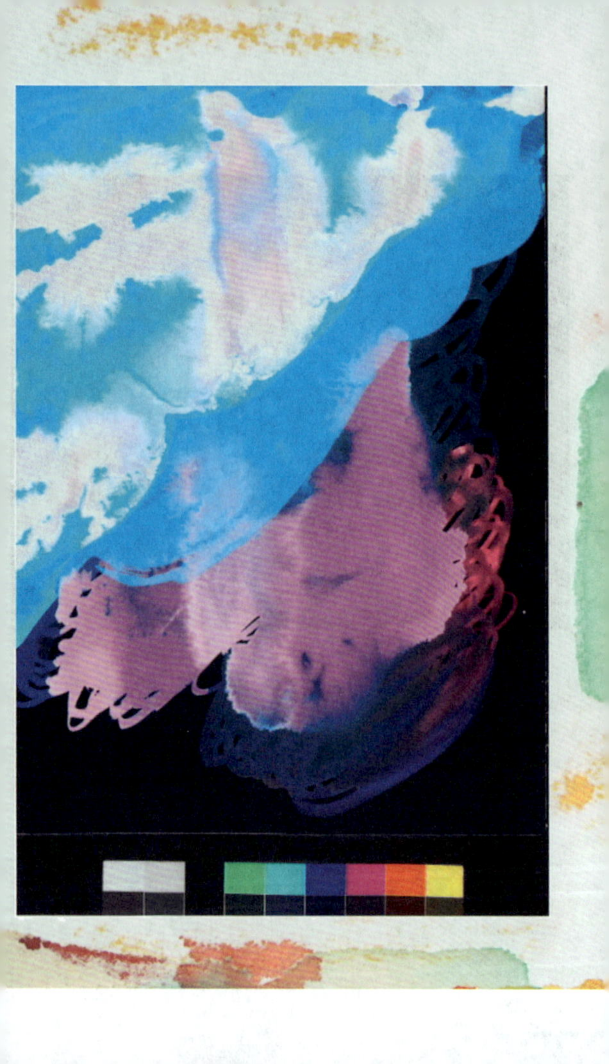

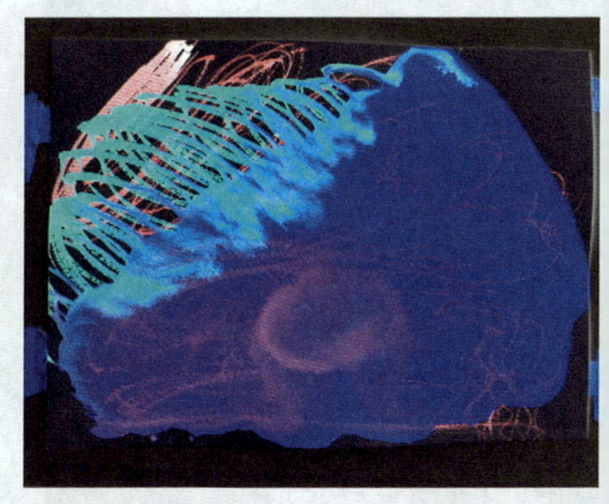

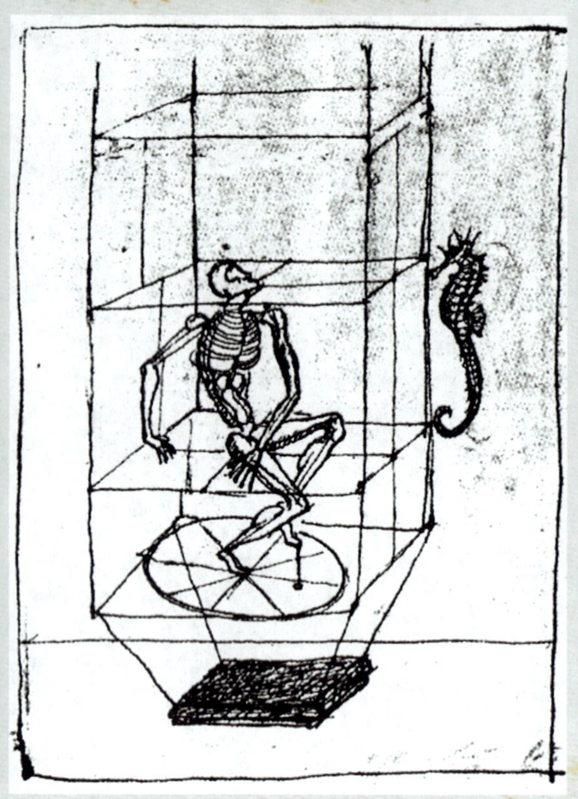

Alberto Giacometti,
Ohne Titel

8

“Lights in the Harbor”

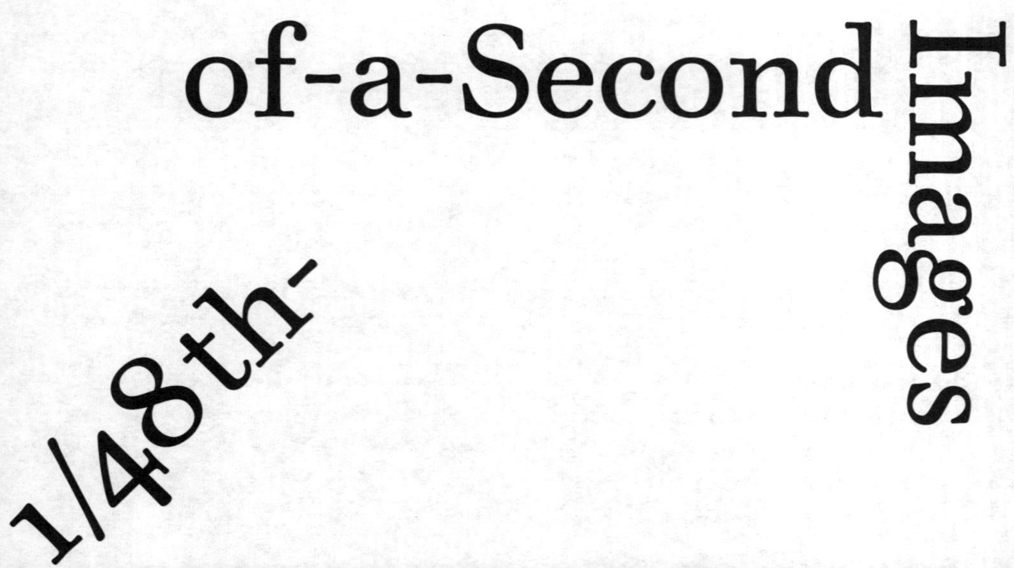
1/48th-
of-a-Second
Images

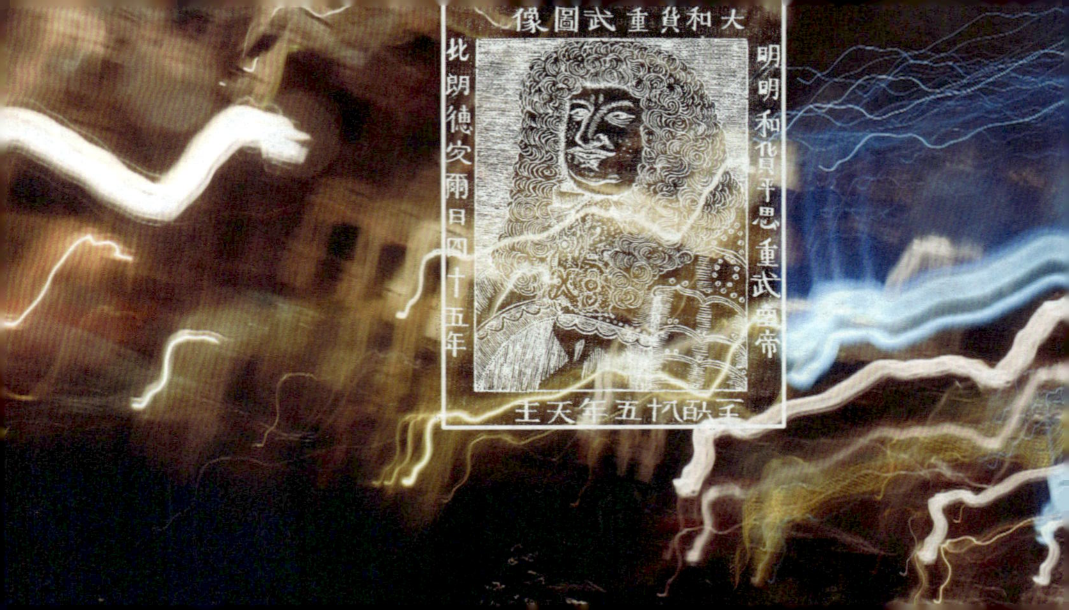
大和貨重武圖像
北朗德安爾日四十五年

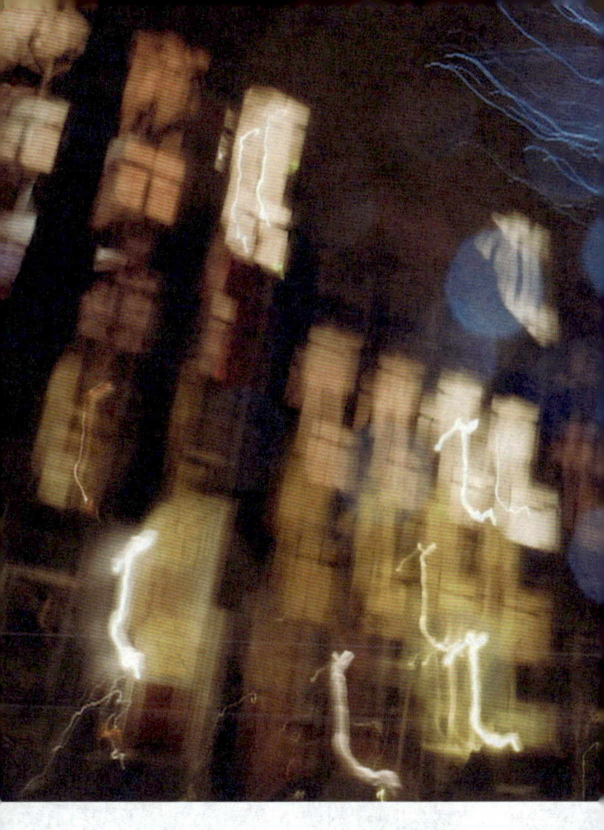

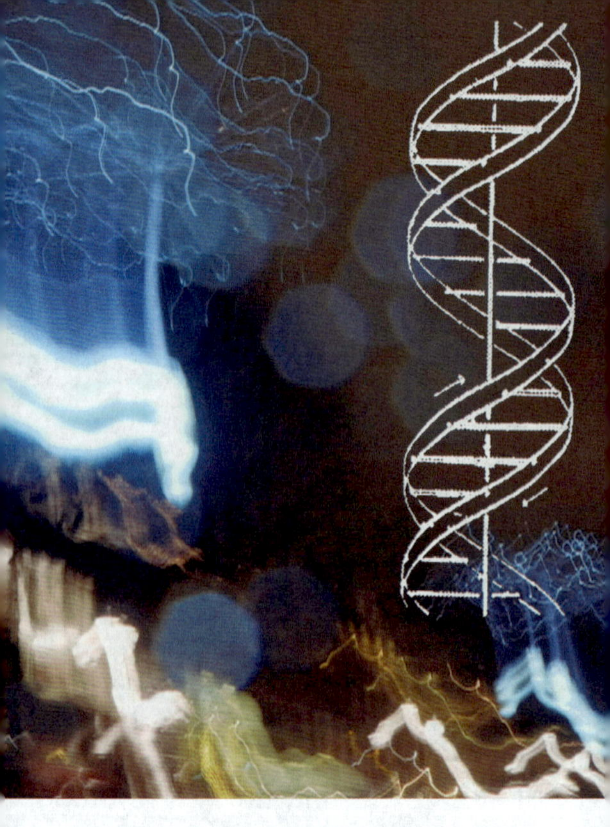

HELIX IN THE HARBOR

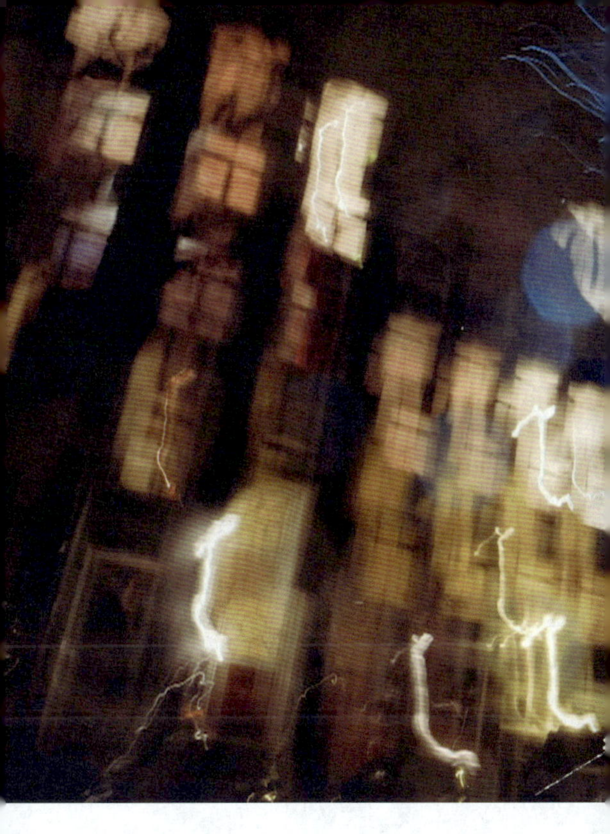

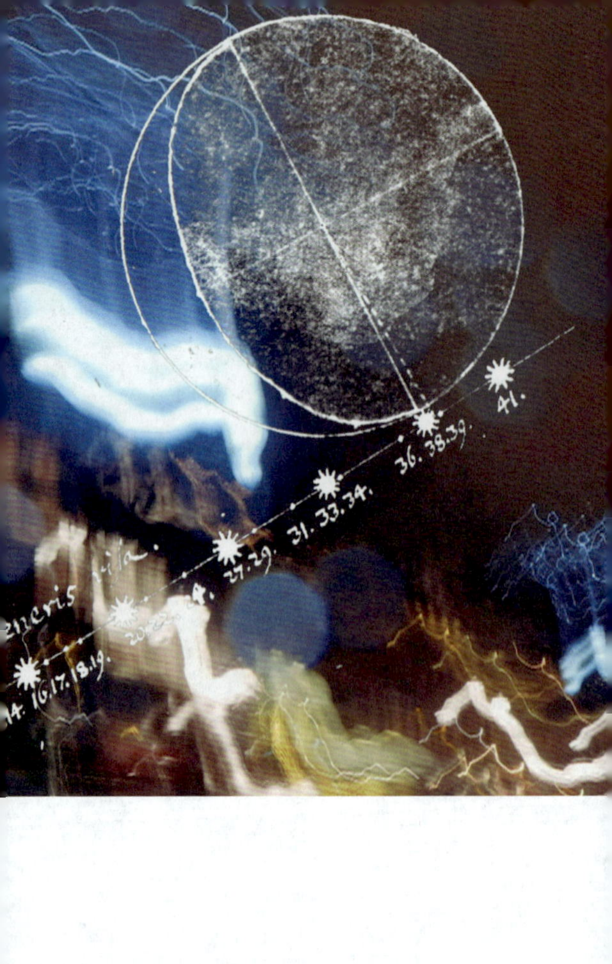
14. 16.17.18.19.
27.29.
31.33.34.
36.38.39.
41.

Shooting with the Silent Movie Camera Askania-Z
02:10

Evolution's Sparkler: The Eye
02:30

CAMERA IMAGES OF LIGHT CONDITIONS / "LIGHTS IN THE HARBOR"

Camera images of light conditions the human eye cannot perceive, film stills, "1/48th-of-a-second images" providing the background for images.

In a classic film camera (Debrie, Arriflex), a time lapse is made by decreasing the number of frames per second (or an ever longer time for extreme time-lapse). The presentation is made at the normal speed of twenty-four frames, plus twenty-four moments of the transport phase (when the image appears to be "dark"). A classic film presentation thus consists of forty-eight units per second. A timelapse recording, on the other hand, which produces a long period of time (e.g., exposure of several minutes for one image) generates a TOTALITY OF TIME in this way. Quasi an overview or a data memory of time lapse. If you fix the single image of 1/48th of a second, then you have the opposite pole of the time totals, a SECTION OF GROSS TIME. I believe that what dragonflies see with their multifaceted eyes is something like this; we humans, however, cannot imitate this "view of the camera."

Classical time-lapse, as practiced by the Bauhaus and used by Walter Ruttmann in the recording technique for his film *Berlin: Symphony of a Metropolis*, represents a TOTALITY OF TIME only in the form of speed. On the contrary, in the reverse method, which captures detail, the

1/48th-of-a-second image (which, interestingly, corresponds to a much longer exposure time) doesn't capture the rapidity of events, but swirls amid inherent movements of light. The camera is a "light catcher," a "light eater." And thus this "massive collection of random light" doesn't have to do with any "dominion over time" or "dominion over scenery," but the opposite: a higher degree of freedom in which lights, coincidences, and particles of reality show themselves in their own form. "A weather of light."

In the present case, this is the method my cameraman Thomas Willke used to film in the port of Amsterdam at night. The still images of the water in constant motion, the light of the harbor facilities and houses, show the autonomous movement, the swirl of light, upon which images can then be imposed when filming is resumed. All of these are artifacts, examples of "condensed chance." For film and literature, neither of which can paint, this is an authentic form of expression.

THE PLANNING OF A NEW KIND OF ACADEMY

G.W. Leibniz pursued a plan of creating a European academy that would be filled exclusively with Chinese scholars. Leibniz felt that just such an implant into one of the capitals of Europe would force a confrontation between the arts of sciences of the West and those of China. From such a separatrix, i.e., that concentrate of opposites, he expected great gains for Western science.

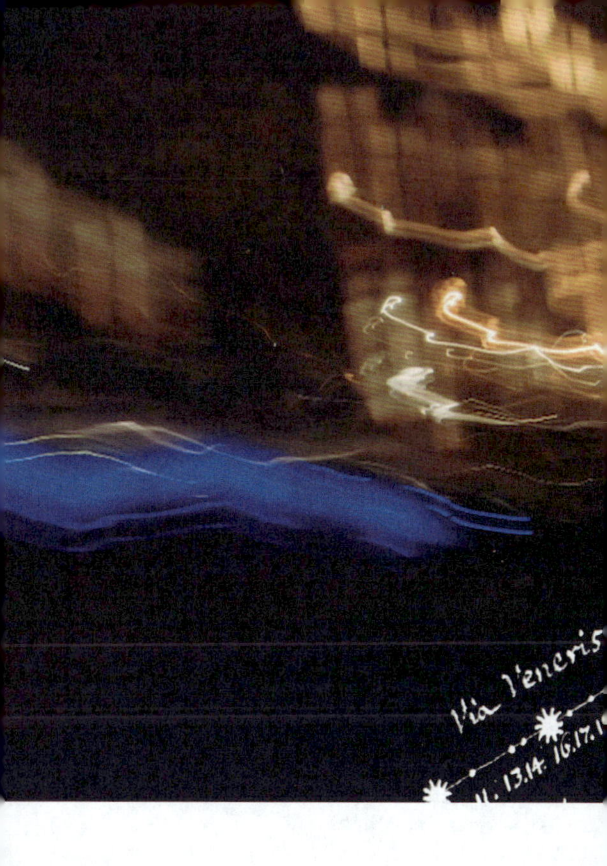
Via Veneris

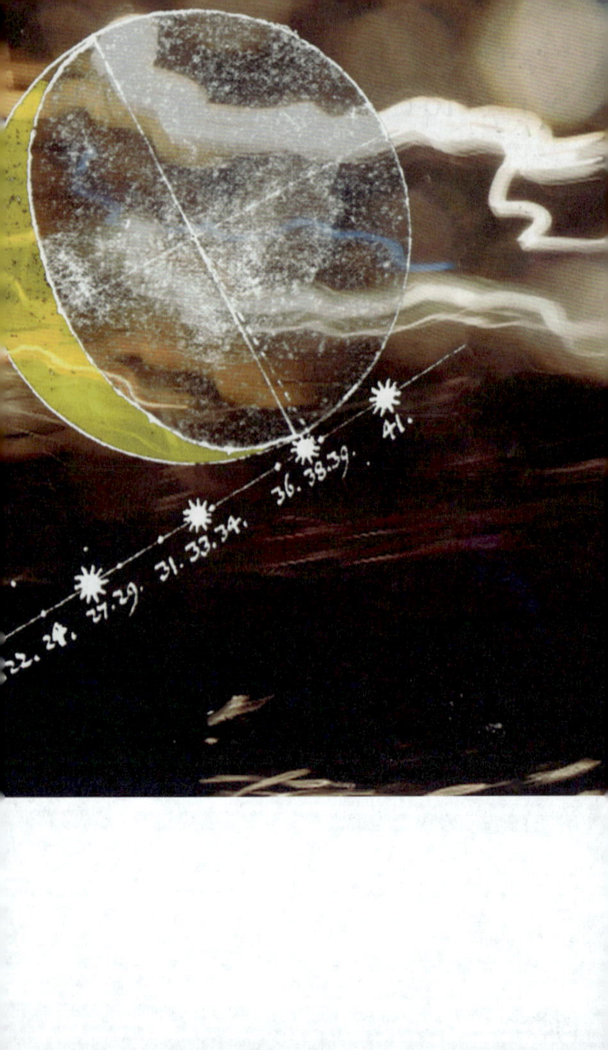
22. 24.
27. 29.
31. 33. 34.
36. 38. 39.
41.

“Let go of the four angels
bound to the Euphrates’ flow!”

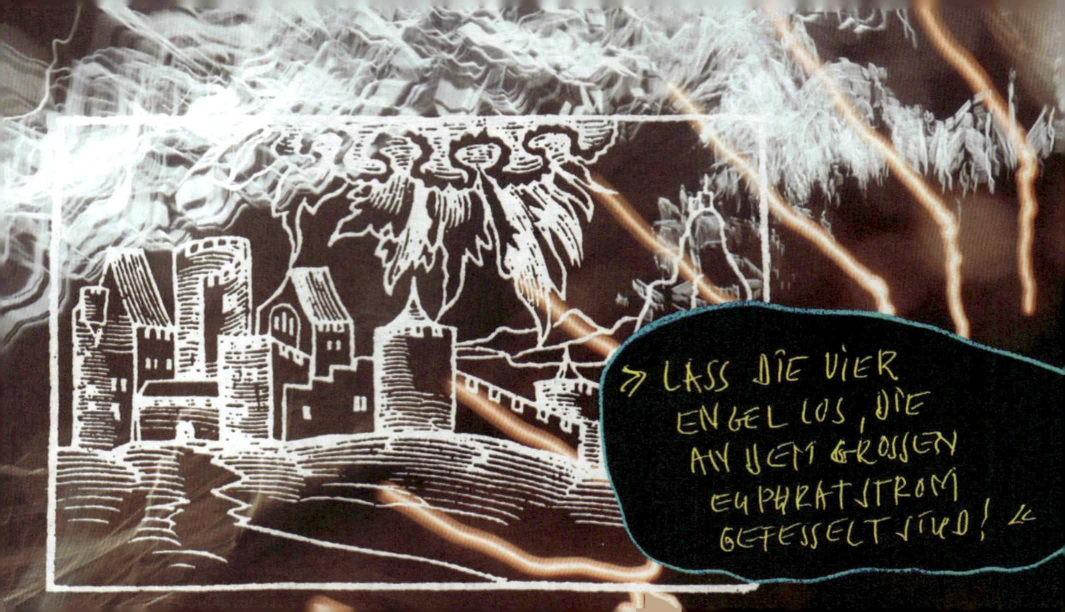
»LASS DIE VIER
ENGEL LOS, DIE
AN DEM GROSSEN
EUPHRATSTROM
GEFESSELT SIND!«

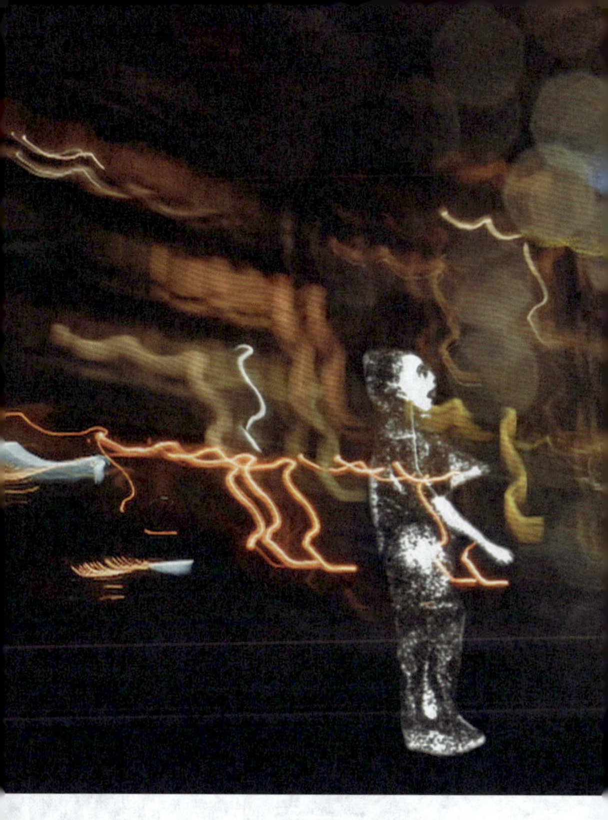

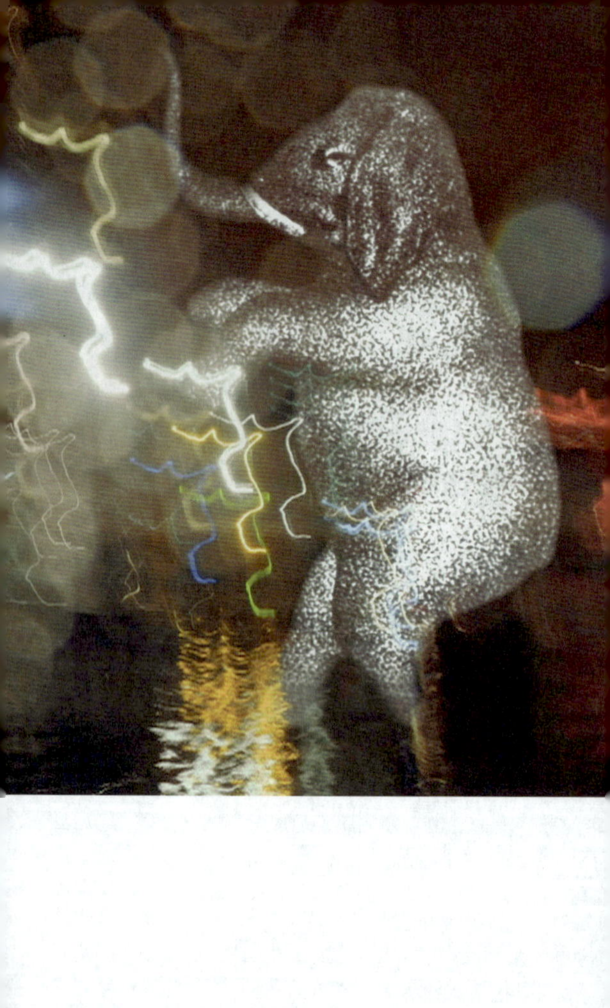

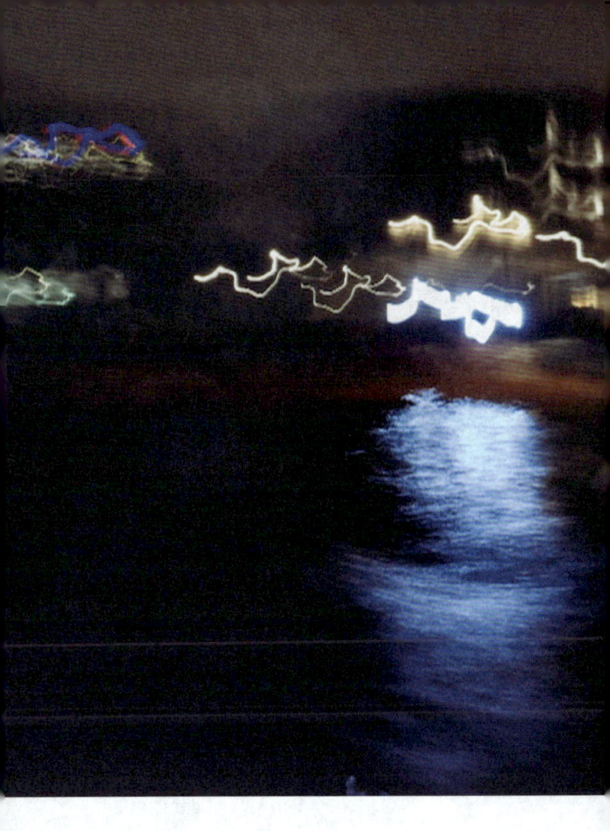

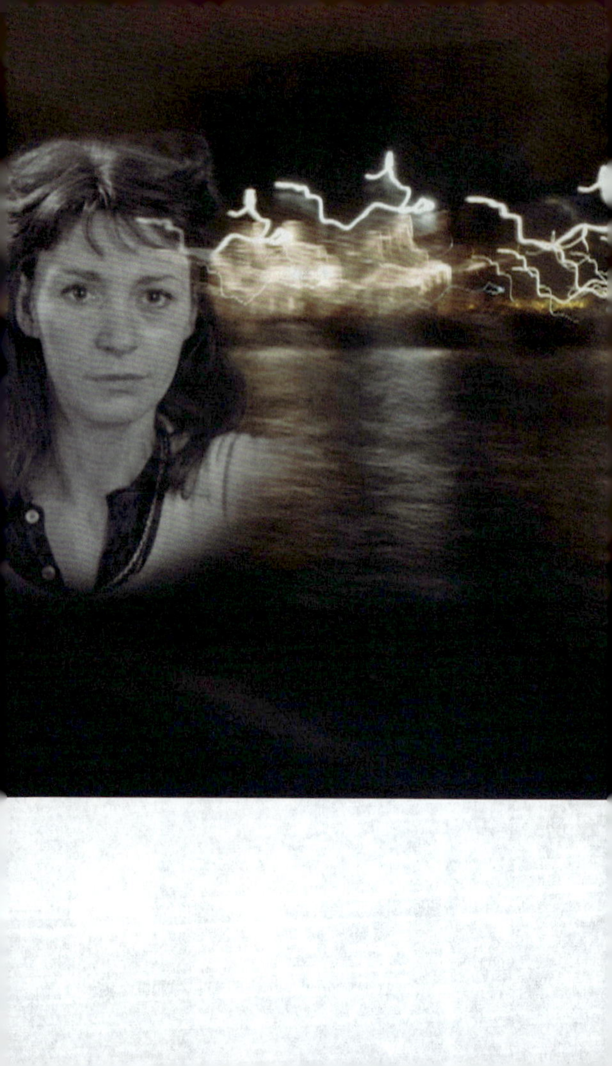

'IHR WORTE, AUF, MIR NACH! /
WEITER, ZU KEINEM ENDE GEHT'S'

Ingeborg Bachmann

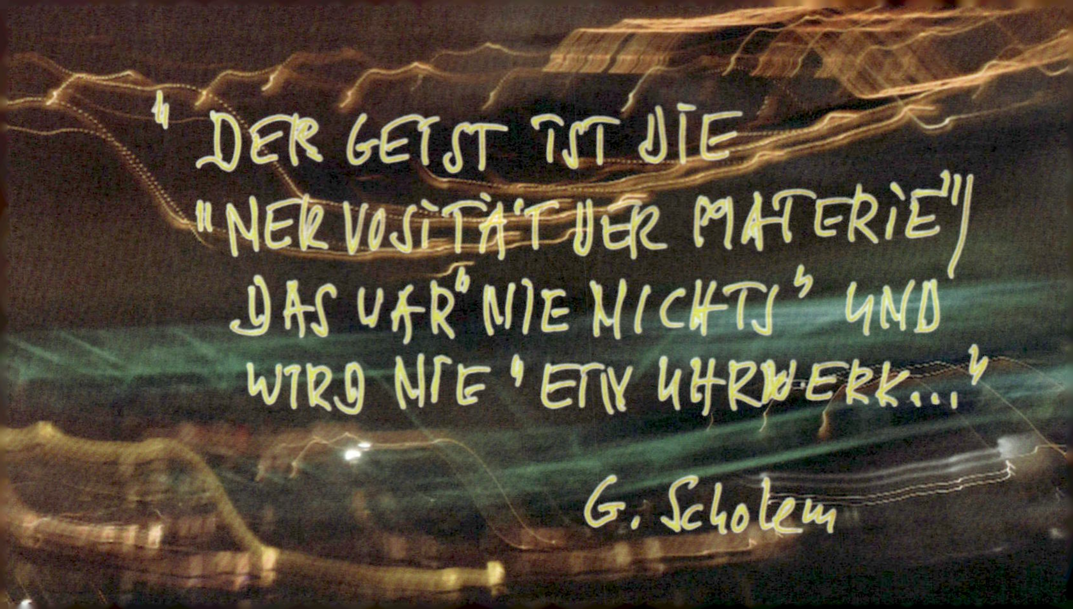

„DER GEIST IST DIE
"NERVOSITÄT DER MATERIE")
DAS WAR NIE NICHTS" UND
WIRD NIE 'EIN UHRWERK...'

G. Scholem

UTOPIE

HETEROTOPIE

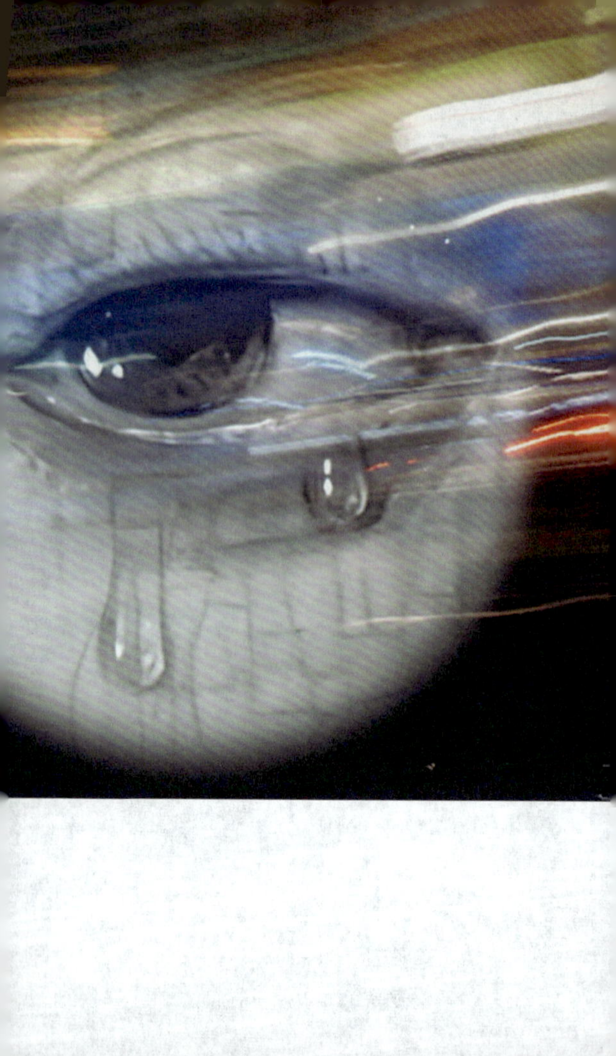

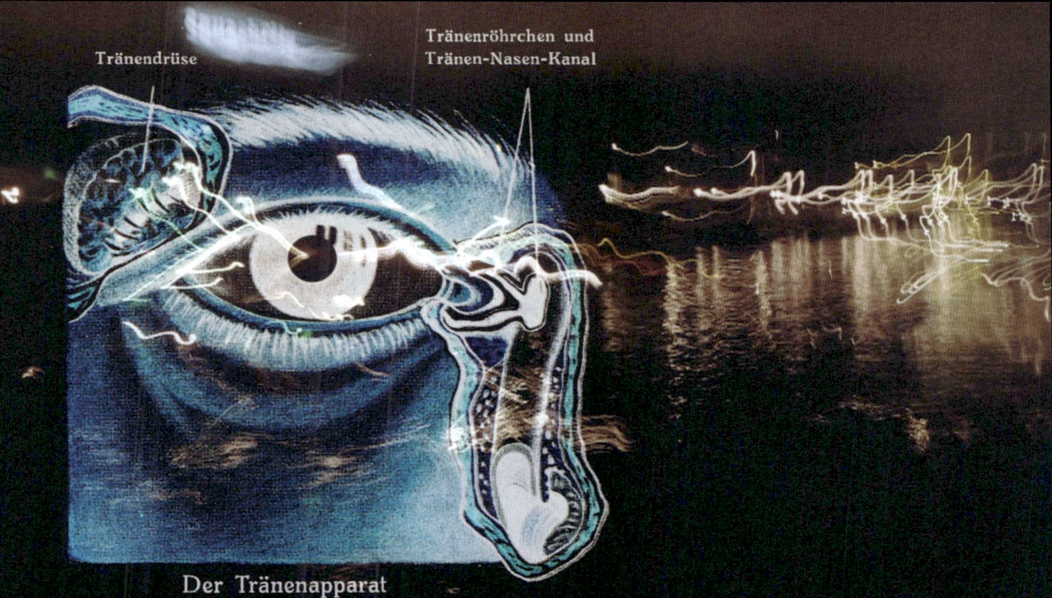

Tränendrüse

Tränenröhrchen und
Tränen-Nasen-Kanal

Der Tränenapparat

"THE IMPOSSIBILITY OF NOT CRYING"

It is said that sea animals alone transport salty liquid from their bodies to the outside. We humans are able to sweat and cry as a result of our descent from such sea animals (a great many years ago). A puma is faster than any human at chasing a gazelle. But after four hundred meters of such running, it must give up its attack, overheated: it is unable to sweat. Our ancestors, on the other hand, on their feet much slower than any predator, their sweat cooling them, would pursue gazelles until the animals finally sank down tired. Then their necks would be cut, and the prey dragged back to the human cubs in the cave. The LACRIMAL APPARATUS is quite different. The fact that greed, aggressiveness, and hardness can be mourned, indeed, that a human being would be unable to stop their eyes from crying when things become terrible, belongs—as *lamenti* in their position as the core of all operas prove—to the spontaneities, the authentic characters of the human race. When the stony heart liquefies, something both inside and out changes. Metamorphosis, the ability to cry, is the root of all poetics.

Lamento on the Death of a Mole
02:35

Rules for Crying
03:44

RULES FOR CRYING

When damp wood sings as it burns, it is the crying of poor souls. When the wind whistles in the firewood and around the corner of the house, the unbaptized children are crying. In the valleys of the North Harz Mountains (especially up in Schierke and Elend), the godfather must buy the newborn baby's cries on the third day after birth. He's supposed to put money in the baby's cradle. If a pregnant woman cries, she'll have a baby that screams and bawls. My mother, as noted above, cried bitterly in February 1937, but the child she bore on 2 April 1937, my sister, has always been cheerful, and never screams at people, as her father and I definitely do.

In Switzerland they say children must be left to cry, for while they cry their hearts grow. In Homer, among the Sioux, on the Andaman Islands, and in New Zealand, people returning home are received with tears. That, says Derrida, is not an expression of emotional agitation, but rather a force meant to avert evil. They wish the homecomer well, and wish him to import no evil.

The tears of those left living—those who loved the dead man—burn in the deceased like fire. The more the dead man is wept over, the more water he must bail in the underworld. Thus, in a side valley of the Adige, where an old Latin dialect is spoken, it's said that one should shed at most a cup's worth of tears for a dead child. The deceased see all that goes on for two days after

their death, and so there should not be too much weeping in these days.

Deceased children, suffering from their mothers' tears, appeared in the house and pointed to their wet, heavy little shirts. They lugged along a pitcher, filled to the brim with tears, and wouldn't let themselves be laid back in the grave until their mothers promised to stop crying.

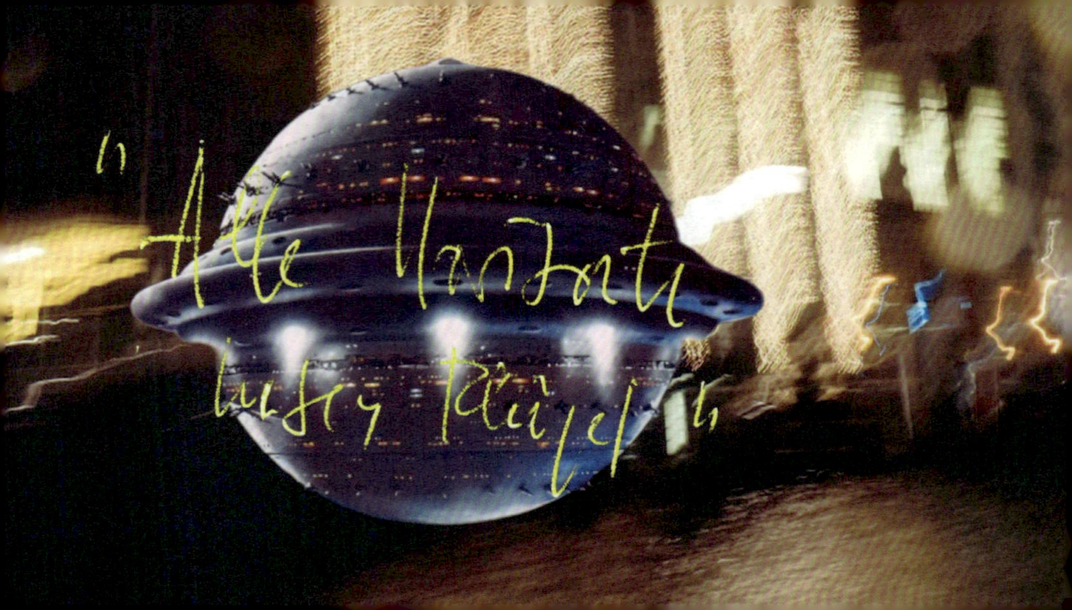

DIE 3 COUSINEN DES „PURSUIT OF HAPPINESS“*:

DIE HOFFNUNG, DER SCHLAF, DAS LACHEN

* Artikel der VERFASSUNG DER USA:
„Jeder Mensch hat das Recht auf Glückssuche“.

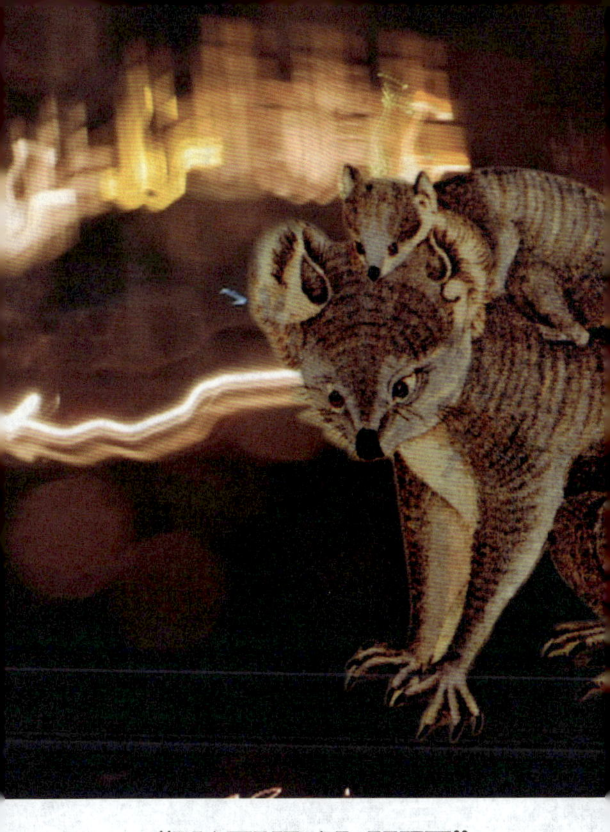

"NATURAL WIT"

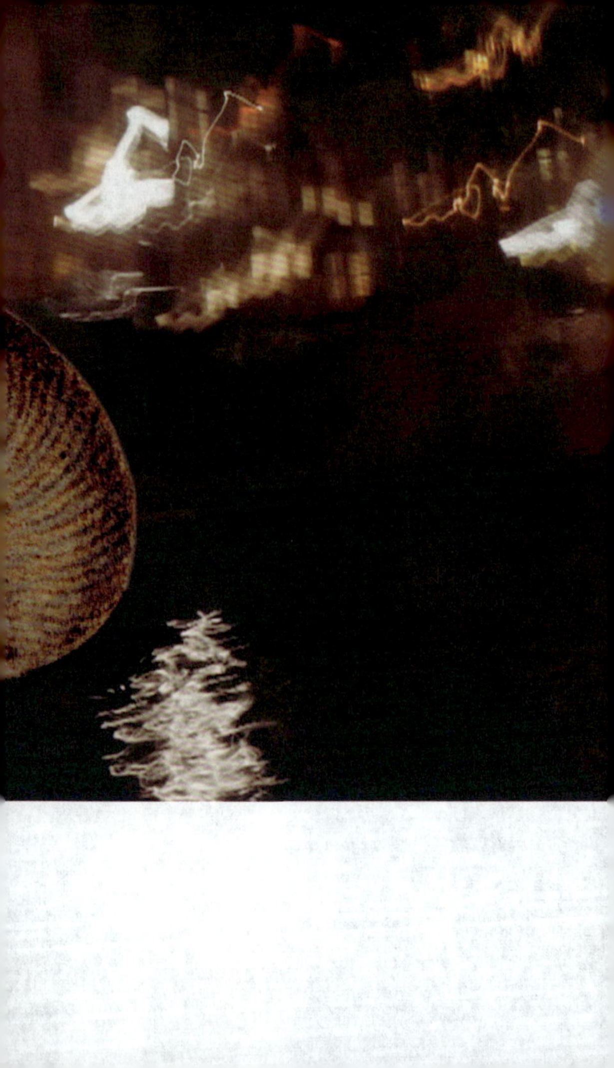

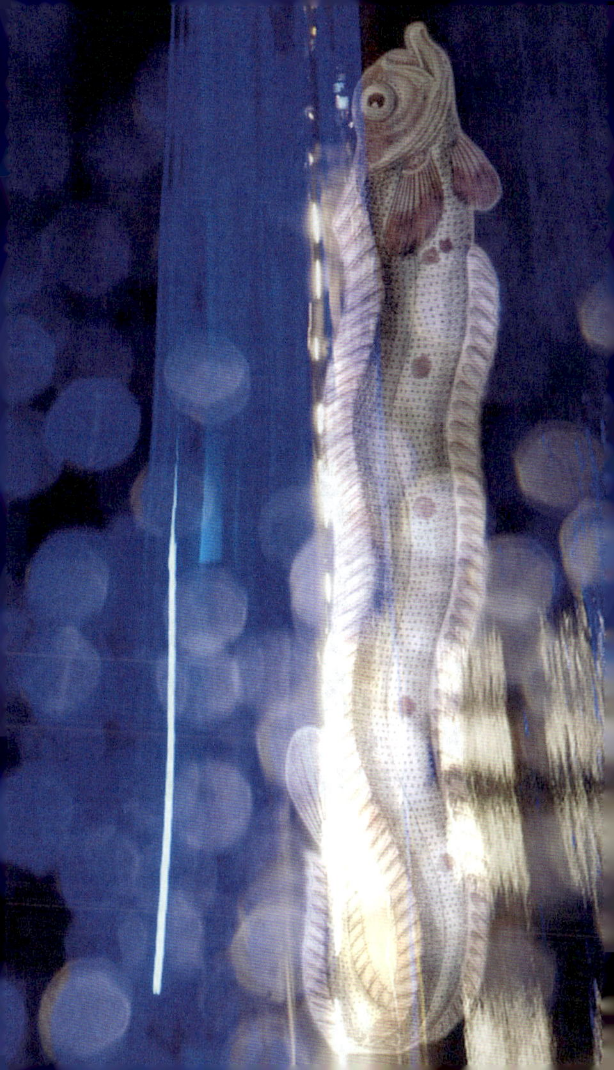

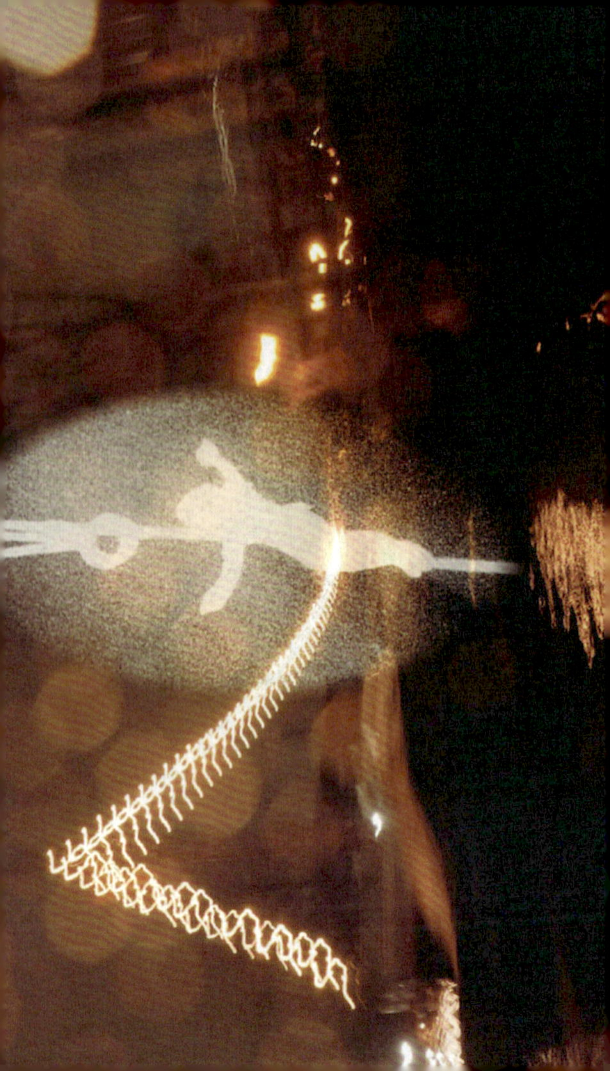

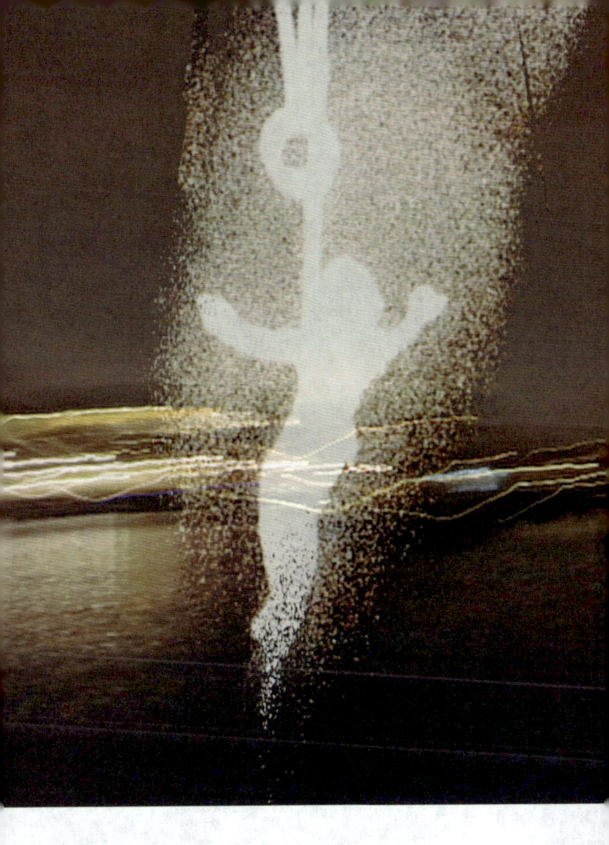

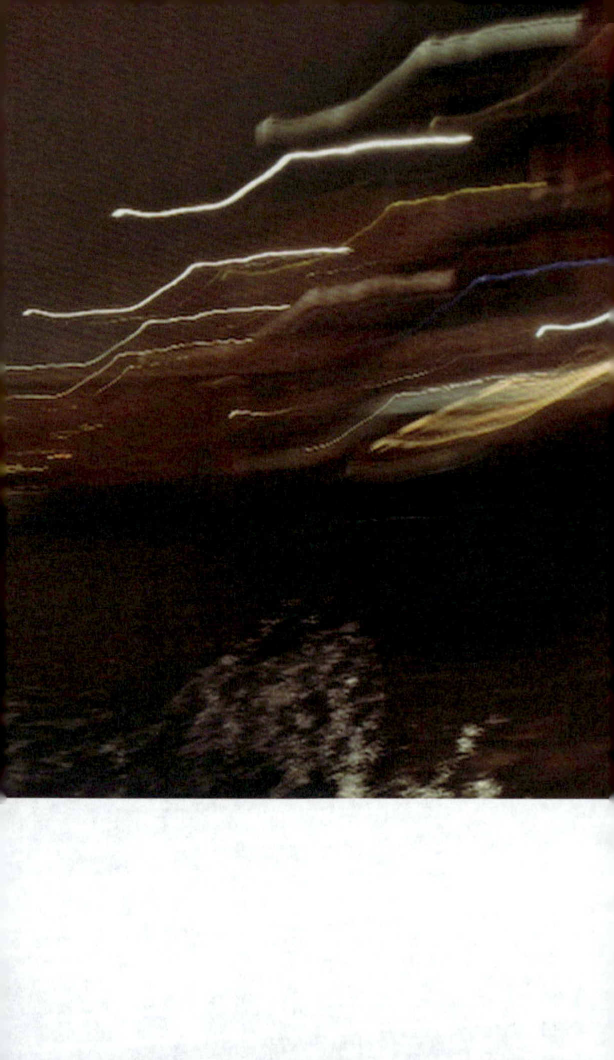

A REPORT ON GUARDIAN ANGELS IN THE CIRCUS

Beneath the circus big top, you can often see guardian angels bounding about. But just who is up for deciding whether they're artists or angels? It's a mistake to believe that you can make out angels' wings against the spotlights. A guardian angel in the circus could only be perceived on account of their intervention: by their rescue of someone falling—against all odds. Artistic angels (whose wings the audience would see) wouldn't have any persuasive power. What scientist would confirm that it wasn't an artist's unexpected, skilled grip that saved their daring colleague, maybe even an artist they secretly loved, without ever being heard, and who was about to fall, but, on the contrary, a god-sent guardian angel, a messenger of the improbable, which is, in fact, life?

„Wirft sich die Trapezkünstlerin vertrauensvoll in die Arme des Fängers, so nenne ich den Klick des gelingenden Sprungs den Augenblick der „Erkenntnis"…"

Fanny Peltzold, Zirkuskünstlerin

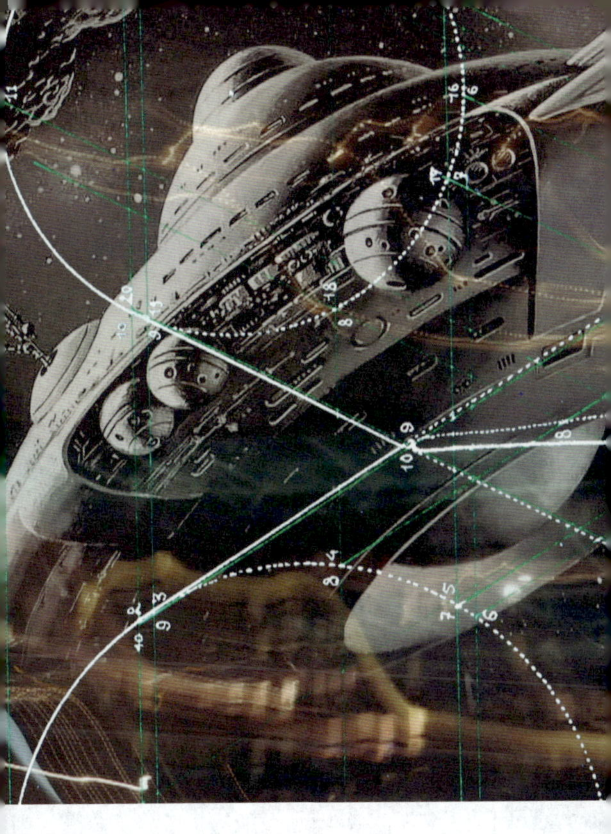

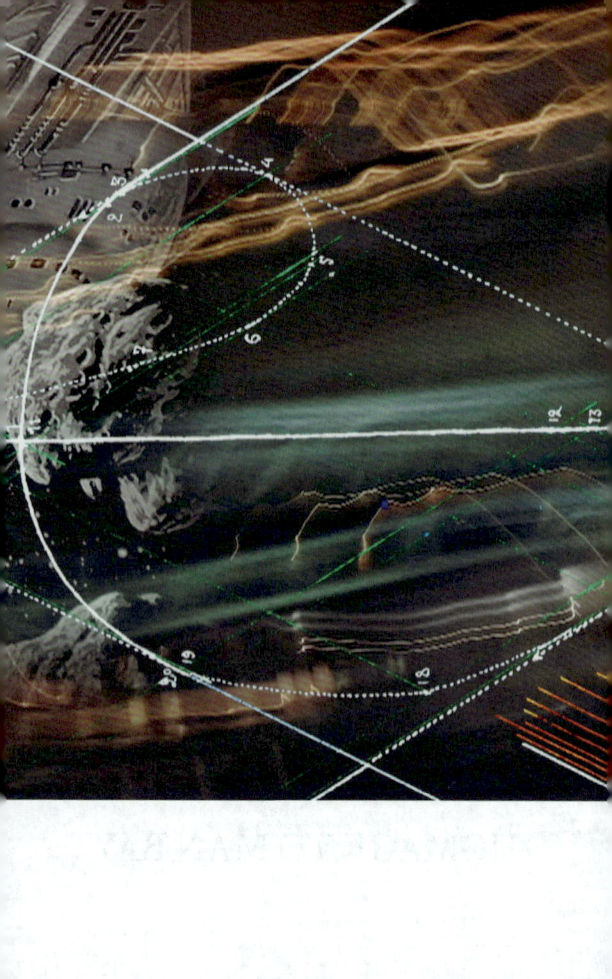

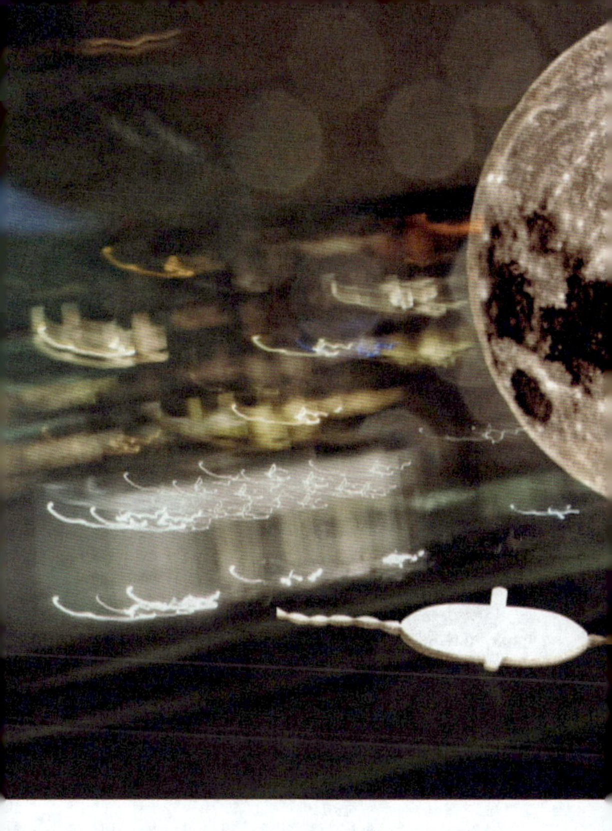

HOMAGE TO MAN RAY

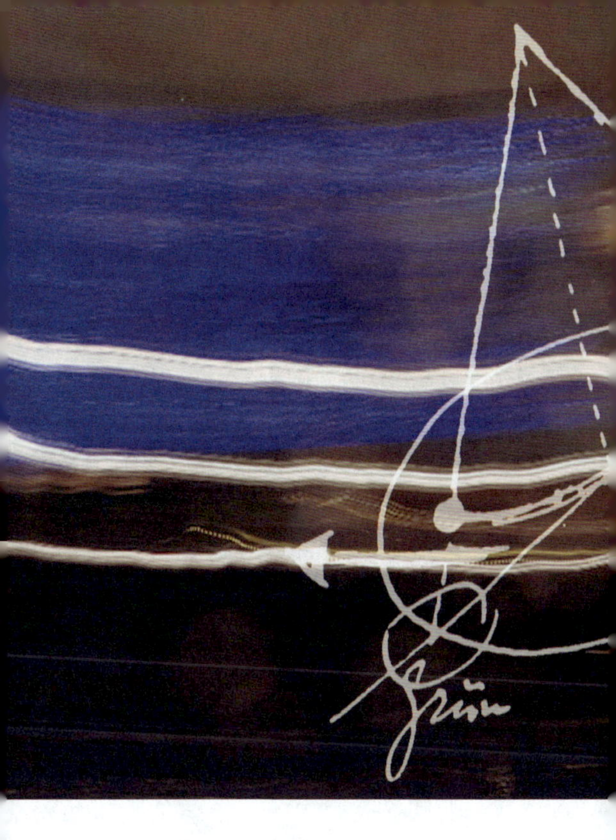
Grün

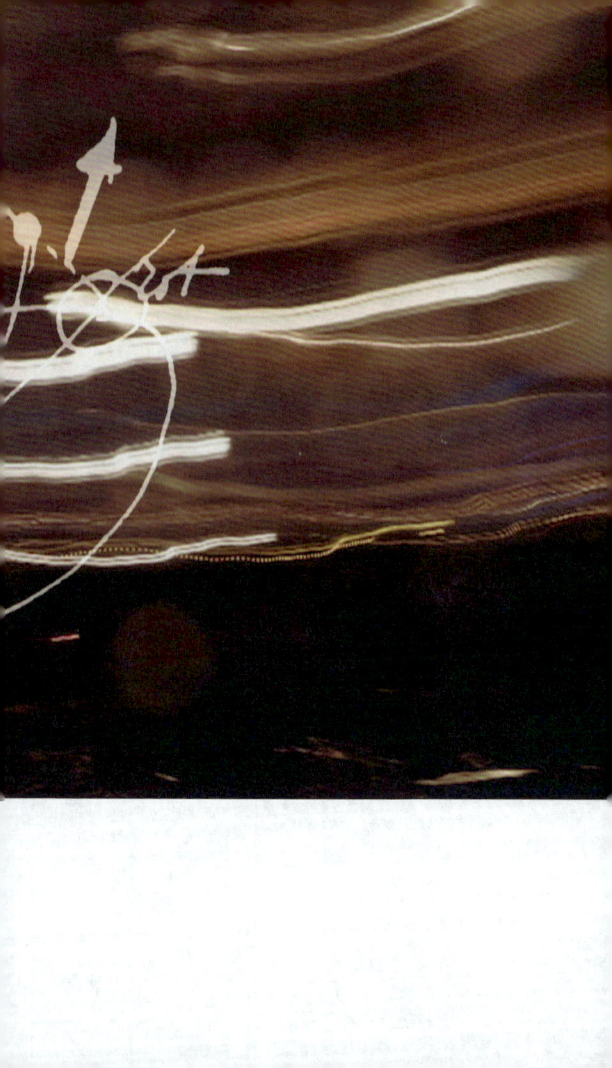

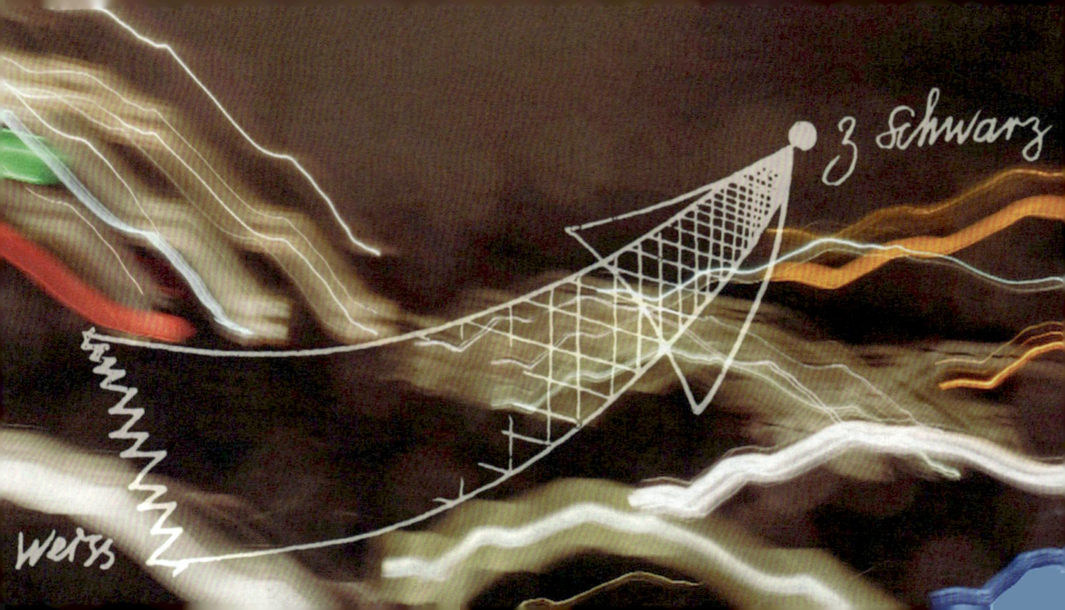

3 Schwarz
Weiss

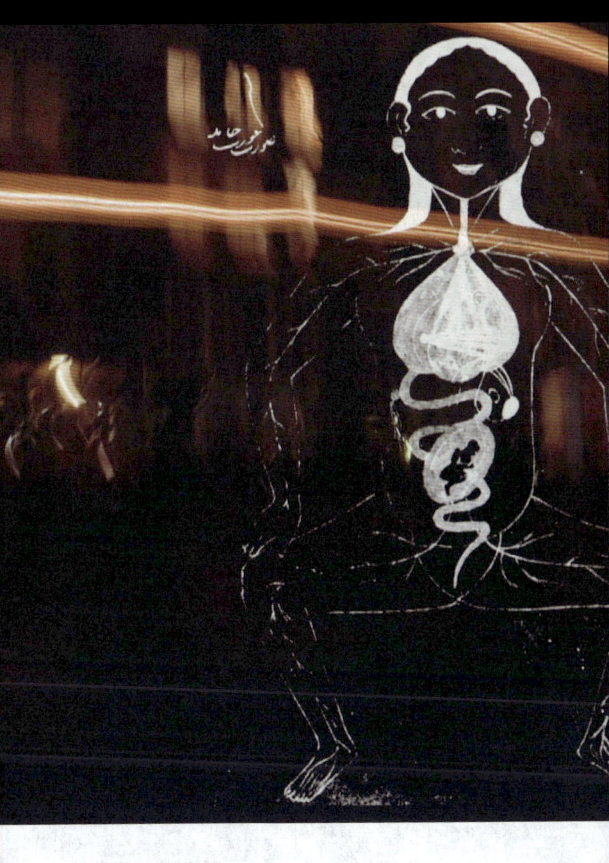
صورت عورت حامله

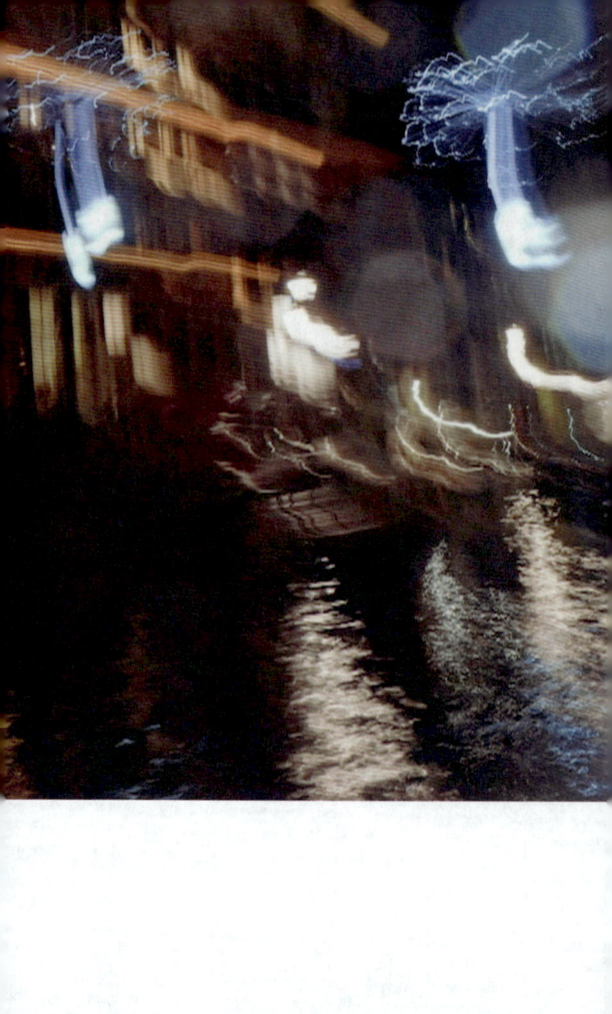

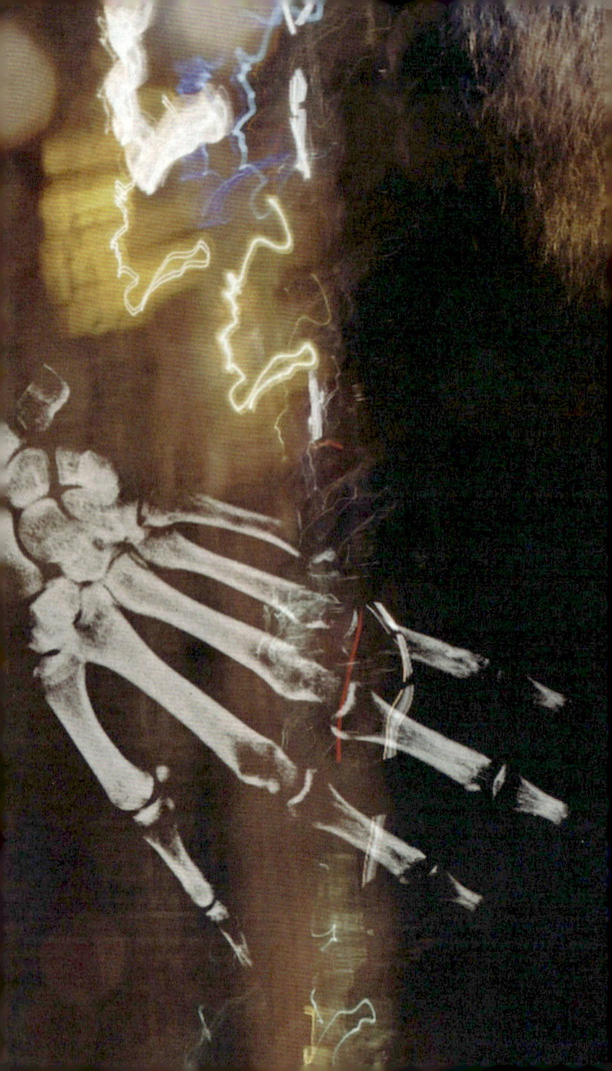

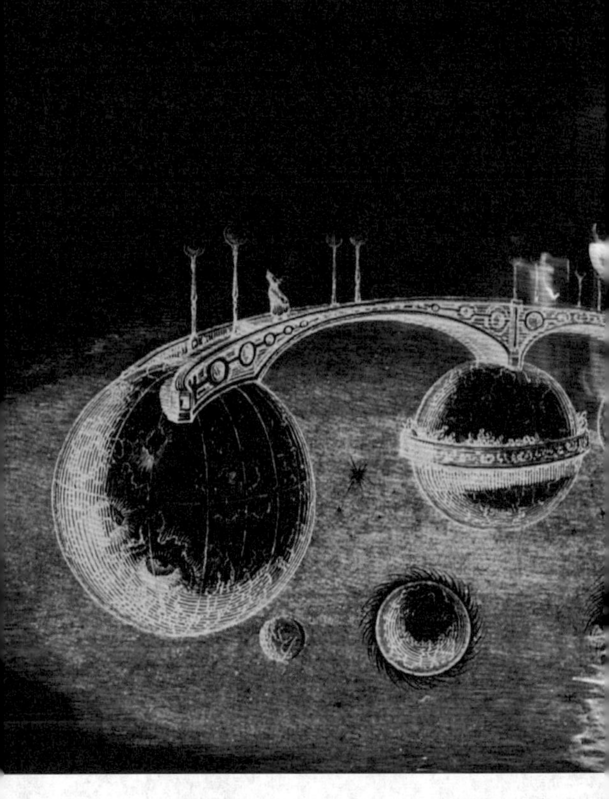

“A BRIDGE LEADS FROM ONE WORLD TO THE NEXT”

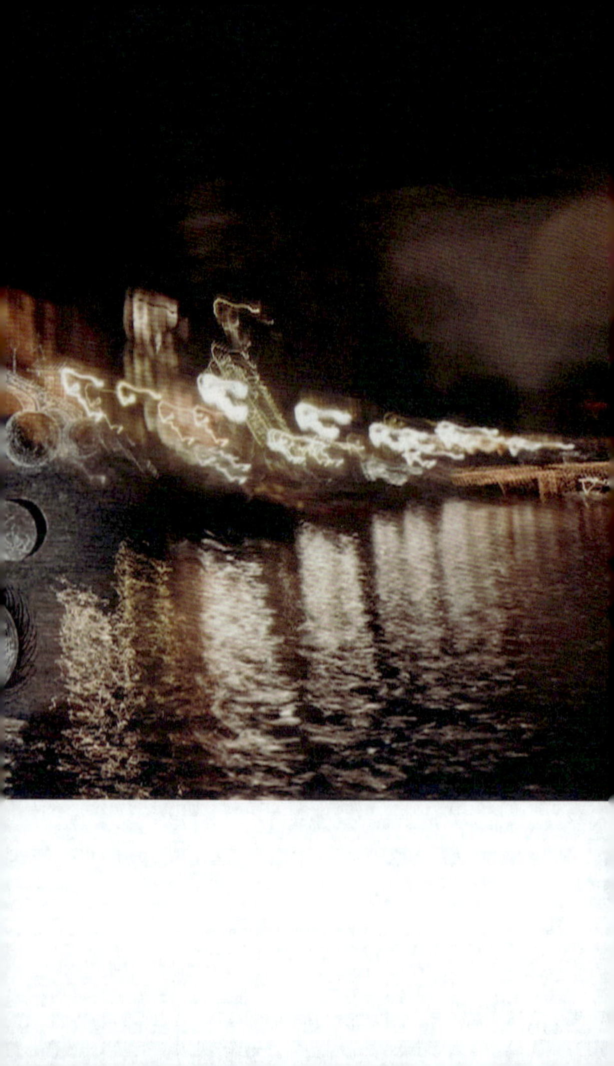

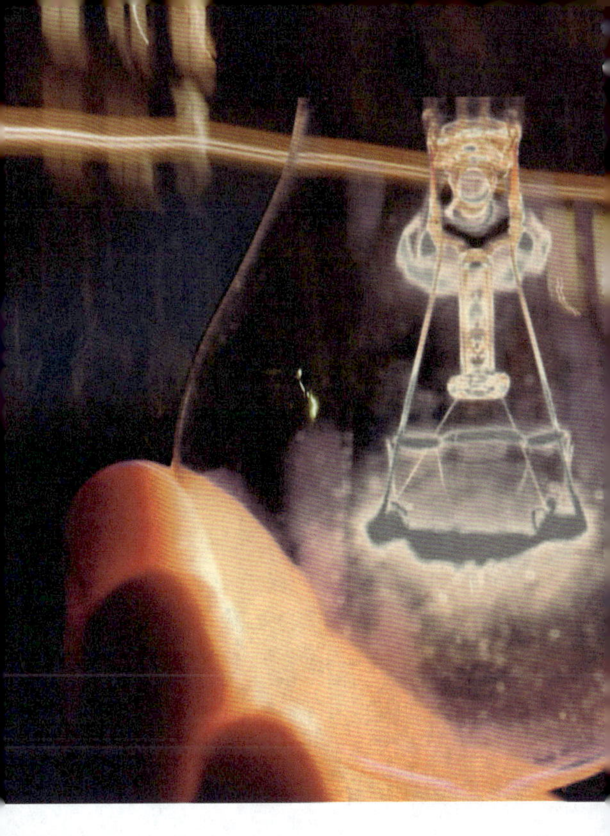

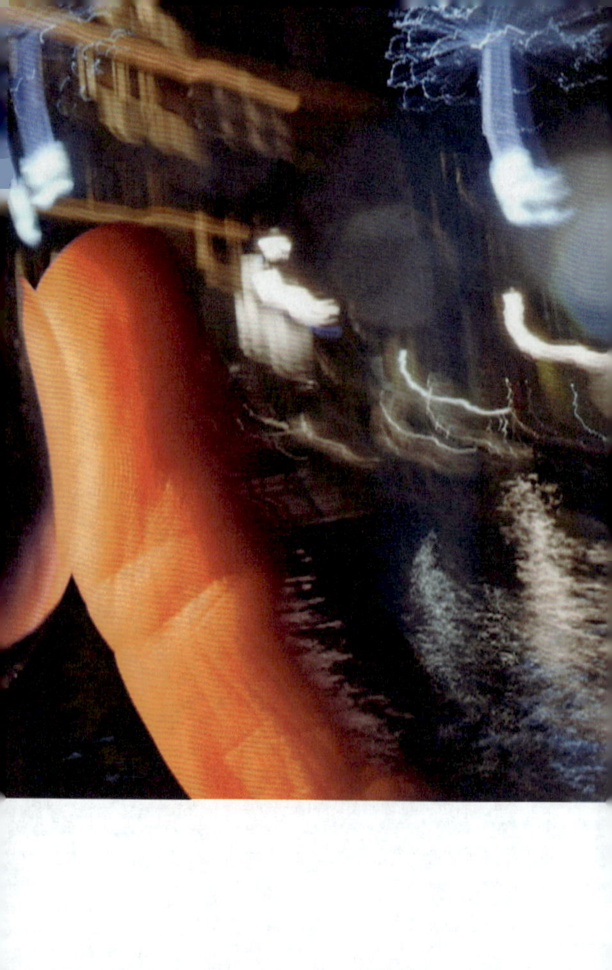

Lights in the Harbor
02:37

DRUNK WITH LIGHT

One hundred years after Lichtenberg's death: on all the continents Edison's lightbulbs overwhelm the night. Light nightclubs. An orgy of entertainment. What has become VISIBLE ELECTRIC FORCE is recorded using film cameras and can be projected onto a wall. The lightbulb conquers the night. What are colonies when compared with the conquest of the dark hours? For illiterates in Siberia: time to read. In some nights, swaths of the earth's population are "drunk with light."

HUMANKIND'S VICTORY OVER NIGHT AND DESERT

A few years after Verdi's *Aida* and the opening of the Suez Canal, Luigi Manzotti's ballet EXCELSIOR, featuring a score by Romualdo Marenco, began to be performed in opera houses and entertainment venues. Concerning a confrontation between the SPIRIT OF DARKNESS and the SPIRIT OF LIGHT, it was performed by a 120-person-strong professional group from Paris. In the third scene, light penetrates all the nocturnally dark zones of the earth. In the sixth scene, at the close of day the spirit of darkness appeals to its last untouched territories in the desert. Hardly a flash of lightning, nothing that could be used for fire. At best, the stars, and they have not been made by man. A whole train of torches would barely bring any light to these dunes. When, suddenly, dancers dressed as lightbulbs, the HOSTS OF THE ELECTRICAL INDUSTRIES, break into the dark spirit's paradise, chasing it and its ballet of shadows off. Thanks to wind machines, the sand that has been heaped into wandering dunes moves across the stage from left to right. Behind the piles of sand, in the background, one spies steamers passing by accompanied by great plumes of smoke, from right to left. Binoculars, but searchlights too, illuminate the ballet, the piles of sand, the steamers, the ramps, even the audience.

A foursome of figures representing England, China, Turkey, and Spain dance Sebastián de Yradier's "Habanera."

9

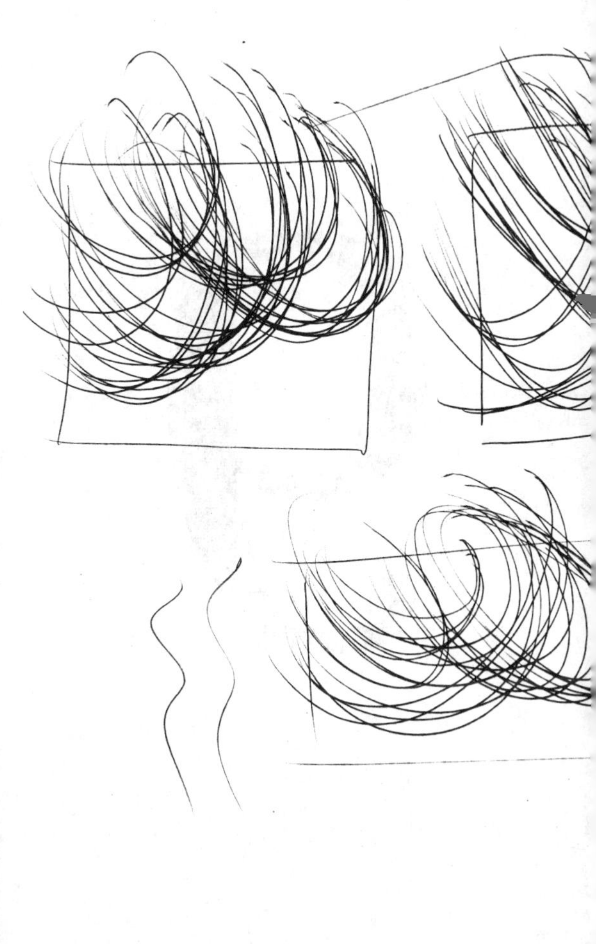

II

Watercolors

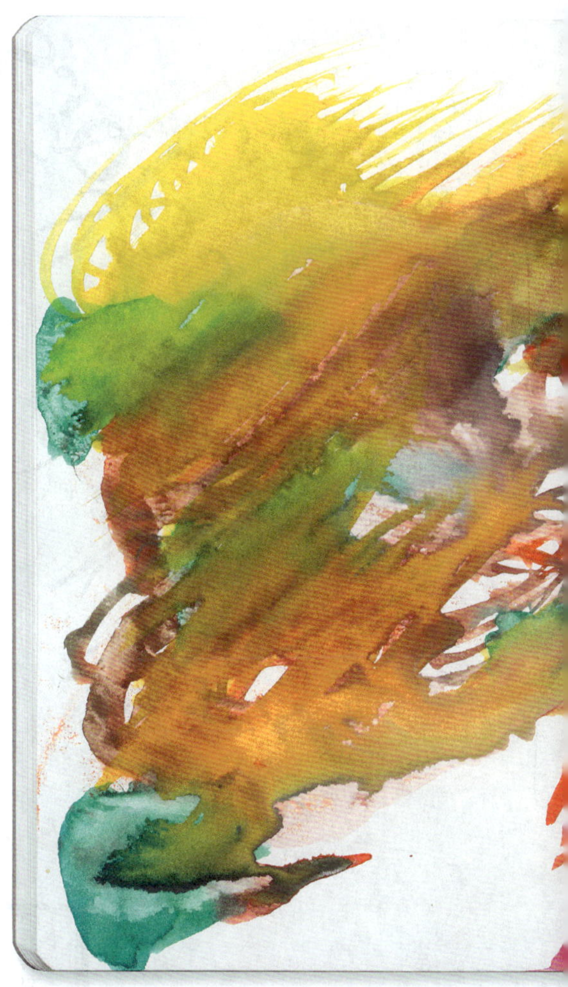

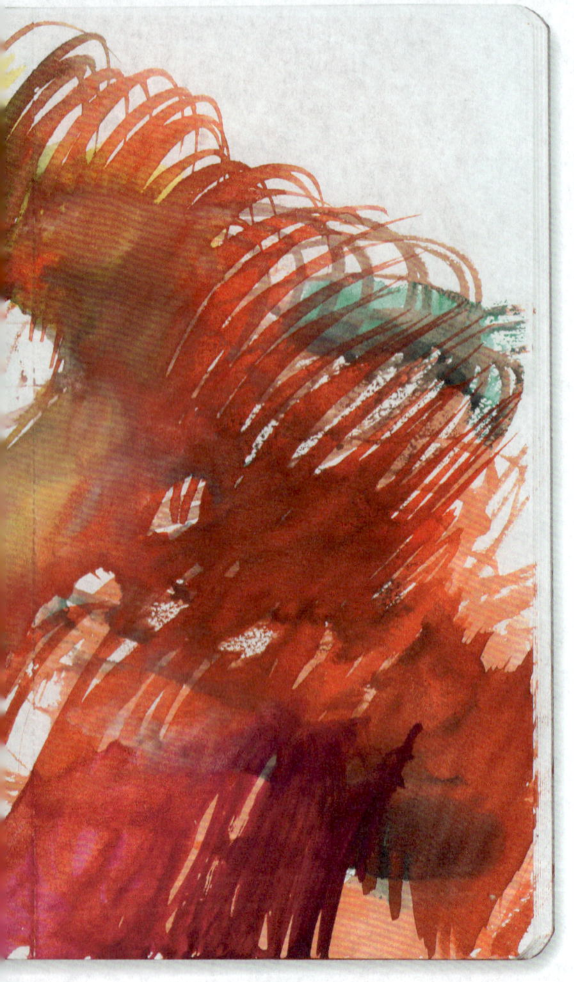

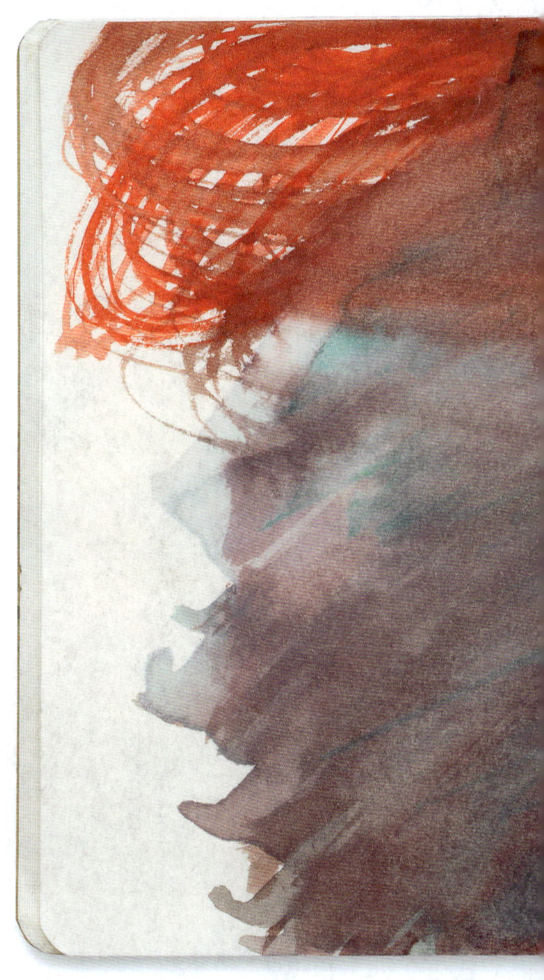

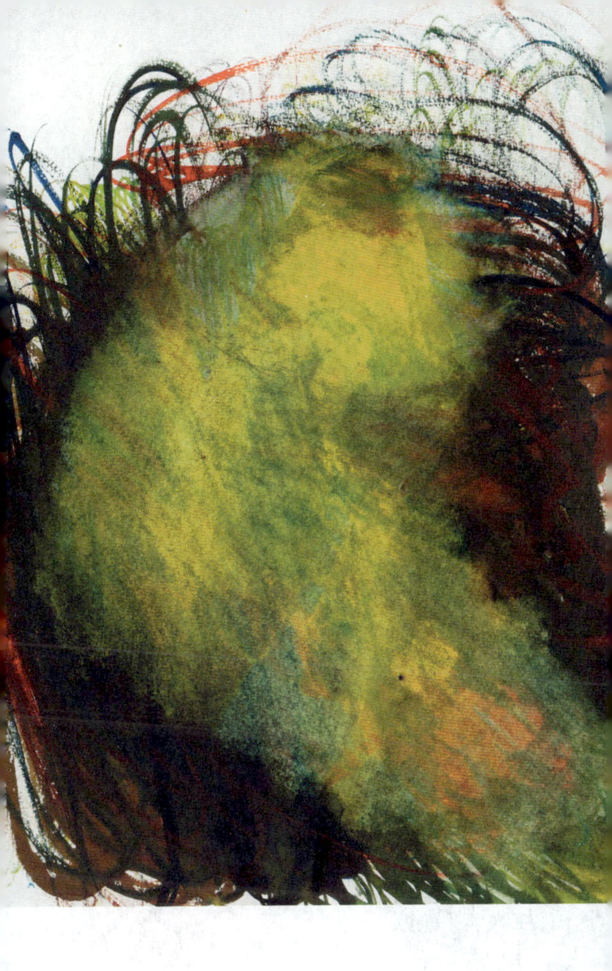

SNOW,
LESS DENSE THAN AIR

That is the snow that cools the hearts. It makes activists into observers. Walled-in soul-space made from such material might be compared with the hangars of the nuclear bombers in Greenland, which for a long while were stationed in the north of that island and watched over the world's safety by extinguishing—by their presence alone and their impregnability four thousand yards beneath the snow—all the world's hot spots. Thus far the metaphor.

The actual experience, meanwhile, is that within each flame of love, at the place where the flame shades into plasma, a soft snowfall is gathering. One time an officer, seeing that his wife and his closest comrade had betrayed him in a momentary aberration, granted the two their freedom while UNDER THE INFLUENCE OF SOFT SNOWFALL IN HIS GREAT SOUL, thus sparing himself the fate of King Mark.

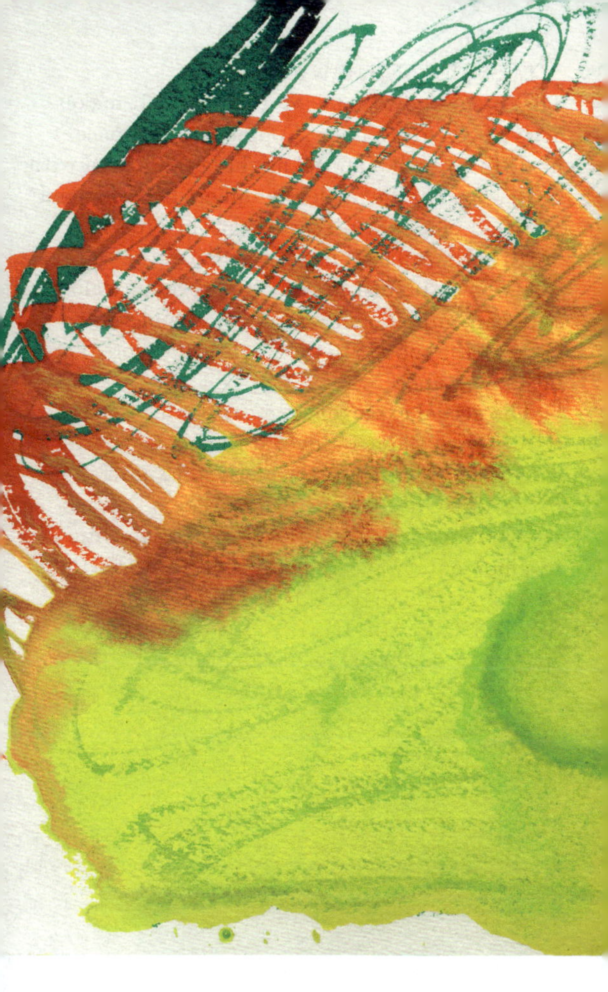

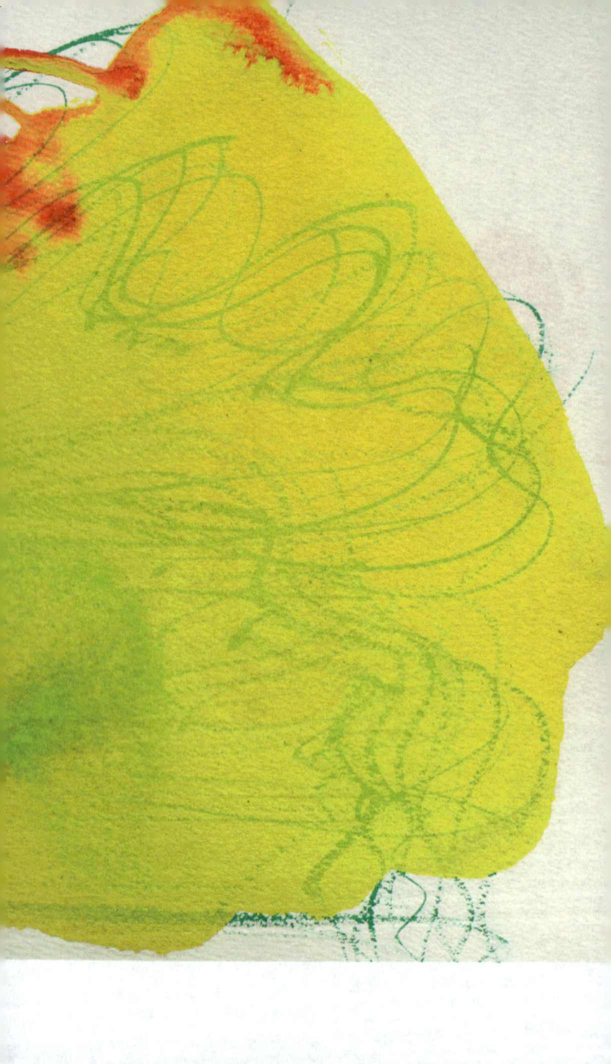

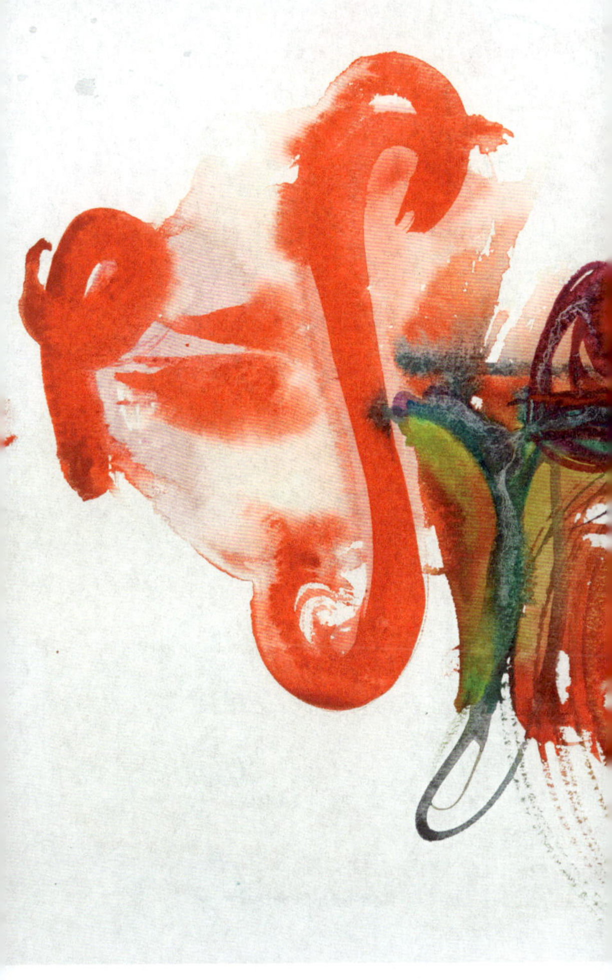

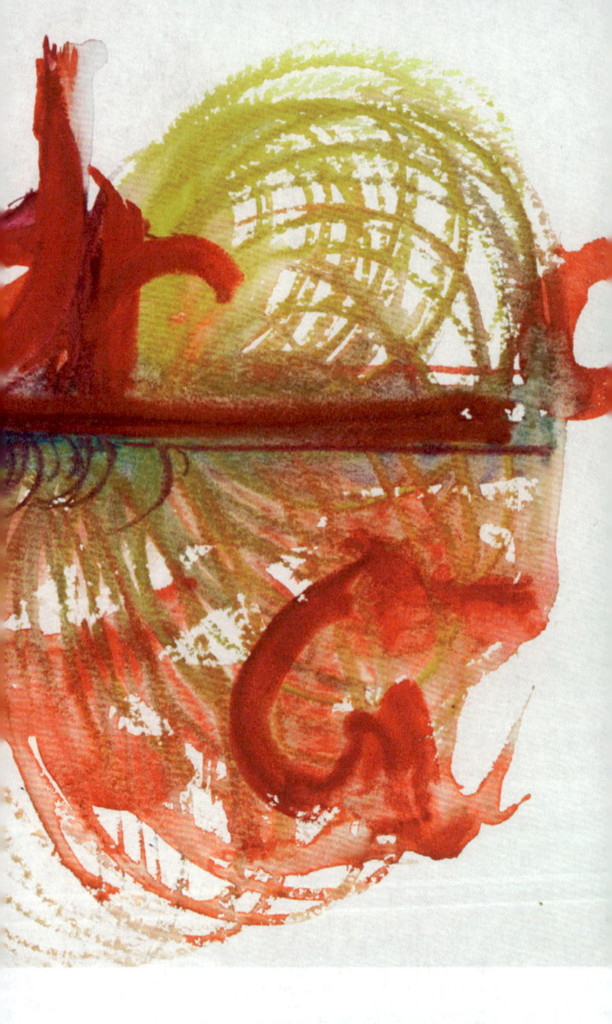

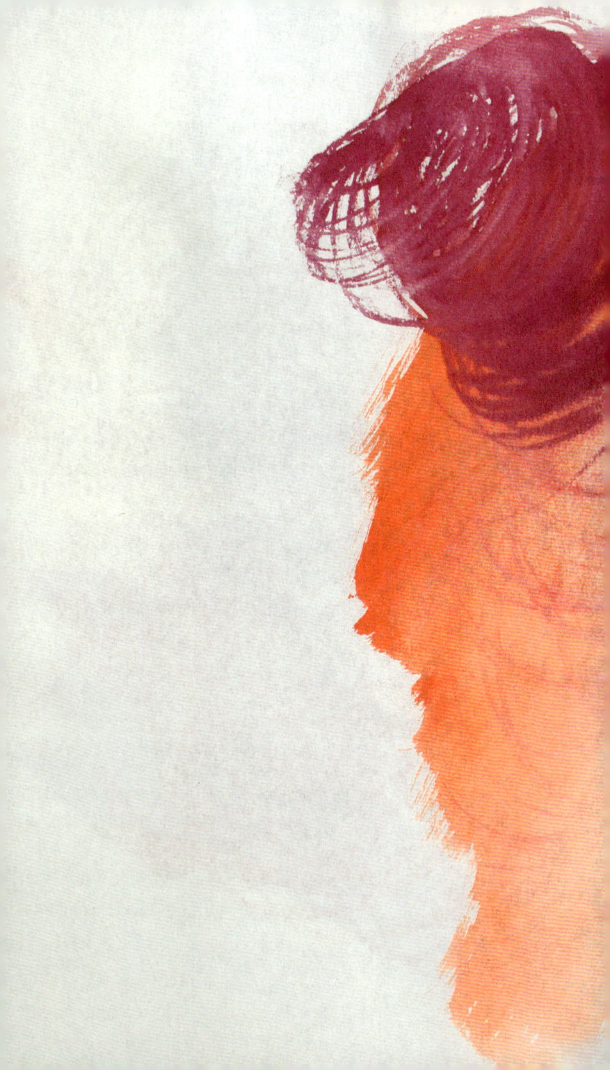

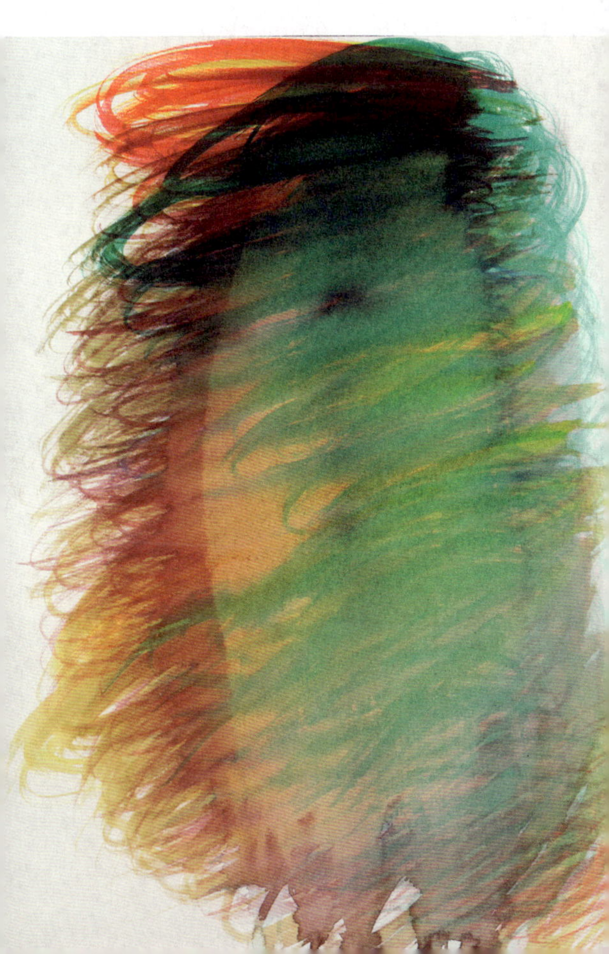

BY NIGHT IN THE LAGOON'S WATERS

While in Venice, the young Lord Byron, all naked body, went swimming in the lagoon. Steps from the palazzo led deep into the water. With his left arm the poet parted the waves; his right hand held a torch.

But then he ventured out into the open waters toward the Lido—with his British-thin arms, the arms of an aristocrat who administers country estates, or with the arms of a writer; not, at any rate, with the well-trained muscles of a sailor, a woodcutter, or a professional swimming teacher. The risk never lost its thrill for him. How eerie were the masses of water closing in on him outside the torch's light. He could not be sure of reaching the safety of the shore, for the final weakness, the depletion of strength that precedes drowning, is felt only on the way back.

Any bandit might have taken the poet prisoner and held him for ransom, and one never knew whether one of the night fishermen working all around from their boats, when faced with a dazed moon-swimmer, might transform back into the original predatory creature from which all the fishermen of Venice descend.

The radical poet escaped these dangers, later succumbing to a paltry case of pneumonia in the Peloponnesus.

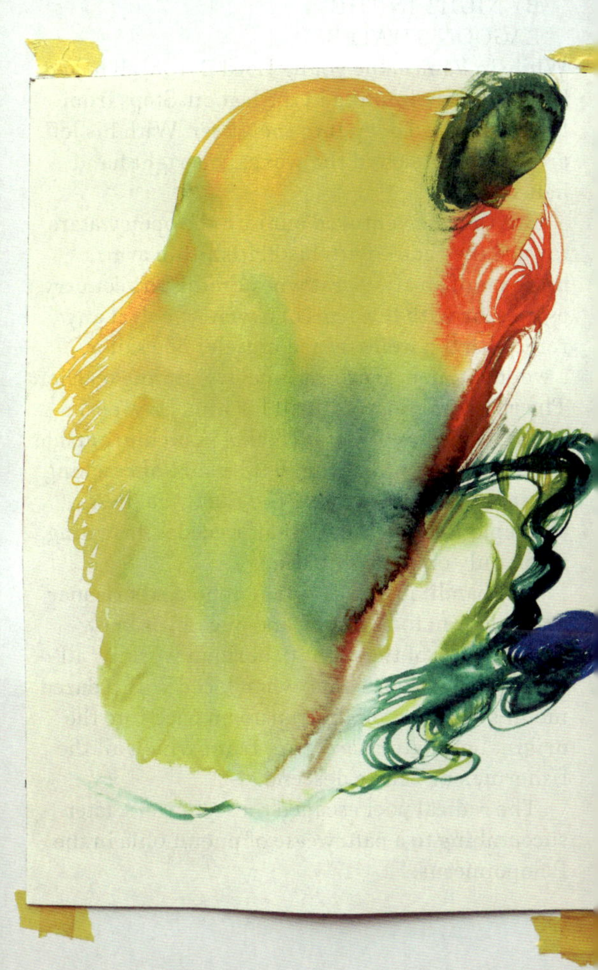

"COUGHING / BLOOD INTO A HANDKERCHIEF IN RUSSIA"

—Ben Lerner, *Mean Free Path*

The commander of a partisan unit, a forty-year-old woman who derailed seventeen German supply trains near Minsk in 1944 (thus sealing the legendary collapse of Army Group Center), in other words, an independently minded person, had, twenty-eight years previously, felt helpless in her affection toward political commissar Gerasimov, her superior. The current, the act of baptism by which his closeness, his daily presence, submerged her in the emotional waters in which our powers of decision swim, had such gravitational force that she was interested in nothing any longer but this political man of skin and bones (no other man, no woman, no obligations of friendship, no rest by day or by night, even work was something she managed only for his sake). She wasted away. In mind and then in body. The man she loved took no notice of her. His duties left him no time. With sunken cheeks he struggled to lend urban cohesion to the provincial backwater where headquarters had posted him, to make it into a city populated, ideally, by Bolshevik people (not just communist minded, but communist *acting*).

Then it grew plain that he was coughing up blood. Now it was shown that the love of Ludmilla —for that was the name of the woman who later became a resistance fighter—was no mere consumptive idealism, but a material force.

She traveled to the capital. She set in motion cycles of authority. Counter to all routine and probability, her beloved, who, as noted, was unaware of his belovedness, was quite unorthodoxly provided with hard currency and sent to a Swiss sanatorium. There—apart from the oxygenated quality of the mountain air—the art of healing had accumulated over decades (what with all the futility of the struggle against treacherous tuberculosis). The man was healed, and served his fatherland for forty more years. He was surprised at the fervor of his benefactress, a subordinate who until then had served him unobtrusively. But before his departure to the west, coughing blood into his handkerchief, he was too weak to put the matter into words. Soon after his return the war broke out. And so his angel went undiscovered. We know that angels can work serenely only in this kind of invisibility. When the eyes fix upon them, they freeze.

*

In the Khrushchev era, rising in the hierarchy, as a militant patriot highly decorated (by motivation, admittedly, she was but a servant of love), but as a woman already downgraded, Ludmilla promoted a project for building tuberculosis sanatoriums in Russia. But throughout the entire vast continent the air was too "viscous," the mountains were either too low or too far away from the centers of

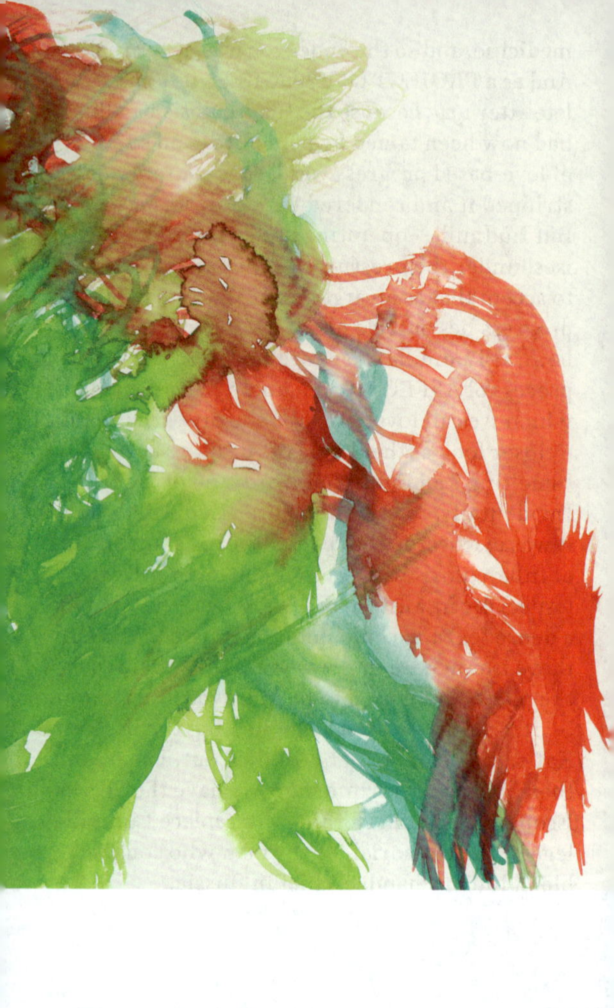

medicine, and so the endeavor was never realized. And as a PROJECT OF PROGRESS it became obsolete after 1945 because the tuberculosis bacillus had now been tamed by penicillin. And so a piece of love-based progress was lost as causality outstripped it and rendered the effort unnecessary. But Ludmilla—operating under socialist premises! under the pressures of solidarity!—refused to accept that as an argument. As a piece of life, progress lies outside purposes, like poetry, for both, as Ludmilla knew, are rooted in the smelting process of AFFECTION, namely, private passion, which we call love. Nor was she prepared to take a closer look at the illogic of speaking both of "smelting," an industrial word, and of "roots." Incidentally, in 2017, long after Ludmilla's death, it was discovered that penicillin-resistant strains of tuberculosis were reviving in greater Russia (especially in western Siberia, where the air is like a dense fog) and could not be combated. And still there is nowhere in the vastness of Russia like the places there used to be in Davos. But even in Switzerland itself the art of healing the illness Kafka died from has almost died out. Where once there was a sanatorium, now we have the World Economic Forum. Nothing can replace Ludmilla's legacy, the memorial for the man who coughed blood into his handkerchief in Russia.

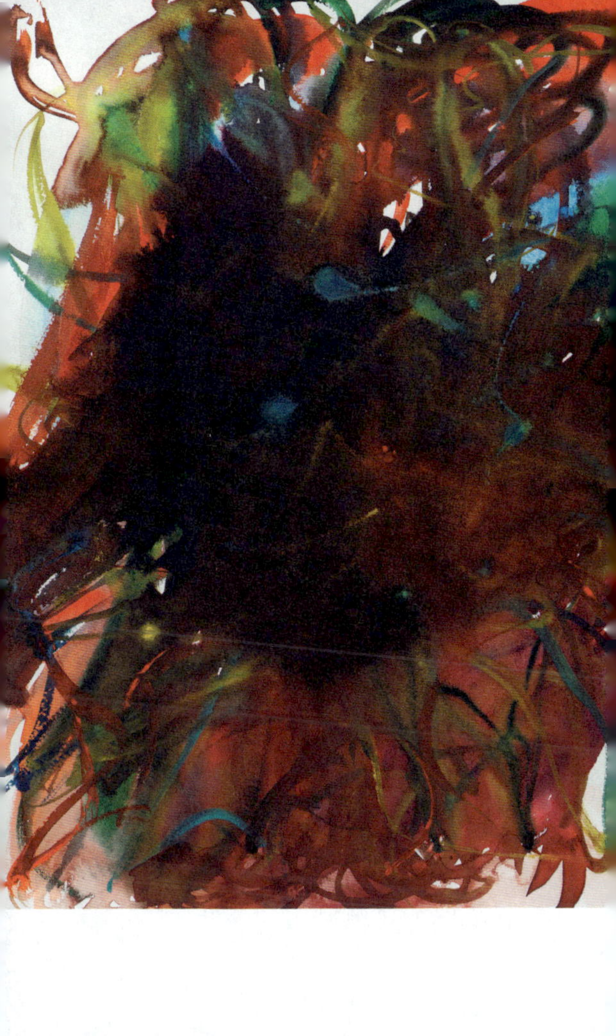

"NUMBERS LEANING AGAINST THEIR RADICALS"

The number beasts (numbers "dressed in animal skins") support themselves with one hand on a torn-down oak. Holding them up against every wind are the roots of this tree. They point to the sky. The roots cannot nourish the tree this way. The number brothers, in turn, lack the strength to move the tree. It is hard work, you see, to bed the roots back in the ground.

"THEORY, LIKE SWIMMING IN A STORM"

Storm birds, descendants of the dinosaurs in a different way than we, swim opposite to the troughs of low pressure, westward across the Atlantic. Their capacity for theory is shown by the elegance of their wings. They give a wide berth to the cloud of plastic particles, which are microscopically small, but slice alveoli like shards of iron or glass. Where is the seat of their confident knowledge? What does the "poetic force of theory" mean for them?

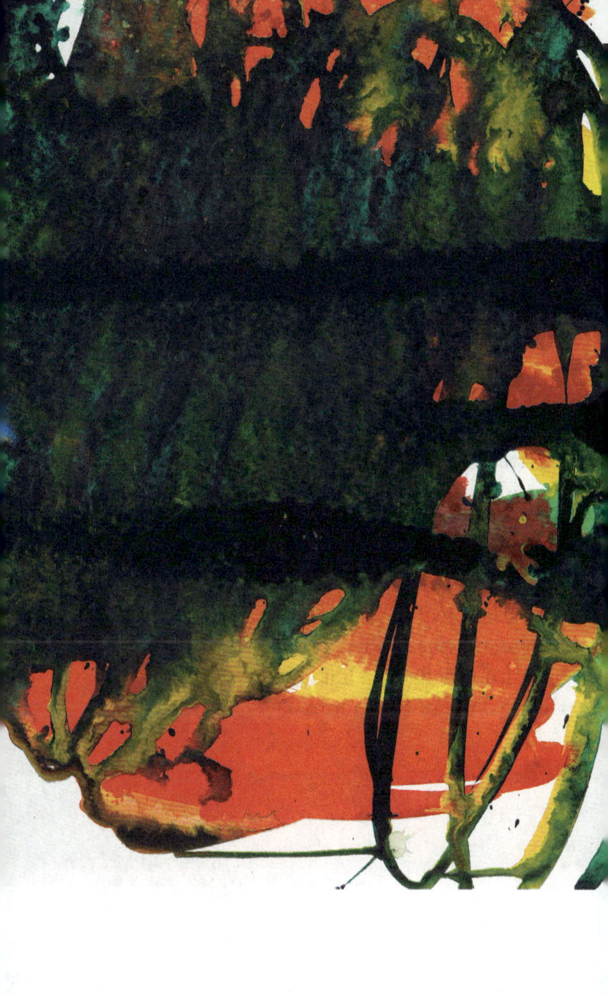

I BELIEVE THAT THE SOUL WHISPERS RATHER THAN SPEAKS... At the age of four I suffered from nightmares. My nanny found me hanging off the side of the bed with my head to the floor, screaming. Her calling out my name and calm words did nothing to bring me back to myself. She began to whisper. I responded to whispers. When I am alone, memorizing something, speaking with myself, I do so in a whisper. As far as my attention span is concerned, the older I get the more speaking in a normal tone becomes muddy. I believe that I have already heard, already understood what is being said, even at the moment of its saying, and my senses begin to wander. I still show interest, but I'm no longer paying attention. What comes in a whisper, however, wafts like the wind along telegraph wires, far up above and deep down below, in the subtext.

At the Munich Security Conference, in one of the interpreters' booths, I notice twenty-six interpreters. Speaking quietly into their machines. When rival parties get excited onstage, raise their voices, thunder against one another, the interpreters' volume automatically goes down. Almost to a whisper. The interpreters' soft tones reach the speakers through their headphones. Having said that, I have never observed an excited or downright hostile debate ever become any milder because of it.

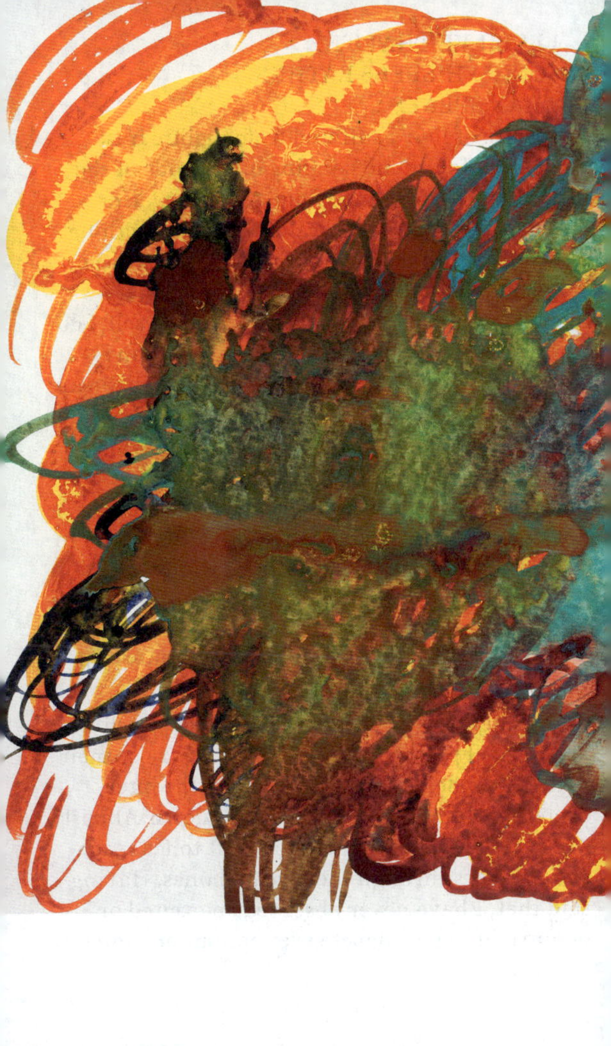

EVIL IS A PIECE OF DEBRIS

Evil, Anselm of Canterbury (*De casu diaboli*) believed, was deserted good will. When evil is metaphorically disrobed, behind its mask, its disguise, a long "account" emerges, one that brings to light all the damage done to the good, gradual forgetfulness, the "secret of evil," a DESTRUCTION OF FREEDOM. What belongs to the evil of evil, Anselm says, is that it opposes every order, even that of understanding. It is a piece of debris.

In our century, Prof. Dr. Rupert Sheldrake, a member of the British Royal Society, added an important observation. A force of attraction of morphogenetic nature like the gravitational effect emanates from larger accumulations of such pieces of debris of former goodwill, of failed god-inhabitation: one misfortune draws in the other.

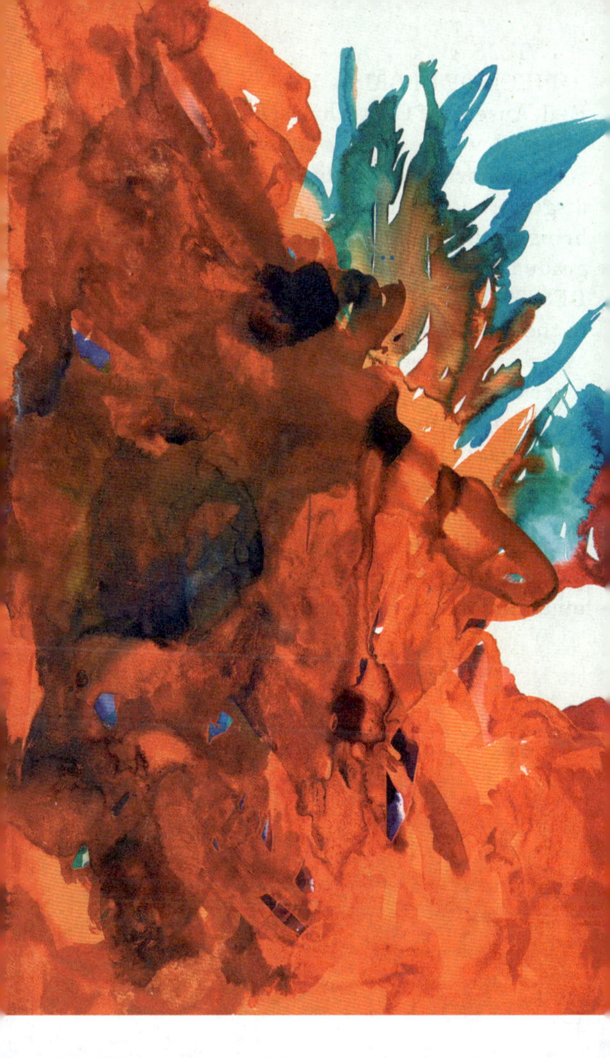

A HAPPY ACCIDENT

The beanstalk of a boy about five years old ran down the jetty with great excitement, yelling

—Yach!,

before slipping on the topmost rung of the iron ladder into the lake, his little head whipping backward and missing the hard edge by a millimeter, that hard edge the back of his head would have hit were it not for a lot of good luck hidden within the wriggly movement he made. Otherwise, he very well might have died, toppling, the back of his head split open, into the water and drowning. There were no skilful rescuers in sight, just well-meaning lay people, and it remains doubtful whether one of the older women observing the whole affair from the side of the lake would have taken the right decision to inform one of the hotel waiters who in turn could have tracked down a lifeguard ... All of that would have taken longer than the little bit of life the boy would have had left, had he not had good luck, that is, the wriggly luck of that tiny twitch that saved him, making it possible for his head, which he no longer could control, to miss the rung. Now the boy is swimming in the lake, calling out:

—I've got to jump in one more time ...!

He simply has not realized the danger his young life was in, that he was his own lifesaver, that something within him, stronger than chance, had governed his movements there on the slippery ground.

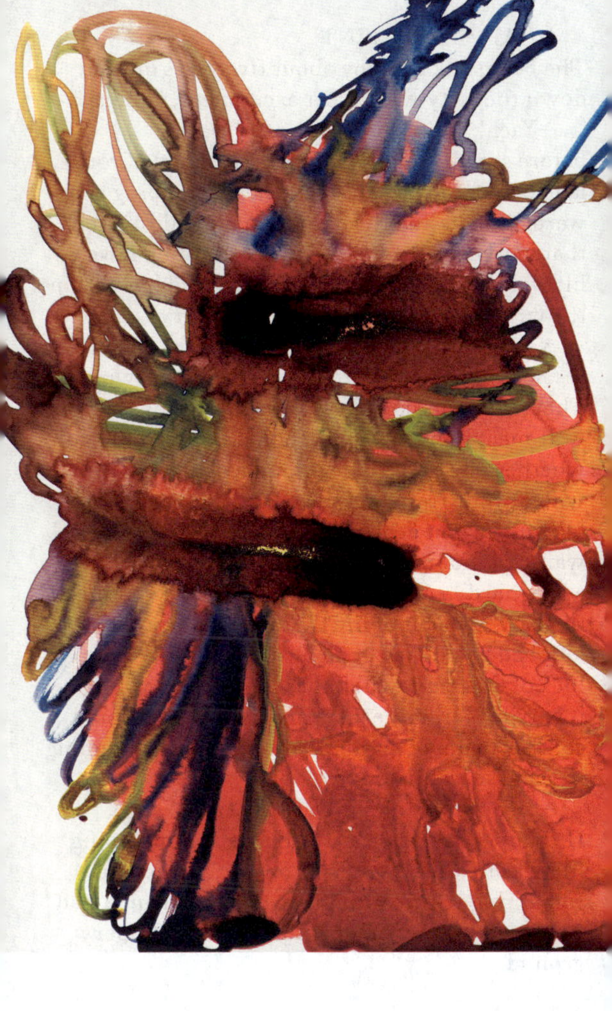

"DER STARKE GLANZ DER BLUMEN"

The frog "smells" the lilypads' bright blue flowers, though presumably he can't see them with his eyes. Frogs are shortsighted. The prince hidden inside them is not thought to be much of a colorist. Presumably the frog is more interested in having his hind leg stroked by a neighboring frog than in the brilliant hues of the flowers. Things have been this way for a very long time. Turtles, by contrast, are very strongly attracted to color. Their slow-moving, centuries-old eyes possess four color receptors (while we human beings only have three). What would a painter paint if he could see the world like a turtle? Crocodiles, by contrast, inhabitants of the Nile, remain age-old and color-blind.

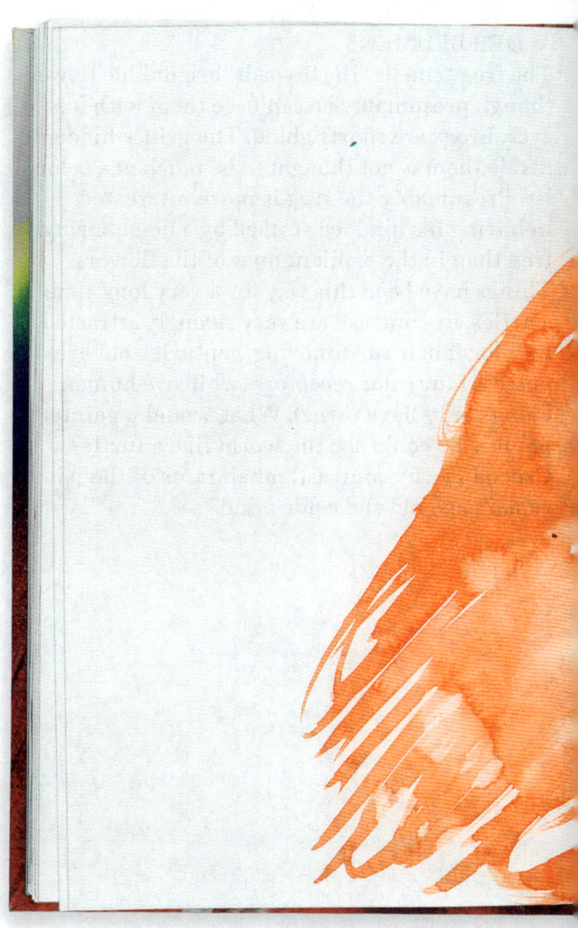

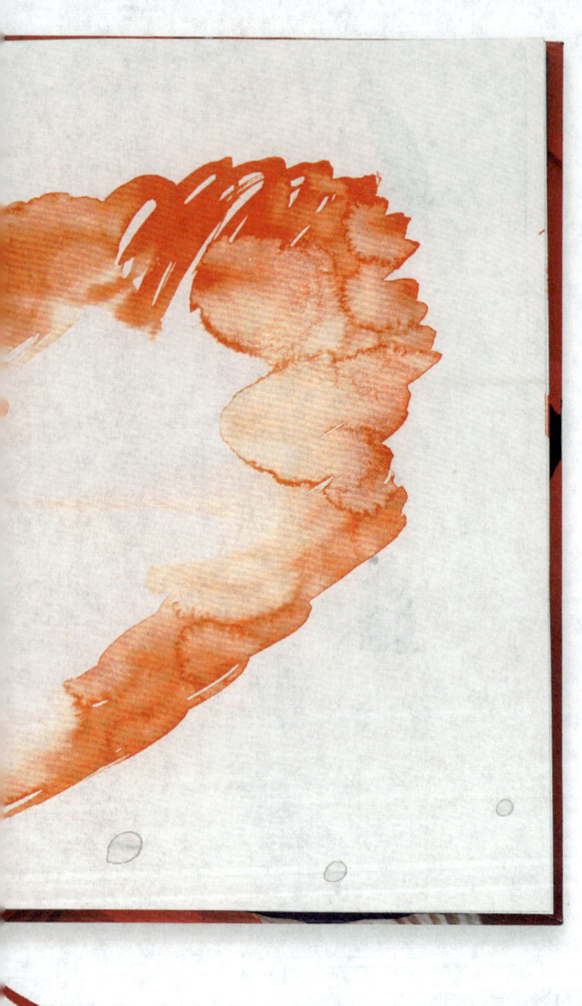

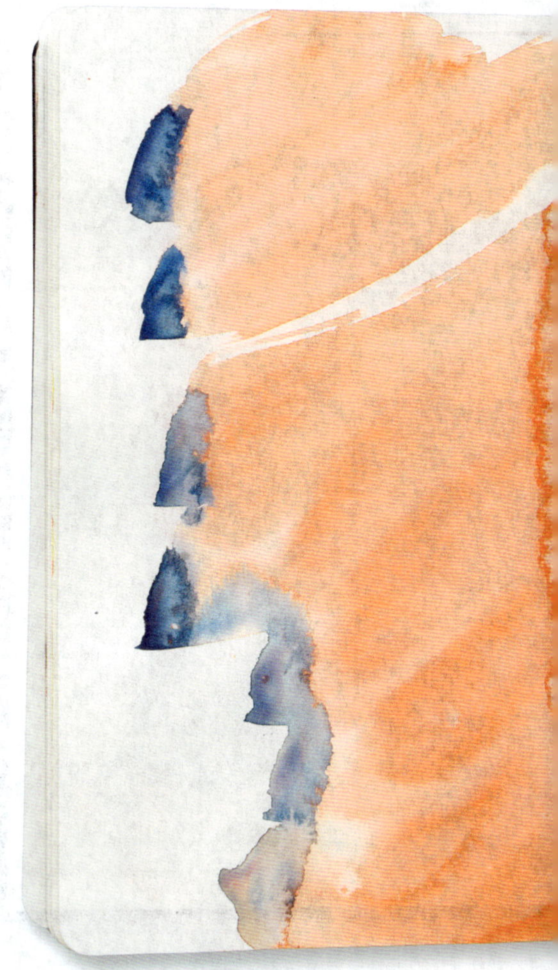

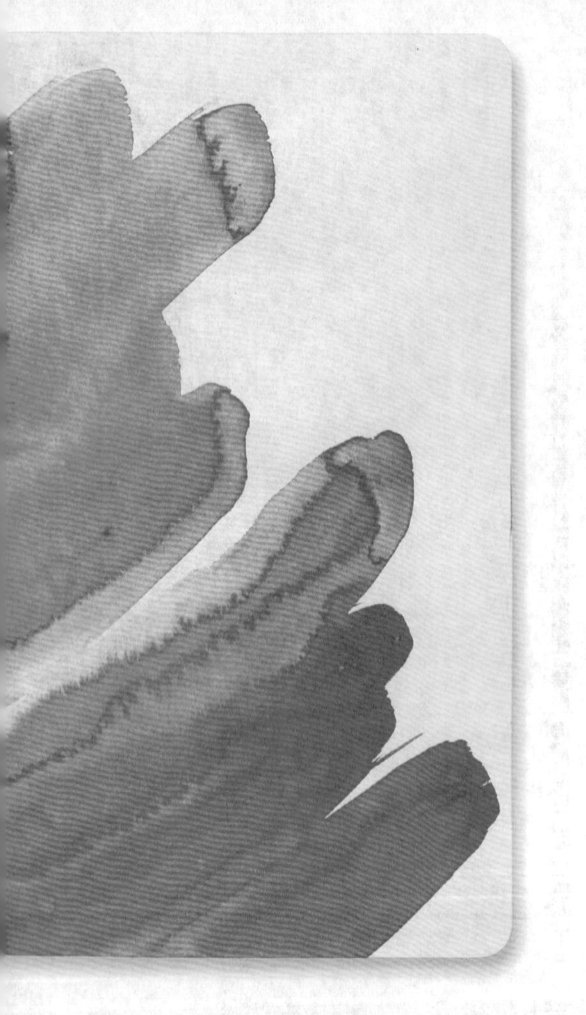

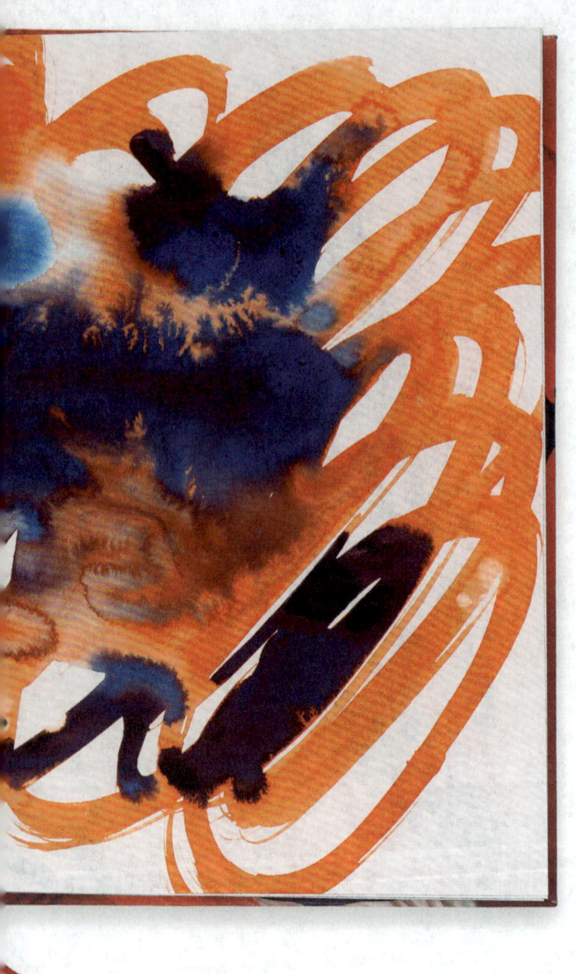

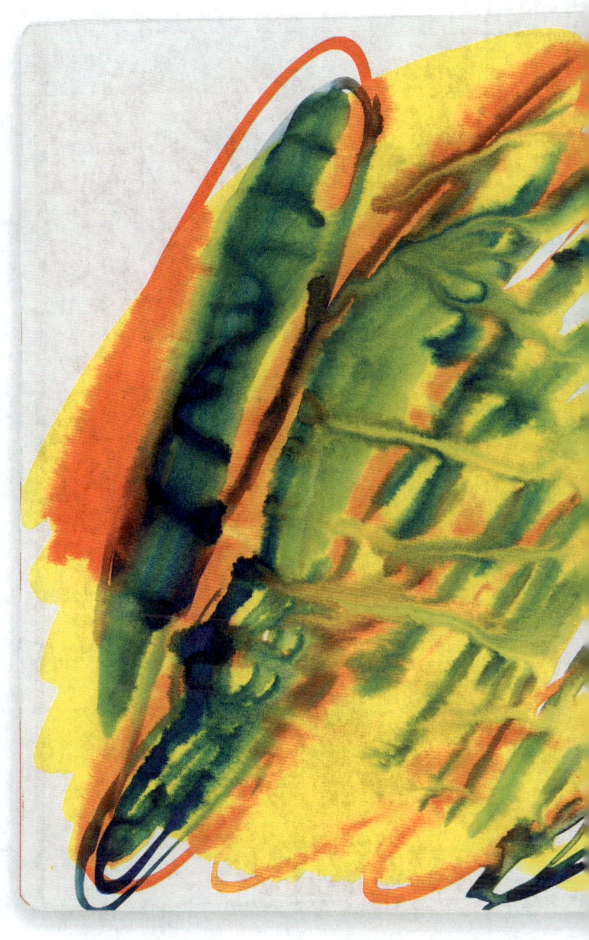

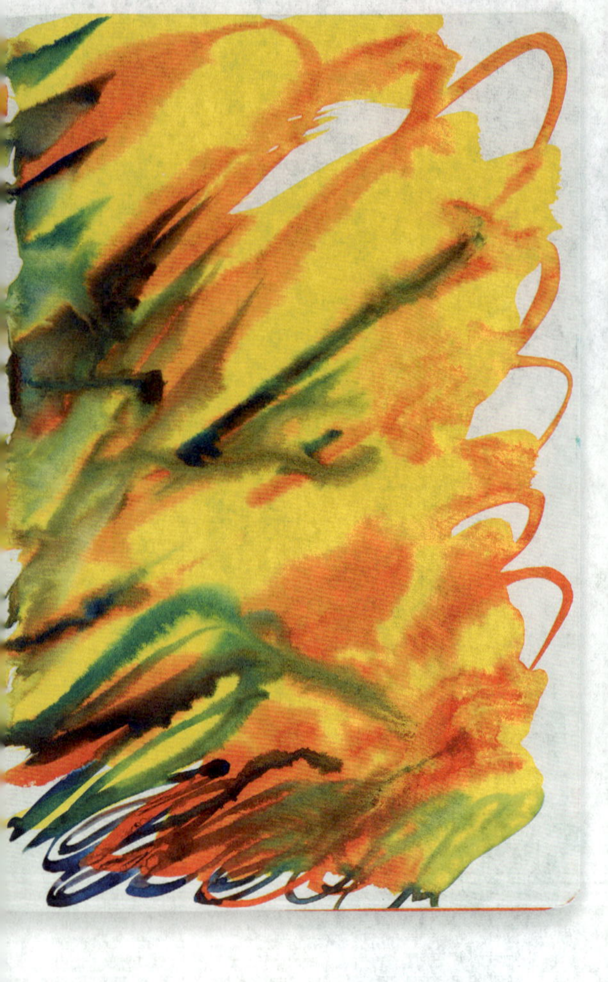

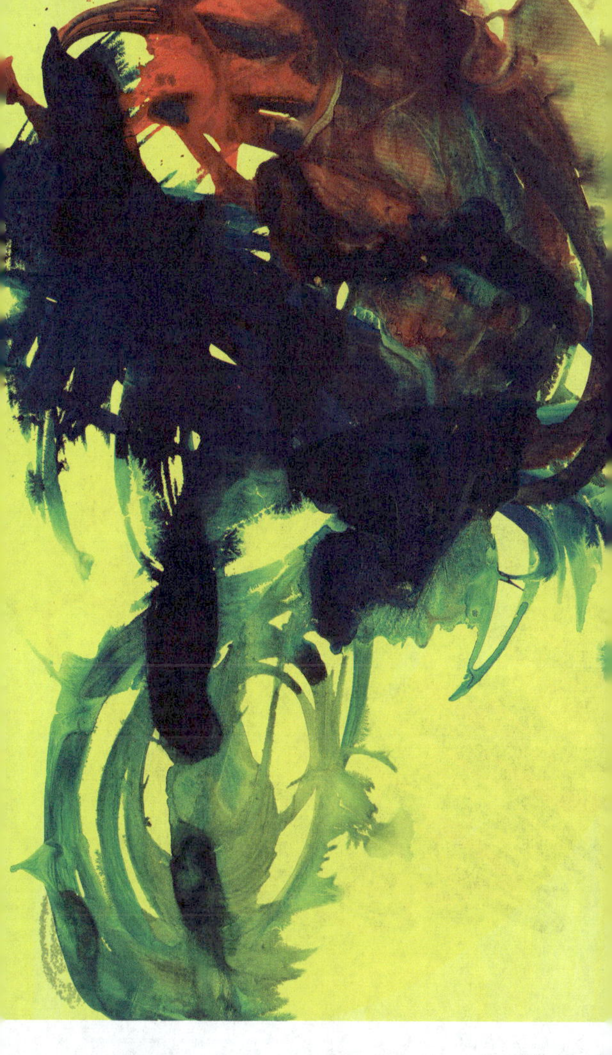

I TAKE A PHOTO

I take a photo. A moment is recorded in it. The skin of the image consists of a thin layer that could almost be called "non-material." What the image records, the exposure, is not something material like paint applied to canvas or ink dabbed on a piece of paper. In digital photos, this "technical spirituality" is even more intense.

At the same time, one cannot speak of a "crystallized moment." The instant of time that the photo wins from the intractable flow of reality is shorter than the blinking of an eye (the German word for "moment," *Augenblick*, literally means the "glancing of an eye"), it is shorter even than the eye's own capacity to distinguish the objects it sees. A photo should be called a "detail" or a "fragment." In a series or a collection, photos establish contact with one another. EVERY PHOTO THAT EXISTS LEADS ITS OWN LIFE AT NIGHT.

10

Strategies from Below

Strategies from Above

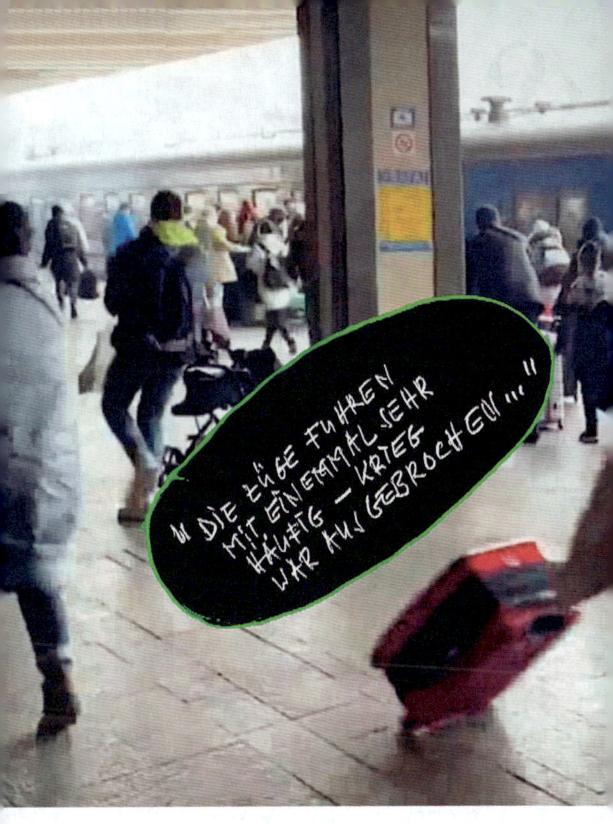
„DIE ZÜGE FUHREN
MIT EINEMMAL SEHR
HÄUFIG – KRIEG
WAR AUSGEBROCHEN …“

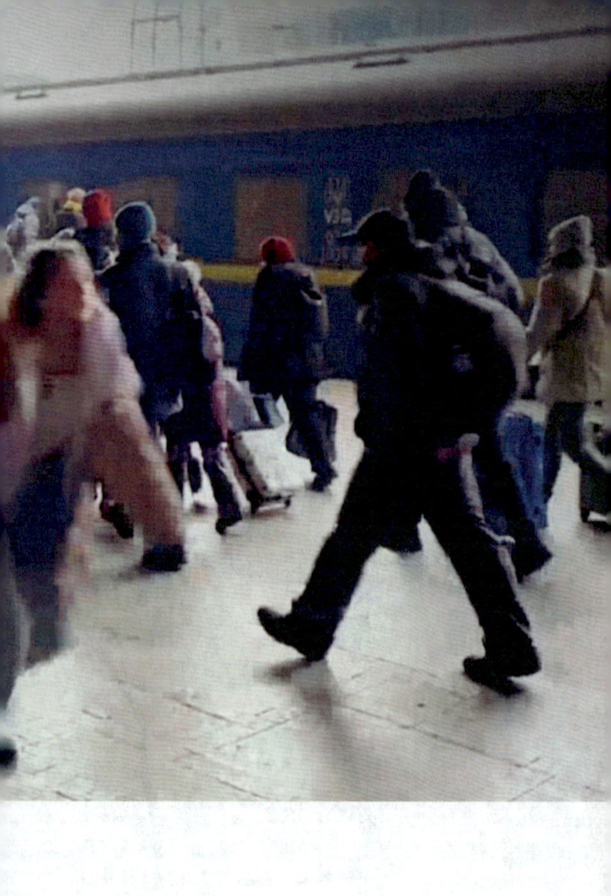

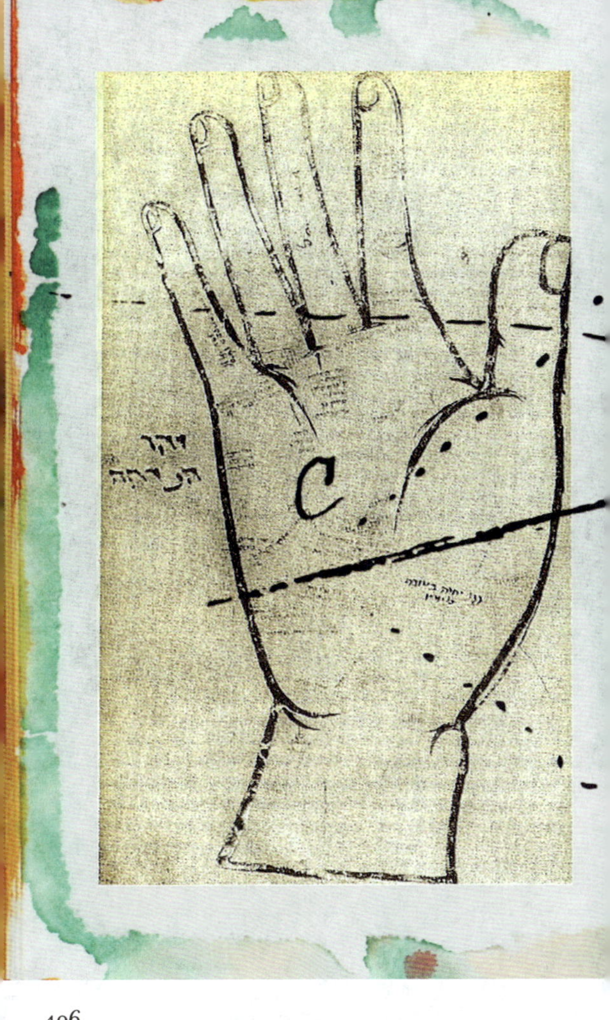

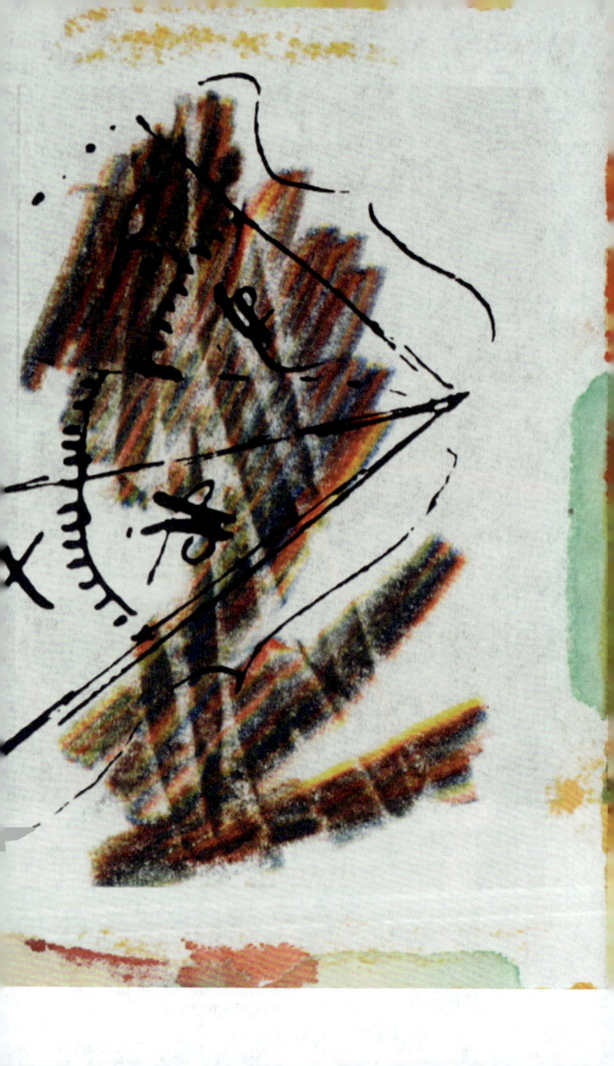

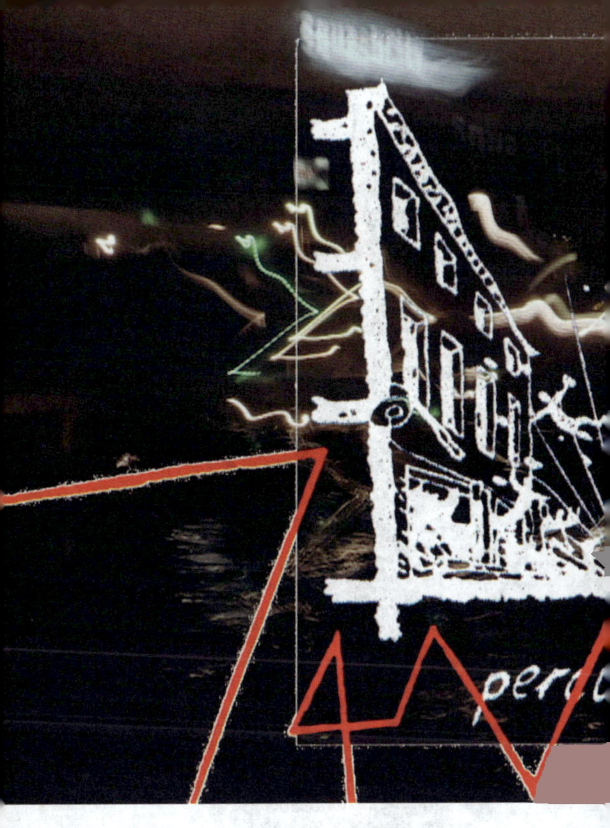

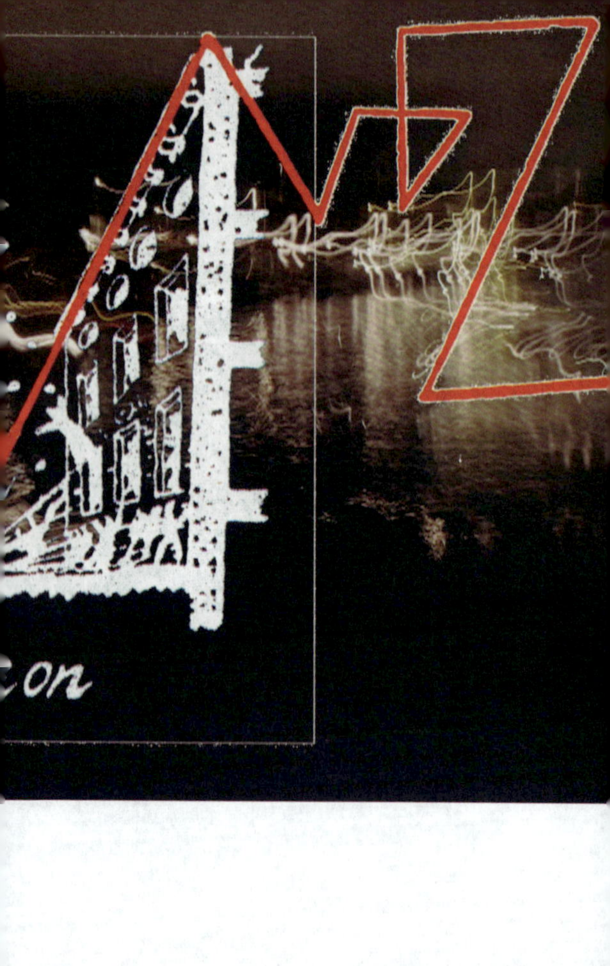

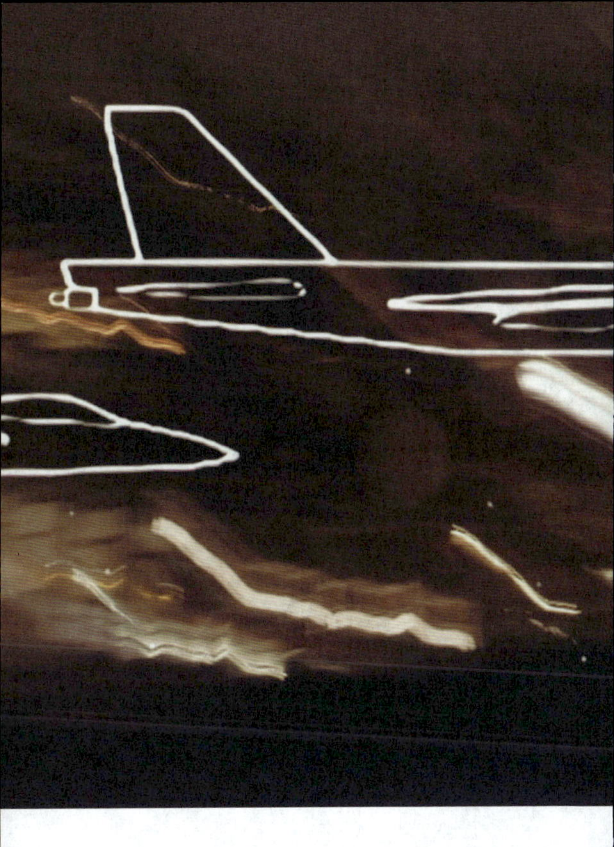

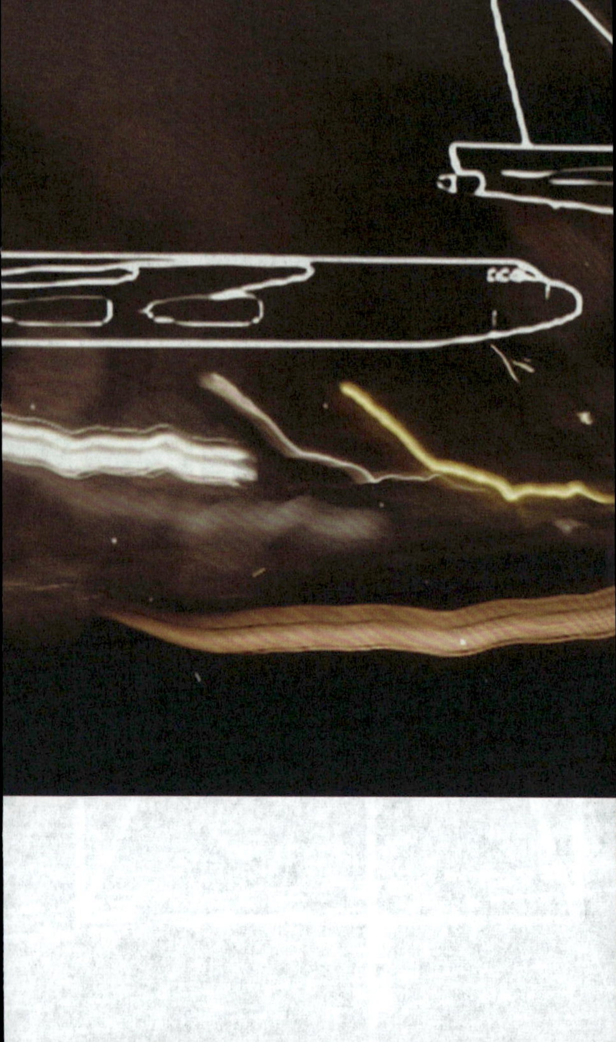

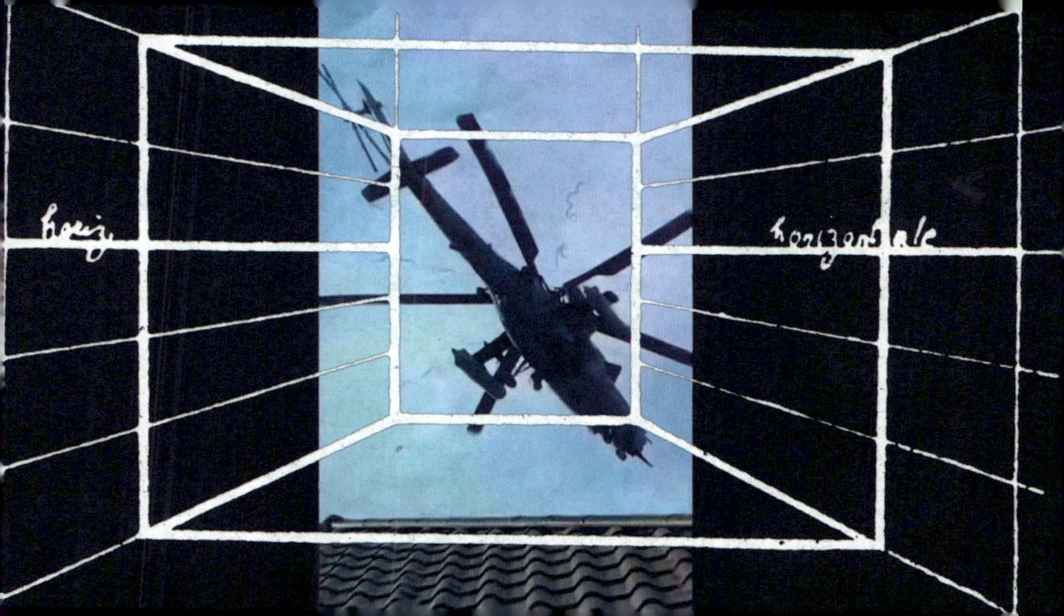
horiz
horizontale

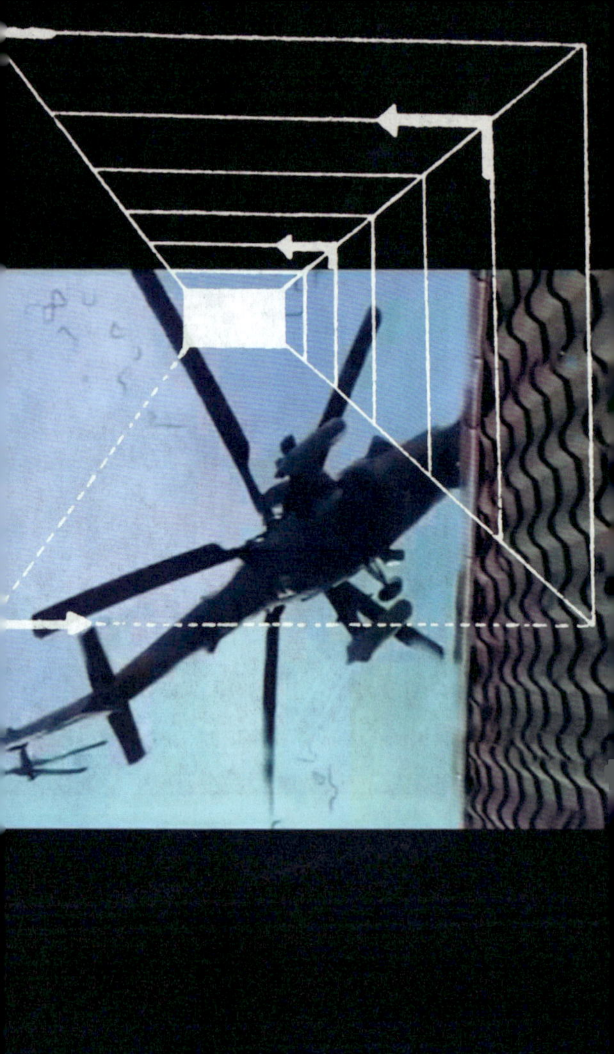

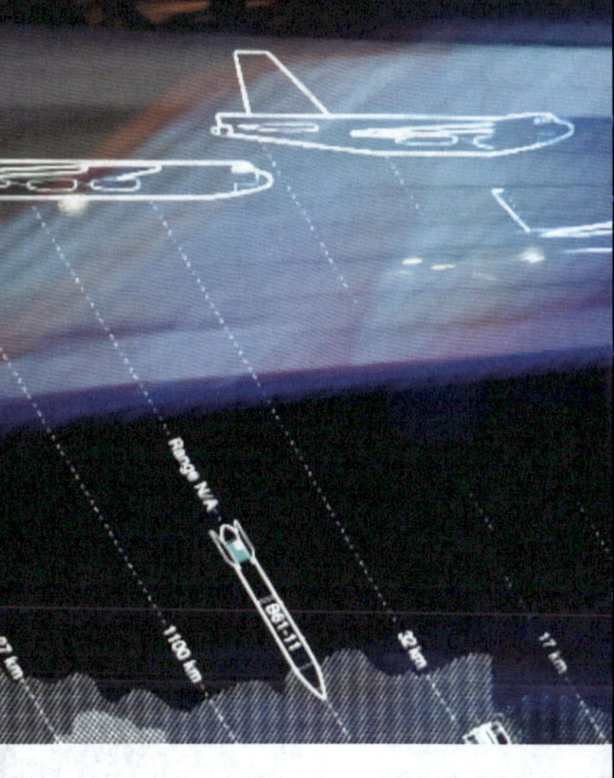
Range N/A
1100 km
32 km
17 km

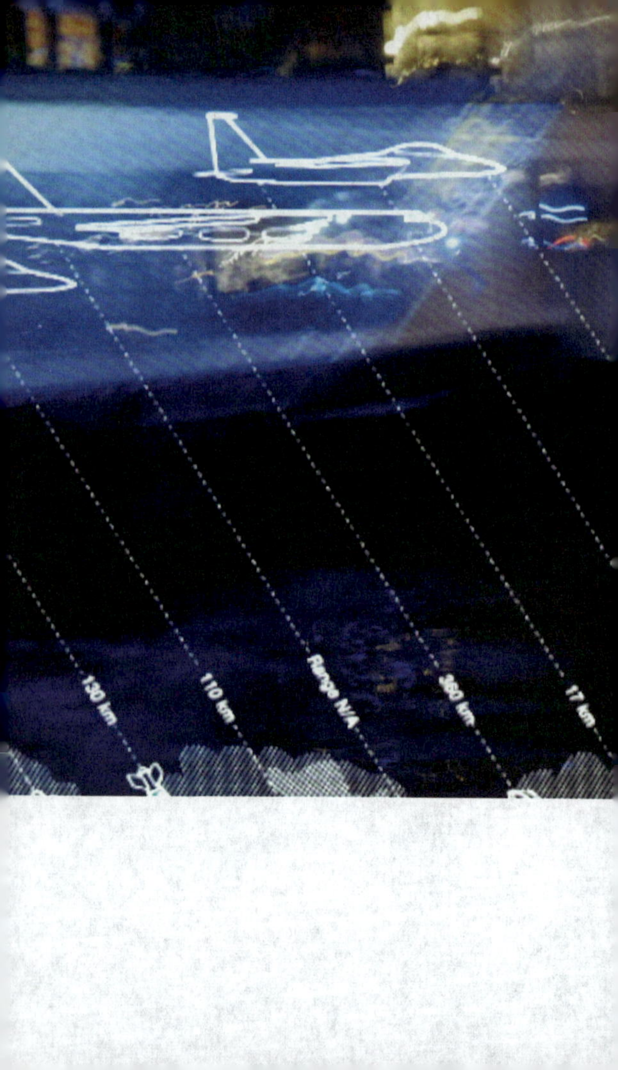
130 km
110 km
Range N/A
360 km
17 km

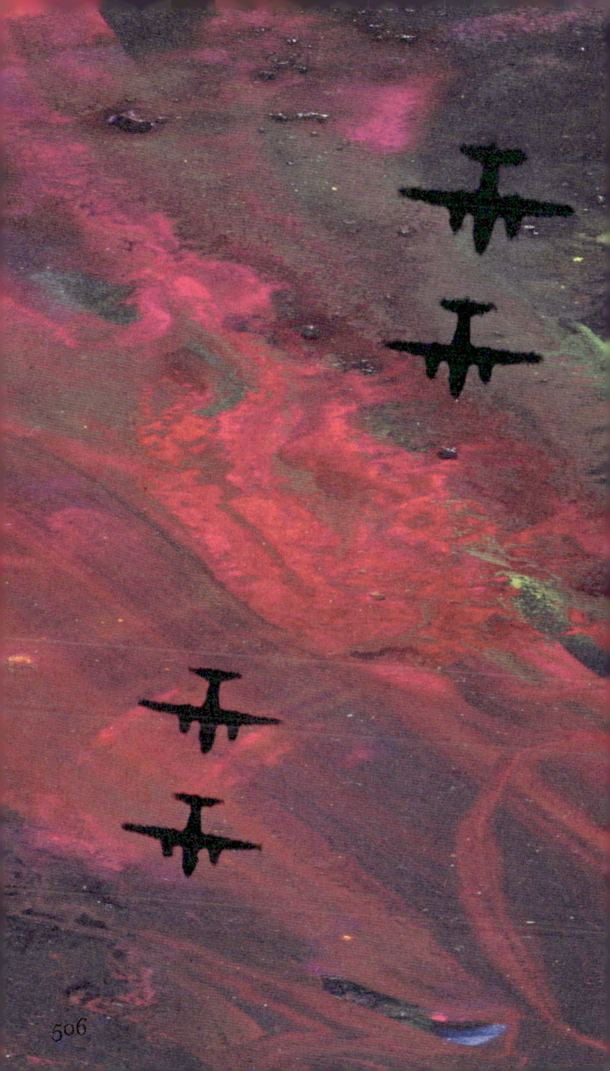

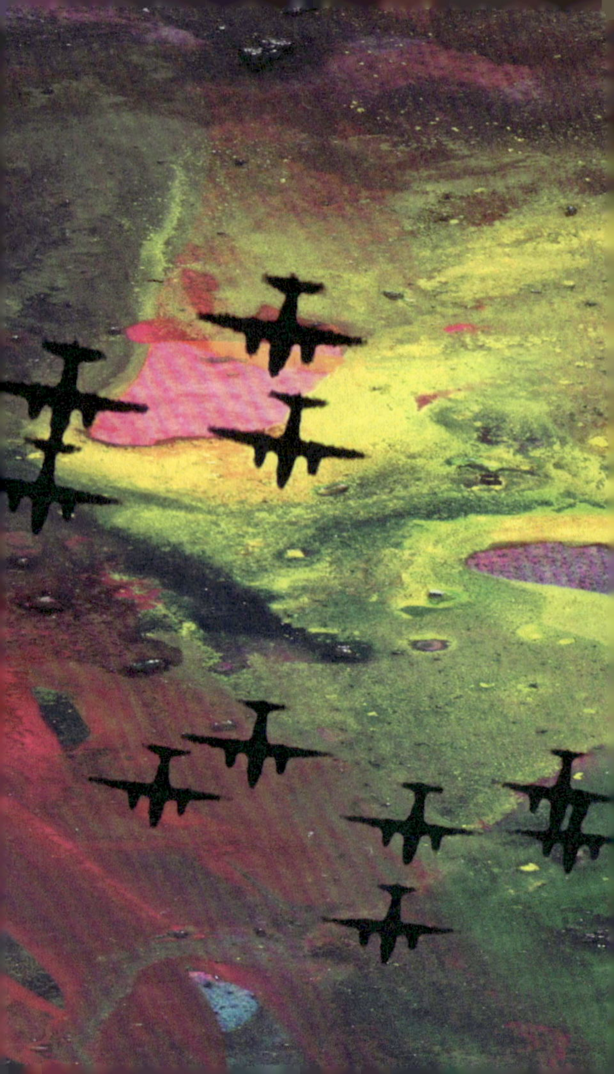

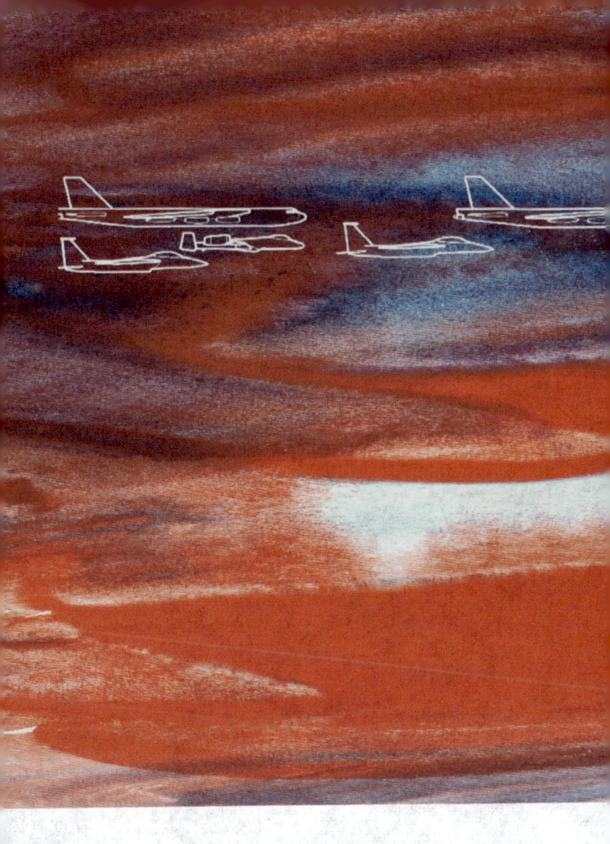

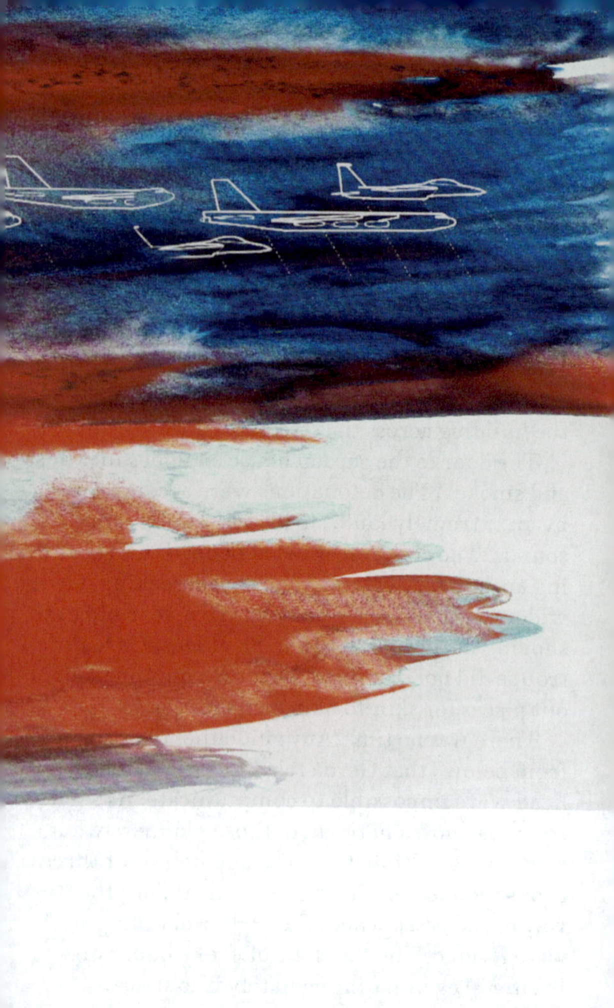

STRATEGY FROM BELOW IN SPRING 1945

The evacuee from around Gelsenkirchen, a primary school teacher now obligated to serve as a munitions worker, Gerda Baethe, together with her three children aged nine, seven, and five, is living in the cellar-less garden house at Breiter Weg Nr. 55/57. At 11:32 a.m. she hears the full-alarm siren, a bomb attack in the distance. She has just finished dressing the children when high-explosive bombs hammer into the air-raid shelter of Nr. 9 (the Koch print shop), Nr. 26, and Nr. 69, the building across the street.*

The door to the garden house explodes into dust and smoke. "The detonations were accompanied by an extremely loud, shrill, and unpleasant sound." The children crawled beneath her, crowding around her legs, neck, her head, seeking out wider expanses of her body, the five-year-old even shoving his head beneath it. So at least Gerda's troupe did not scatter to the four winds but sought out places for skin-to-skin contact.

There was no time. Any guidelines of a "strategy from below" that Gerda tried to gather in her head were impossible to communicate. As seen from way down here, up to those planners who remained invisible to Gerda at a height of three thousand meters above the town, and all the way to the bases where the higher planning staff were located. The top floor of every house on Breiter Weg burst immediately into flame.

* The eighteen people who had sought shelter there are asphyxiated. Gerda Baethe is unaware of this.

STRATEGY FROM ABOVE
1945

The bomber group of around 200 aircraft—which was being followed by another 115 aircraft at a distance of ten flight minutes, that is, over Nordhausen—was flying toward Halberstadt from the southwest at about seven thousand meters. The formation "as if ordered to attack" had a traditional calvary-like appearance but had been *calculated*, this was no parade but a position in which, were they to be attacked by fighters, the aircraft could close ranks to escape fire; if shot at by the flak guns, spread apart.

The pioneering phase of such air raids of four-motor, long-distance B-17 bombers (each one a workshop but an entire factory when the compact formation was together) had taken place three or four years before. The completion of the process managed to separate as irrational factors that had played a role in that initial phase such as trust in God, the world of military forms, strategy, internal advertising to crews to make them willing to attack, references to peculiarities of the target, the purpose of the attack, etc.

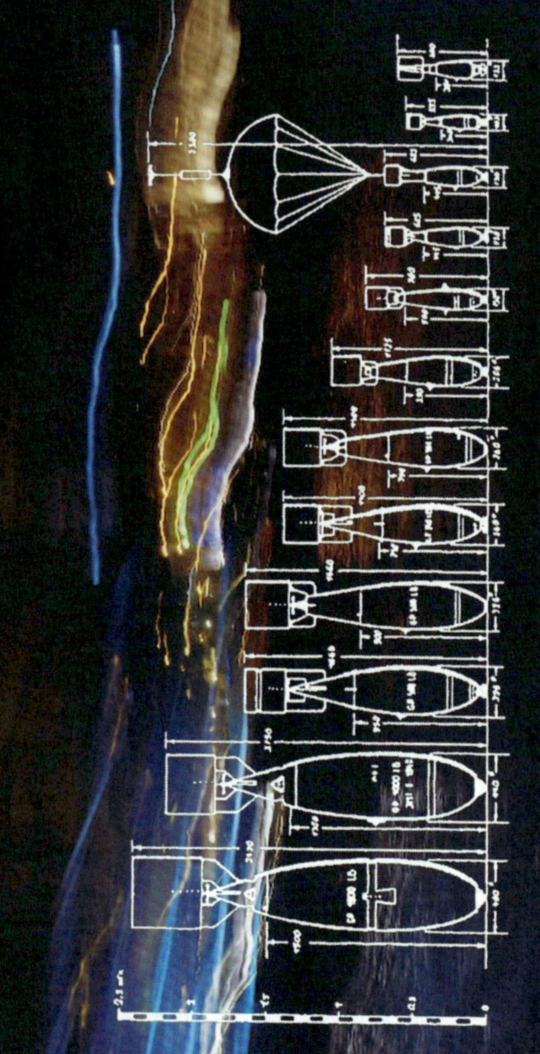

DER LUFTANGRIFF AUF HALBERSTADT

AM 8. APRIL 1945

GERDA BAETHE'S STRATEGIC PERSPECTIVE

To open any kind of strategic perspective—something the "well-done" Gerda Baethe would have liked in her hideout on 8 April, especially at night when the heat was at its worst—seventy thousand determined teachers, all like her, would had to have taught hard in every one of the countries involved in the war, for twenty years apiece, beginning in 1918, but at a national level as well: pressuring the press, the government; only then would all the young, so educated, have been able to take hold of scepters or reins (but scepters and reins aren't strategic weapons, there would have been no model for the use of force required here). "It's all a question of organization."

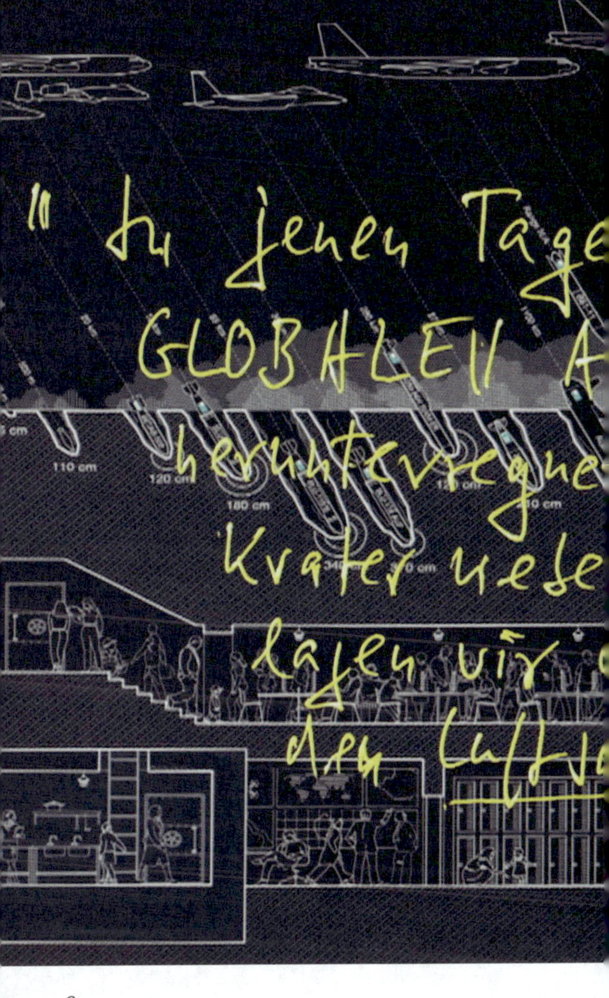
„In jenen Tage
GLOBALEN A
herunterregne
Krater
lagen wir
den
110 cm
120 cm
180 cm

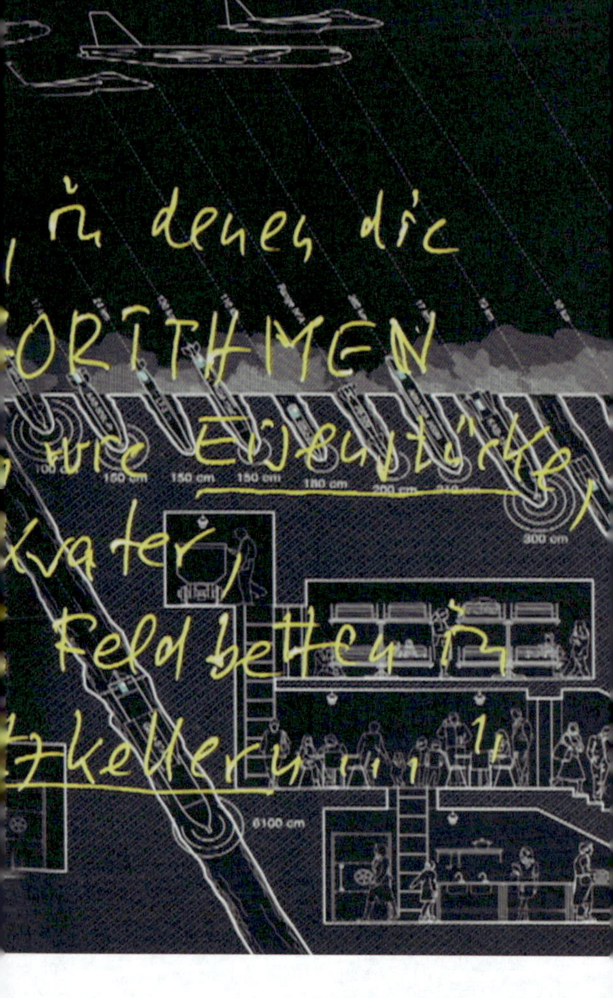

in denen die
ORITHMEN
wie Eisenstücke,
xrater,
Feldbetten im
tzkellern
150 cm
150 cm
150 cm
180 cm
300 cm
6100 cm

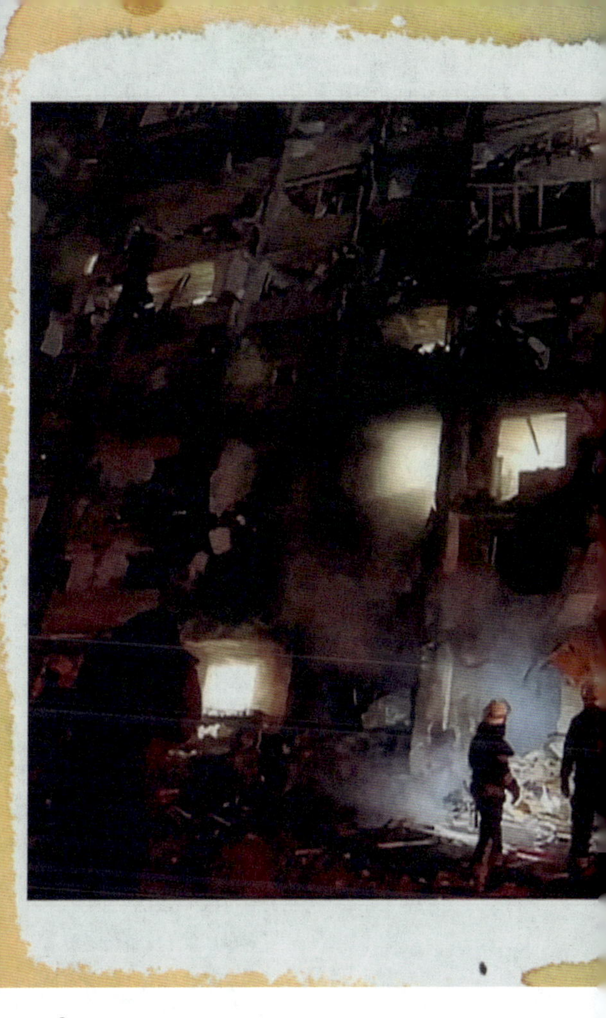

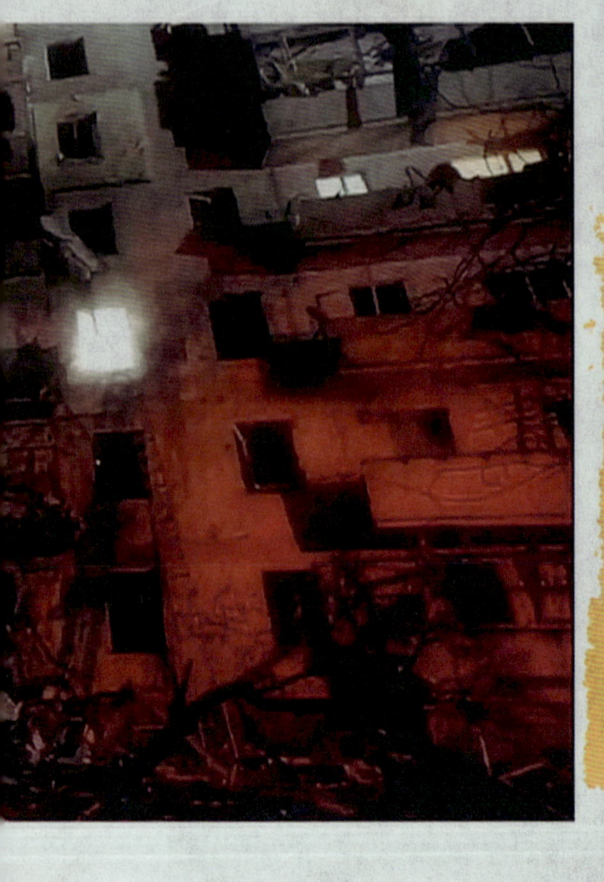

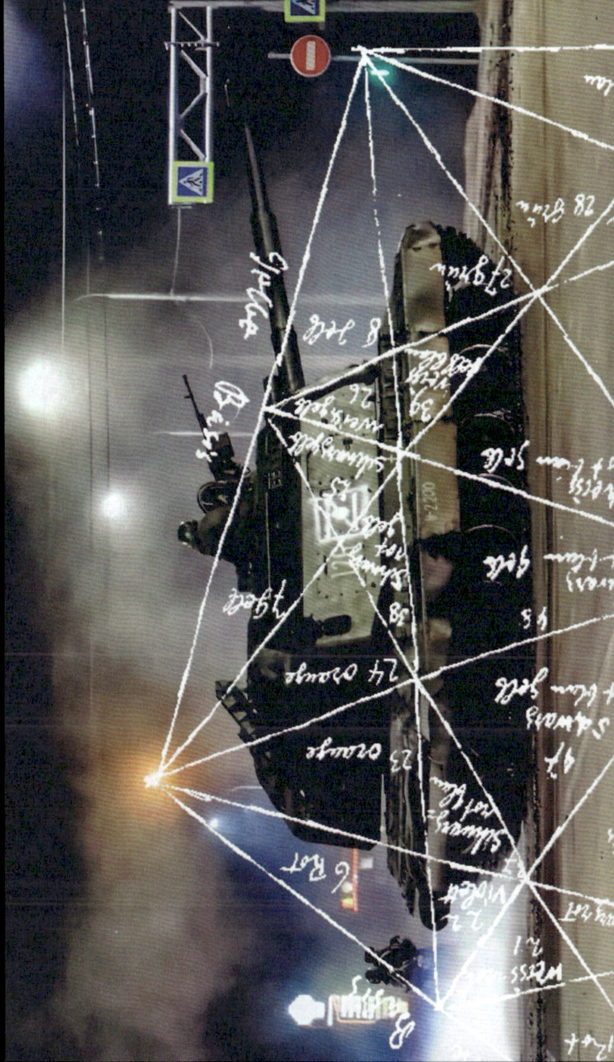

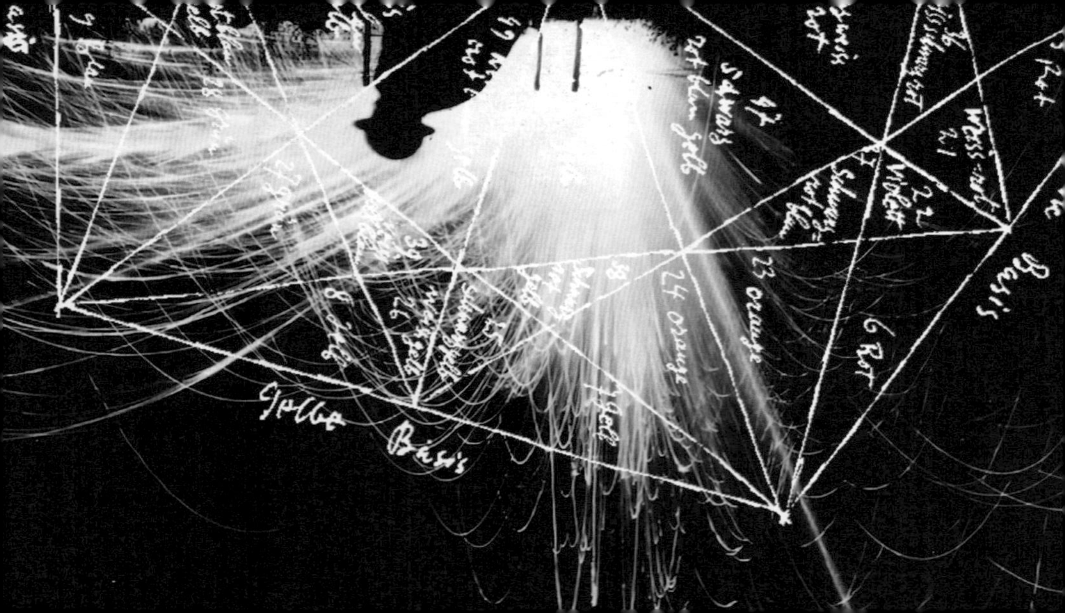
Gelbe Basis
Basis
6 Rot
23 orange
24 orange
47 Schwarz rot blau gelb
22 Violett
8 gelb

The Circus in War
01:49

Armor’s Utopia
02:10

Desire is the father of all things/
War is no father
02:24

STRATEGY FROM BELOW IN THE UKRAINE CRISIS

Those who flee from war and those who die are not strategies. I don't know what kind of concrete chances people susceptible to Russian attacks in Ukraine have. That goes for the young people in uniform too, those who get burned alive in their tanks when the latter are turned into fiery caskets. In April 1945 Frau Anna Wilde of Halberstadt, mother of five, bombed out of her home, said: "Once you've reached a certain point of misery, it doesn't matter who caused it. It just has to stop." Strategy from below is synonymous with ceasefire. Nothing counts except for just such an end to the war.

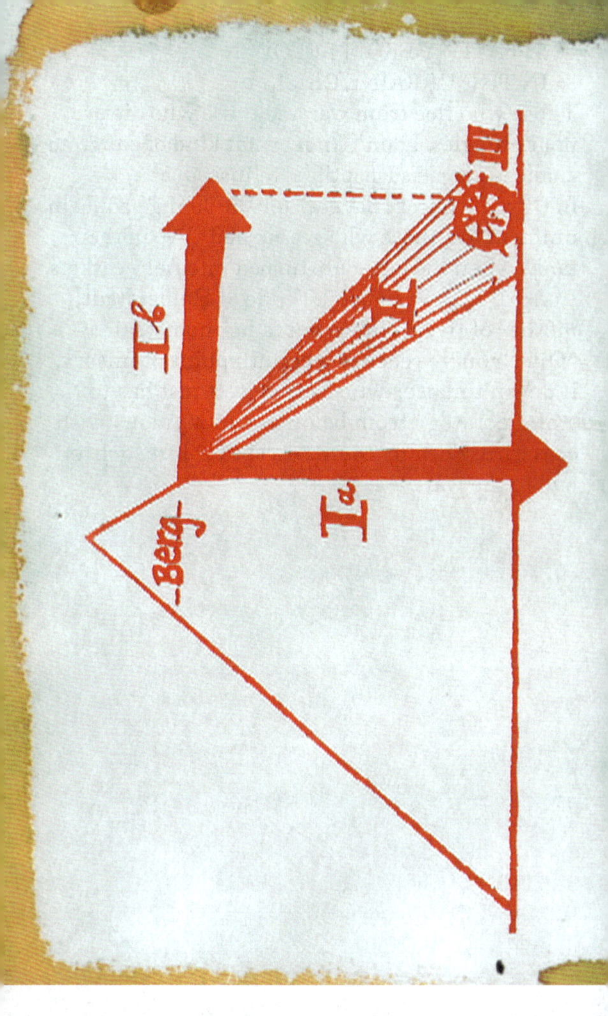

Berg

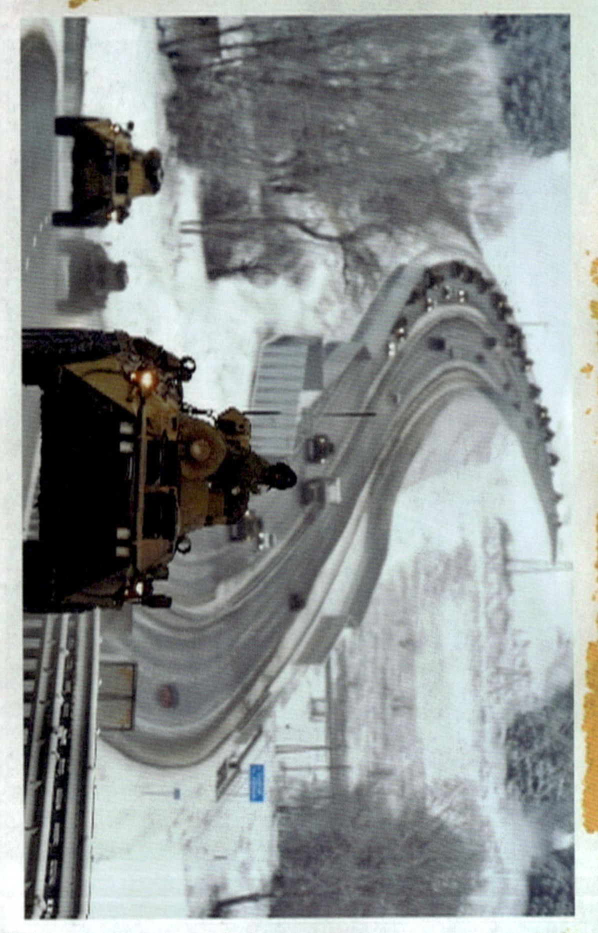

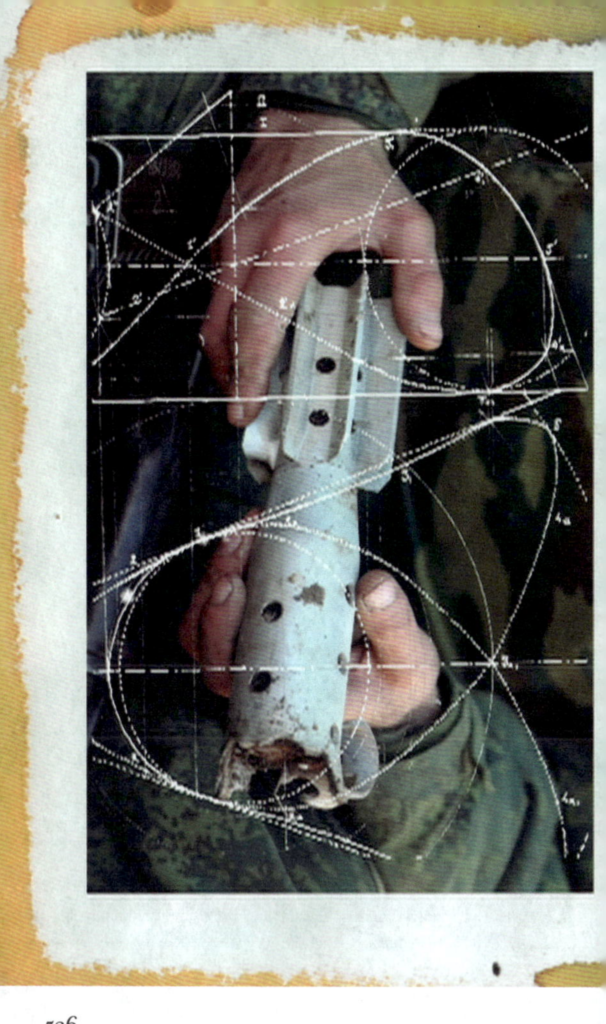

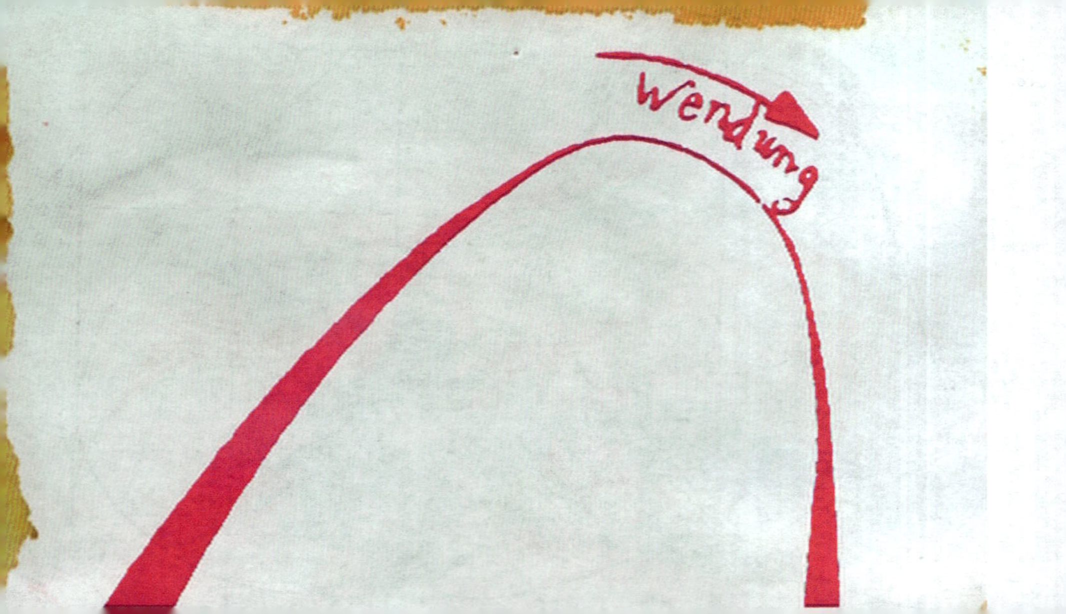
Wendung

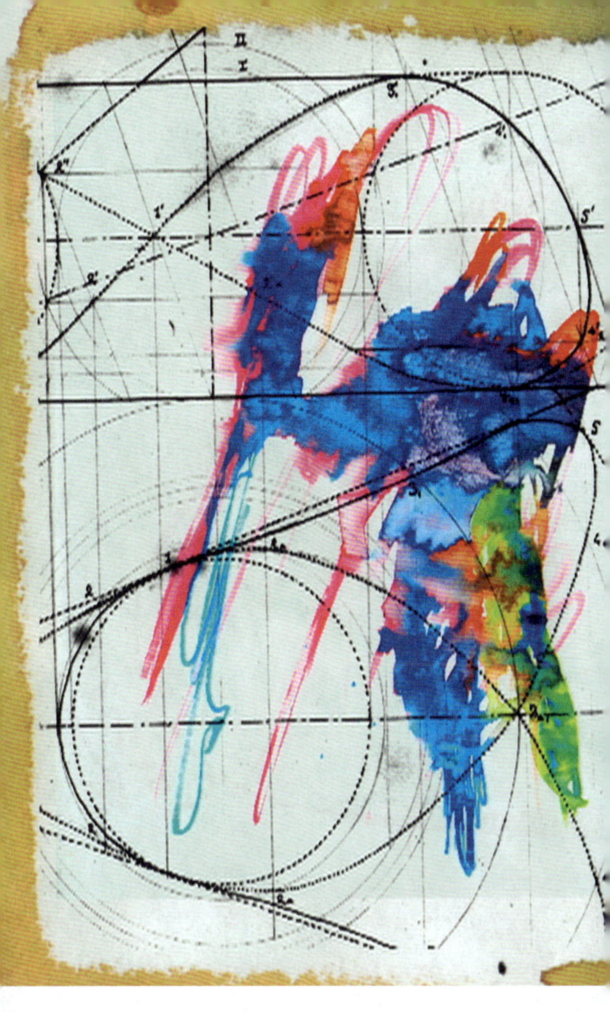

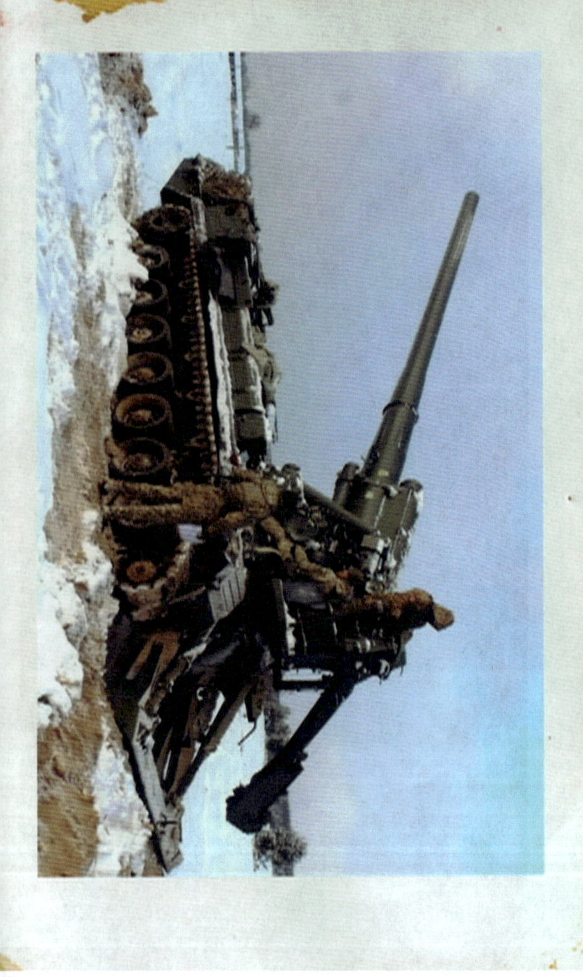

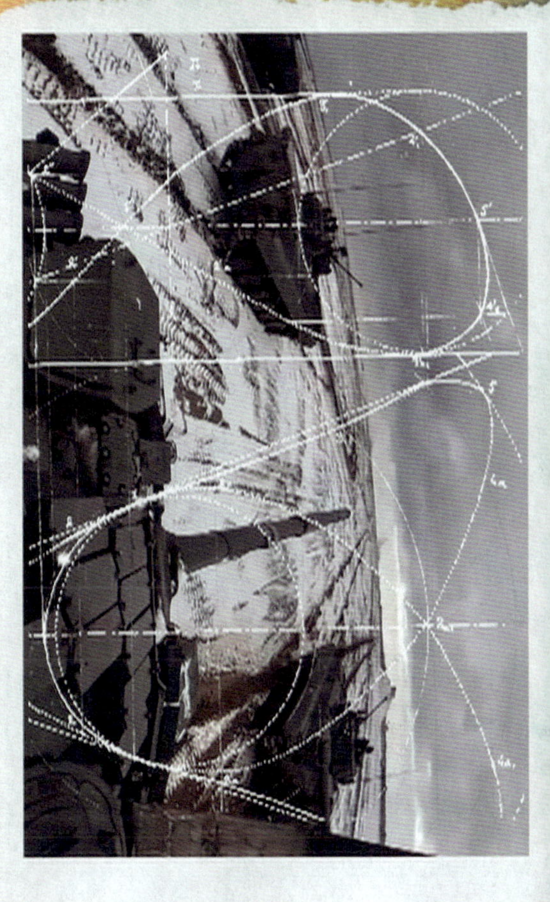

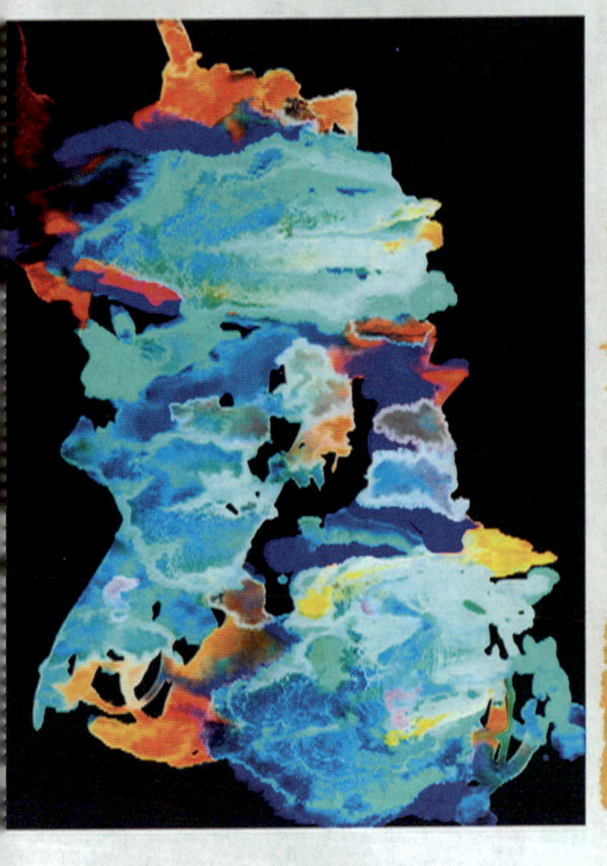

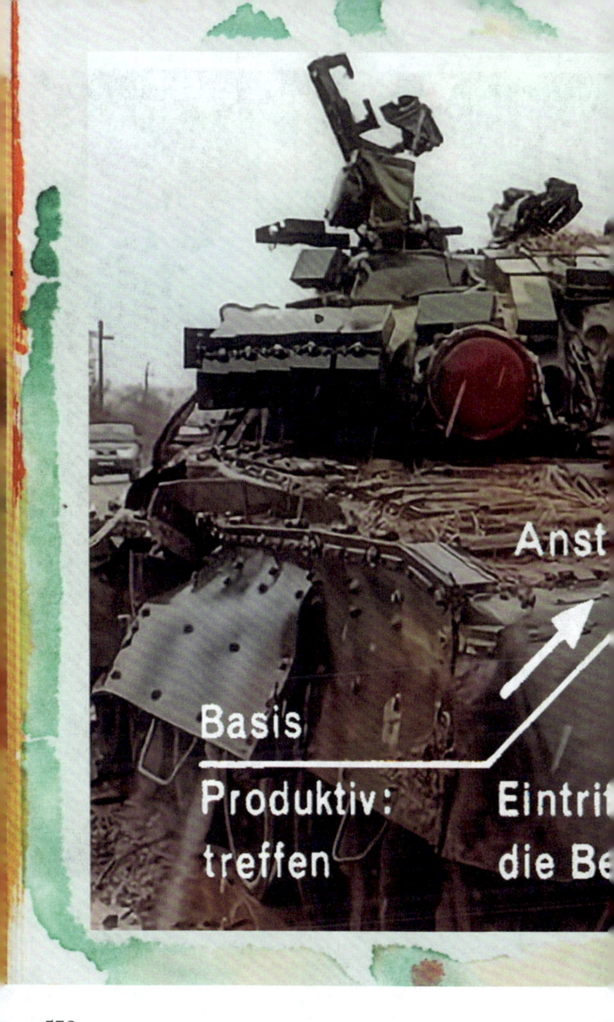
Anst
Basis
Produktiv:
treffen
Eintrit
die Be

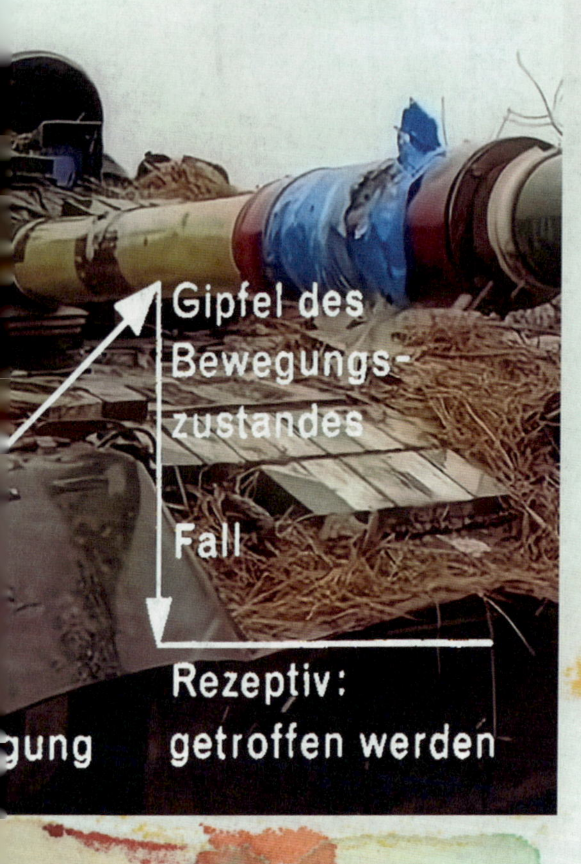
Gipfel des
Bewegungs-
zustandes
Fall
Rezeptiv:
getroffen werden
gung

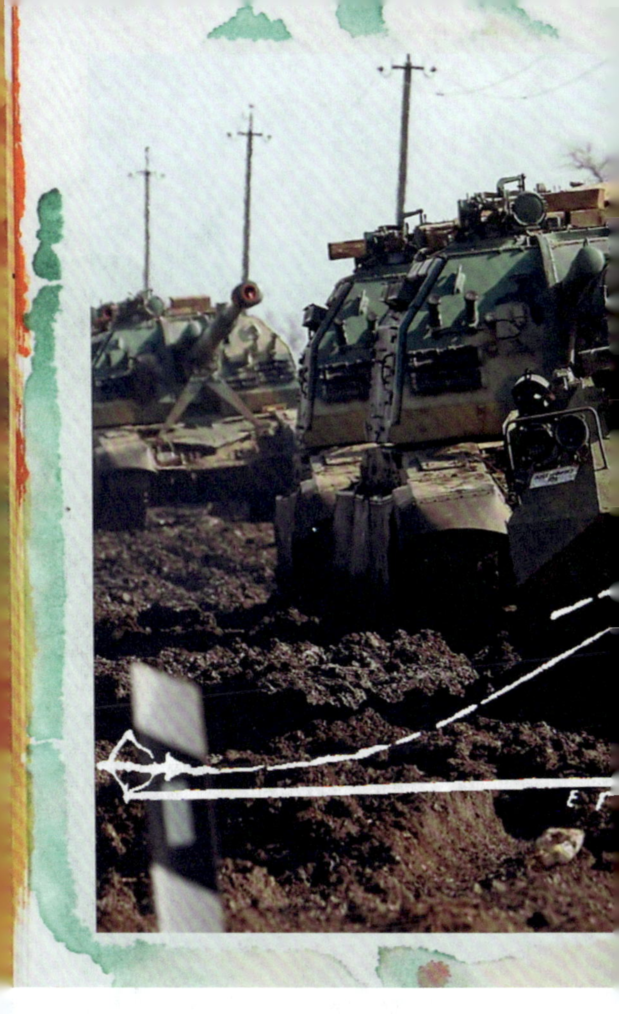

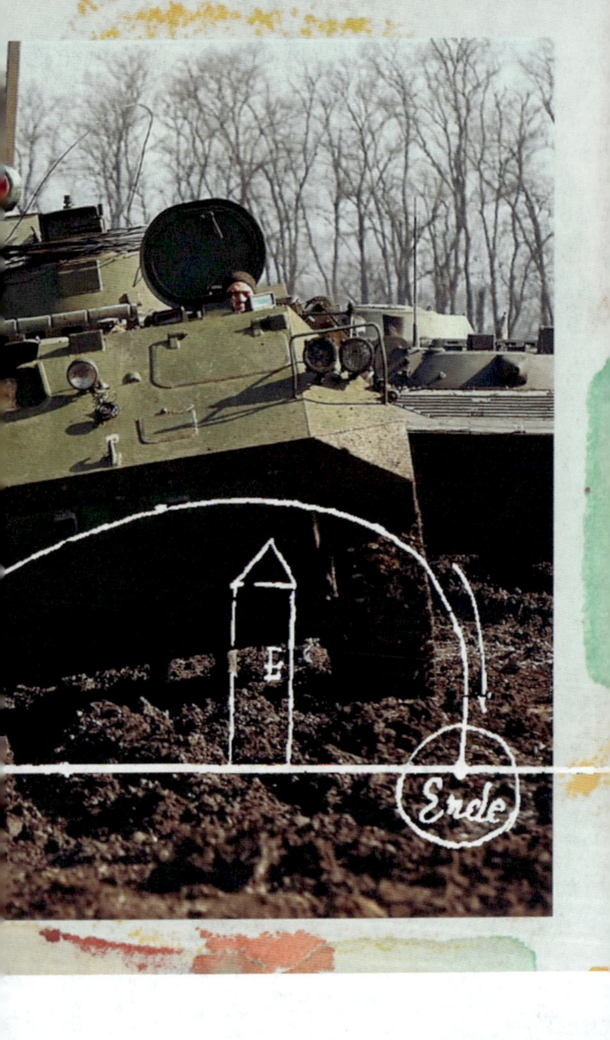
E
Erde

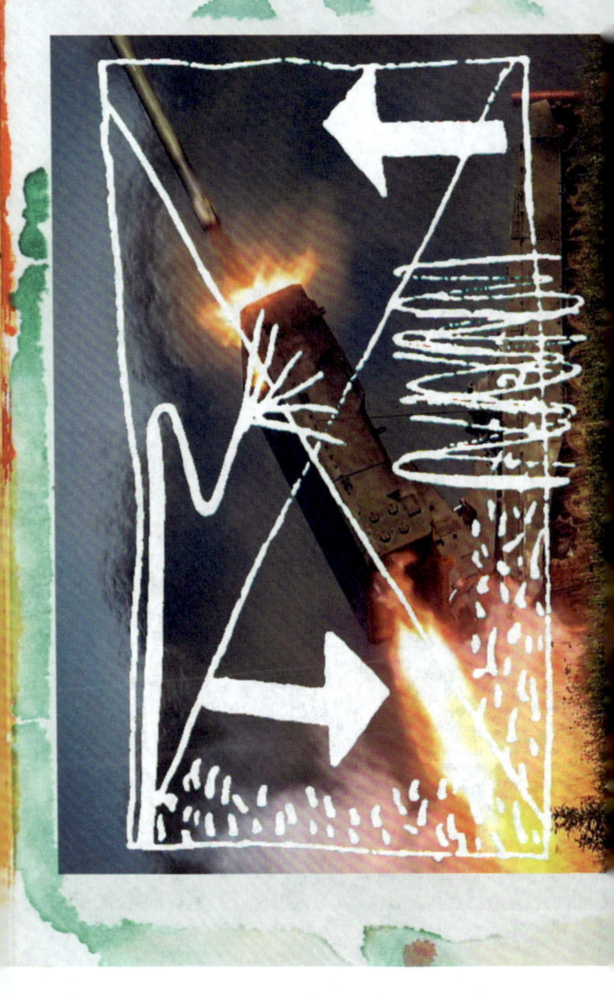

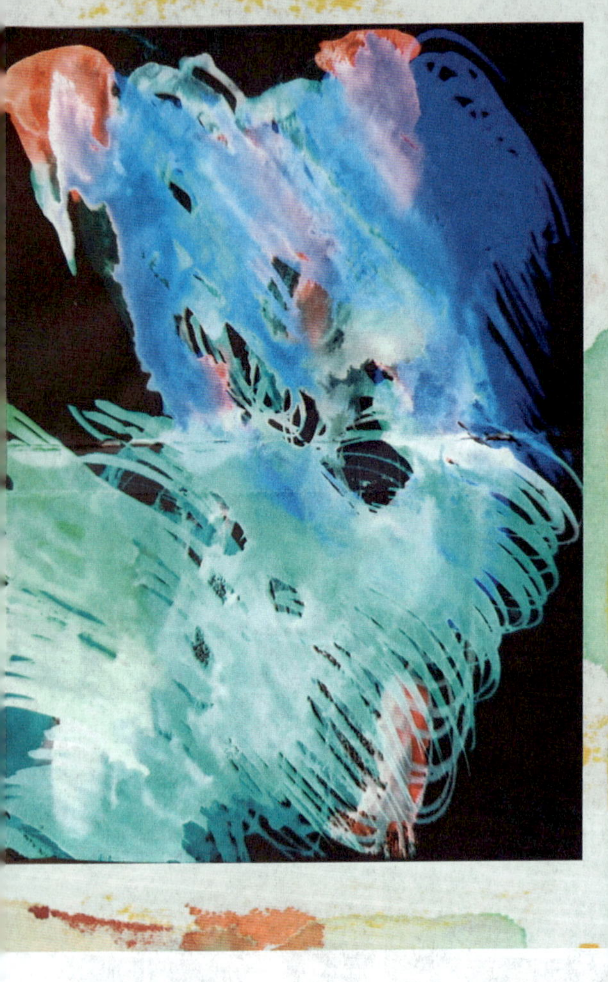

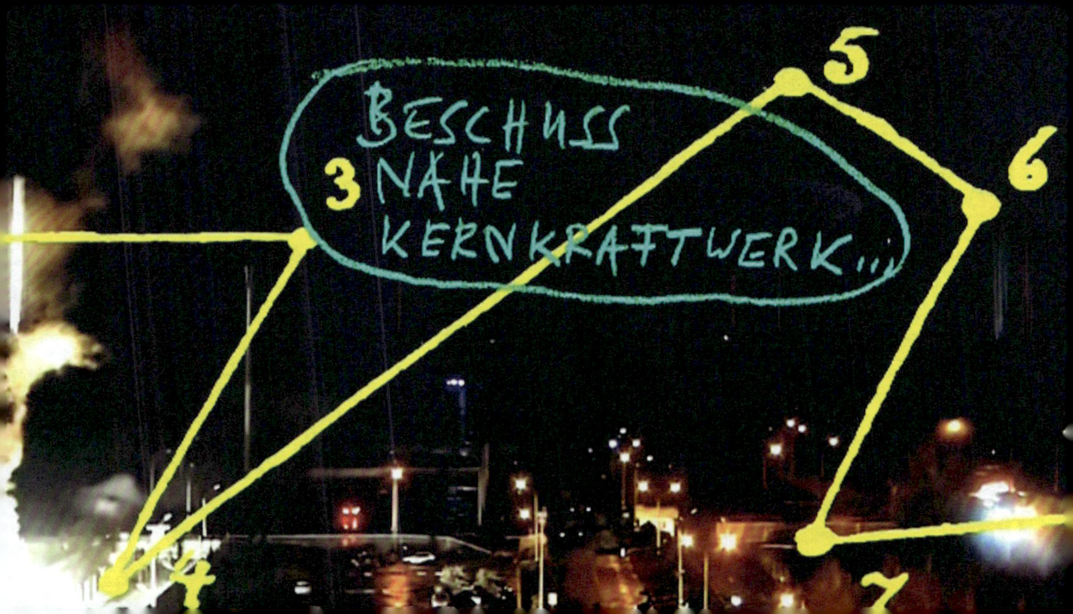

3
BESCHUSS
NÄHE
KERNKRAFTWERK..
4
5
6
7

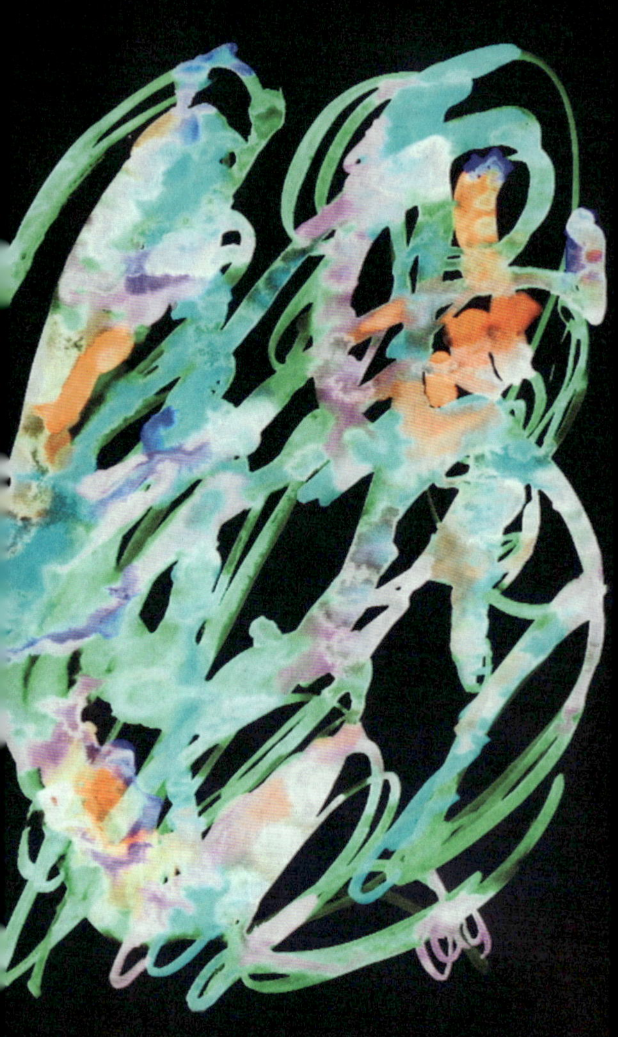

THE DARK SIDE OF PROBABILITY

In the hurried days of September 1983, military psychologist I.V. Smirnoff gave a lecture to a subcommittee of the Central Committee, which had a little more time to listen than the people in the Politburo. He pointed out the "sediment" of mentally unstable suicidal types and paranoiacs (in the latter case, fanatical patriots with obsessive ideas) who—once they got their hands on a dangerous weapon—would not hesitate to use it. He put the probability of such a threat of war at

0.3 percent, while he put the probability of an attack by the Western Allies (given that their command centers would have half an hour's survival time after an attack on the Soviet Union before they were wiped out by the counterattack) at 0.001 percent. And the four-eyes principle? It won't prevent a determined perpetrator suffering from self-aggression from doing anything, as they will kill whatever comrade is there to control them before being stopped.

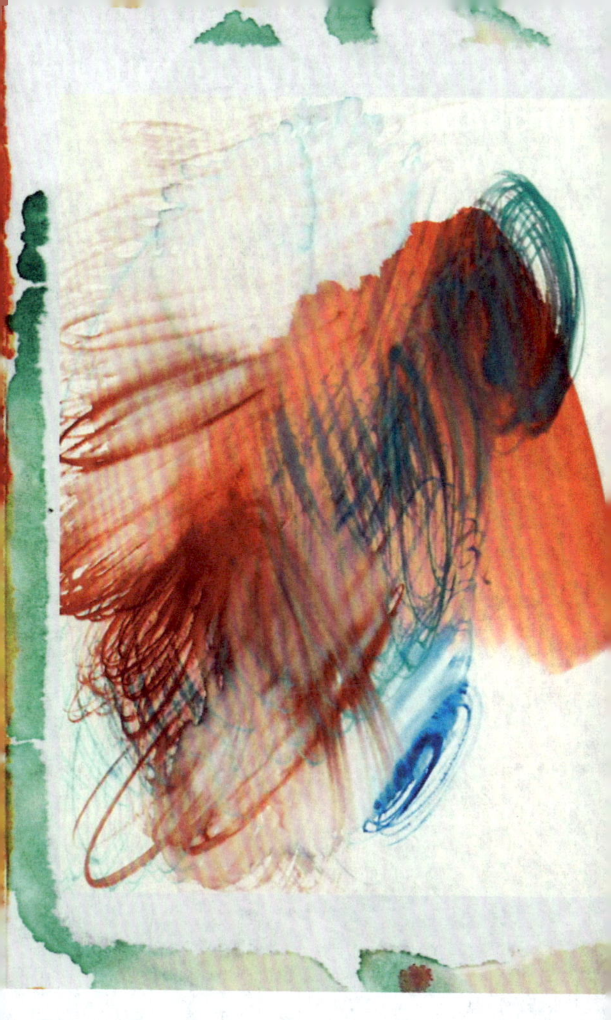

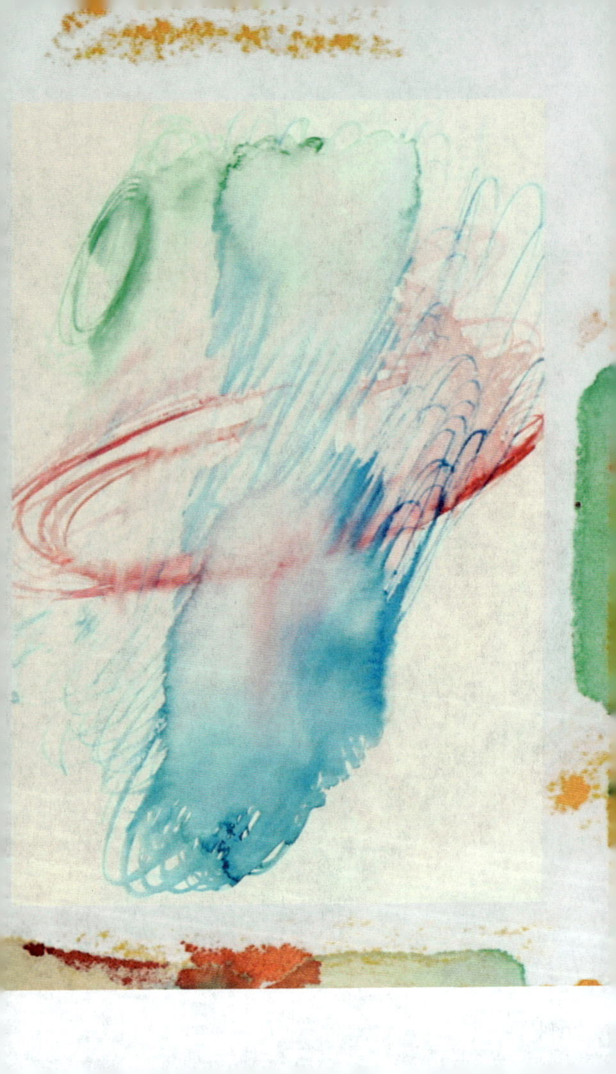

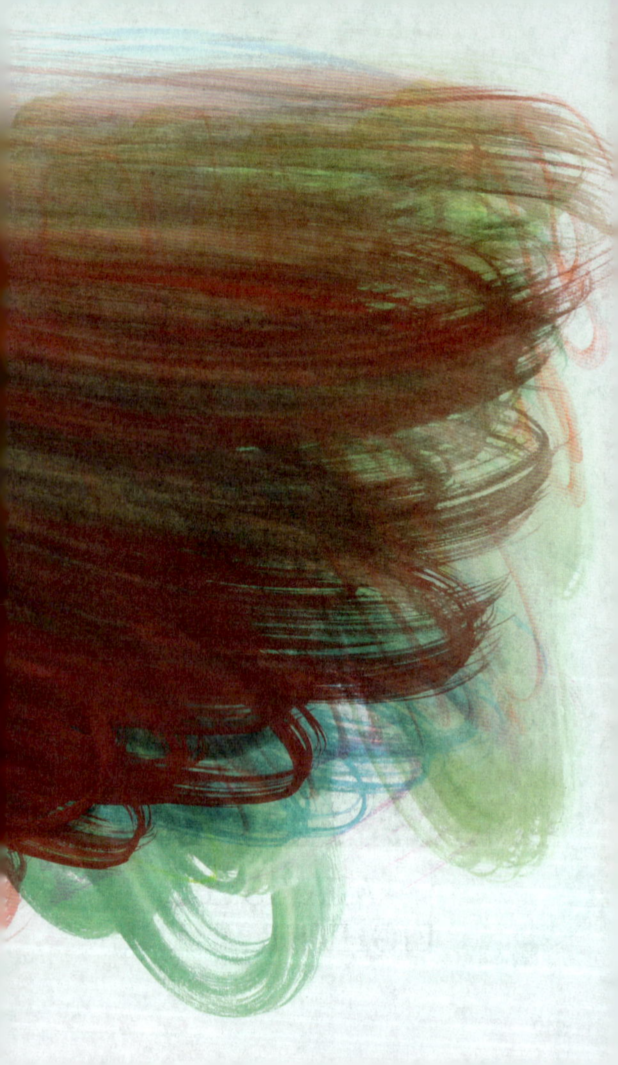

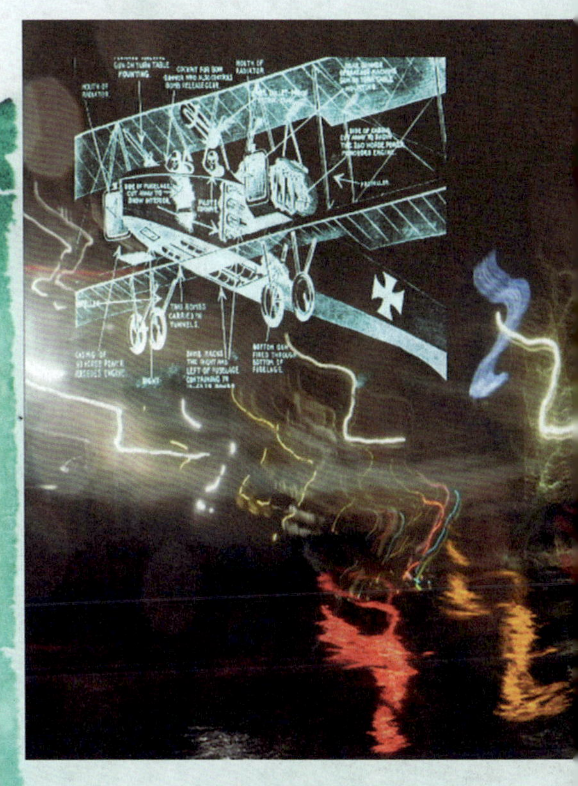

ATAVISTIC FIGHTER PLANE

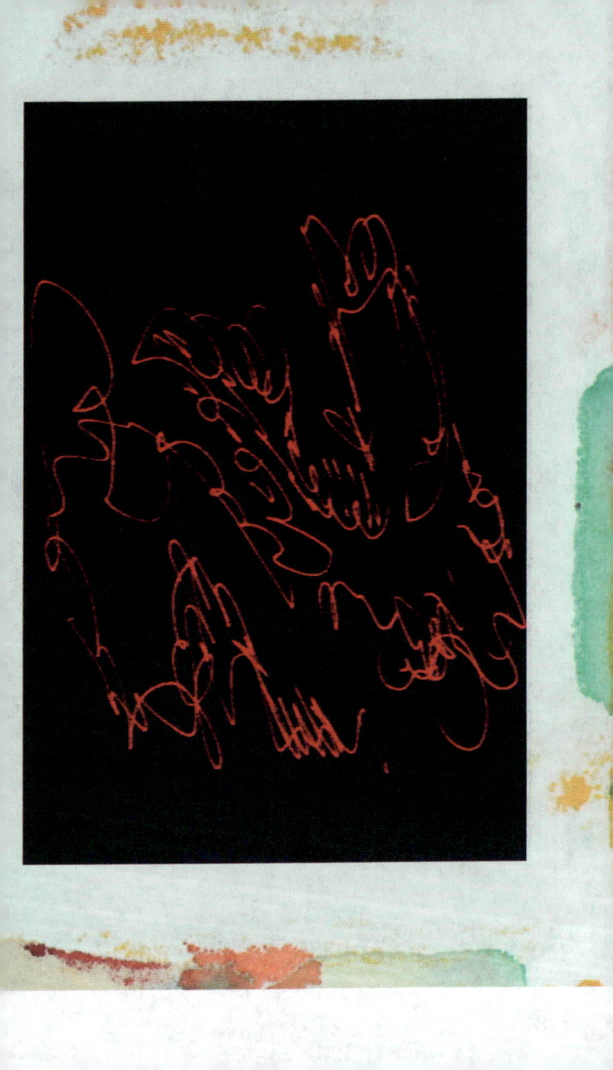

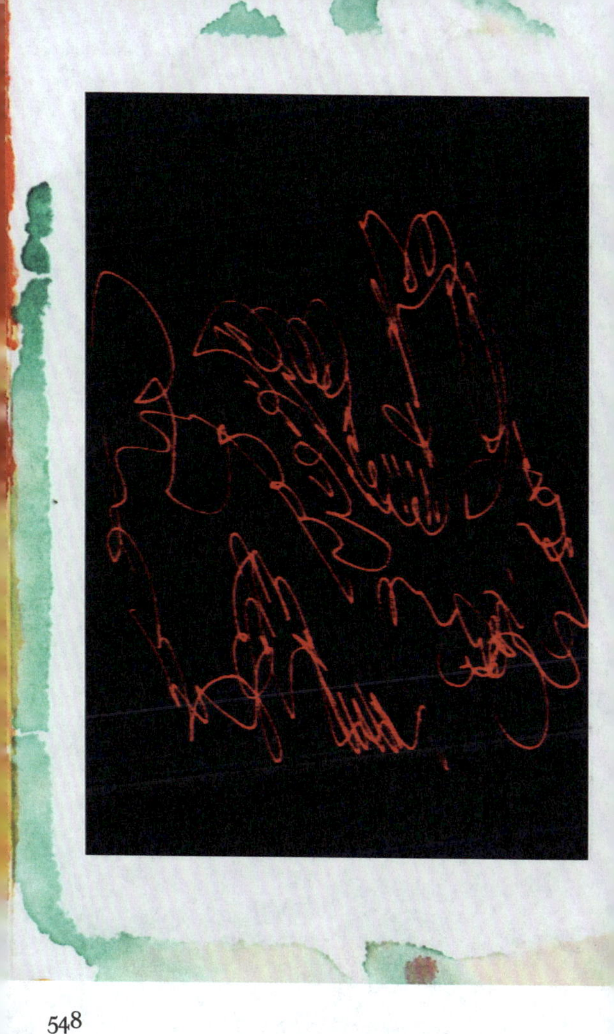

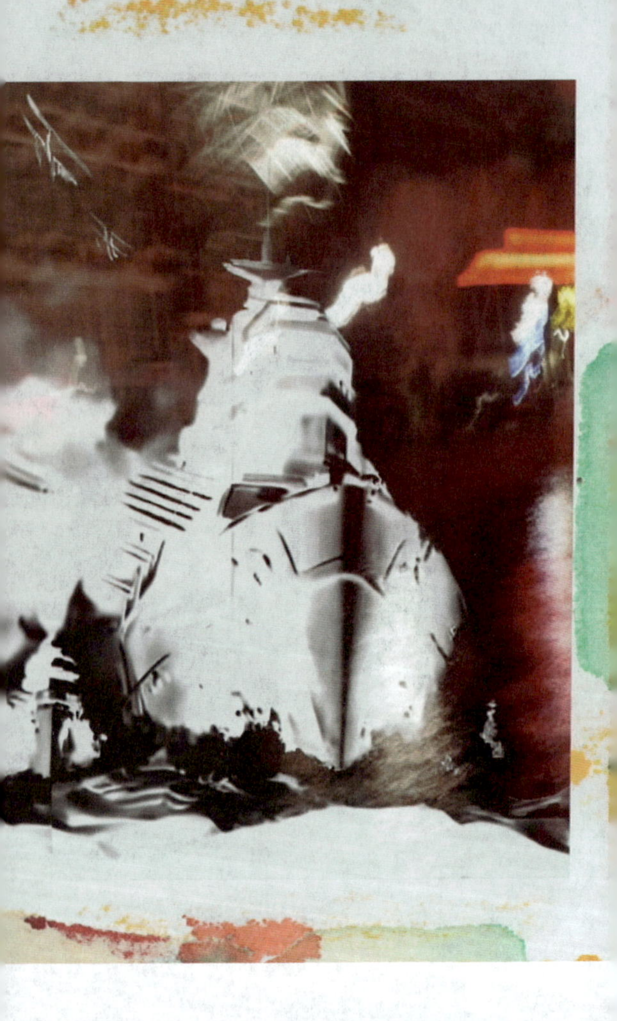

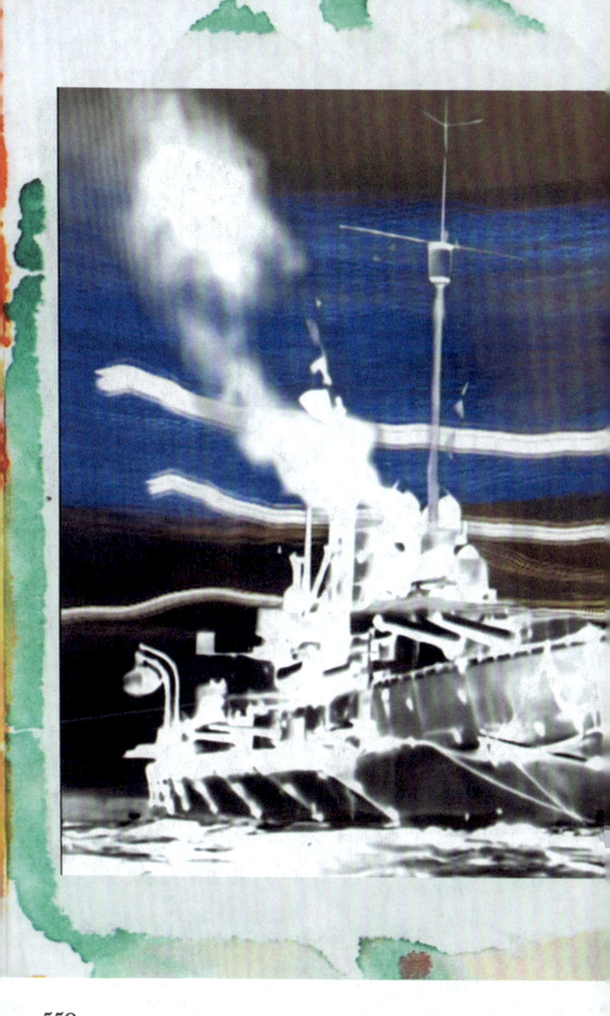

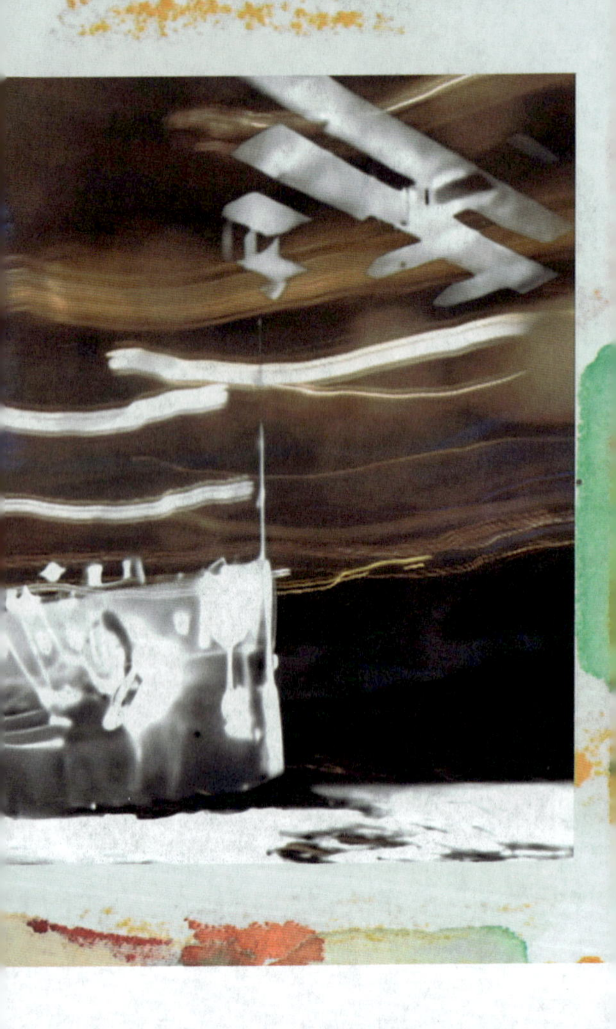

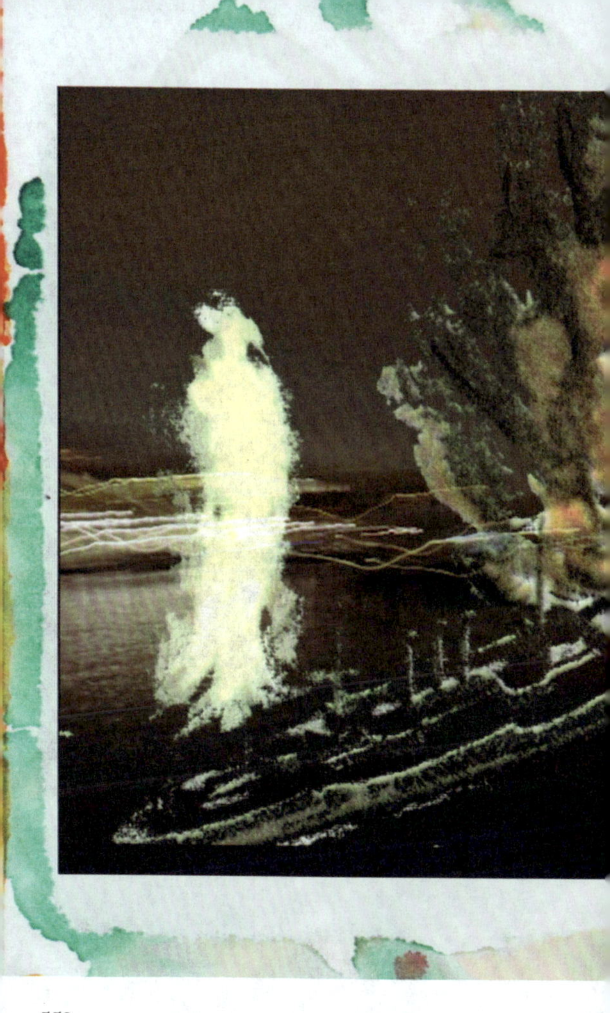

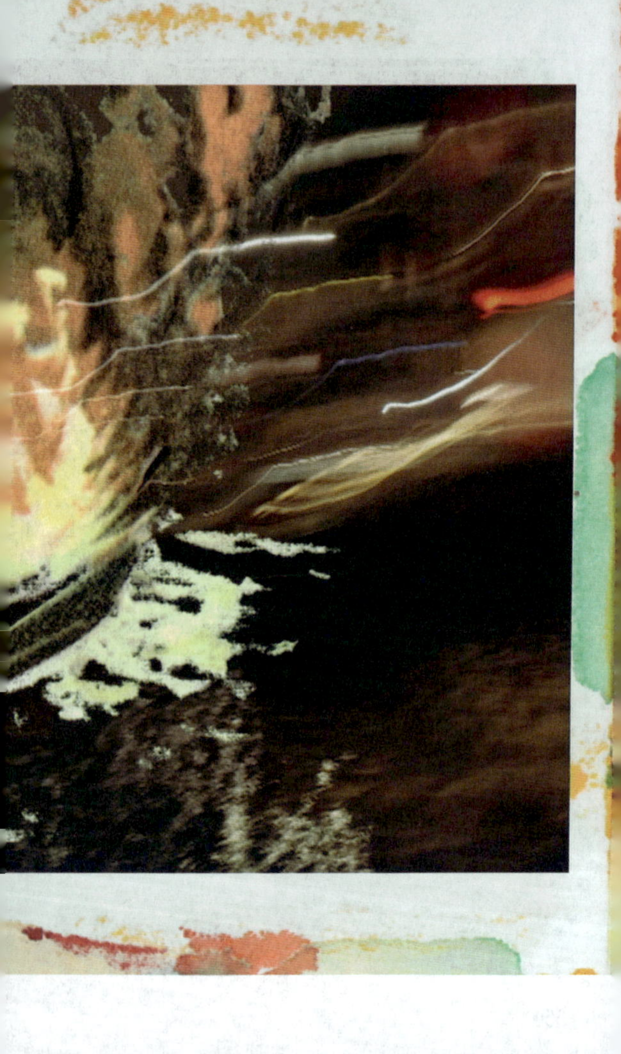

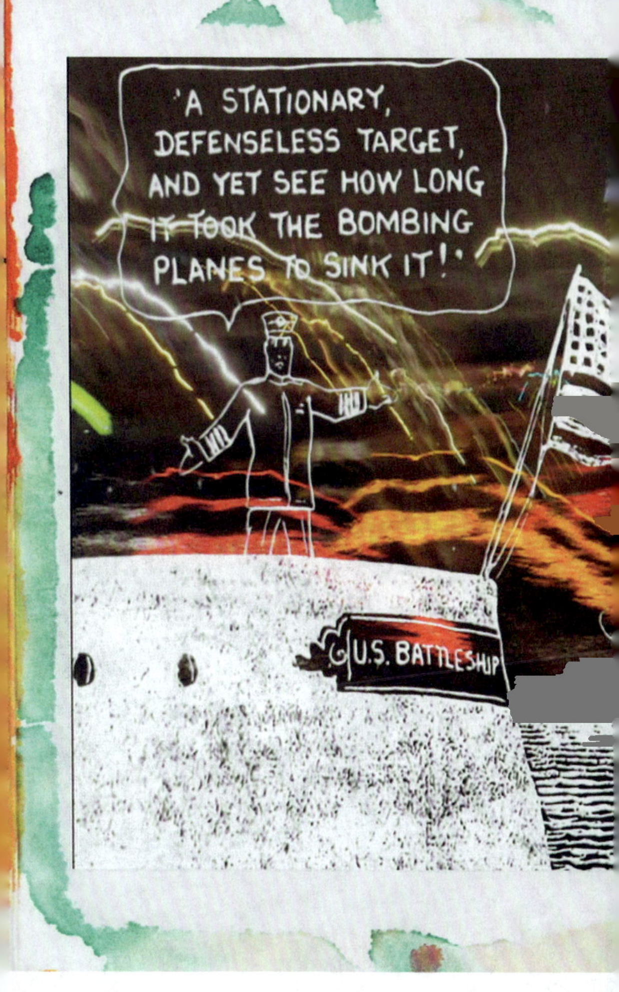
'A STATIONARY, DEFENSELESS TARGET, AND YET SEE HOW LONG IT TOOK THE BOMBING PLANES TO SINK IT!'
U.S. BATTLESHIP

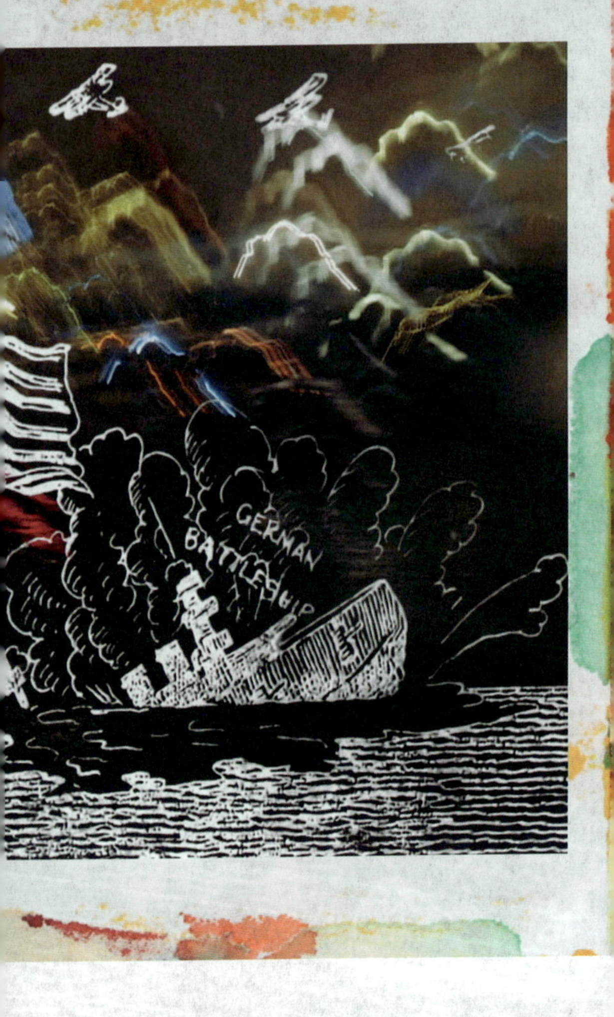
GERMAN
BATTLESHIP

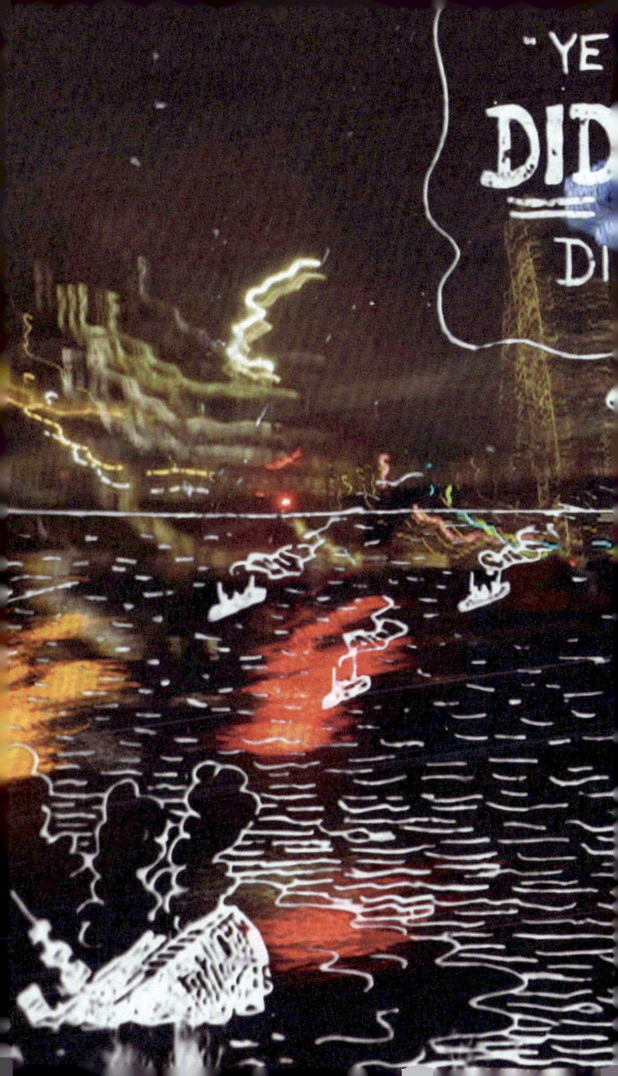

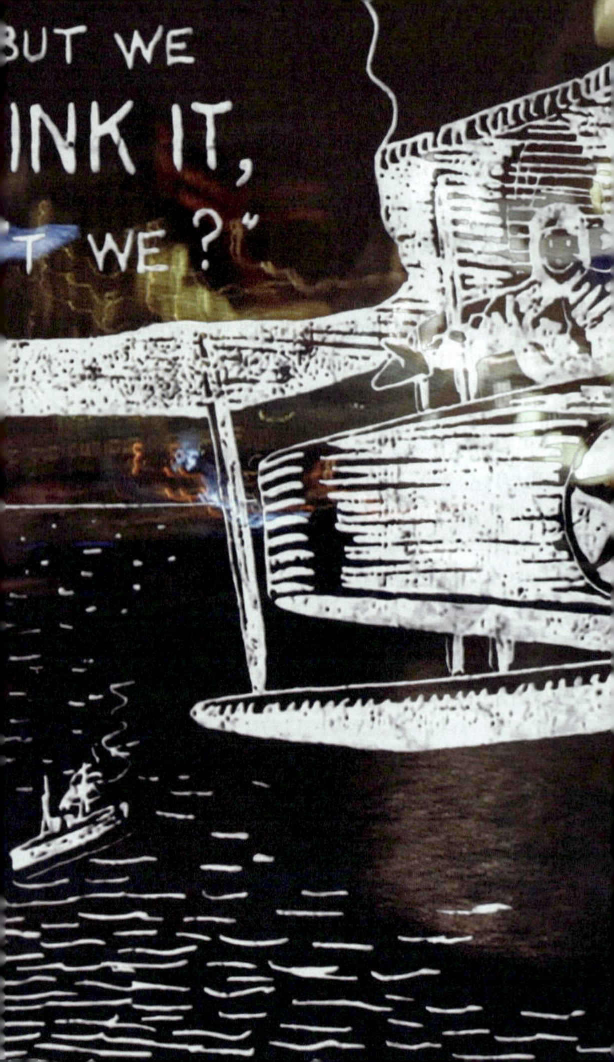
BUT WE
INK IT,
T WE?"

THE FLEET
HAS TO CARRY GRIEF

We still had no theory at all about what happened. Our pride spoke against the enemy hitting us, our *Moskva*, our flagship, in such a blatant way. Moreover, the chains of command were broken. The orders in circulation contradicted each other. In their sudden, omnidirectional mass, they formed BALLS AND KNOTS. They had to be unrolled, reinstalled, and there were no addressees for the majority of the orders.

Tugs were now approaching. In addition, three corvettes pressed against the side of the ship facing the storm, which had intensified powerfully. This causality was visibly unrelated to the catastrophe, but it fuelled the imbalances as immeasurably as the original catastrophe had. These kinds of northern storms on the Black Sea are treacherous. Unlike in the Mediterranean —in my estimation as a naval officer at least— they carve deep hollows into the masses of water that then come crashing down onto the seagoing vessels LIKE SOLID OIL. If the vessels are intact, the "drifting mountains" merely throw them off course, pushing them around over the surface of the sea. A wrecked ship, however, will be smashed and crushed by these towers of water and—in the depths of the notches or valleys too—by the mechanical forces as if they were being worked by iron-processing machines or the steam hammers of a scrap-metal recycling plant.

We thought we could take our ship to a port and repair it there. Until late at night, we assumed—with the remnants of our pride—that we'd get this expensive wreck so dear to our hearts home. The tugboats only made headway meter by meter. The accompanying corvettes, which couldn't effectively fight the storm as they were exposed to it themselves, however, offered comfort.

Ultimately, it was the lasting power of the sea against our lurching, storm-tossed ship, battering our hawsers to the tugs, that brought the end like a ram. We were still puzzling over the cause of the accident. Grief slowed every reaction. We were exhausted. But even had we been perfectly awake, we could not have prevented our *Moskva* from sinking into the depths. The word "depth," referring to the structure of the Black Sea, is not a dimension that can be measured in meters. It has to do with different levels. Down to the very bottom, we're talking about heavily salted seawater. Then, there in the deep floor of this strangely ancient sea, is the original freshwater lake, in whose dark waters (hence the name Black Sea) there is no life. We assume that our ship hit the bottom with its torn parts sometime late at night. We've got to ensure that no enemy intelligence services can reach the sunken ship with special submarines. Therefore, we're guarding the sea and the site with special electronic equipment. The ship is a whole treasure chest of secrets. How exciting it must be to approach the wreck as an

enemy and to bring its trove of electronic experience to the surface! Year after year, refinement after refinement, our naval command built up the ship. It's a veritable inventory sheet of our modernity. I don't know if the enemy—essentially, the USA—would have been able to launch an underwater operation quickly enough. And I also think their divers would've been disappointed. Thanks to the explosion, it would have been impossible to extract any information from the chaotic and randomly jumbled collection of metal, plastic, and steel components, and the equipment jammed inside them, above water or below.
I imagine—with a mixture of pleasure, sadness, and pride—the spies slitting open their diving armor in the narrow remnants of the ship, riddled with sharp cracks, and then dying themselves in the putrid groundwater.

All the same, at this point—the entire Russian fleet had gathered around the spot of the sinking in a kind of funeral procession—nothing larger than a mouse would've been able to wriggle through to the site of our *Moskva*'s grave. By now, all our weapons are on alert, which they hadn't been at the time of the catastrophe. In the meanwhile, we cannot rule out enemy activity. Neptune rockets must have ripped open our flagship's belly. And yet, everything we feel—stable, counterfactual—denies this possibility.

Underwater drones (which we also possess) are the size of a wolf, a large fur-bearing animal, or a

young deer. Not the size of a mouse. They're good for inspecting wrecks. In modern warfare, we're beset by dangers the students at our naval warfare schools had no idea about ten years ago. For our most beautiful ships the rule is: in the event of war, hide! This valuable and intelligent PORCELAIN OF WAR is too good to be destroyed as quickly as it has been recently.

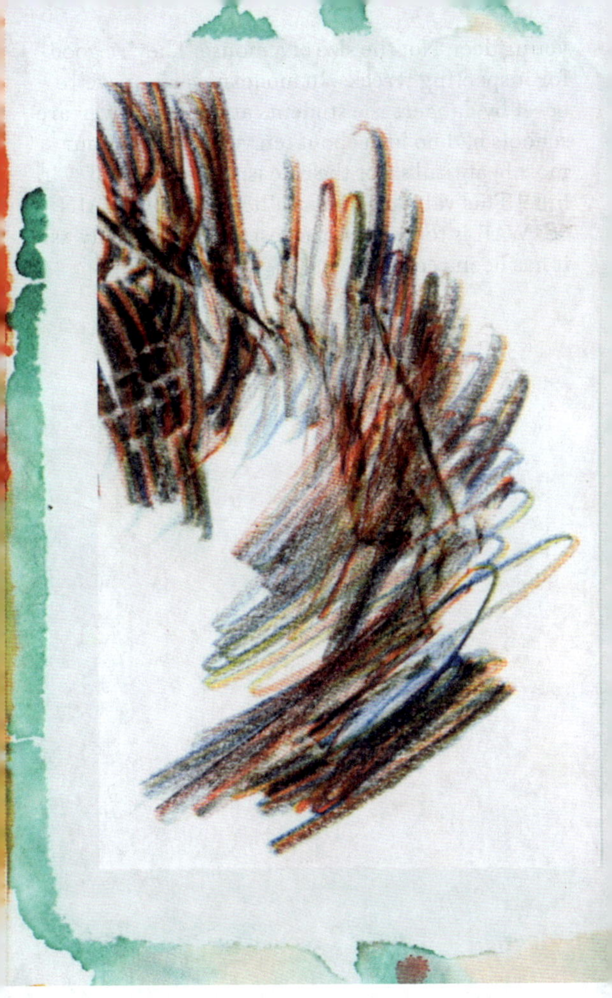

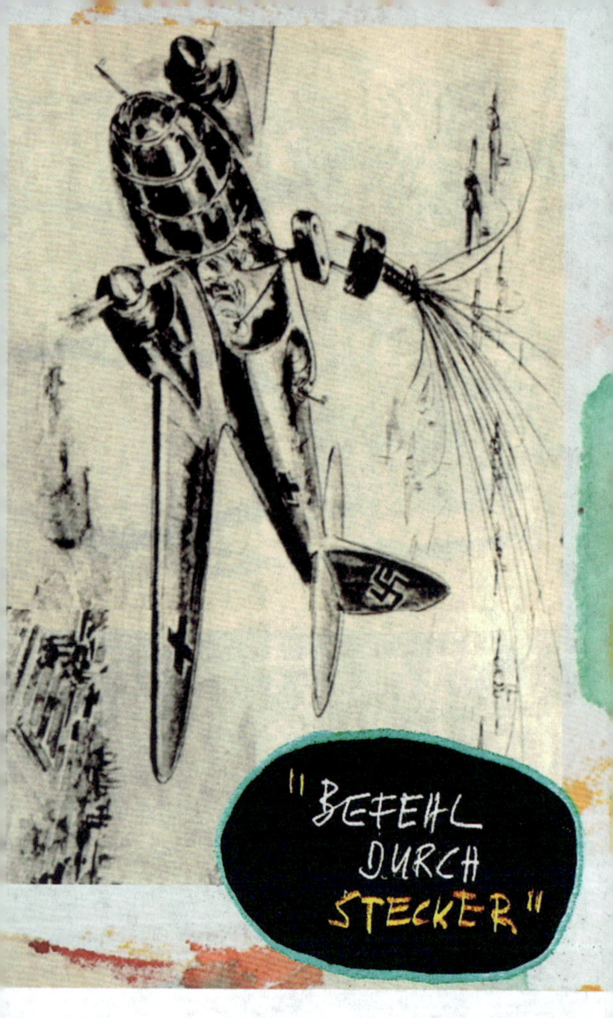
"BEFEHL
DURCH
STECKER"

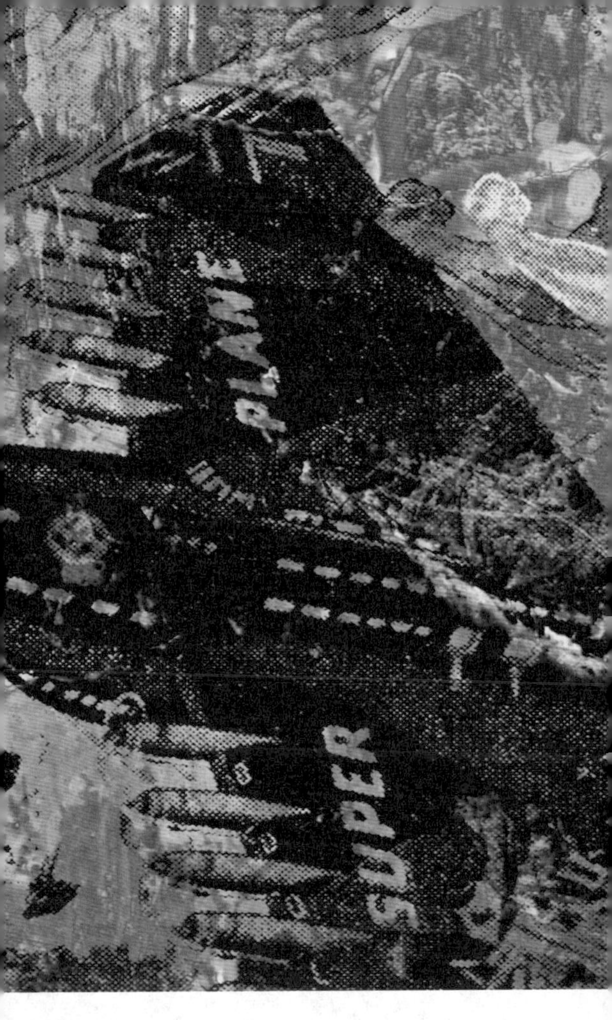
PLANE
SUPER

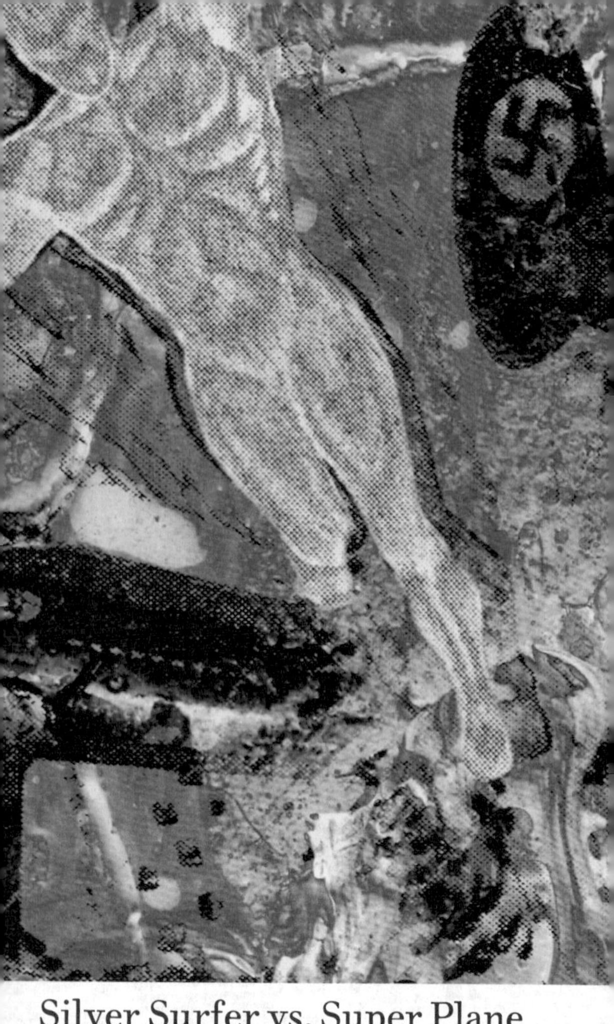

Silver Surfer vs. Super Plane

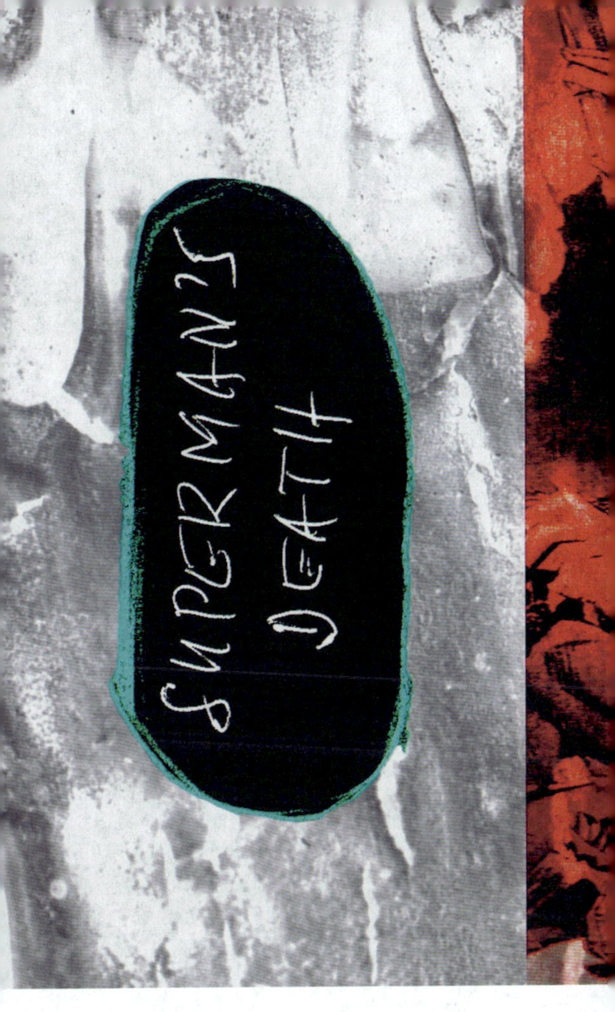
SUPERMAN'S
DEATH

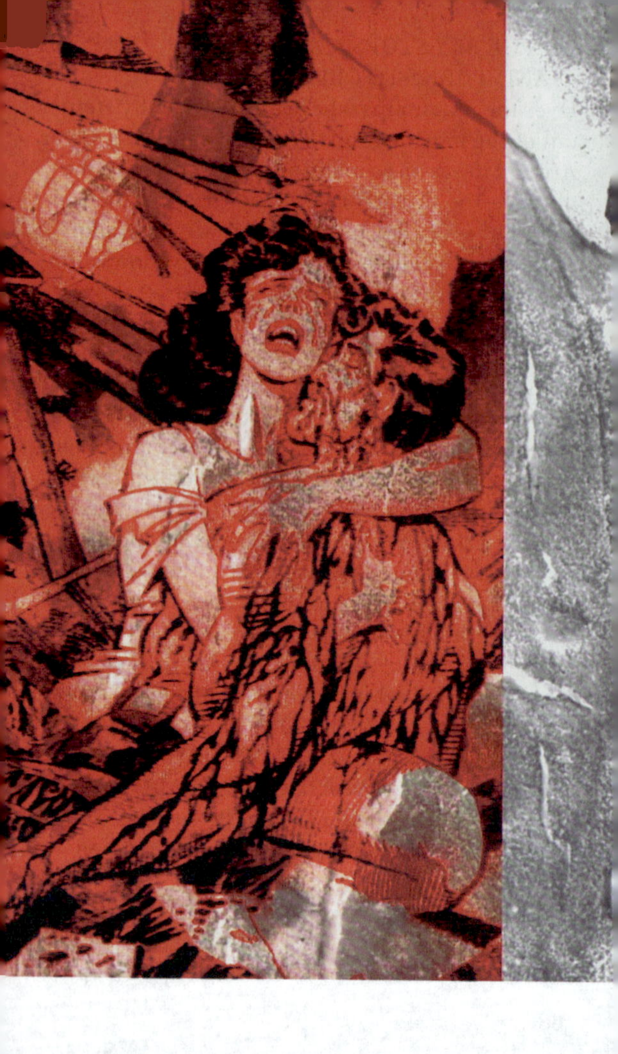

“THE SKY STOPS PAINTING AND TURNS TO CRITICISM”

Over the mountains where the sun usually steps out of the morning mist: a row of sparkling silver. Around it—as on so many other days at this time of year—the sky, according to witnesses, changed color but every day in a different way: the color of gooseberry, perfectly blue, flannel-yellow, shimmering red, the color of angels, hysteria-white, pink-melange. And always the echo on the opposite horizon, to the west. Still in darkness, responding to the splashes of light from the east.

The abundance of color destroyed the still tiny artifacts, the engine noise of which preceded their appearance in heights. Dots. And yet their sound (“the trumpets”), namely, the anticipation, attracted the viewers’ attention all the same.

Twenty minutes later the town was destroyed. Though it required six or eight such attacks to truly erase it—and then there are always still nests of human spirit, people trying to save themselves and set up anew. The airplanes’ attack, that impact of ARMED INDUSTRY, of ENGINEERING-CENTERED HEAVENLY POWER, contains a strong thrust of CRITICISM.

In the air-raid shelter the question: Where was the last diversion for me and my children when it comes to escaping the doom that will fall upon us from an altitude of two miles? Twenty years ago? Could I have escaped yesterday? Where? Knowledge of safe places is the beginning of philosophy.

This is how the CHANGING HEAVEN ABOVE criticizes the body, the senses, and the mind, and urgently calls for the Homo Novus, as last envisioned by the Biocosmists of the Russian revolution in 1917. Where, brothers, are you now in my hour of need? There was time enough to contact you, but I was busy. I have tried to count the crystal colors of the sky. The sky at dawn and dusk is a gifted painter in this part of the world. When I have enough time, I suck on the teats of the she-wolf to fill myself up with the miracle.

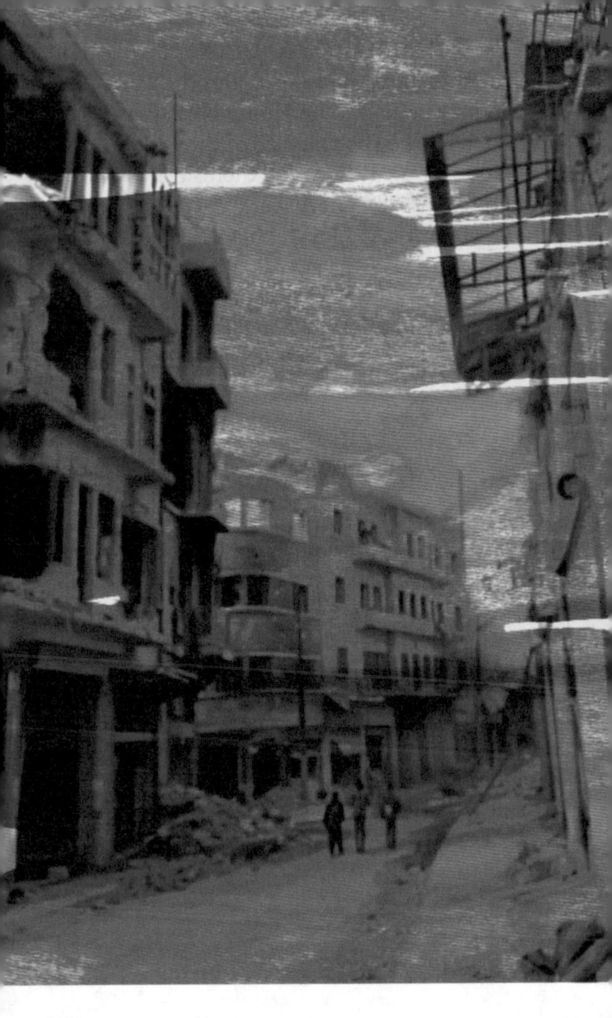

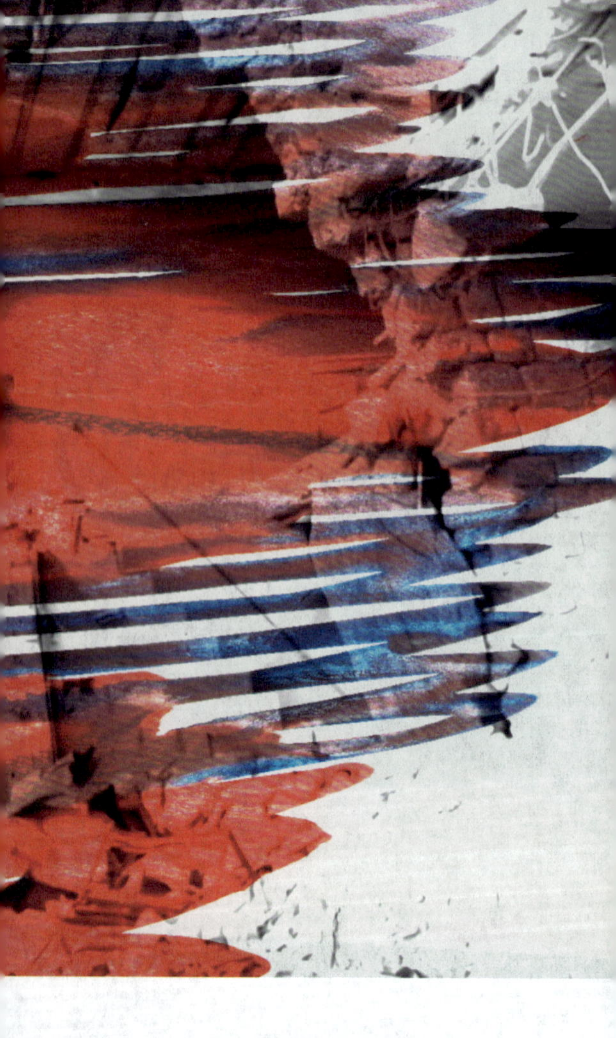

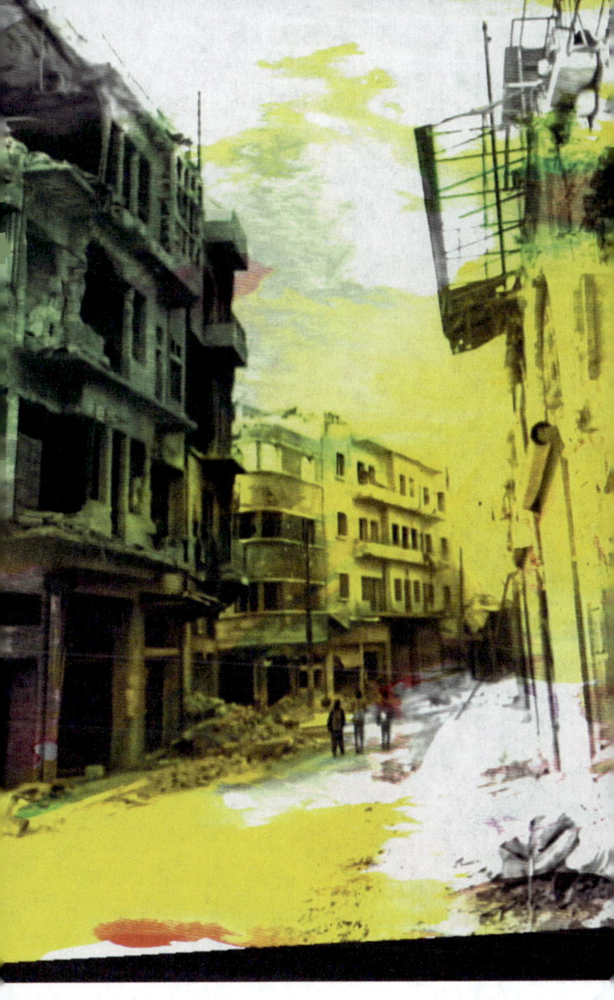

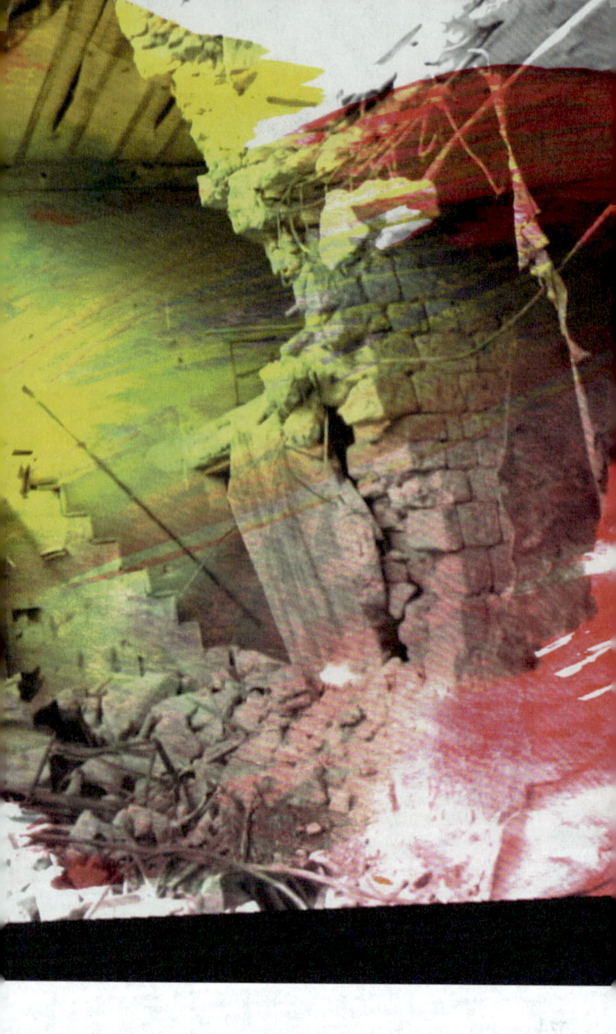

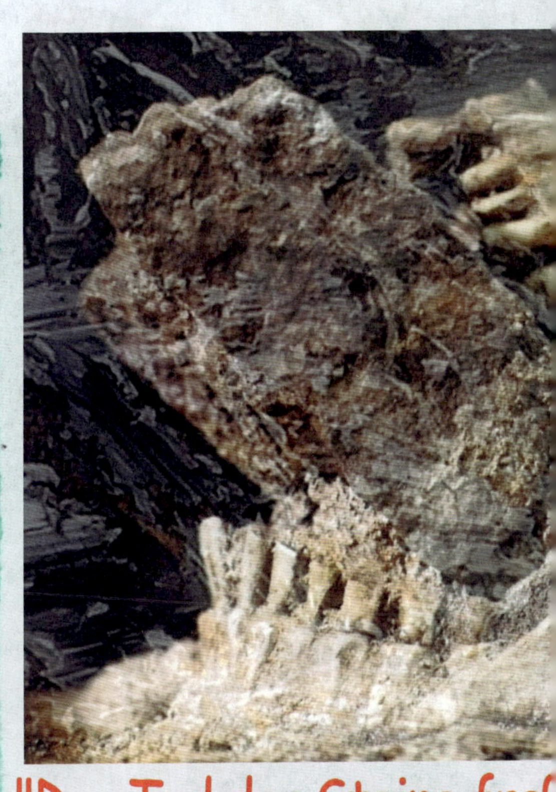

"Der Tod der Steine fraß

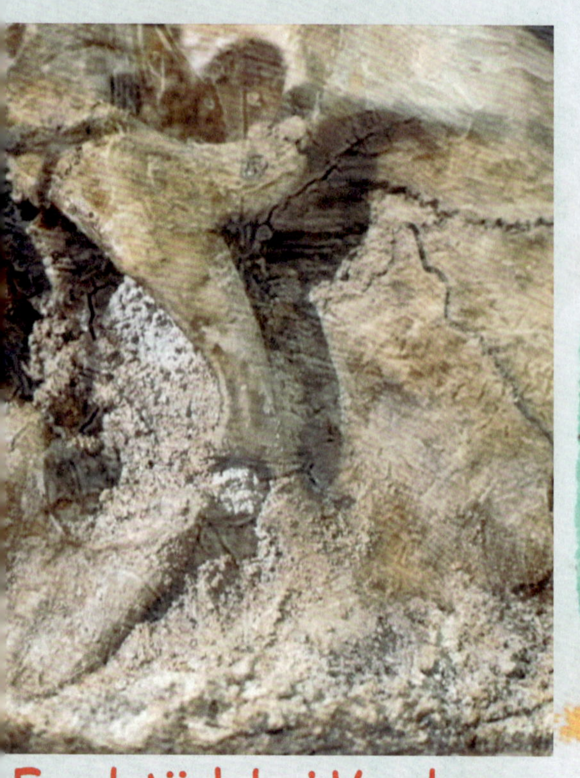

Fundstück bei Verdun

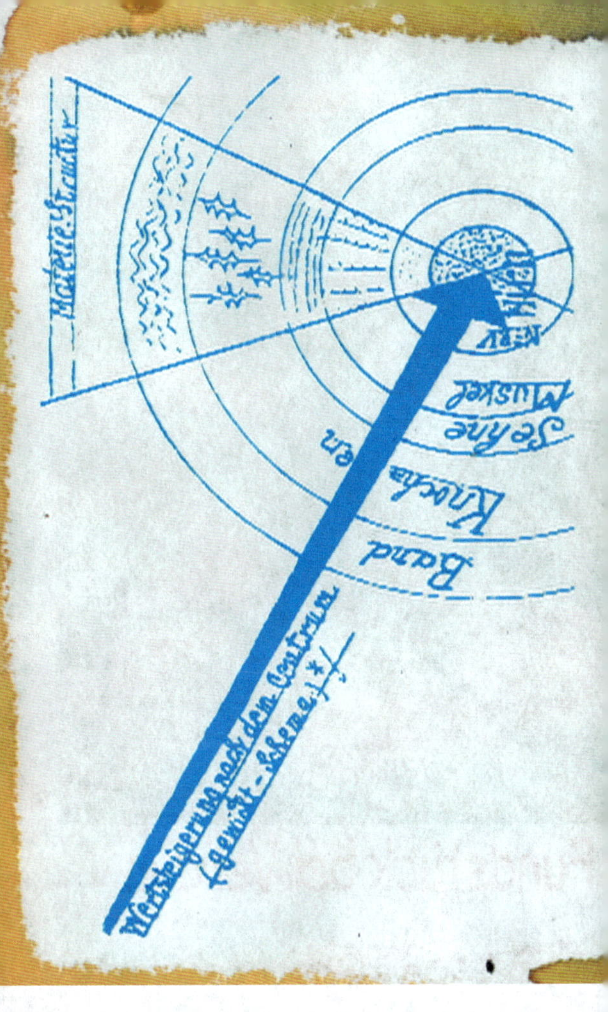
Materie Structur
Band
Knochen
Sehne
Muskel
Nerv
Wertsteigerung nach dem Centrum
(Gewicht-Scheme.) *

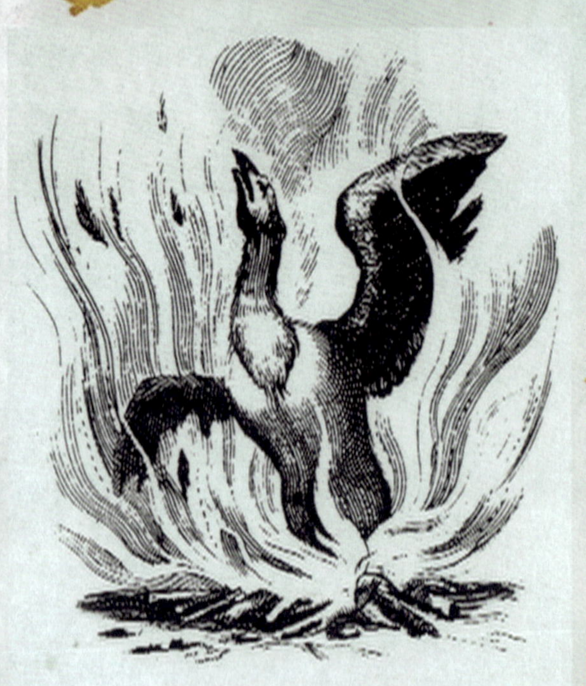

"Phönix
aus der Asche"

11

Heraldic Animals of the Enlightenment

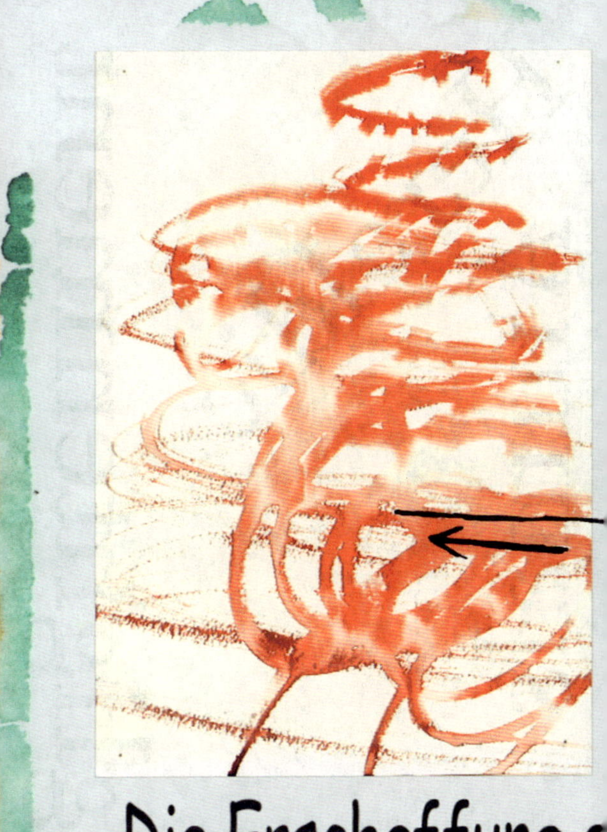

Die Erschaffung c

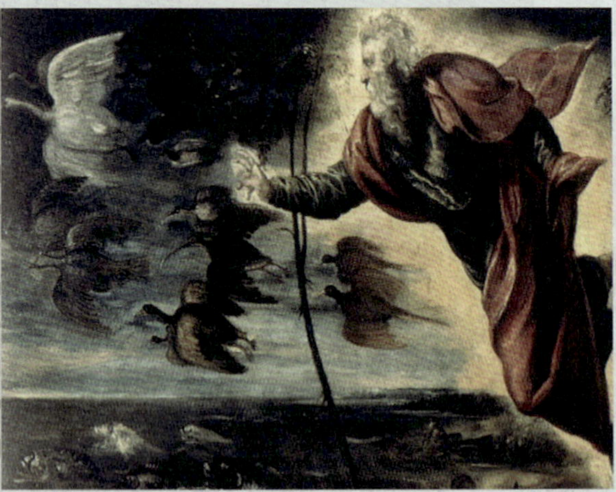

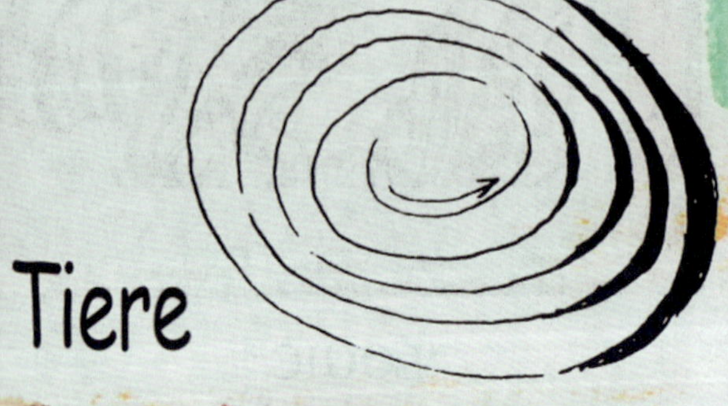
Tiere

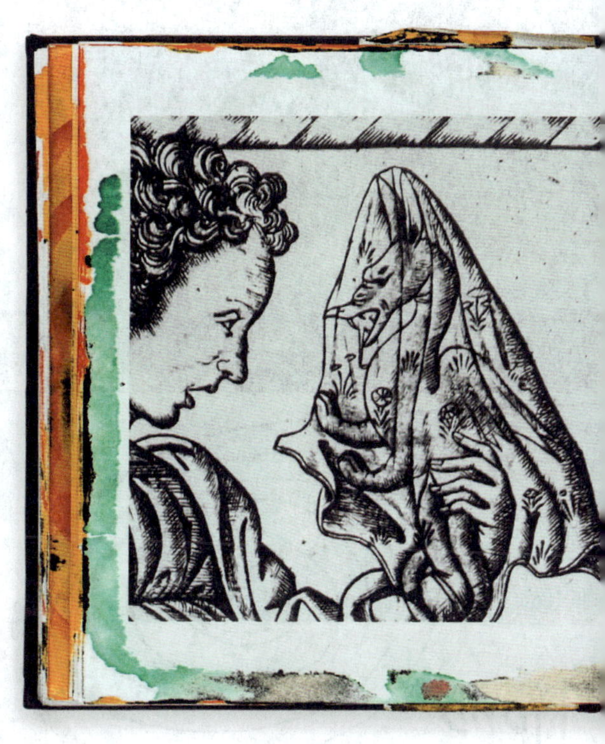

“LOGIC”

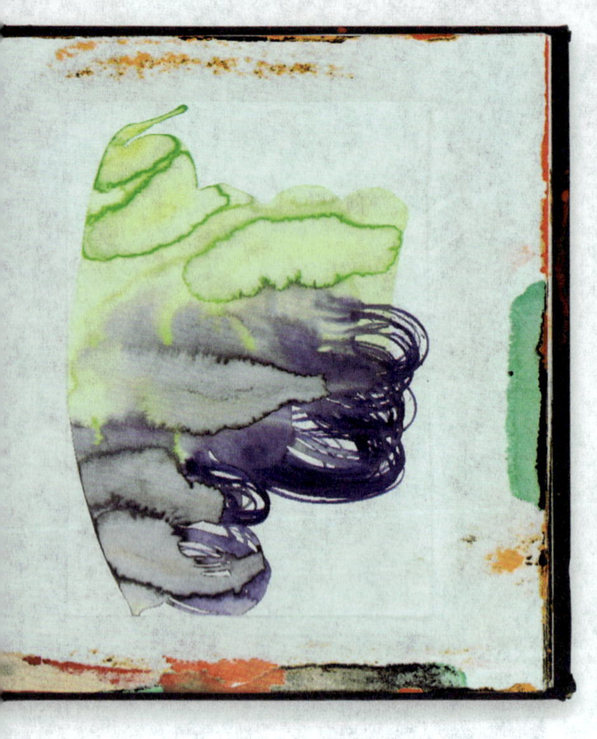

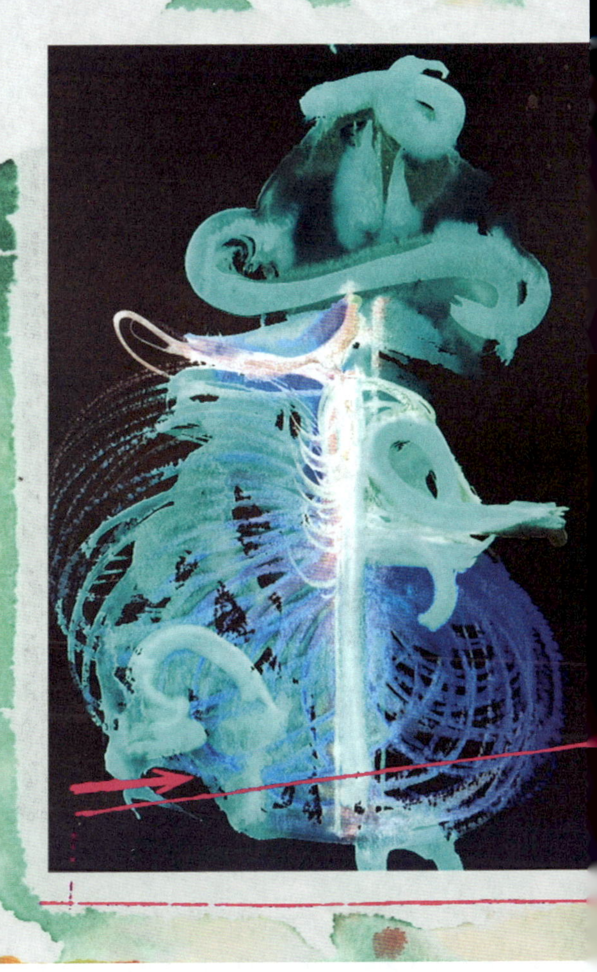

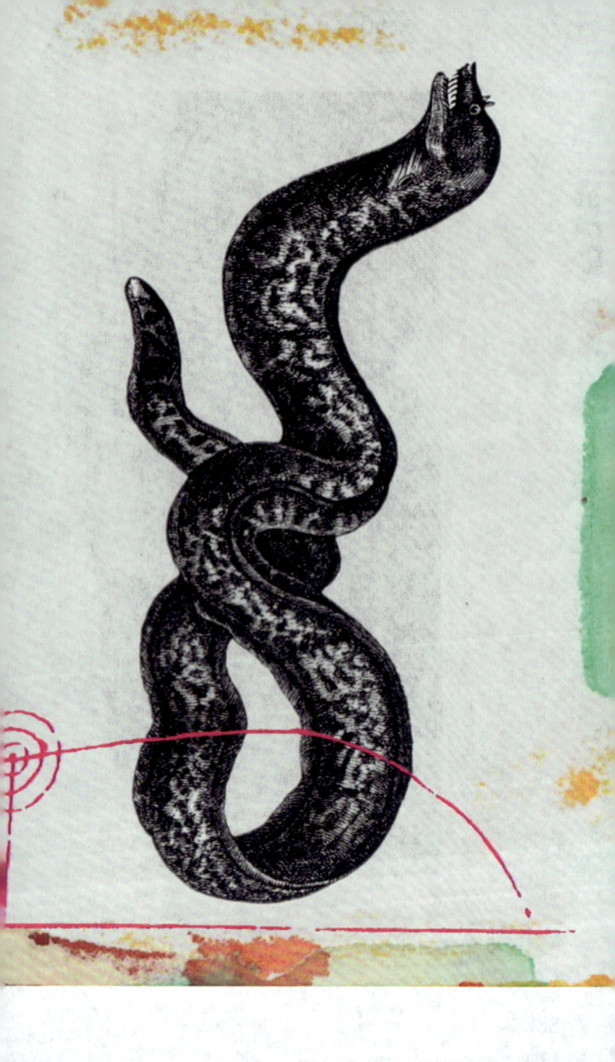

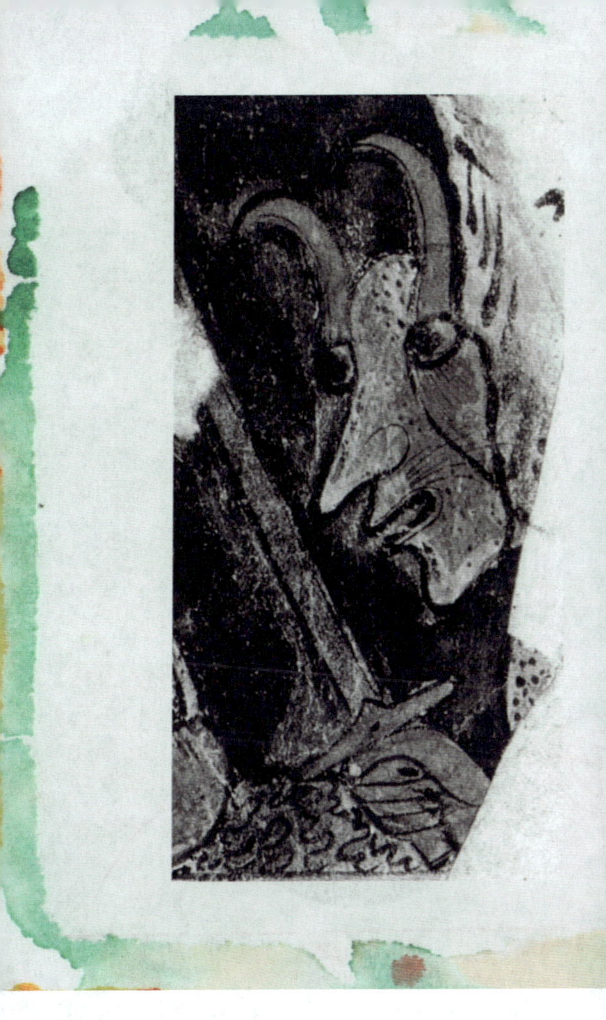

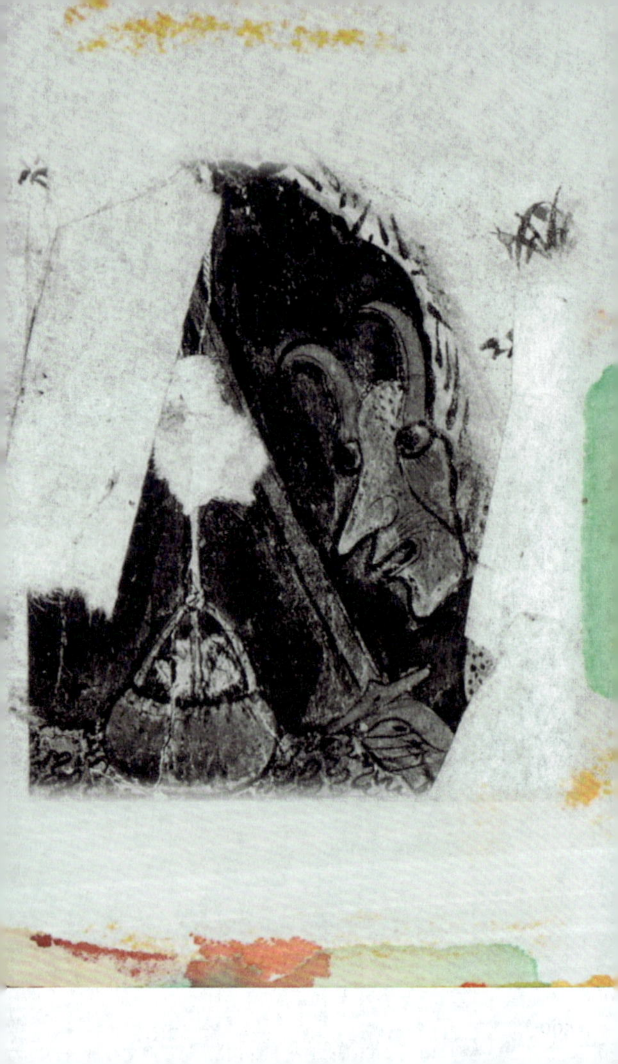

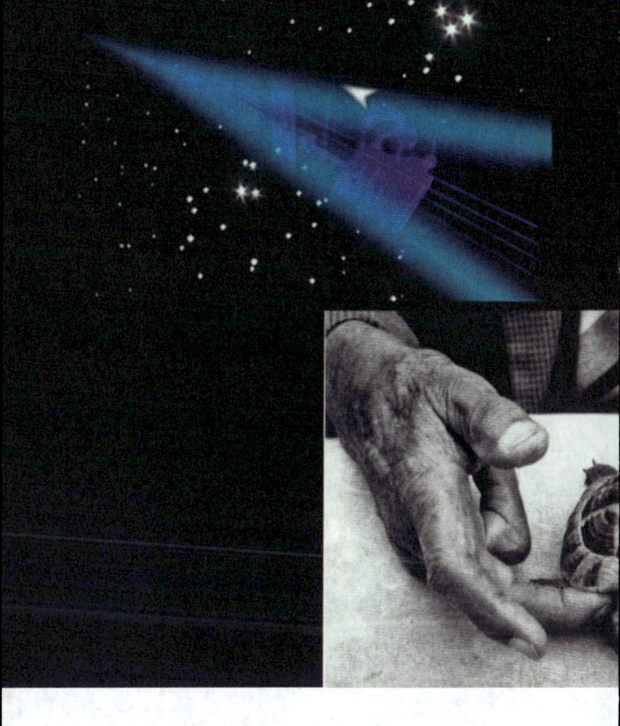

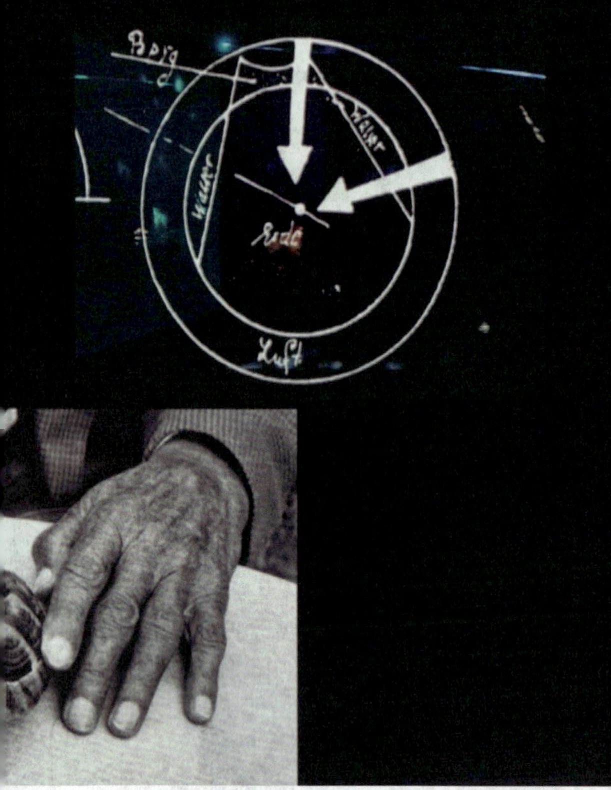

TURTLE WITH ERNST JÜNGER'S HANDS

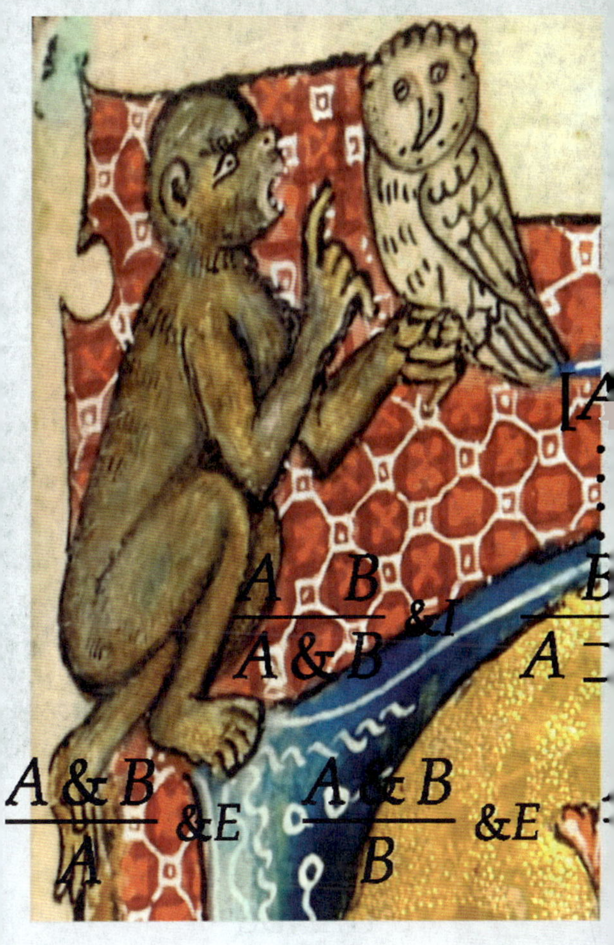
A B / A & B &I
A & B / A &E
A & B / B &E

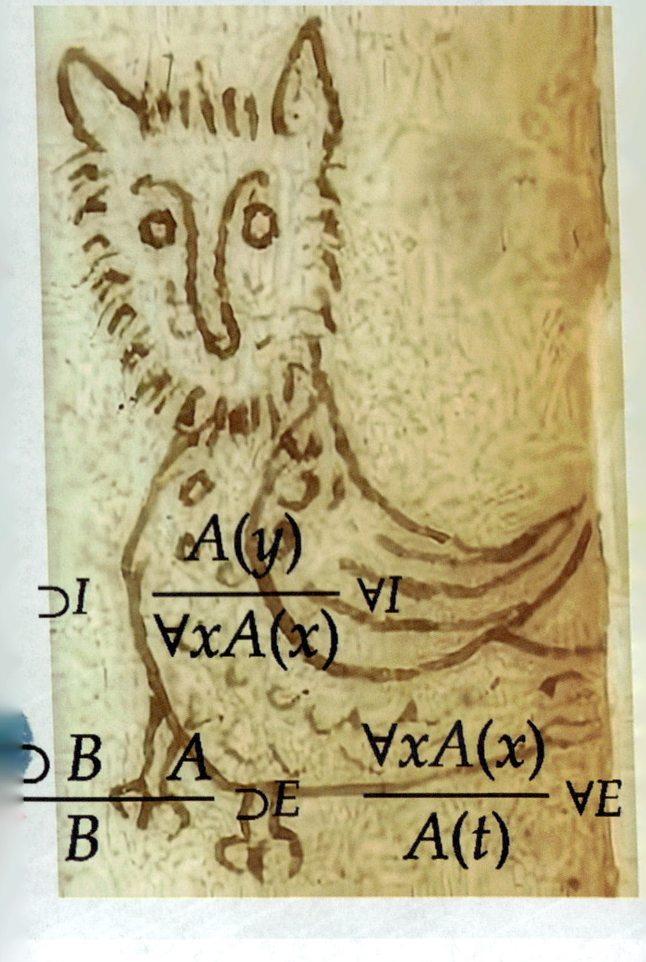

⊃I
A(y)
∀xA(x)
∀I
⊃B
A
B
⊃E
∀xA(x)
A(t)
∀E

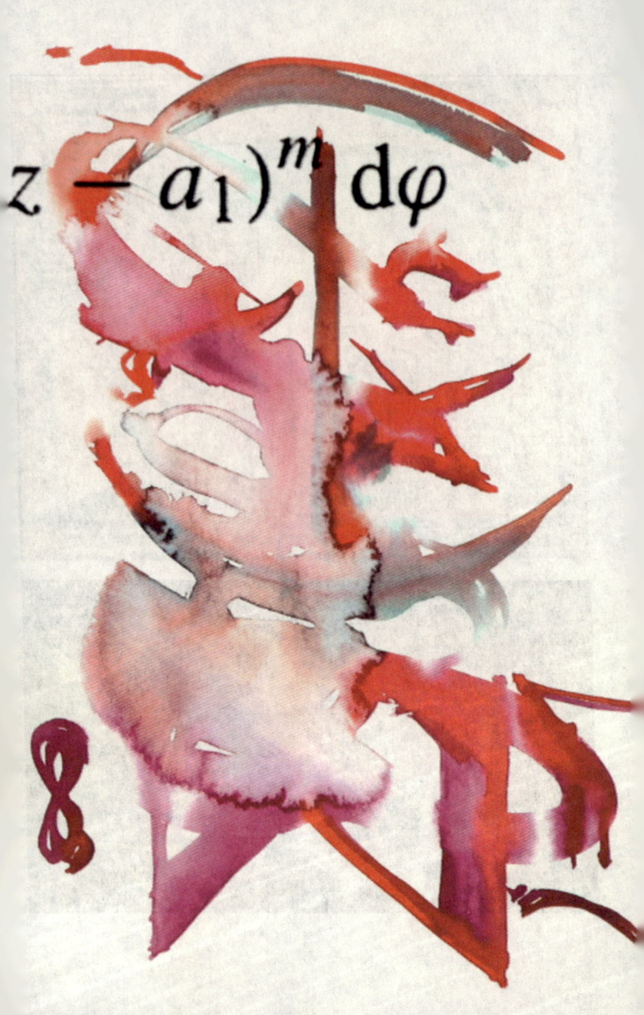
$z - a_1)^m \mathrm{d}\varphi$

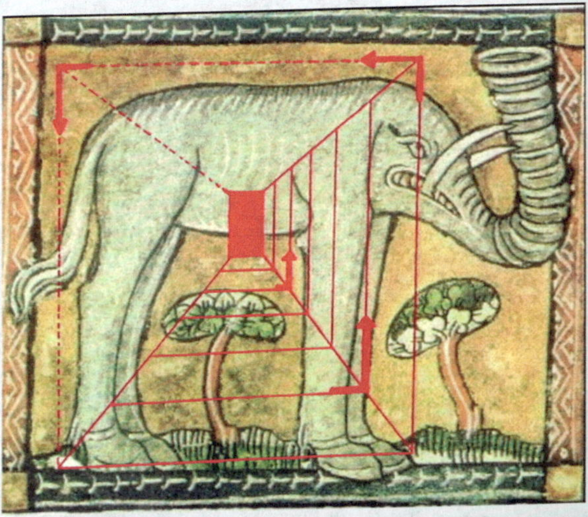

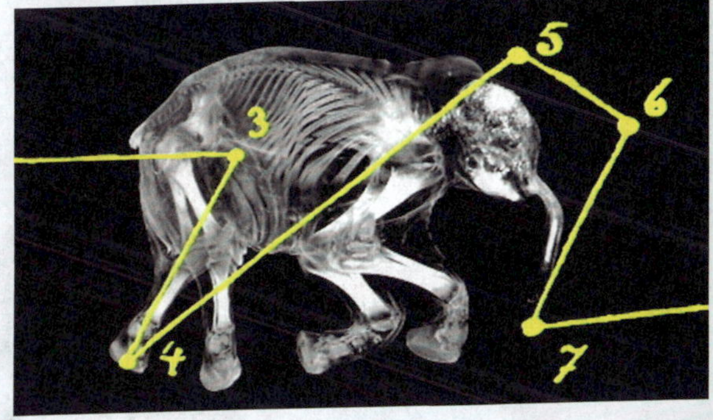
3
4
5
6
7

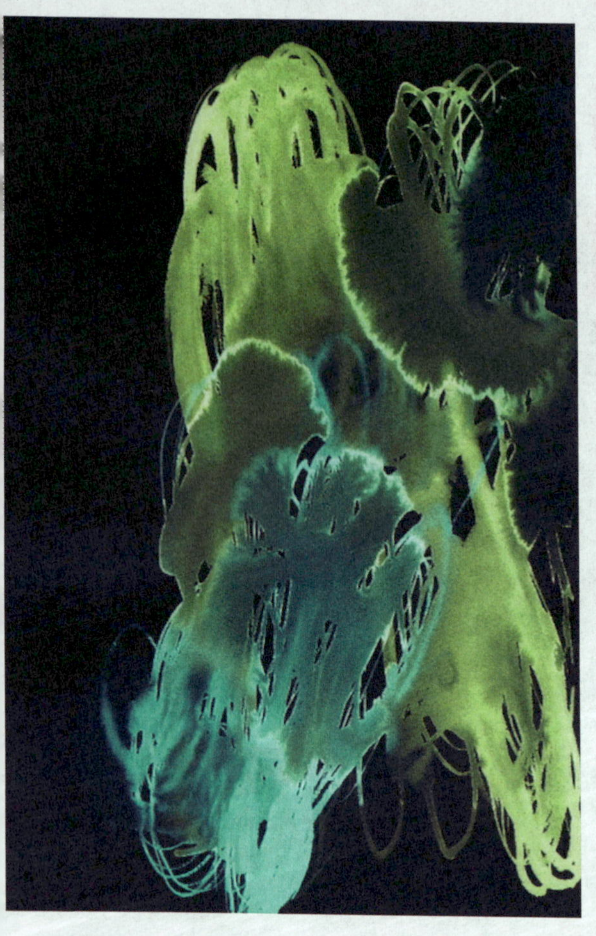

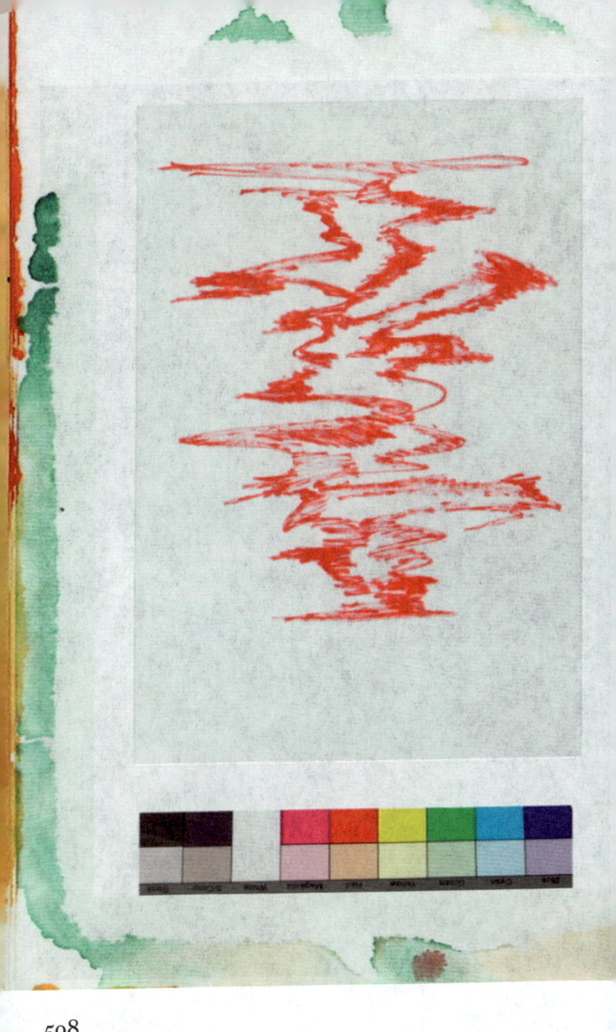

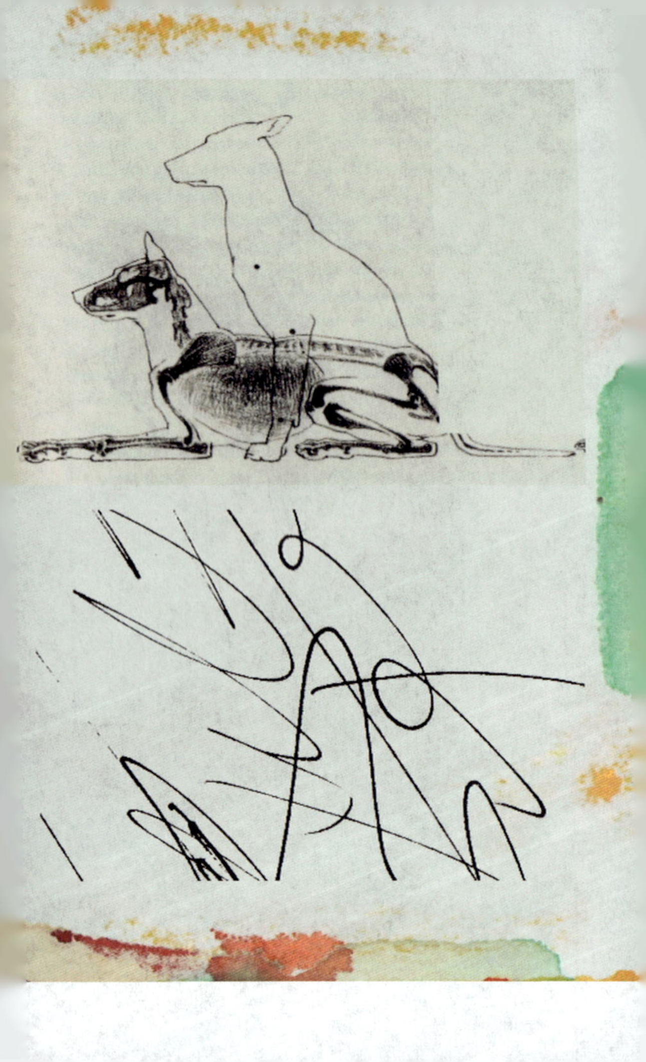

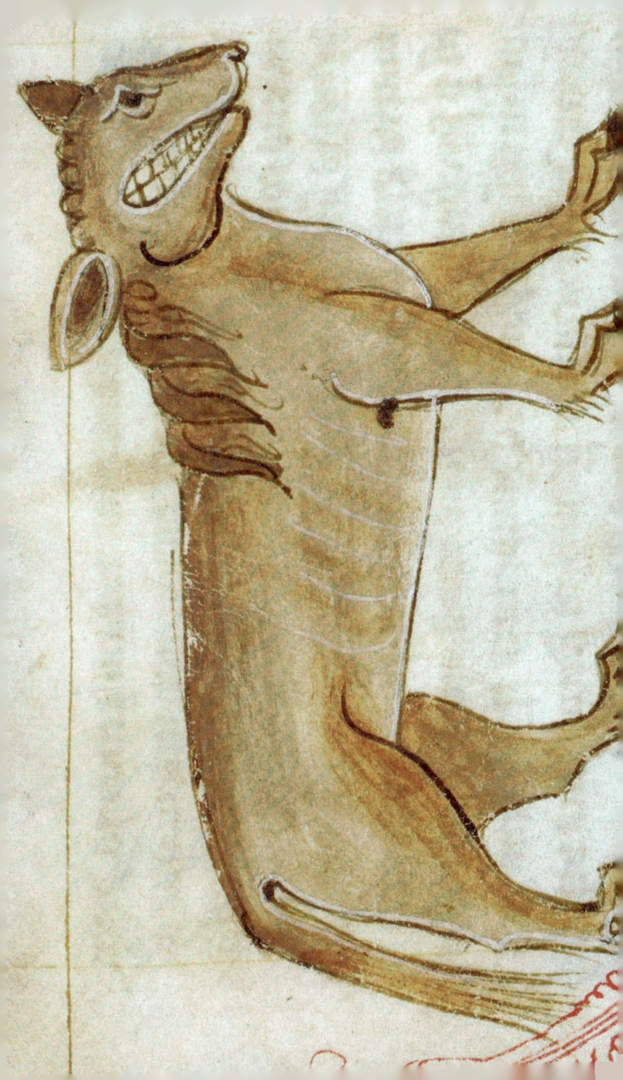

THE WOLF AS REASON'S HERALDIC ANIMAL. WOLVES DO NOT ENGAGE IN CIVIL WAR AMONG THEMSELVES

At one point during the Age of Enlightenment, when slaves from Africa worked the sugar plantations in Haiti and sugar was refined in complicated machines (supplied from Europe) before being shipped to England as a luxury item, a large bowl of sweet crystals was placed on a table in one of the salons of Edinburgh. The philosopher David Hume spent the afternoon circling this pleasure-bucket and never stopped shoving pieces of sugar into his mouth. Until the host, who also feared for the philosopher's insides, had the jar with the sweets removed, that is.

Separated from the coveted objects, Hume now began to formulate ideas. One man is not another man's wolf. He was refuting Thomas Hobbes's famous statement: *homo homini lupus*. Hume based his argument on a conversation he'd had a short time earlier with his friend Adam Smith on the subject. Humans are more cruel and much less sociable than wolves, Hume said. In general, humans differ from wolves in that they do not possess any consistency of character. Rather, humans' chances depend on the fact that people are always marked by two disparate qualities engaged in constant struggle. That is impossible for wolves. People (and no one interrupted

Hume, who was teaching with as much concentration as he had earlier given to eating sugar) have the GAZE OF IMPARTIAL OBSERVERS and—contrary to it—the penetrating impulse to EMPATHIZE WITH OTHERS. These are two "pincers of feeling" that the world is able to grasp. This is the apparatus of knowledge. This is also the foundation of the process in every WORKSHOP. Having observed the scholar somewhat disrespectfully as a dabbler until just then, those present were now pleased by his remarks and happily watched him as he engaged in his "work of thought," in which he moved farther and farther away from one thing in order to approach it all the more intimately.

Among the salon's guests there were slave traders, physicists, and inventors. As far as their daily praxis was concerned, Hume's insights were of no consequence. And yet it was clear that the MOVEMENT OF INSIGHT in and of itself was something they were happy to observe and from which they hoped to nibble. All of them considered themselves part of the PRODUCTIVE CLASS. Property owners were absent from this meeting. The longer the evening went on, the more a flood of opening doors, an exodus of spaces, seemed to become visible. The hunk of sugar's long journey from Haiti, where sugarcane was harvested with sweat, was not what moved the assembled guests. They neither behaved as impartial observers nor with empathy.

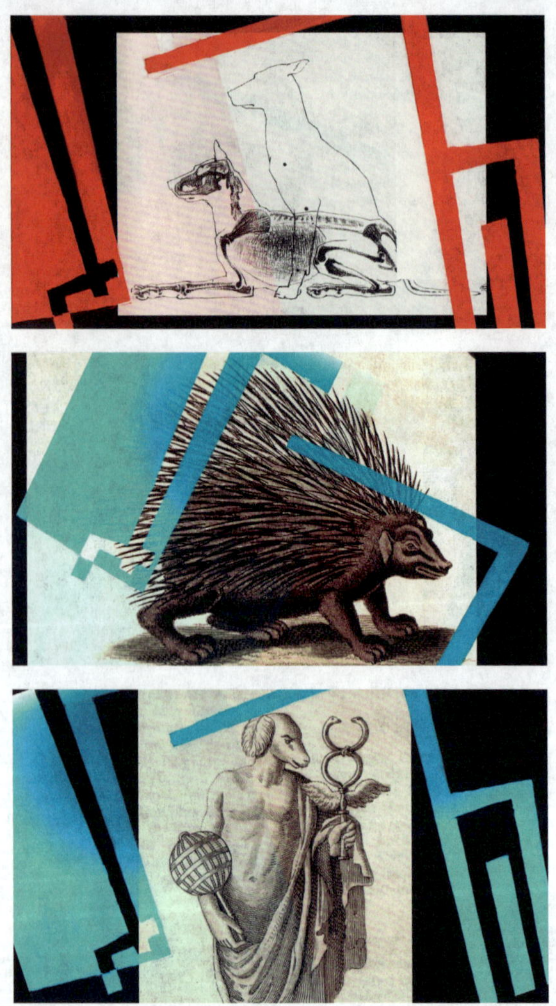

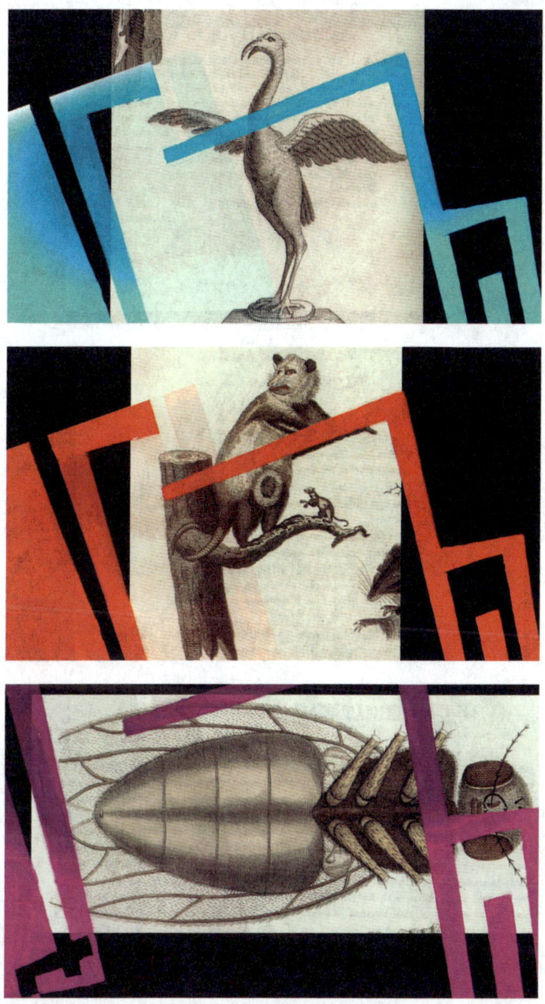

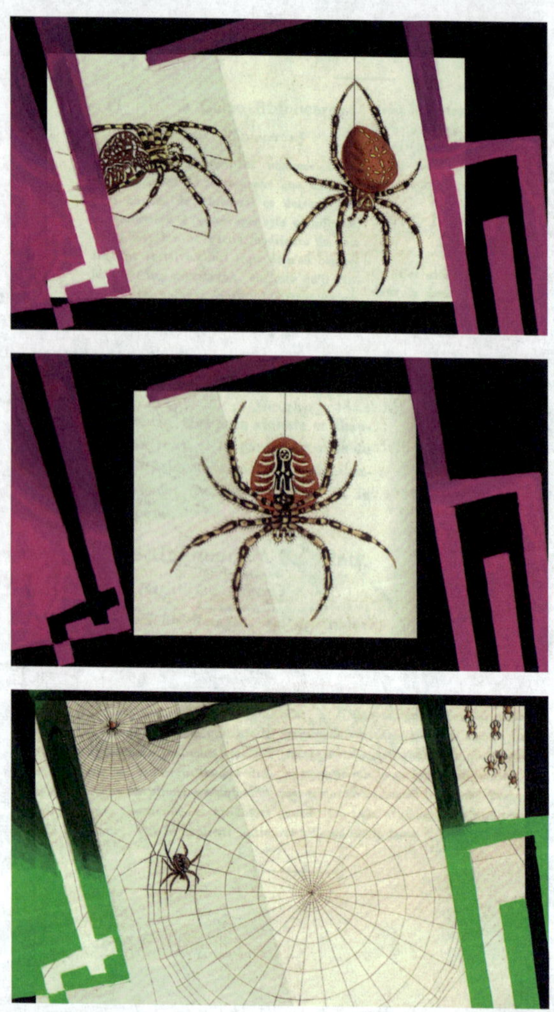

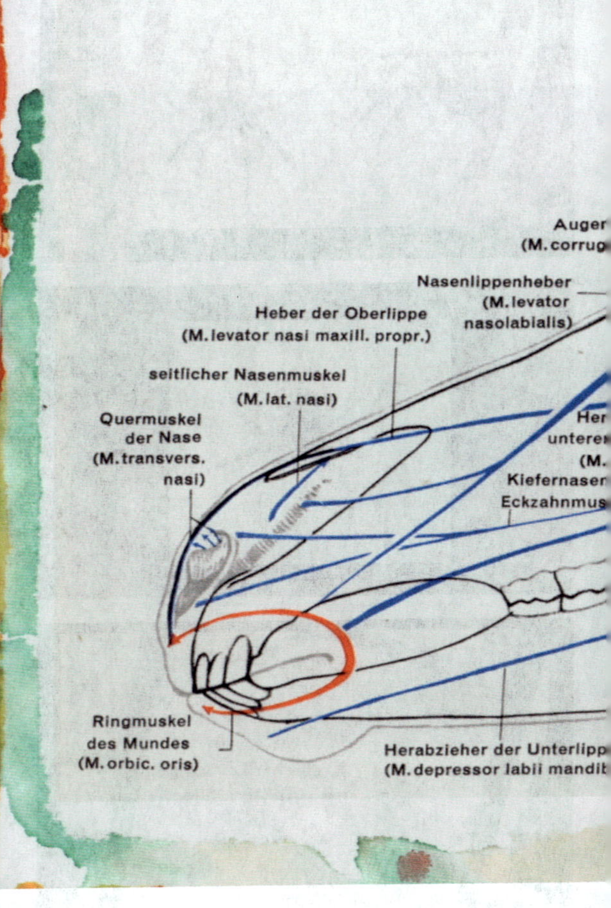

Nasenlippenheber
(M. levator
nasolabialis)
Heber der Oberlippe
(M. levator nasi maxill. propr.)
seitlicher Nasenmuskel
(M. lat. nasi)
Quermuskel
der Nase
(M. transvers.
nasi)
Ringmuskel
des Mundes
(M. orbic. oris)

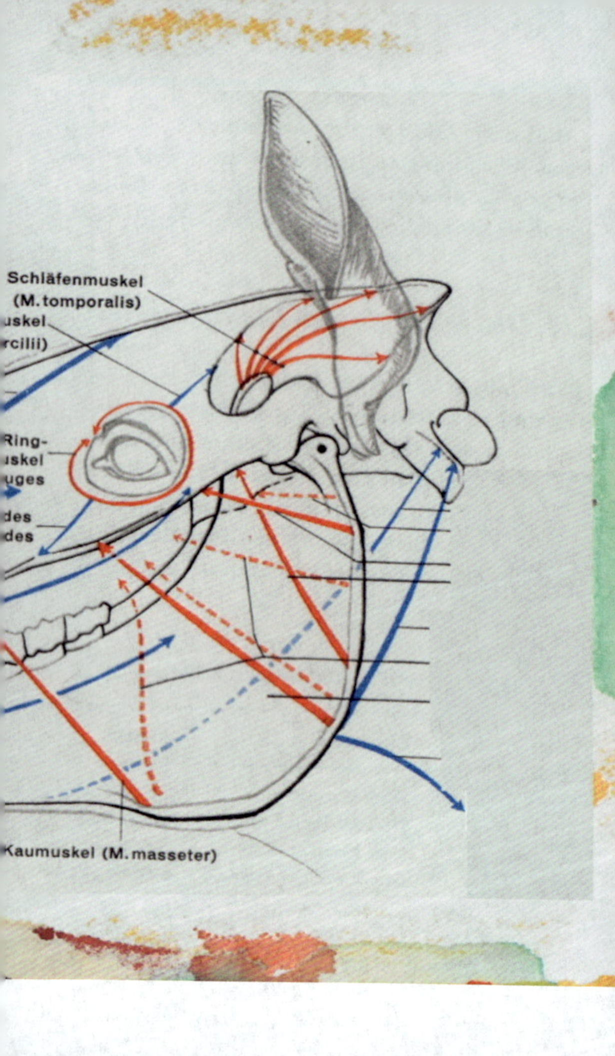
Schläfenmuskel
(M. tomporalis)
Kaumuskel (M. masseter)

Die Phantasie als Pferd*

The imagination is an animal that can take flight like a horse /

It is a POLITICAL ANIMAL /

It possesses countless sources, even ones with sparse and barren vaults. Fountains spring forth that destroy everything in its vicinity /

The most important manufacturing plant for the imagination, according to Theodor W. Adorno, is sorrow /

I have to disagree with him /

I know of fantasies set in motion because of indulgence and elation /

Such an imagination competes with those that serve in self-defence /

"In pointed brackets the burned words"

* Heiner Müller, "Mommsen's Block," in *Heiner Müller Reader*, ed. and trans. Carl Weber (Baltimore: Johns Hopkins University Press, 2001), 122–29. [Trans.].

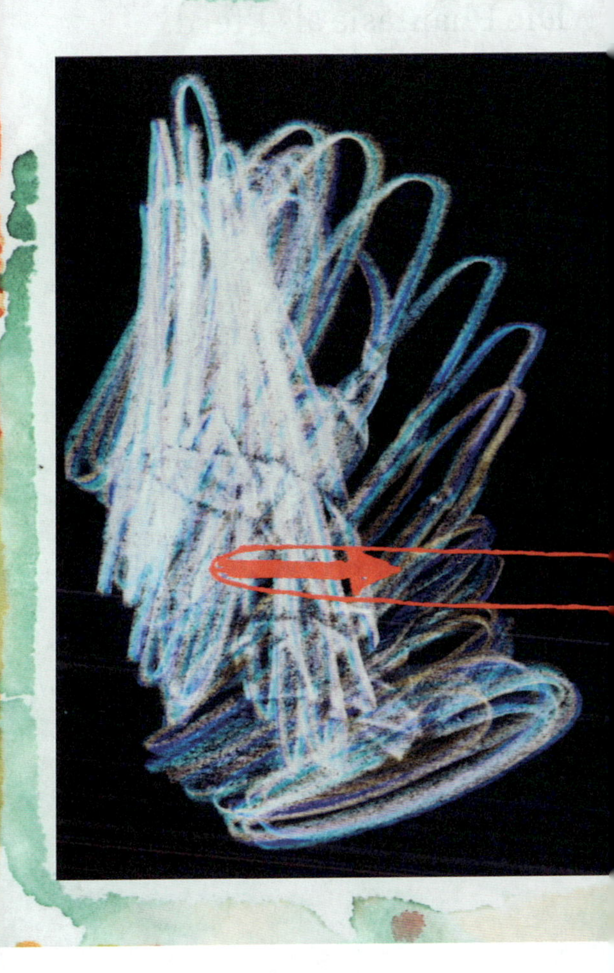

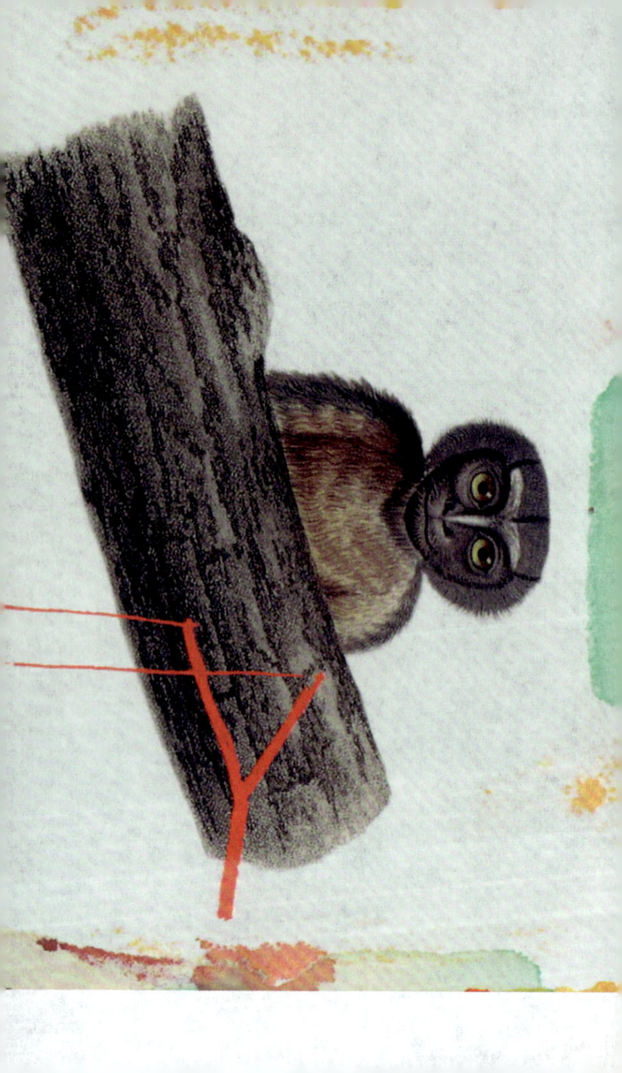

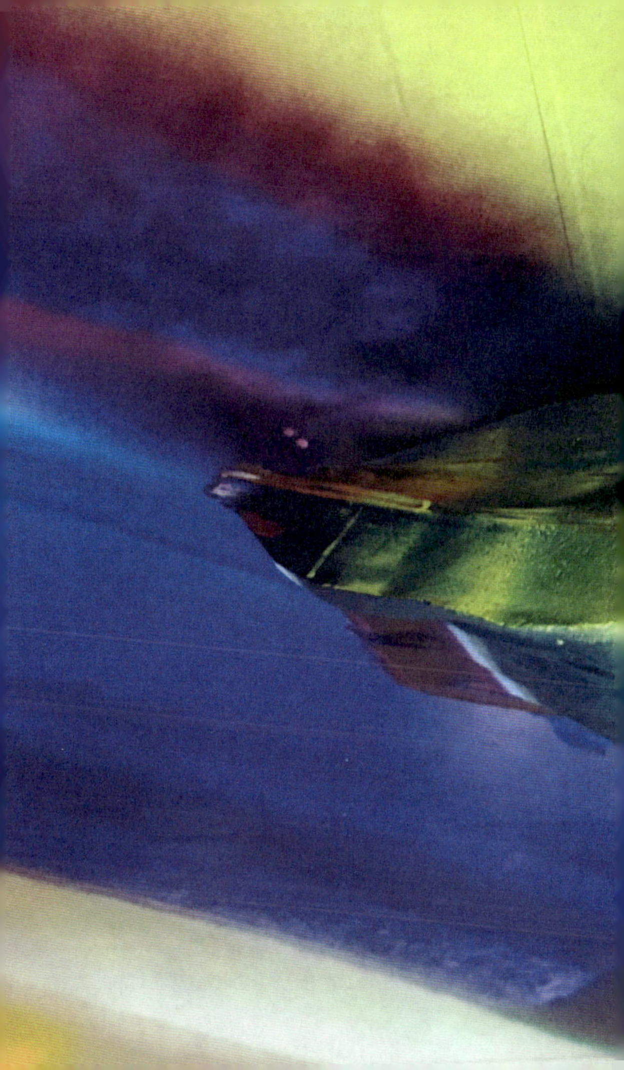

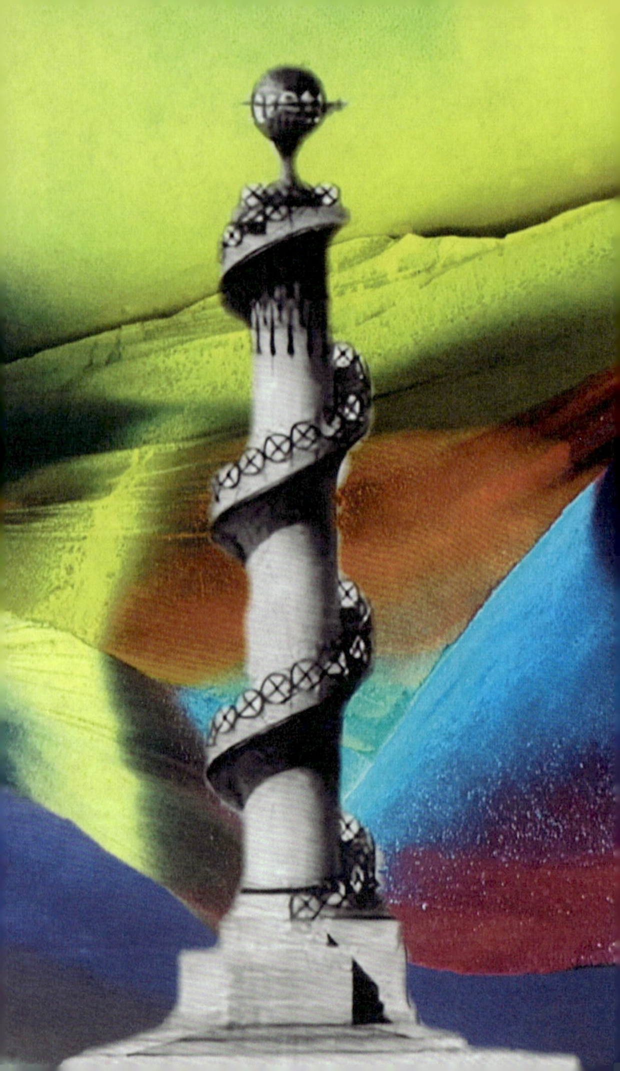

Quod petis in te est – ne te quaesiveris extra.

Persius

Regiom.
d. 18 Mart.
1788

I Kant
Log. et Meta[illegible] P.

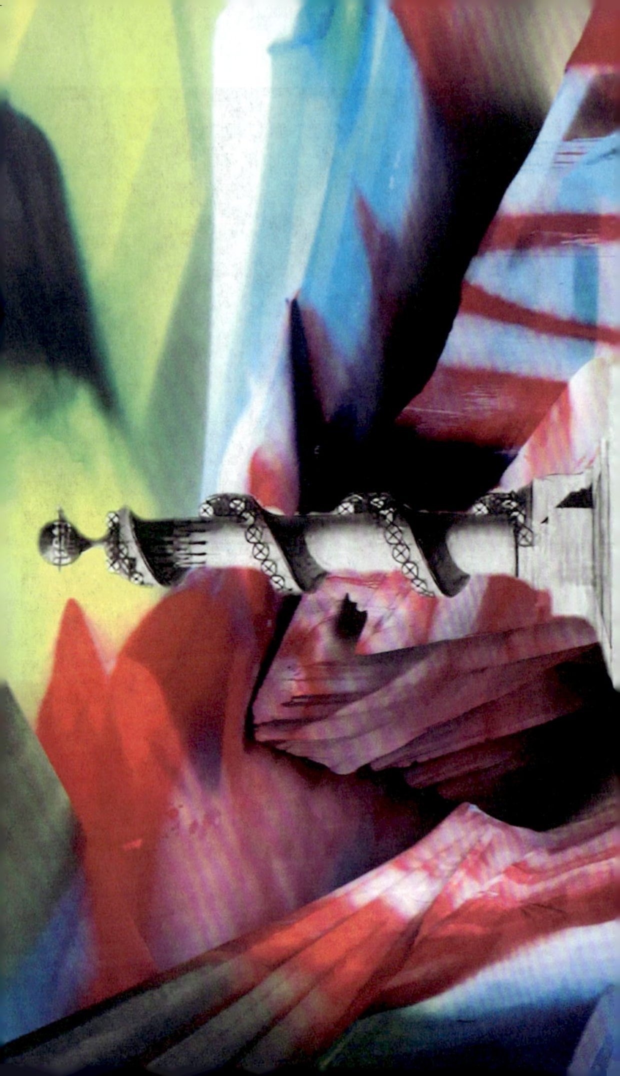

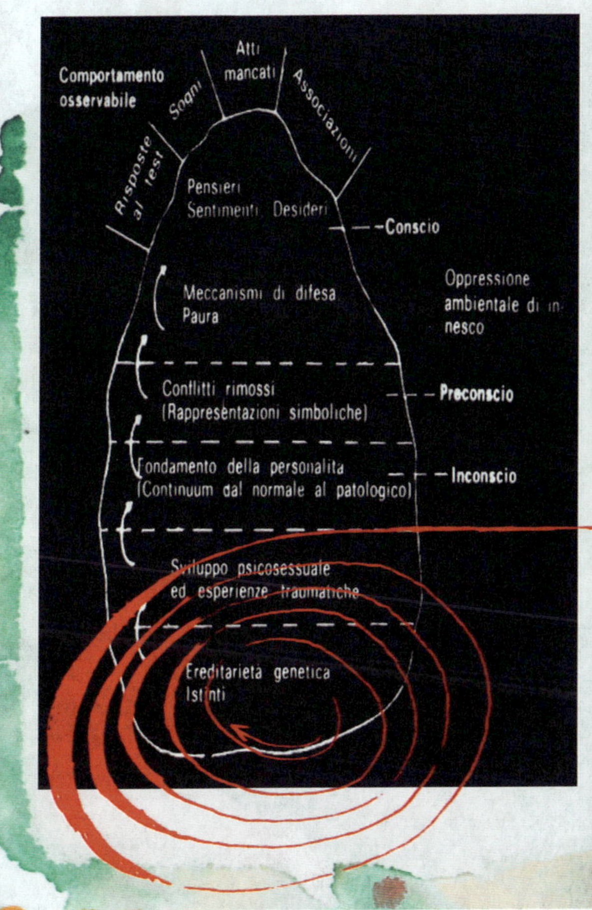
Comportamento osservabile
Atti mancati
Sogni
Associazioni
Risposte al test
Pensieri
Sentimenti, Desideri
Conscio
Oppressione ambientale di innesco
Meccanismi di difesa
Paura
Conflitti rimossi
(Rappresentazioni simboliche)
Preconscio
Fondamento della personalità
(Continuum dal normale al patologico)
Inconscio
Sviluppo psicosessuale
ed esperienze traumatiche
Ereditarietà genetica
Istinti

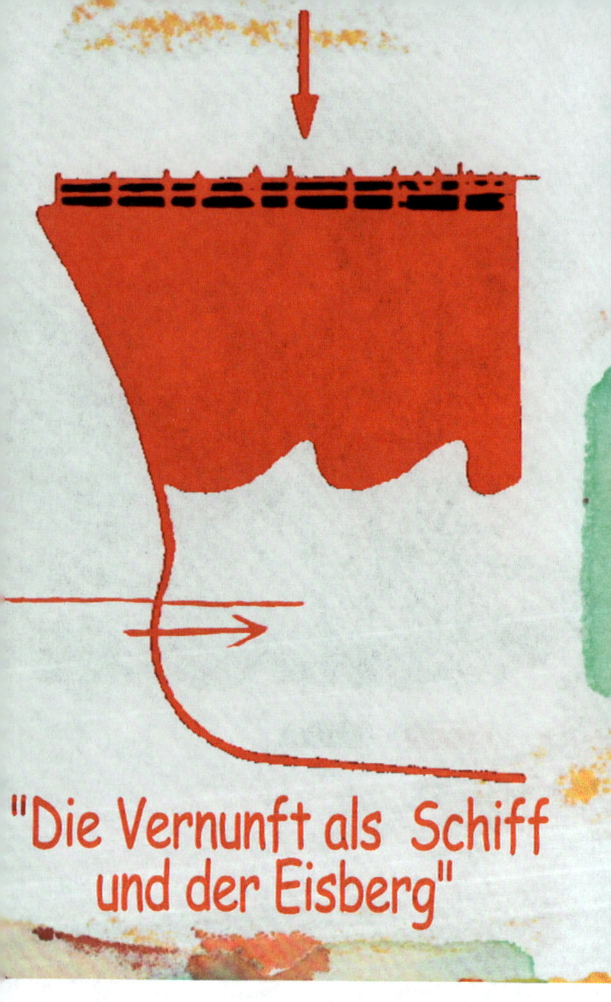
"Die Vernunft als Schiff
und der Eisberg"

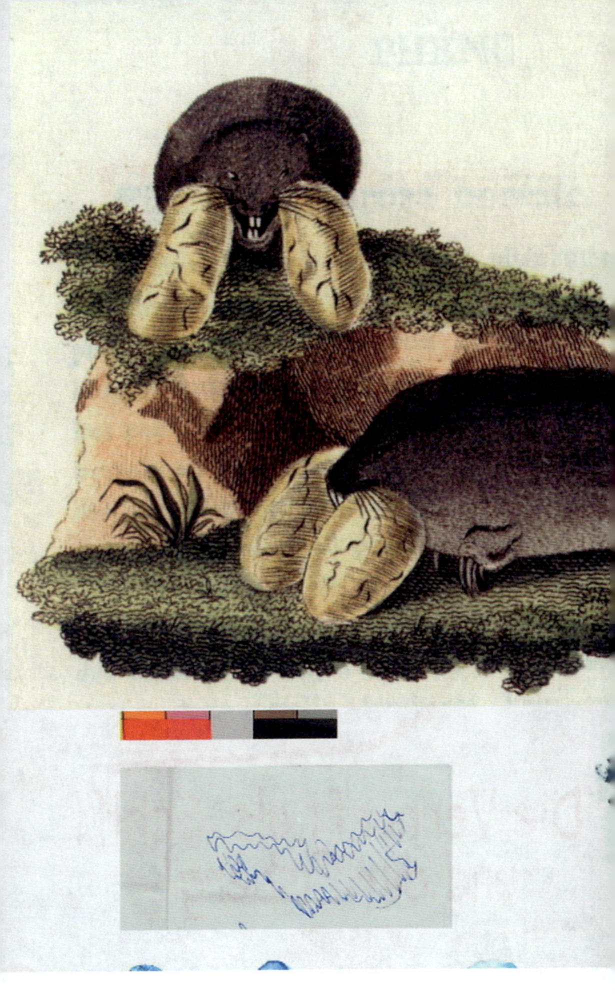

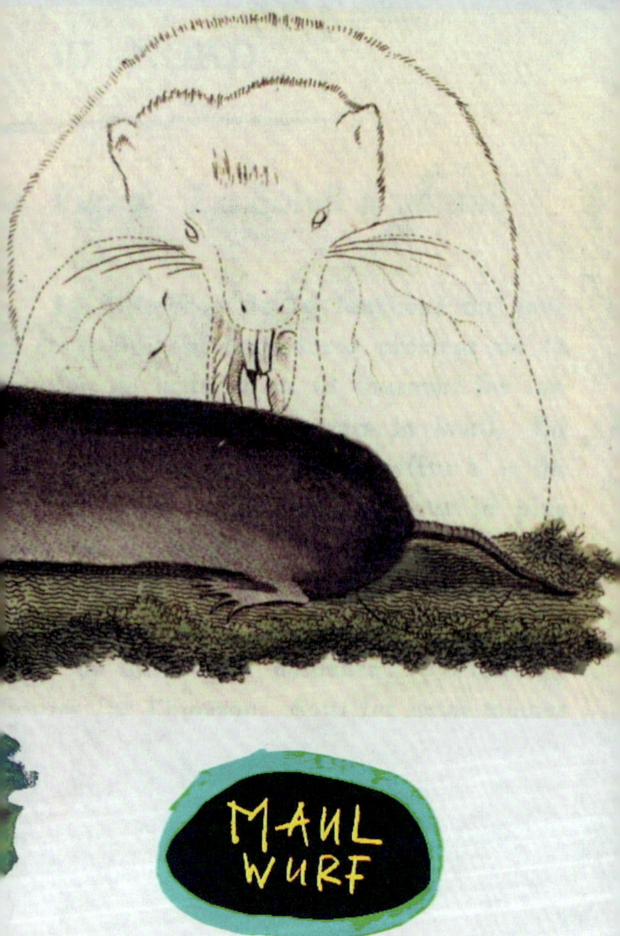
MAUL
WURF

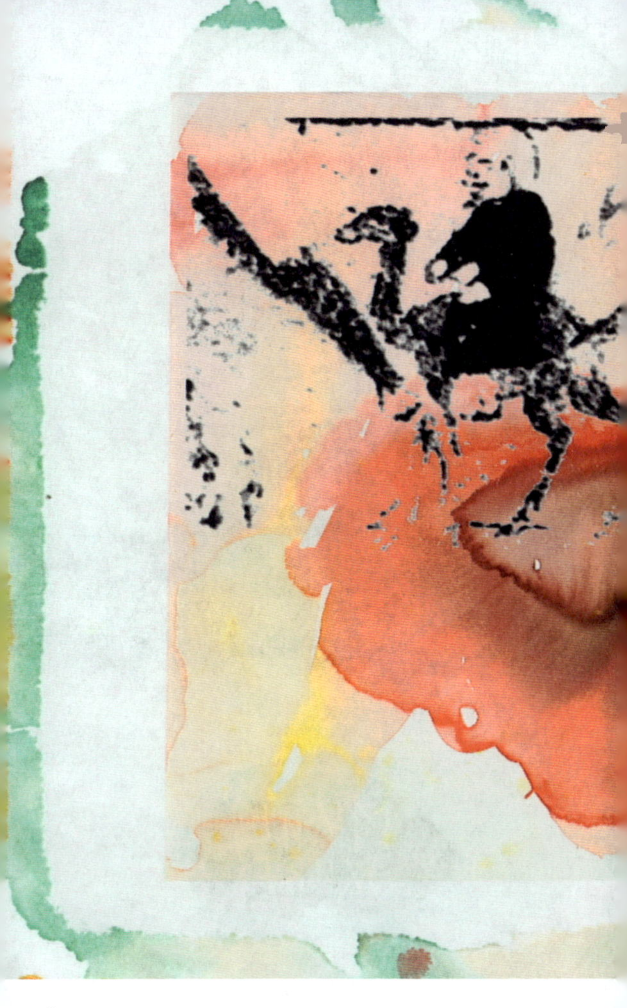

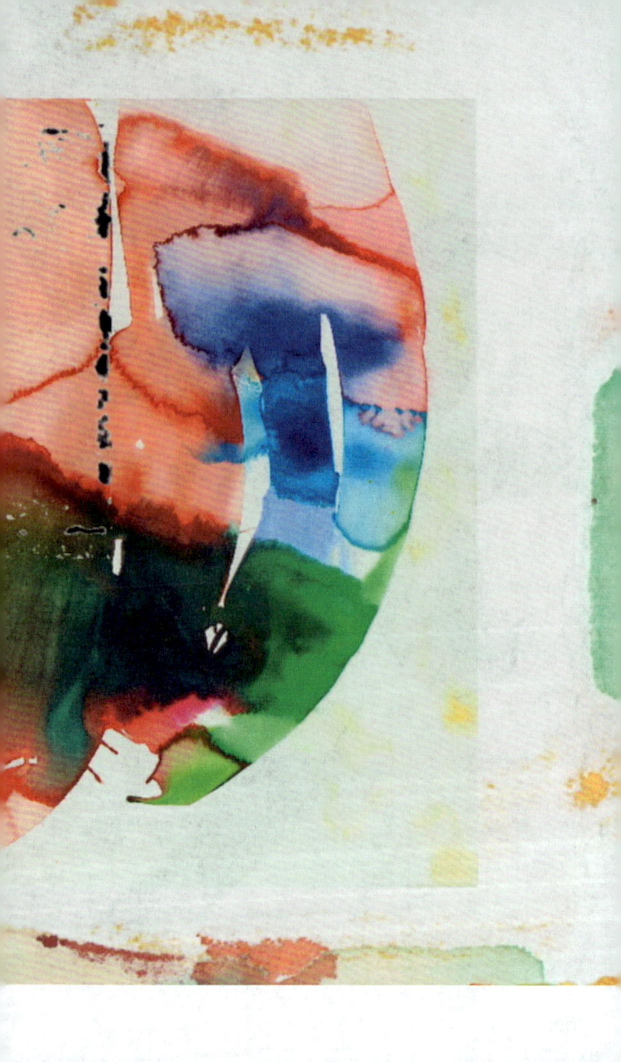

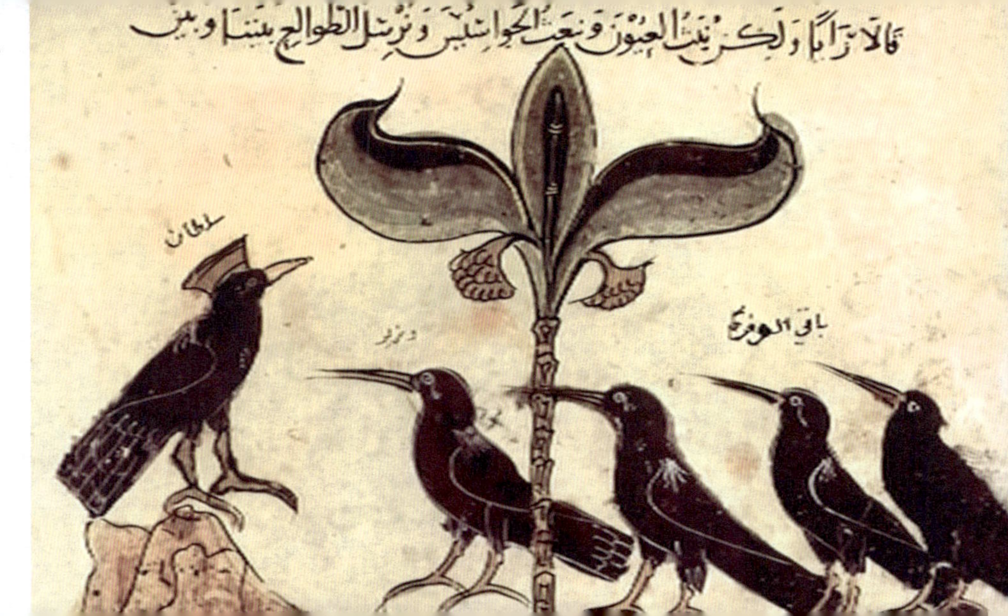
قالا ترانا ولكن نبث العيون ونبعث الجواسيس ونرسل الطوالع بيننا وبين
سلطان
وزير
باقي الوزرا

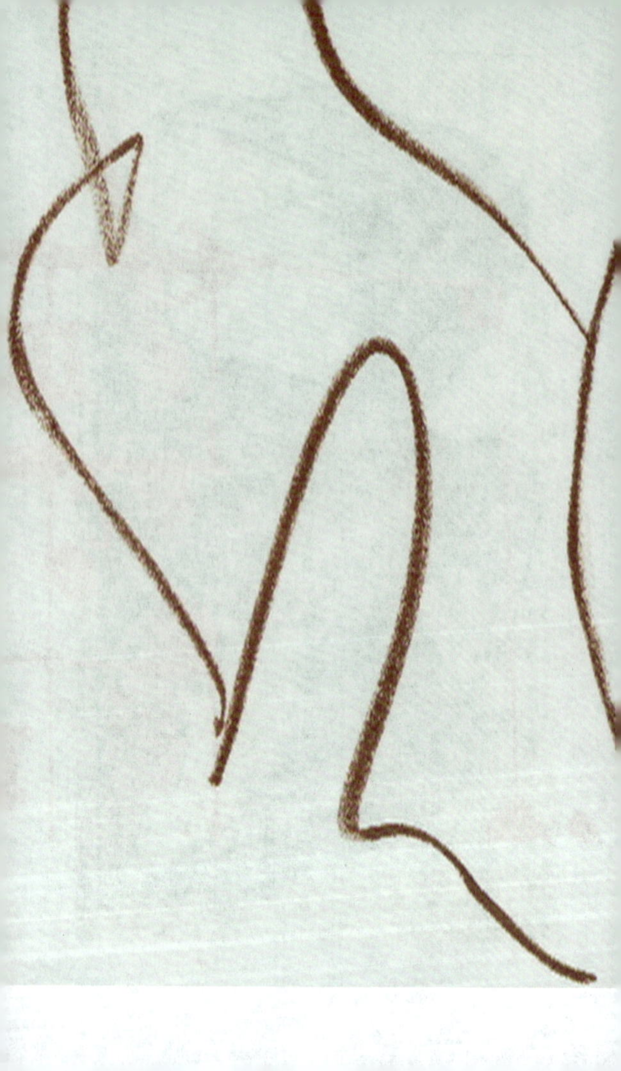

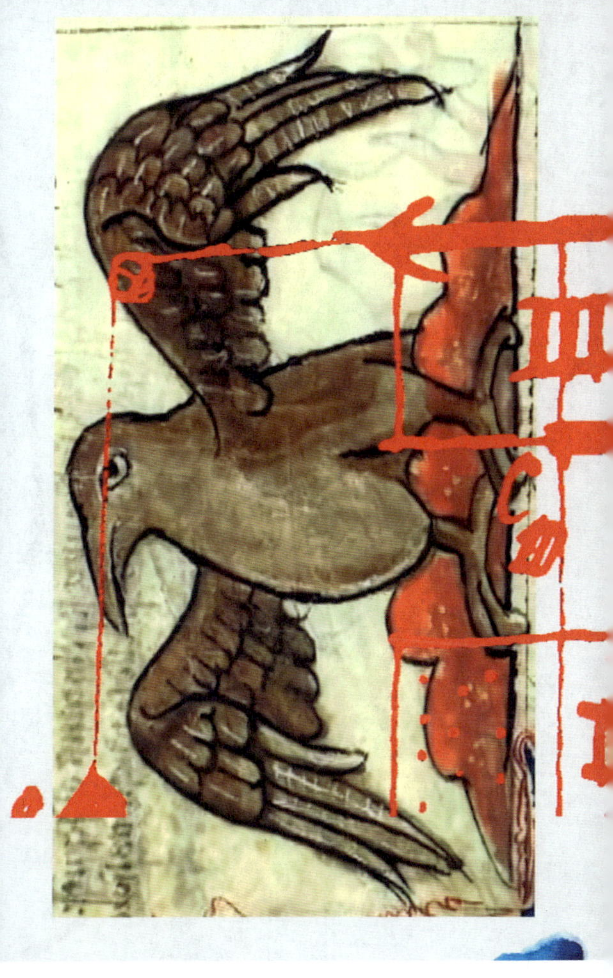

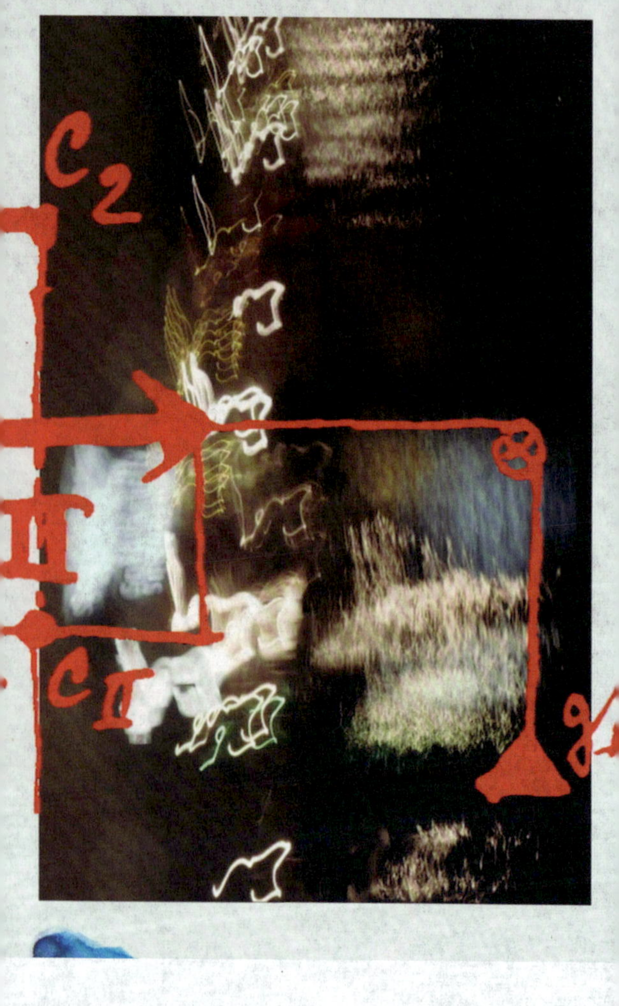

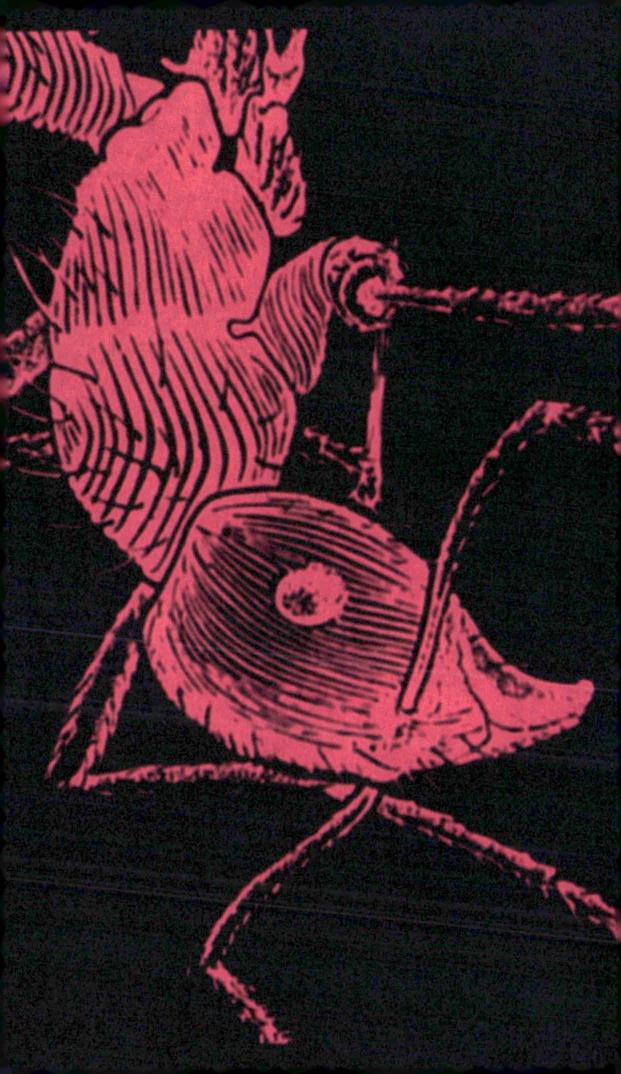

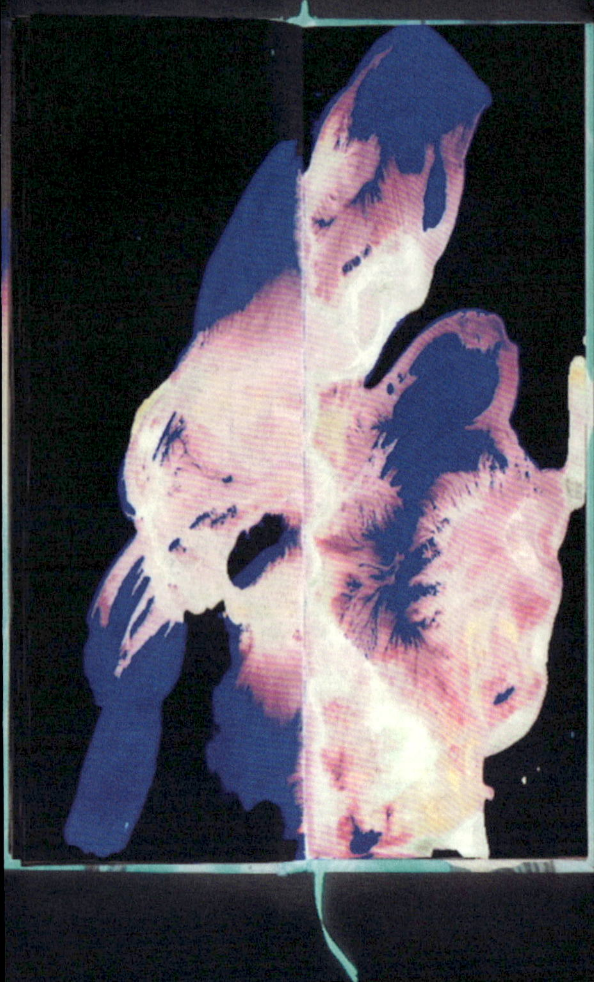

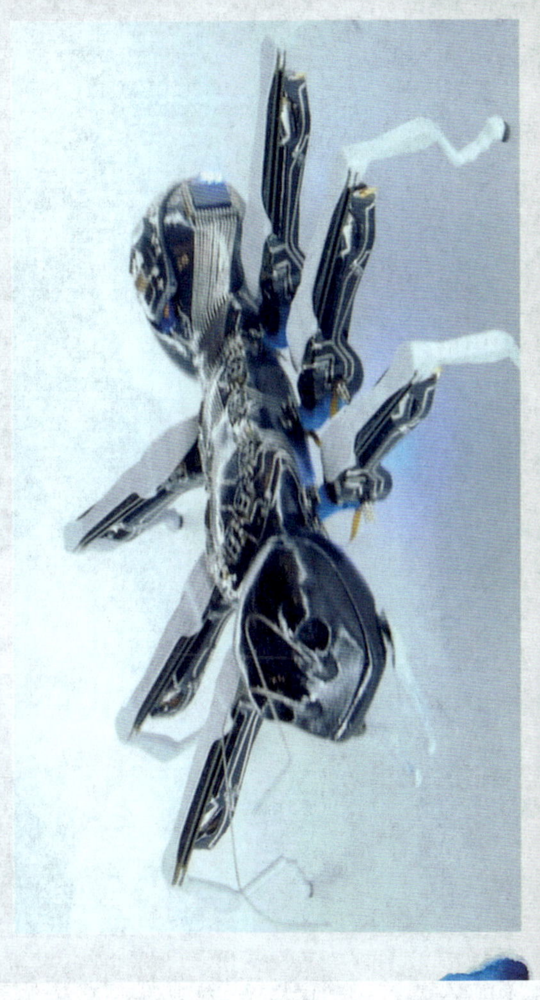

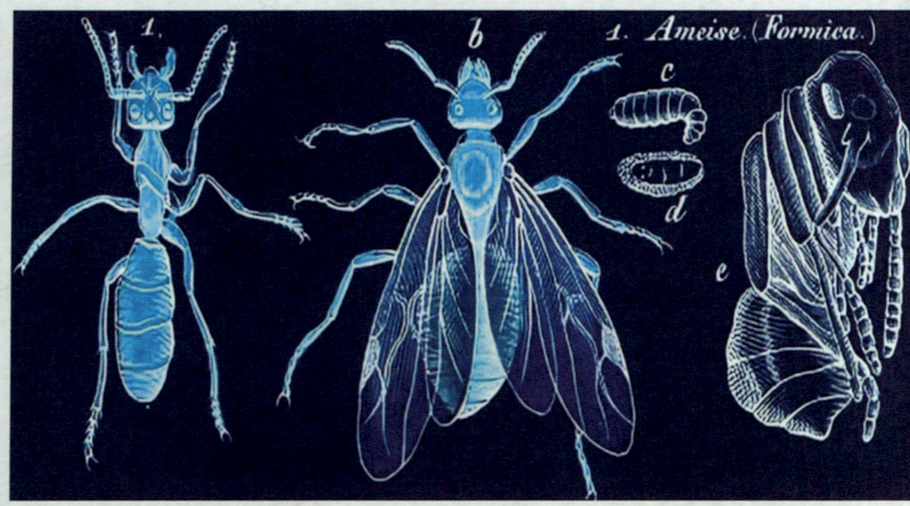
1. Ameise. (Formica.)
1.
b
c
d
e

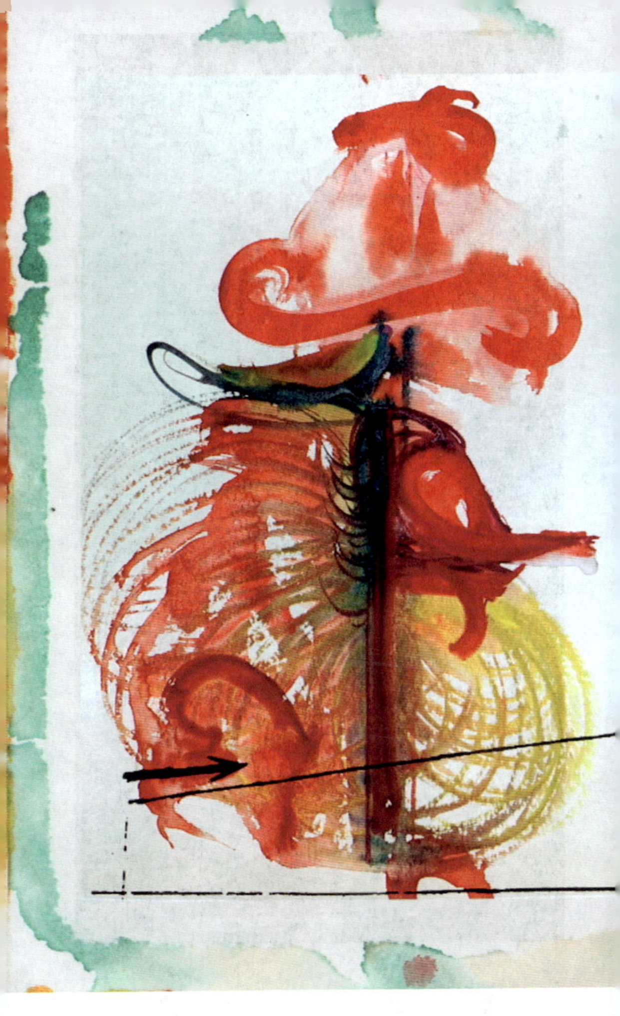

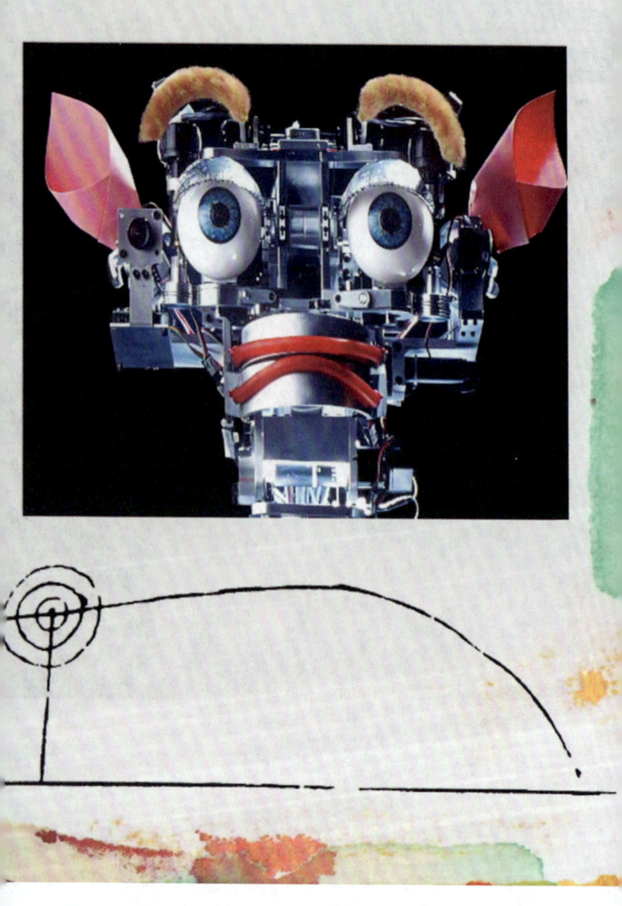

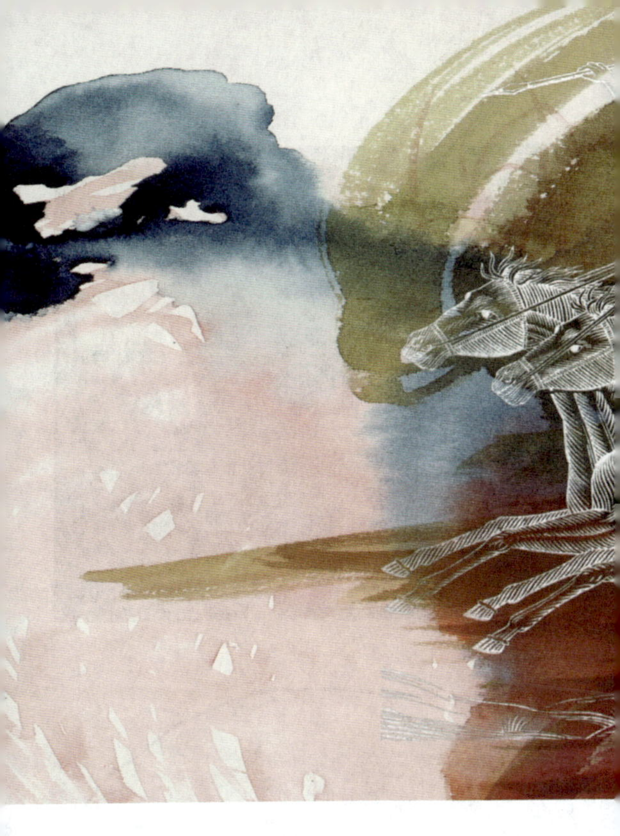

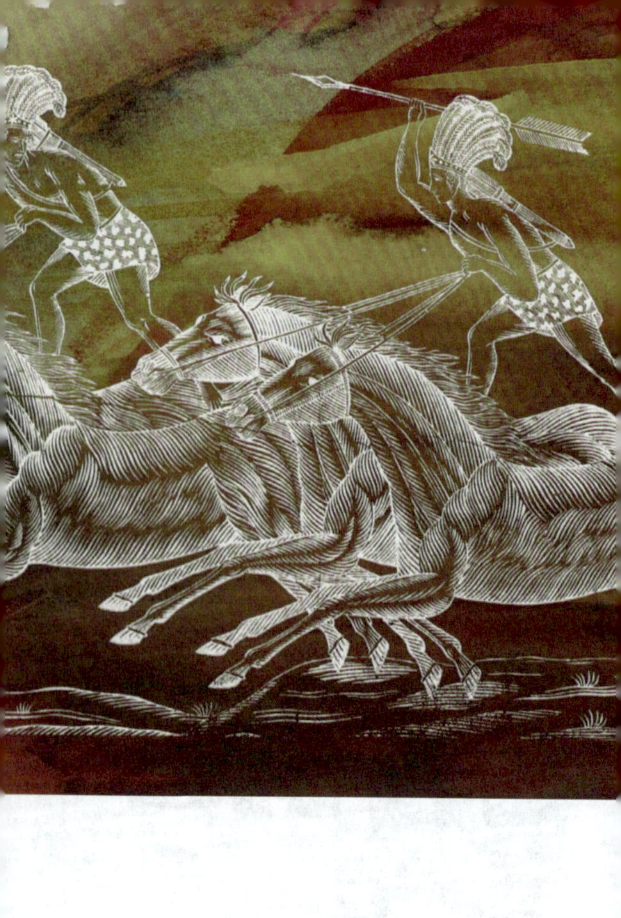

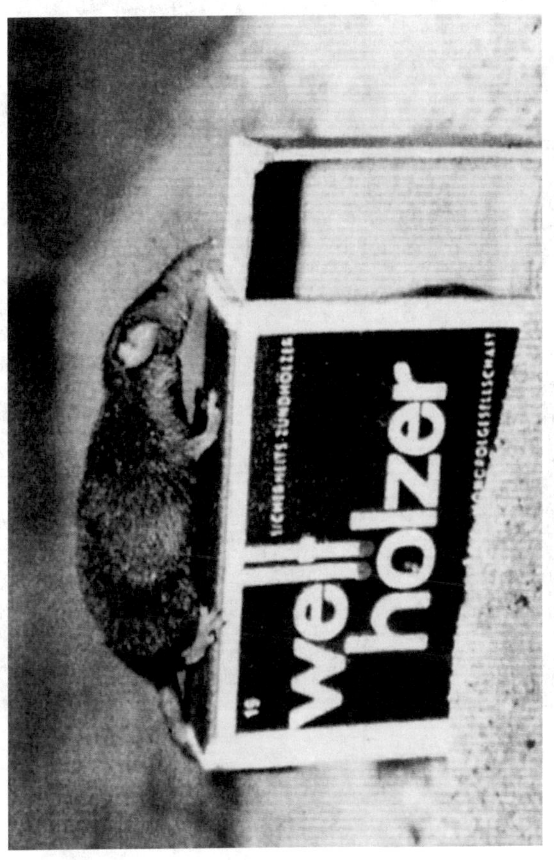
welt
hölzer

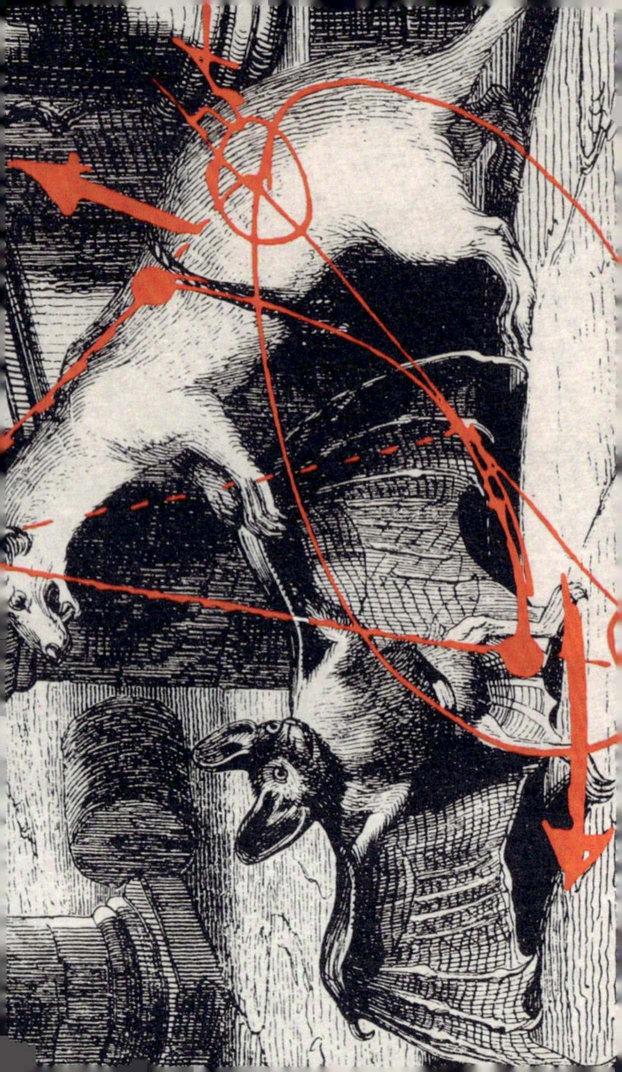

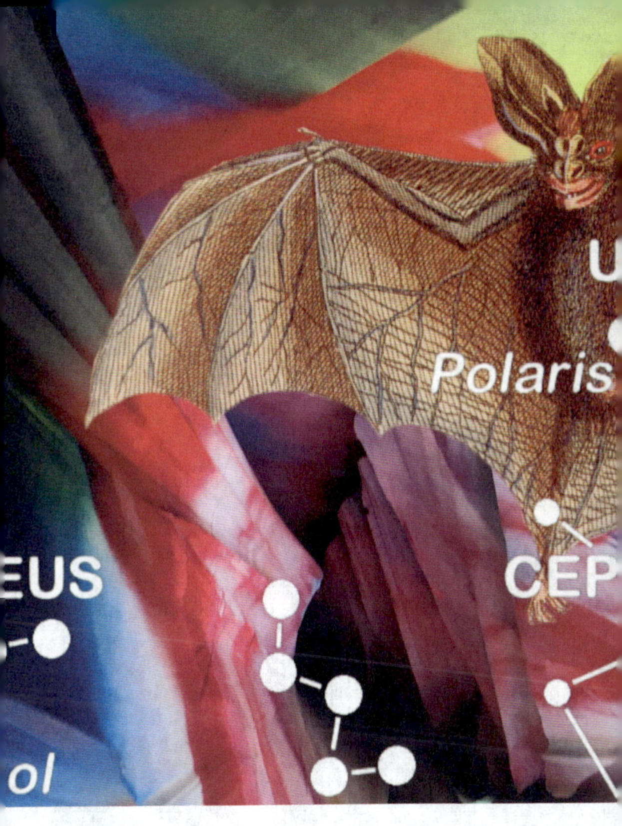
Polaris

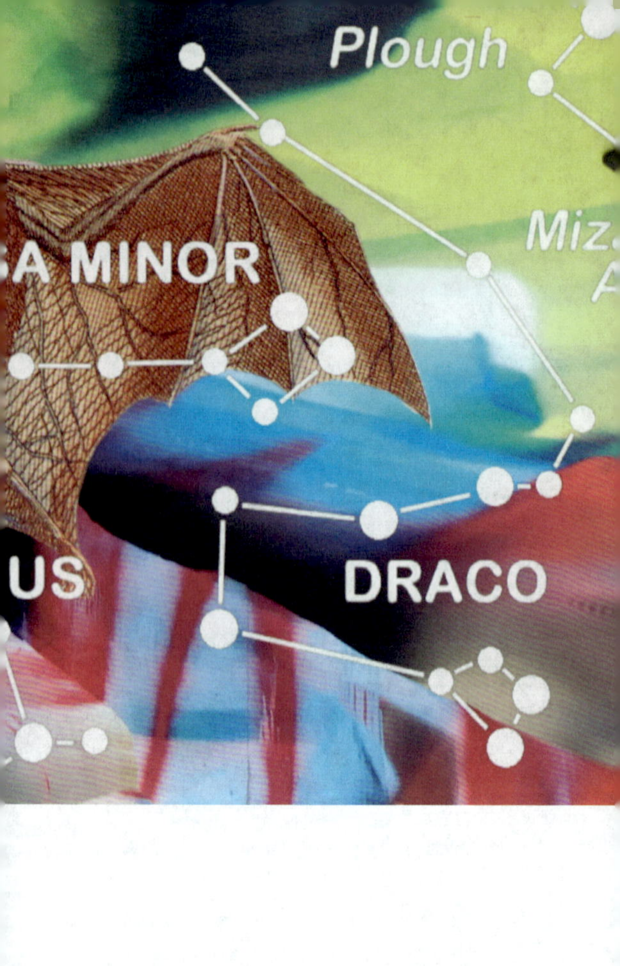
Plough
A MINOR
DRACO

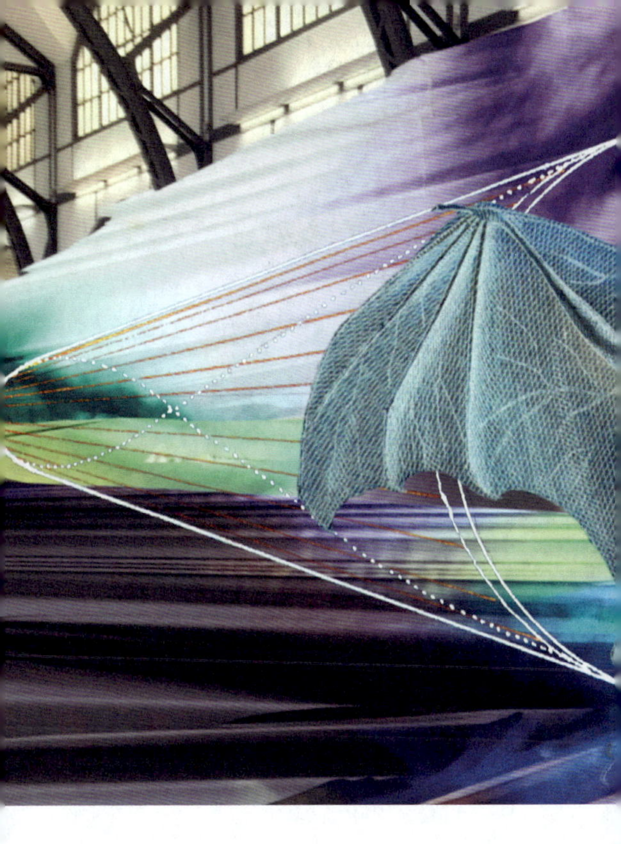

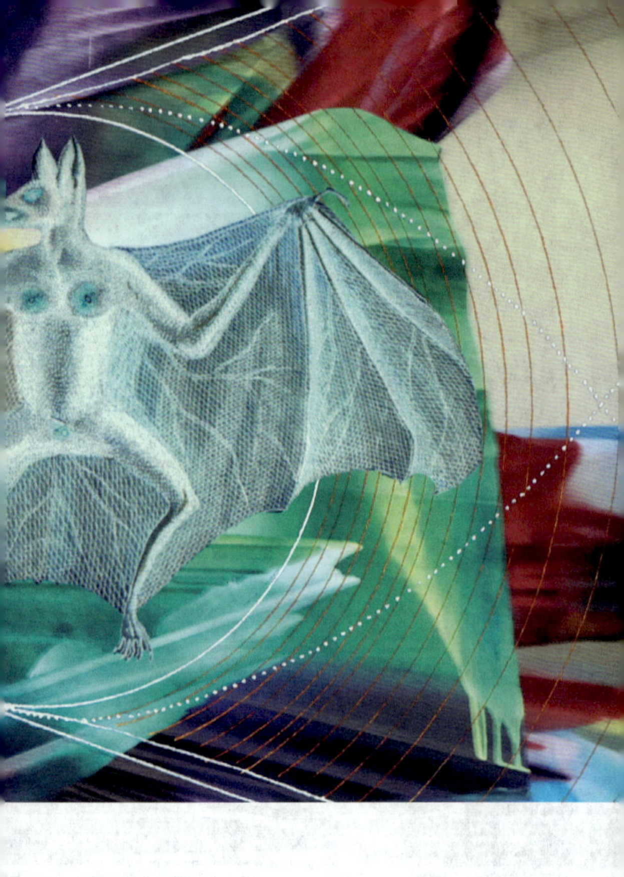

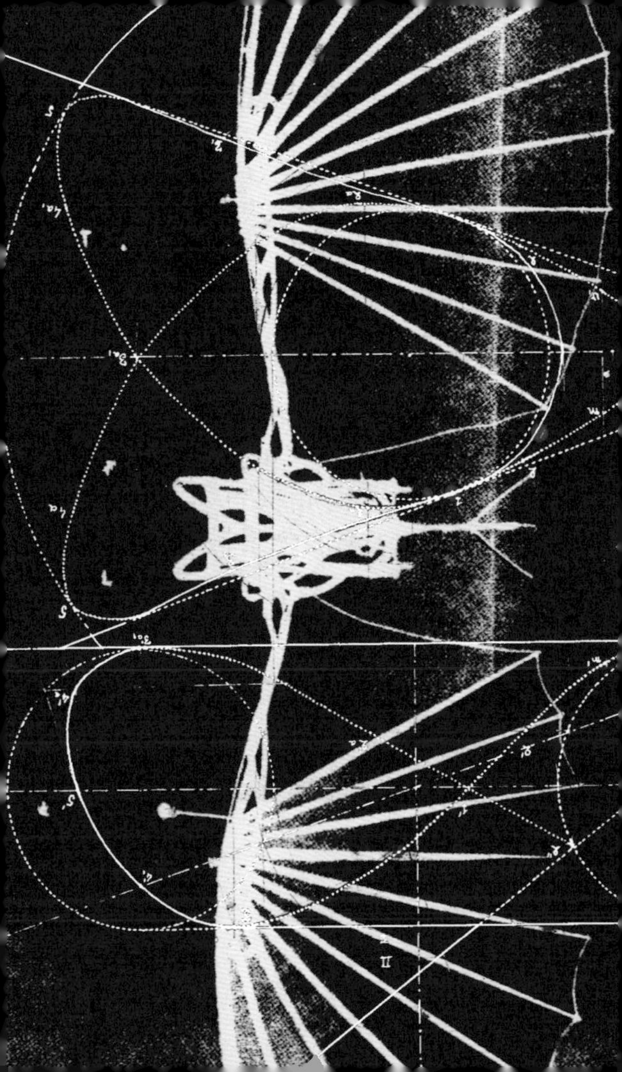

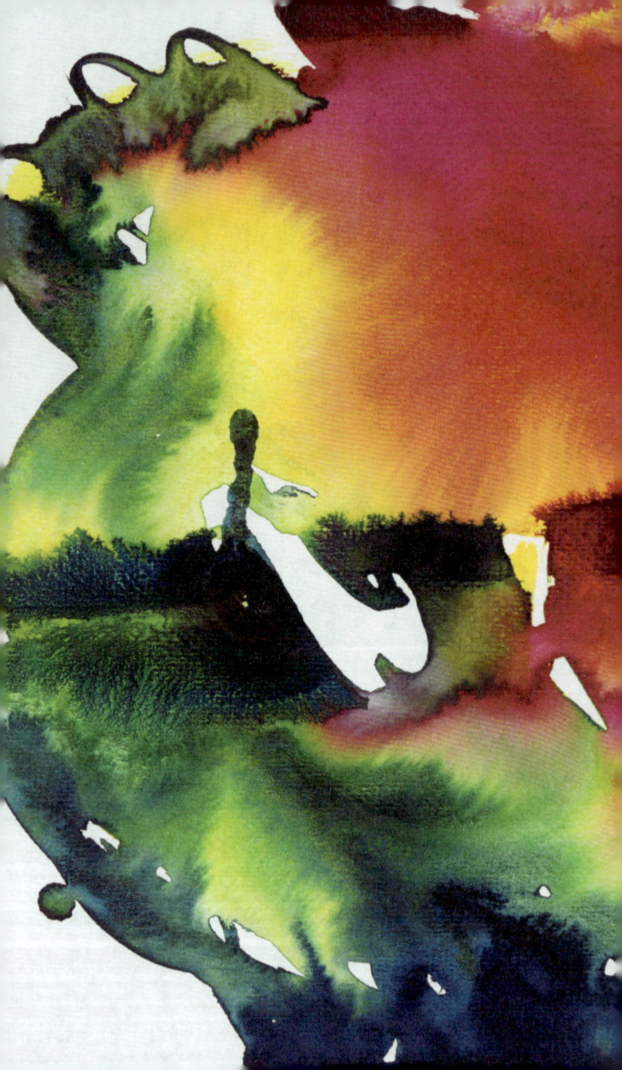

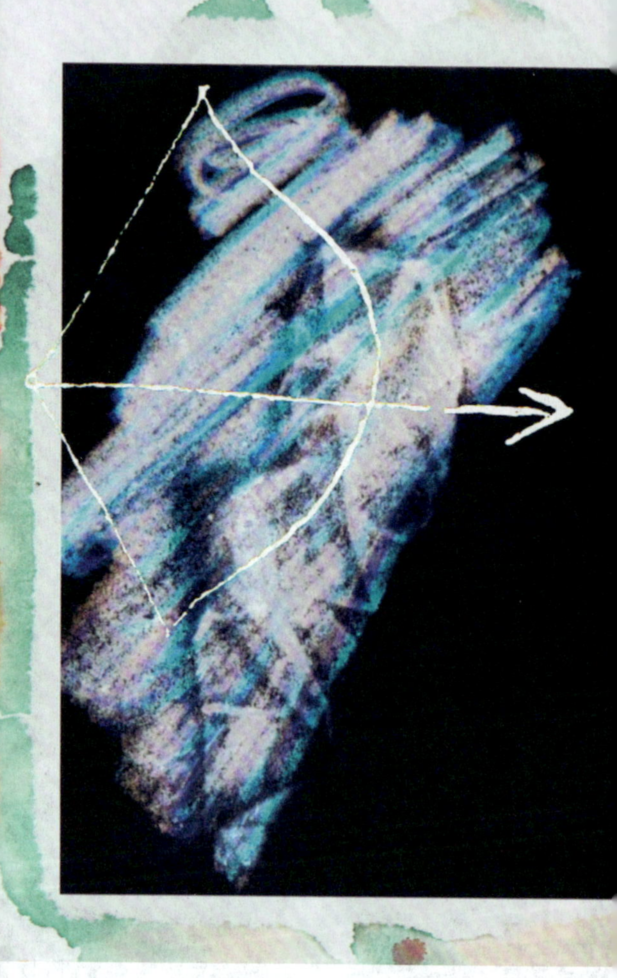

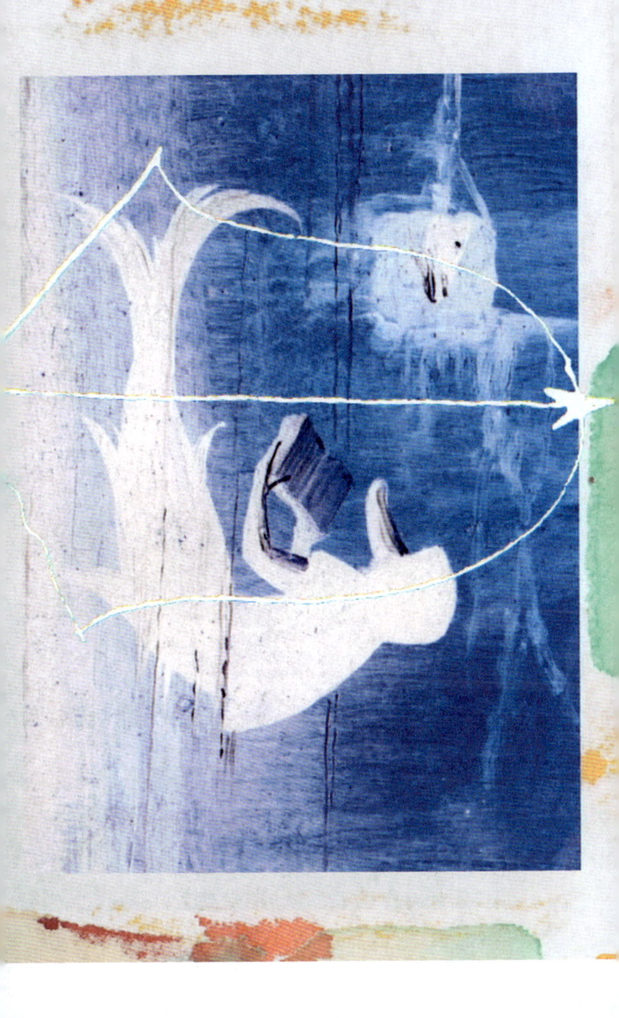

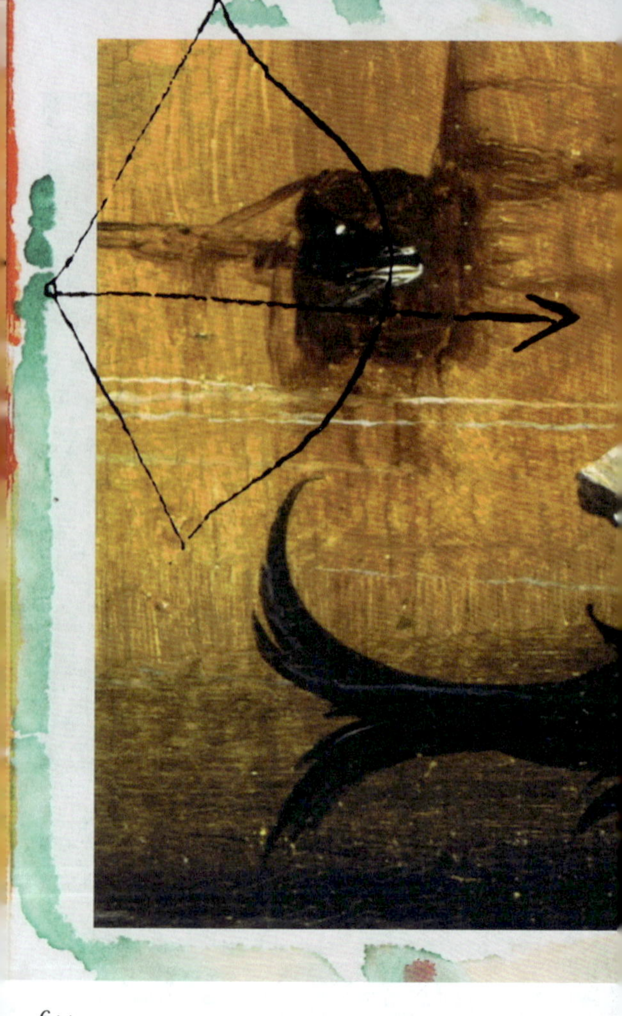

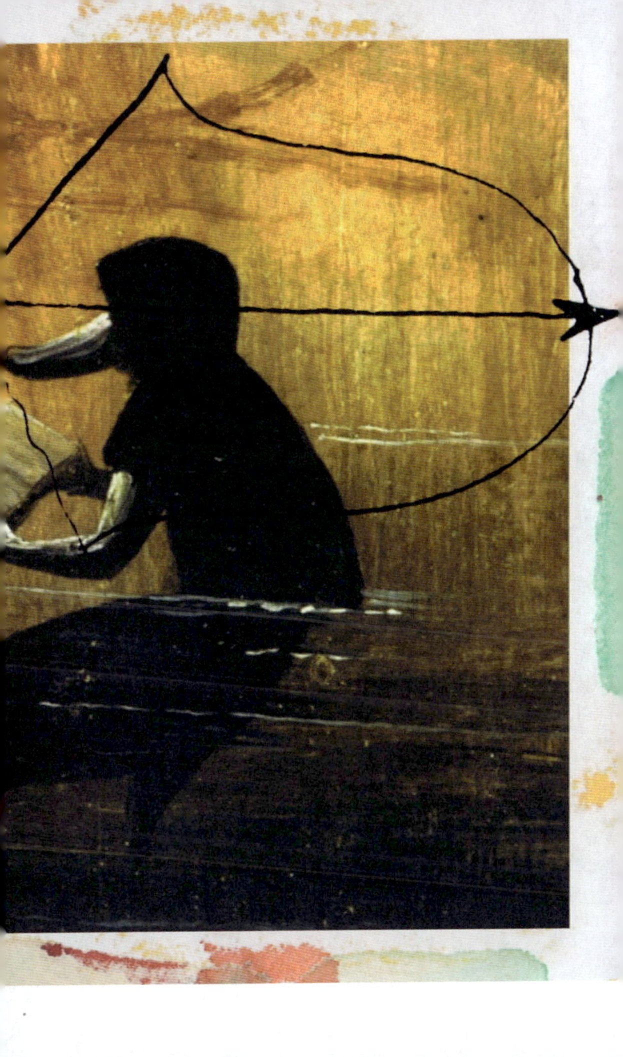

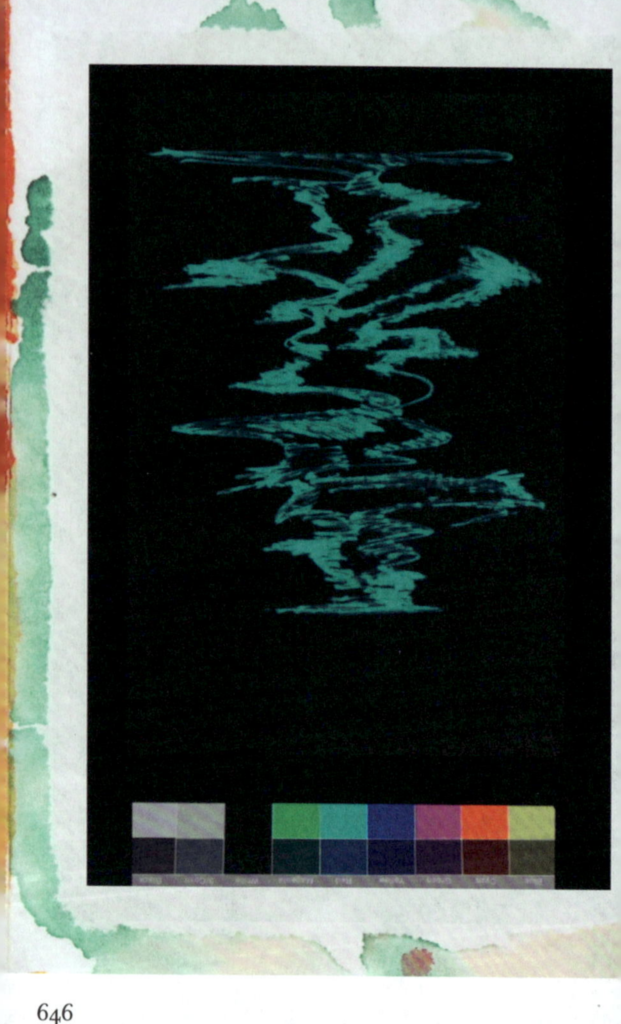

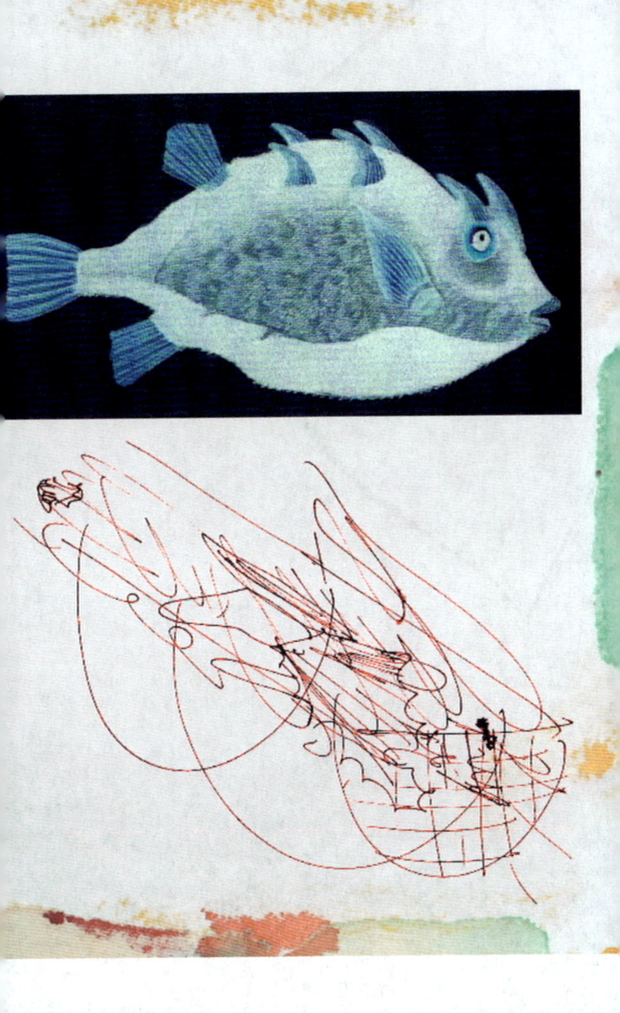

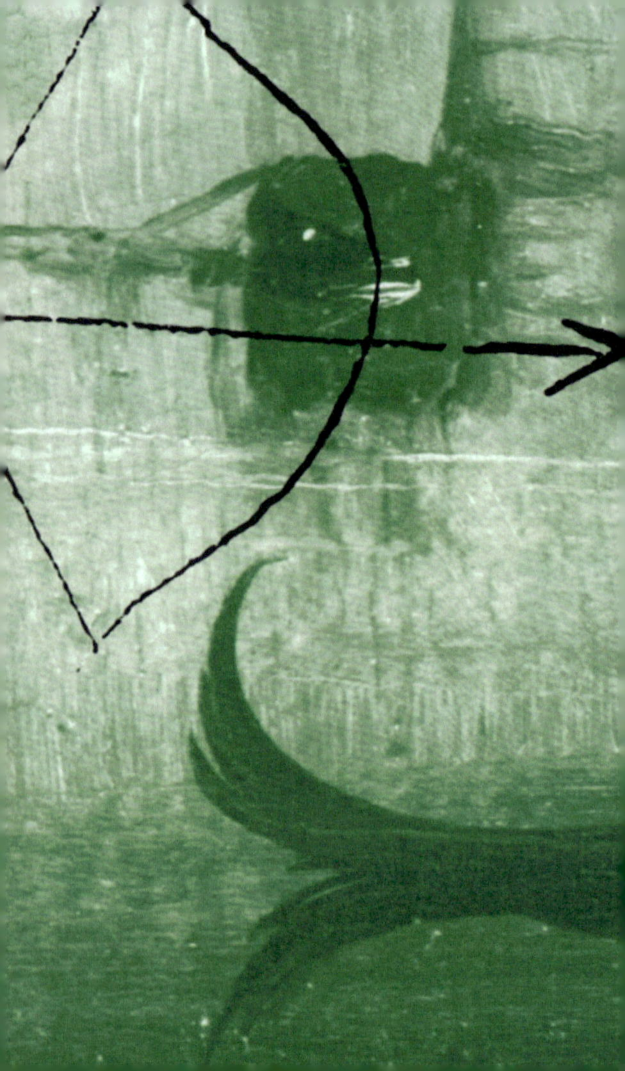

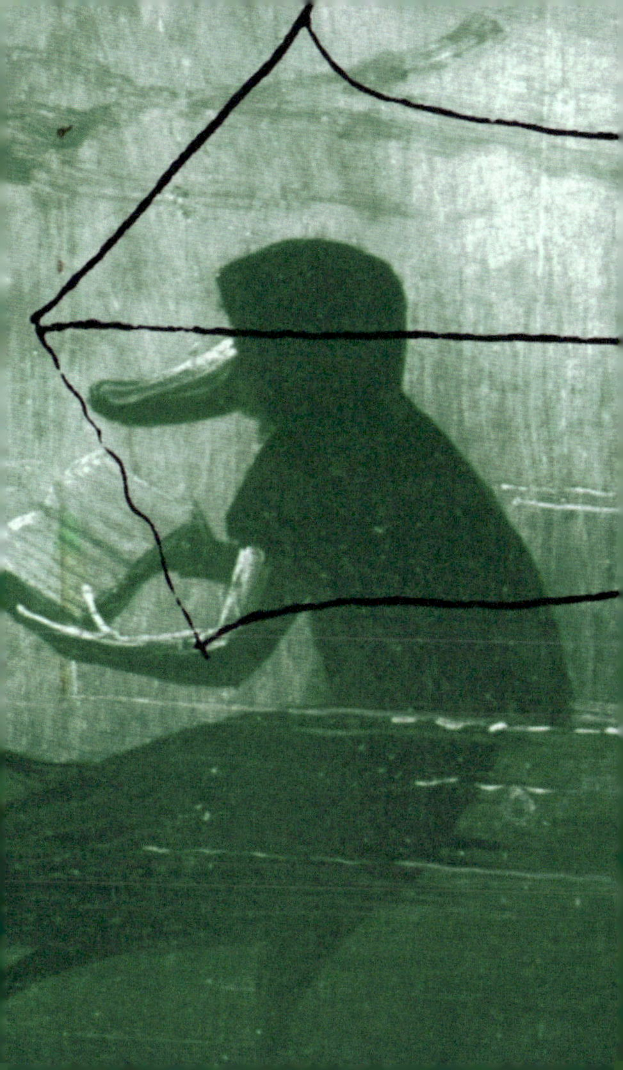

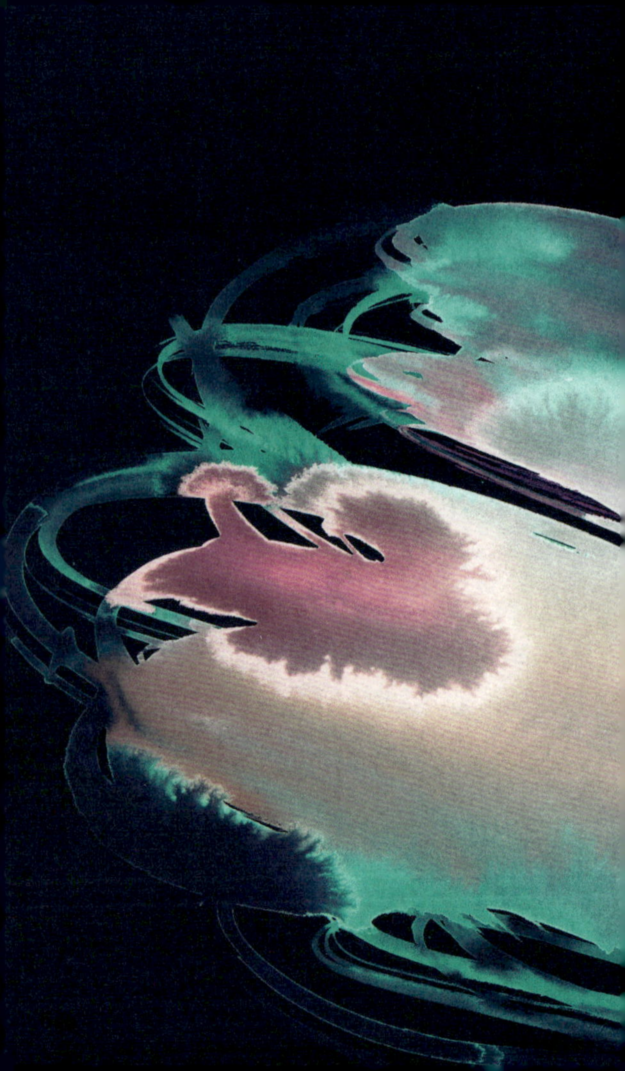

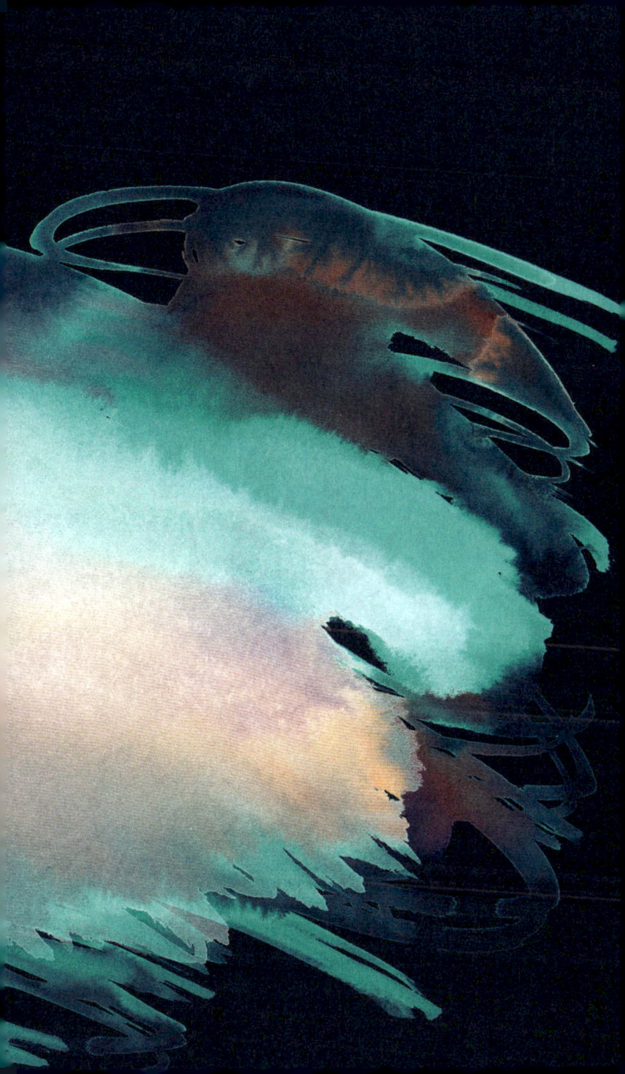

([illegible]
[illegible])

Notes and Sources

In this book, Katharina Grosse's watercolors and drawings come into contact with film stills, cinematographic work, and texts by Alexander Kluge. We have worked together Station for Station (with the exception of Stations 1, 8, and 9), page for page. Attempting to explain all we have done and thought would be inappropriate. Ultimately, decisions are subjective, especially in collaborative work. Oftentimes, it was a case of experimentation, and explanations will become apparent the more we continue to work.

ungefähre

Abweichung

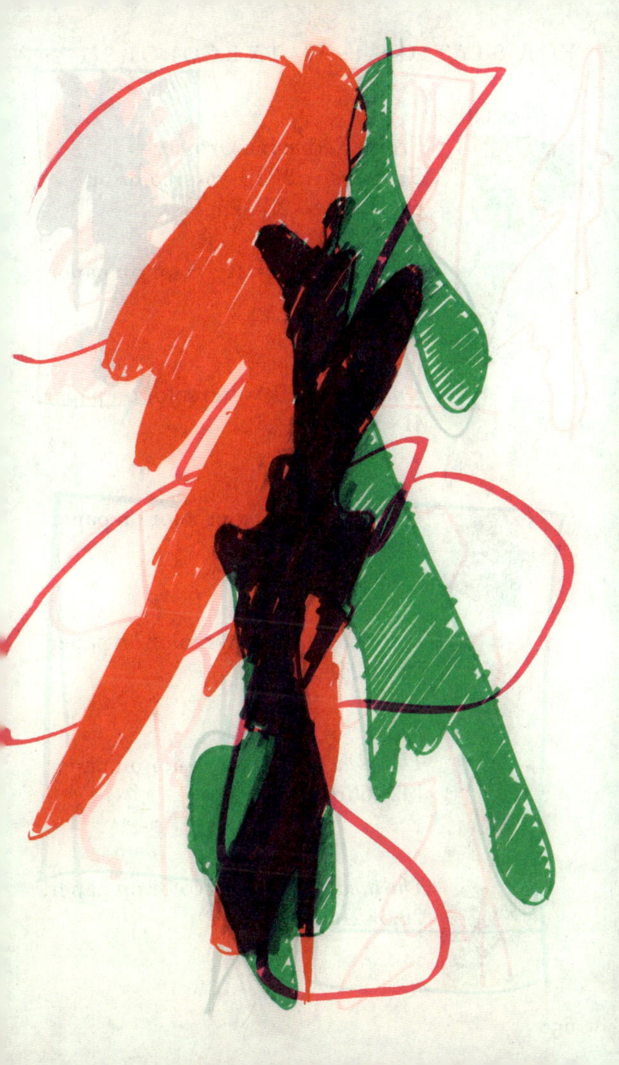

Pages 10–41

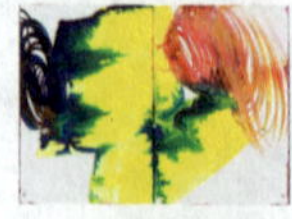

From: Katharina Grosse, *Sketchbook*, 2021, watercolor on paper, 29.8×21×1cm

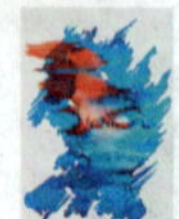

Untitled, 2019, watercolor on paper, 30×21cm

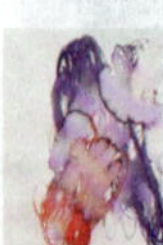

Untitled, 2020, watercolor on paper, 41×31cm

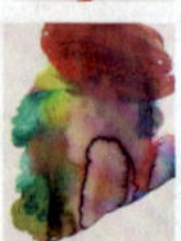

Untitled, 2021, watercolor on paper, 40.5×31cm

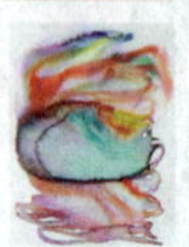

Untitled, 2019, watercolor on paper, 30.5×23cm

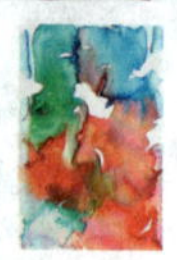

Untitled, 2019, watercolor on paper, 102×66cm

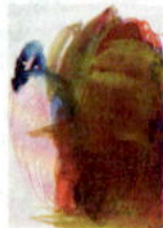

Untitled, 2021, watercolor on paper, 29.5×21cm

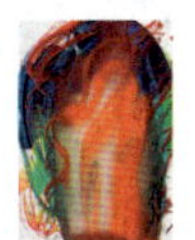

Untitled, 2021, watercolor on paper, 29.5×21cm

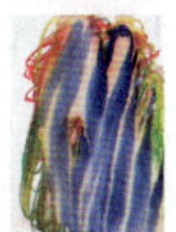

Untitled, 2021, watercolor on paper, 29.5×21cm

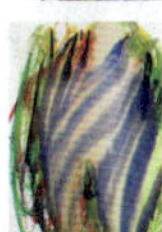

Untitled, 2021, watercolor on paper, 29.5×21cm

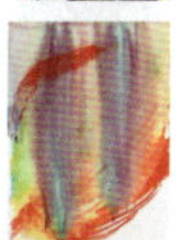

Untitled, 2022, watercolor on paper, 31.8×24.1cm

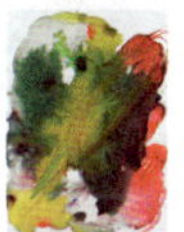

Untitled, 2020, watercolor on paper, 40×30cm

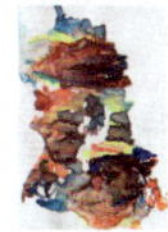

Untitled, 2019, watercolor on paper, 29.3×20.5cm

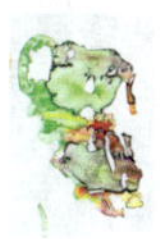

Untitled, 2019, watercolor on paper, 29.3×20.5cm

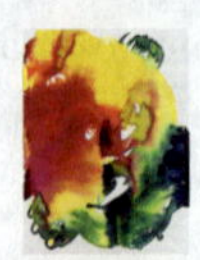

Untitled, 2021, watercolor on paper, 31.9 × 23.9 cm

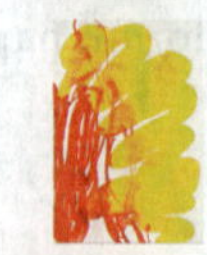

Untitled, 2019, watercolor on paper, 42 × 29 cm

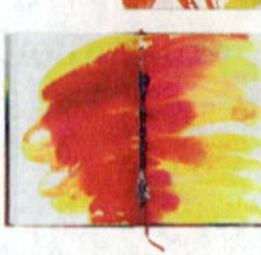

From: *Sketchbook*, 2021, watercolor on paper, 21.5 × 15.5 × 4 cm

FOR STATION 2—LEIBNIZ AND THE SEPARATRIX

Pages 50–51

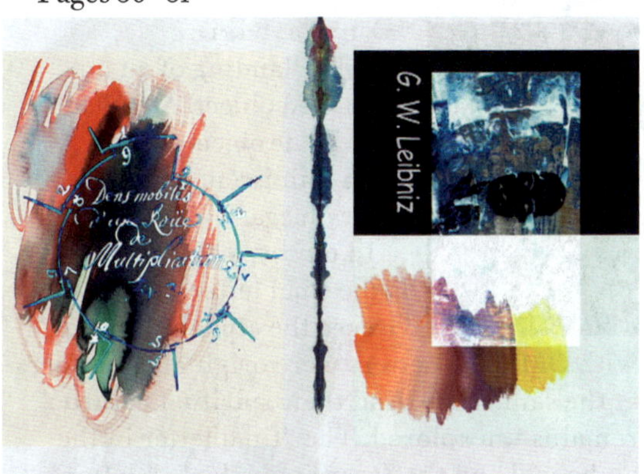

Composite image. On the left, a drawing of Leibniz's, the "stepped reckoner," a mechanical calculator for multiplications, 1673. Placed over a watercolor by Katharina Grosse. In the pages to follow, composite images will only receive comment when any special information linked to them remains unexplained by the image itself.

Page 74

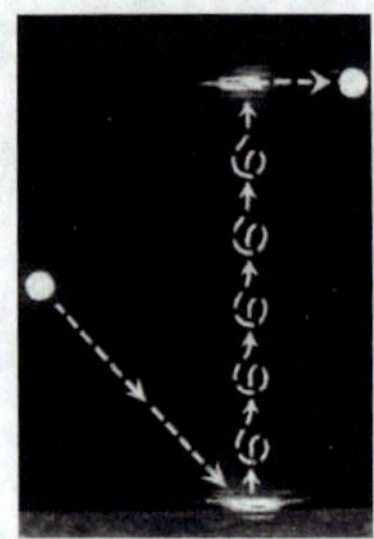

"Omega Rising" Peculiar landing of an unidentified object. At its later launch, the object shows a sign reminiscent of the Greek letter omega.

In our own alphabet Z is the final letter; in ancient Greece the alphabet ended with OMEGA. Letters were originally numbers at the same time. And their spiritual nature remains unexplored. The "final letter in the alphabet" and the "search for the lost letter" within the Jewish tradition, as well as the question regarding the "dark side of the alpha," are just as much of a challenge for the arts and for science today as they were in the past.

Page 75

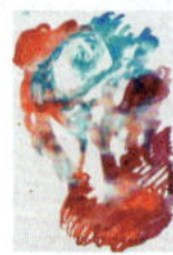

Katharina Grosse, *Untitled*, 2021, watercolor on paper, 29.7 × 20.9 cm

Page 77

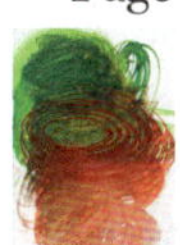

Untitled, 2019, watercolor on paper, 20.8 × 14.8 cm

Page 120

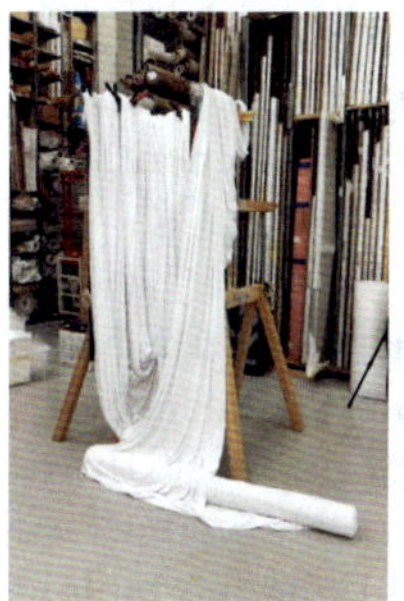

Katharina Grosse, *Der Profit*, 2019, fabric, wooden saw horses, spring clamps, wooden slats, and stretch foil, 226 × 210 × 140 cm, created for the exhibition *Alexander Kluge–DIE MACHT DER MUSIK / DIE OPER–Tempel der Ernsthaftigkeit*, Kunsthalle Weishaupt and Museum Ulm.

Page 121

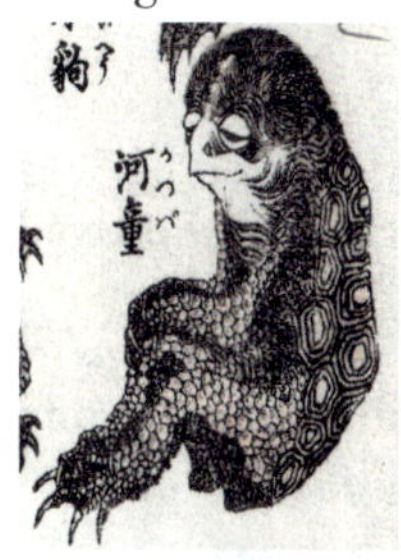

A famous literary tale from ancient China recounts the adventures of the "Golden Monkey." After wandering across the Himalayas and far into the west, he returned home all the more shrewd. The monkey carries a magic wand. Two lines in a poem by Mao Zedong read: "The Golden Monkey wrathfully swung his massive cudgel / And the jade-like firmament was cleared of dust."

FOR STATION 4—THE SOUL SWIMS IN MUSIC

Page 138

Upon Mozart's death. A song composed by Joseph Martin Kraus upon hearing of Mozart's death. Kraus, director of the Royal Opera in Stockholm, was considered the "Swedish Mozart." His opera *Dido and Aeneas* is legendary. Kraus belonged to the *Sturm und Drang* movement.

Page 145

The libretto for Alban Berg's opera *Lulu* is based on Frank Wedekind's original plays. The legendary murderer who kills the soprano in the third act of Berg's opera was—along with his name, "Jack the Ripper"—a creation of London's tabloid press.

Page 153

Prometeo by Luigi Nono. Nono refers to his musical work as a "tragedy of listening." The piece was performed at the Salzburg Festival in 2011. Rehearsals were filmed for the dctp-Kulturmagazin News & Stories *The Ear Swims in Music.* The images are film stills from the same, superimposed with fragments of the score.

"Indiscriminate Gods Have Power Over Life and Death in the Trojan War…"
Film fragment on Joseph Marin Kraus's *Dido & Aeneas*.
07:33

Homage to Luigi Nono
Film fragment on *Prometeo*
04:14

FOR STATION 5—AREAS OF UNQUIET

Page 194

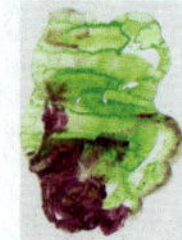

Katharina Grosse, *Untitled*, 2021, watercolor on paper, 29.6 × 20.8 cm

Page 200

"Außerordentliche Wahrnehmung südlich von Afrika." From: Alexander Kluge, "Die blaue Gefahr," in *Die Lücke, die der Teufel lässt* (Suhrkamp, 2003), p. 887. The incredible tortoise was, according to the seamen, the size of thirty sailors.

Page 207

Homage to Edvard Munch, *Tod des Marat I*, 1907. Munchmuseet, Oslo.

Page 209

Berliner Abendblätter. For half a year, from October 1810 to 30 March 1811, the poet Heinrich von Kleist published an evening paper in Berlin. Every day of the week but Sunday. Length: four pages. In addition to official reports from Napoleon's theater of war, the legendary paper contained sensational stories of crime as well as immortal texts from the hand of the master himself. They were written summarily, as demanded by an evening paper. The *Berliner Abendblätter* constituted a "narrow interface, a separatrix," between plebeian openness and high art. During a period of subjective and objective "unquiet" in Kleist's life.

The *Berliner Abendblättern*,
no. 45 (21 November 1810),
had the following to say concerning the
death of Charlotte Corday:

"When Charlotte Corday was guillotined, as is well known the executioner took her head and slapped it. It was said that on this occasion, the girl's cheeks blushed and her eye, before it closed, looked once more unwillingly at the wretch who had inflicted this ignominy upon her. This statement famously gave rise to many physiological disputes between those who had the right to judge: could sensation with consciousness exist in the head that had already been cut off and completely separated from the body? Those who answered this question in the negative had a variety of experiential reasons to do so. Quite recently, Professor Senff of Halle, in the presence and with the assistance of several other insightful physicians, has made experiments on a decollated head, which in the final instance resulted in those present not being able to detect any sensation or consciousness in the thus injured and completely separated body part.

On 8 October, the murderer was beheaded by his two sisters. He was, which is likely of importance here, very calm and composed beforehand. The head was cut off right in the middle of the neck and fell into soft sand. Before the experimenter and his assistants picked it up, the lower jaw moved twice. The bandage was quickly torn from the eyes, which were found to be wide open, but with pupils that were narrower than usual and the eyeballs turned somewhat outward. They powerfully shouted the decollated's name into one ear, but his eyes did not move at all, not even toward the side whence the shout came. A pin was inserted deep into his cheek, but no sign of feeling whatsoever was noticed. Volatile alkaline salt (liquor ammonii caustici) was injected into the deceased's nose, but, again, without the slightest reaction to this violent stimulus, no twitching, no change, however slight, in the features of the face. The time lapse between these attempts and the moment of decapitation was only a few minutes."

Page 225

Gallows. *Le Pendu,* painted by the dramatist and poet Victor Hugo, 1854. Metropolitan Museum of Art, New York.

Pages 234–35

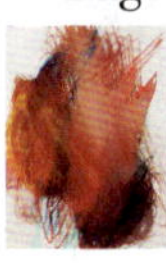

Katharina Grosse, *Untitled,* 2022, watercolor on paper, 41 × 31 cm

FOR STATION 6—THE QUIET CHAPTER

Pages 244–84

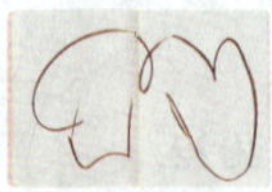

From: Katharina Grosse, *Sketchbook*, 2021, crayon on paper, 25×19×1.5 cm

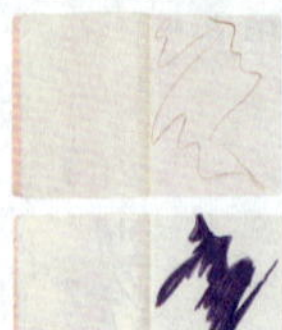

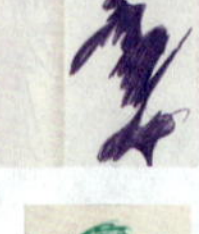

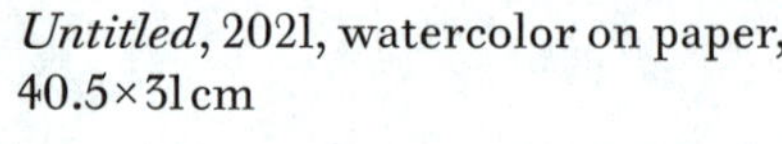

Untitled, 2021, watercolor on paper, 40.5×31 cm

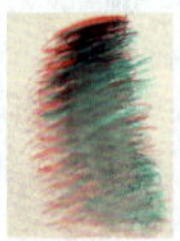

Untitled, 2021, watercolor on paper, 40.5×31 cm

From: *Sketchbook*, 2021, pencil on paper, 14×9×1 cm

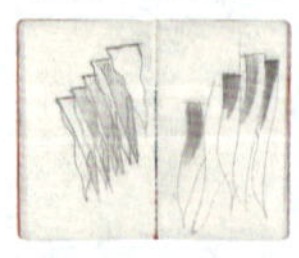

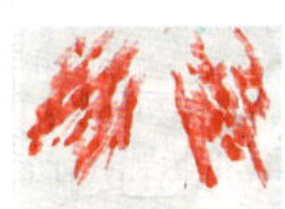

Untitled, 2022, watercolor on paper, 14.8 × 20.7 cm

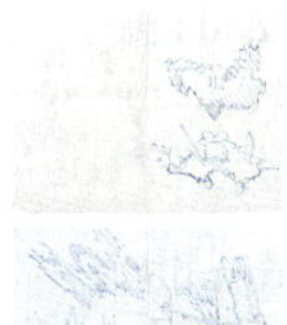

Untitled, 2022, ballpoint pen on paper (front and back), 42 × 29.7 cm

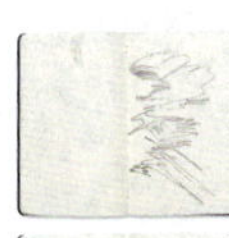

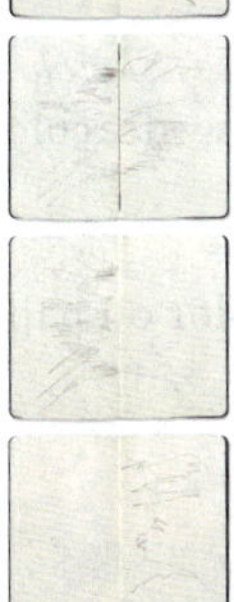

From: *Sketchbook*, 2022, crayon and pencil on paper, 21 × 13 × 0.5 cm

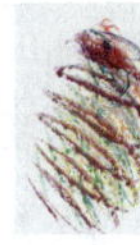

Untitled, 2021, watercolor on paper, 42 × 29 cm

Page 286
"Seminal sprinter." Image of an animal from the Messel Pit. On a watercolor by Katharina Grosse. This sprinter with an "upright walk" belongs to the line of ancestors that leads to us humans.

Page 288
Archaic bat. A skeleton that is a few million years old. The symbiosis between the Corona virus and bats is just beginning. In the image the chest, of interest to the virus as it houses the lungs, is clearly marked.

Pages 300, 304, 316

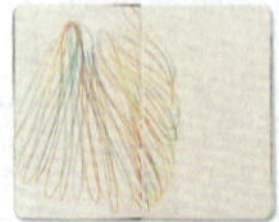

From: Katharina Grosse, *Sketchbook*, 2022, crayon and watercolor on paper, 21×13×1 cm

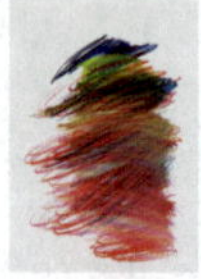

Untitled, 2021, watercolor on paper, 42×29 cm

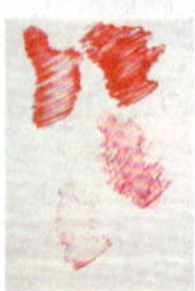

Untitled, 2021, watercolor on paper, 42×29 cm

Pages 318–26

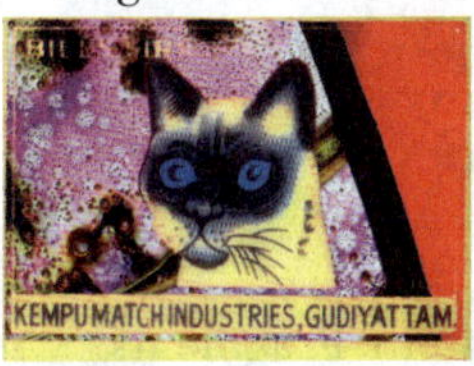

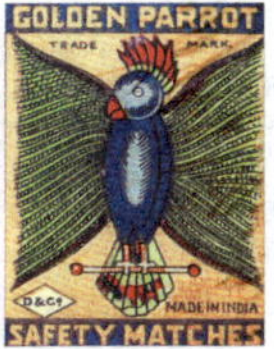

Images on Indian matchboxes.

Page 323

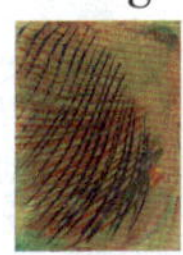

Katharina Grosse, *Untitled*, 2022, watercolor on paper, 39.7 × 30 cm

FOR STATION 7—HOMAGE TO SERGEI EISENSTEIN (with Velimir Khlebnikov, Kazimir Malevich, and Giacometti)

Sketches by Sergei Eisenstein. Fragments of these sketches are combined with watercolors by Katharina Grosse or with those camera images characteristic of the work in Station 8. Eisenstein's sketches refer to works related to his production of Richard Wagner's *Walküre* at the Bolshoi Theater in Moscow, as well as to an unfinished work on the Destruction of Troy and to the making of the film *Alexander Nevsky.*

Page 365

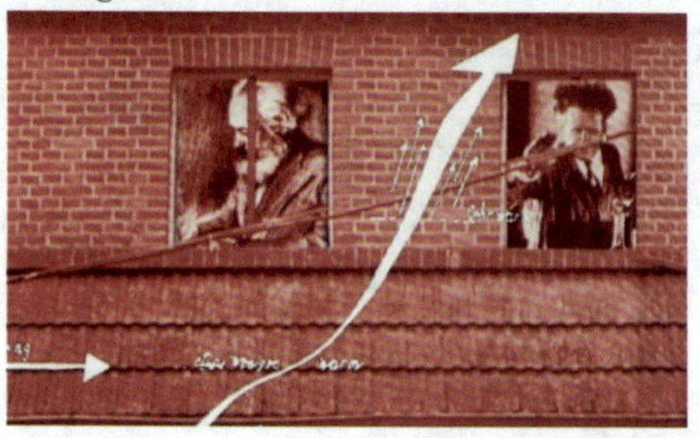

"Eisenstein and Marx in the Same House." Title image of *Alexander Kluge: Nachrichten aus der ideologischen Antike. Eisenstein–Marx–Das Kapital*, suhrkamp-filmedition, 2008.

News From Ideological Antiquity. Abbreviated edition for the Cinemateca Portuguesa, 1h 29min, 2021. Original edition: *News From Ideological Antiquity. Eisenstein–Marx–The Capital,* 6h 8min. Installation for 3 projectors—Biennale di Venezia, 2015. Collection de Audiovisuel du Centre national des arts plastiques, 2021.

Page 367
Sculpture of the young Karl Marx. From: Stefan Moses and Alexander Kluge, *Le Moment fugitif* (Nimbus Verlag, 2014).

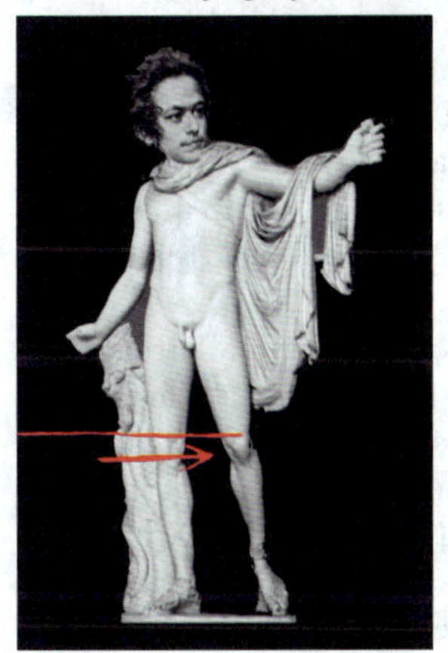

Page 370

The Veiled Marx

An artist loaned to the GDR by the Italian Communist Party—Venice branch—created an unusual Marx sculpture for the capital city of the GDR in metal painted white and pink: the young Marx aged perhaps twenty-five years, completely unclothed.

It could have passed since no one would have suspected that the figure represented the founder of the dialectical materialist method had it not been written on a plaque. Nevertheless, the bureaucrats in the cultural department of the central committee were embarrassed. And as soon as the Italian master had returned to his homeland, they had the structure covered. It was still in this state when the Treuhand liquidators were to decide on what remained. They valued it —also unaware of whose image was in question— only in terms of its scrap value. The artefact was melted down.

A lifespan of a quarter of a century, already covered, and then transformed into a lump of metal. For scrap dealers the lot was too small, of hardly any interest. There is no image of the youthful author of the Parisian "Early Writings" in the world. One thousand years of Harvard research could not offset their élan. The body created by the Italian master possessed an elegant beauty. The sympathies of a whole generation could have been won for socialism if Marx had been shown like this at the right moment, unveiled and in public.

Page 374

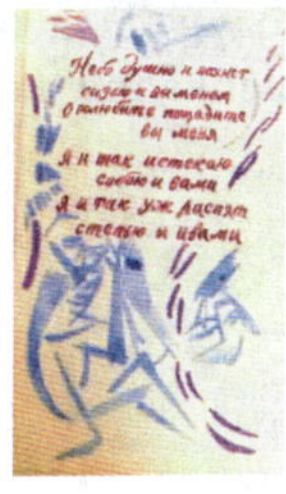

A page from Alexey Kruchenykh's book *Vzorval* from 1913.

Page 372

Top An example of Velimir Khlebnikov's "poetic mathematics."

Page 375

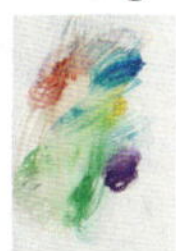

Katharina Grosse, *Untitled*, 2022, watercolor on paper, 20.8 × 14.9 cm

Page 376

Above Film still from *Alexander Nevsky*.
Below Film still from *October*.

Pages 378–81
The image sequence is an homage to Georges Didi-Huberman, *Der Kubus und das Gesicht: Im Umkreis einer Skulptur von Alberto Giacometti* (Diaphanes Verlag, 2014). Cited figures: *Der Schädel* (1923); *Kopf auf einem Stab* (1947); *Ohne Titel*; Kunstmuseum Basel (Kupferstichkabinett).

FOR STATION 8—"LIGHTS IN THE HARBOR" / 1/48TH-OF-A-SECOND IMAGES

Page 402
My sister Alexandra. "Lights in the Harbor." 42×24-cm film still printed on aluminum. Knust Kunst Gallery Editions, 2022.

Page 404
"Up, you words, follow me! / On to no end." From: Ingeborg Bachmann, *Sämtliche Gedichte* (Piper Verlag, 2003).

Page 410
"Tear apparatus." 42×24-cm printed on aluminum. Knust Kunst Gallery Editions, 2022.

Pages 418–19
"Natural wit." Mother animal with cub on its back. With camera image from "Lights in the Harbor." Knust Kunst Gallery Editions, 2022.

The image of the mother animal: from Bertuch's *Bilderbuch für Kinder*, volume 10, table 21: STRANGE PREY ANIMALS. It states the following: "The koala is a newly discovered prey animal from New Holland the size of a medium dog, with long-haired, thick, ash-gray fur, forward-pointing ears, and a black nose. It is similar to a kangaroo in terms of bite, but close to a bear in terms of body movement. The female carries her young on her back, as the illustration shows." F. J. Bertuch had published the volume in 1821.

Bertuch's *Bilderbuch für Kinder* was Walter Benjamin's favorite book. He purchased another copy of it as an adult in 1918. There are a total of twelve volumes.

Pages 421–22
"Lights in the Harbor." With a film still from *Artisten in der Zirkuskuppel: ratlos*.

Page 425
"If the trapeze artist throws herself into the arms of the catcher, then the click of the successful jump is what I call the moment of 'insight.'" On a detail of a watercolor by Katharina Grosse.

Pages 428–29
Homage to a photo by Man Ray. 42 × 24-cm film still printed on aluminum. Knust Kunst Gallery Editions, 2022.

Pages 434–35
Homage to Paul Klee. Anatomical image, Persia, 13th century.

Pages 438–39

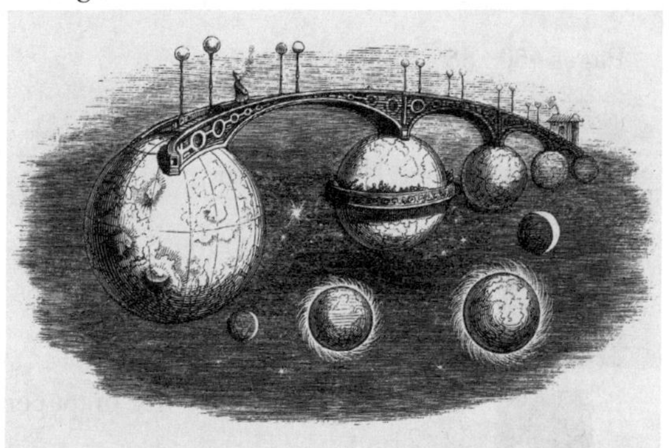

"A Bridge Leads from One World to the Next" by Grandville. In Walter Benjamin's *Arcades Project* this illustration is the final image in volume 1. *Collected Writings*, volume 5, p.1. At the end of the bridge: "Lights in the Harbor."

Pages 450–88

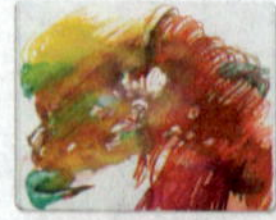

From: Katharina Grosse, *Sketchbook*, 2022, watercolor on paper, 14 × 9 × 0.5 cm

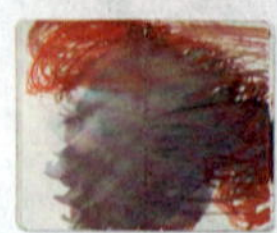

From: *Sketchbook*, 2022, watercolor on paper, 14 × 9 × 0.5 cm

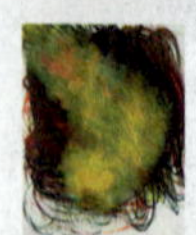

Untitled, 2022, watercolor on paper, 32 × 24 cm

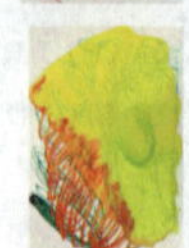

Untitled, 2022, watercolor on paper, 29.7 × 21 cm

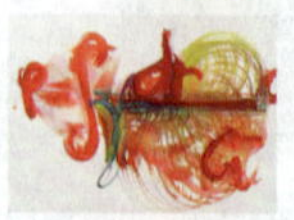

Untitled, 2022, watercolor on paper, 29.2 × 42 cm

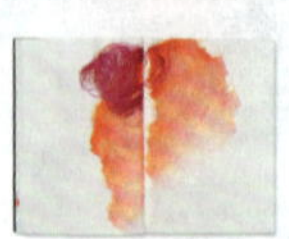

From: *Sketchbook*, 2022, watercolor on paper, 29.5 × 21 × 1.5 cm

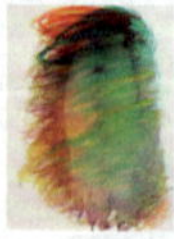

Untitled, 2021, watercolor on paper, 40.5 × 31 cm

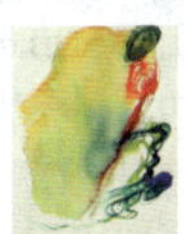

Untitled, 2022, watercolor on paper, 41×31 cm

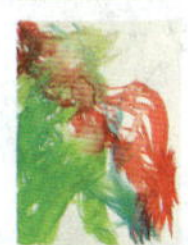

Untitled, 2022, watercolor on paper, 41×31 cm

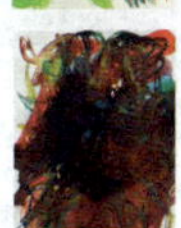

Untitled, 2022, watercolor on paper, 41×31 cm

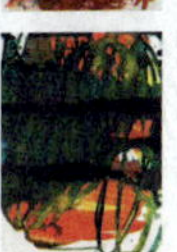

Untitled, 2021, watercolor on paper, 40×30 cm

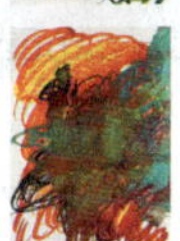

Untitled, 2021, watercolor on paper, 40×30 cm

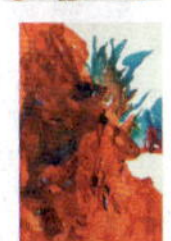

Untitled, 2019, watercolor on paper, 102×66 cm

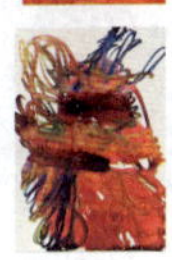

Untitled, 2019, watercolor on paper, 29.8×21 cm

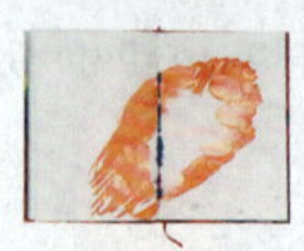

From: *Sketchbook*, 2021, watercolor on paper, 21.5×15.5×4 cm

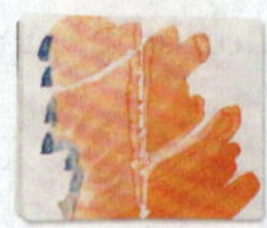

From: *Sketchbook*, 2022 watercolor on paper, 21×13×1 cm

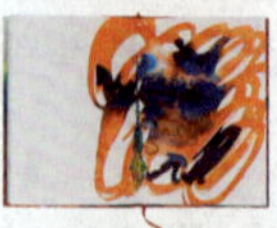

From: *Sketchbook*, 2021, watercolor on paper, 21.5×15.5×4 cm

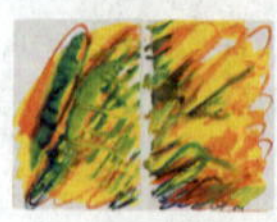

From: *Sketchbook*, 2021, watercolor on paper, 30×22.3×0.5 cm

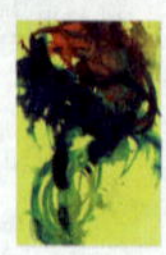

Untitled, 2019, acrylic on paper 101×67 cm

Pages 494–95
Railway platform at Kyiv's main station on the third day of the invasion, 27 February 2022. "The trains began to run very frequently. That was the war beginning." From: Andrei Platonov, *Chevengur*, trans. Anthony Olcott (Ardis, 1978).

Pages 542–44

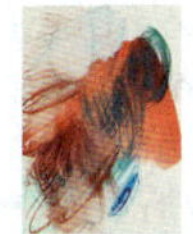

Katharina Grosse, *Untitled*, 2022, watercolor on paper, 41 × 31 cm

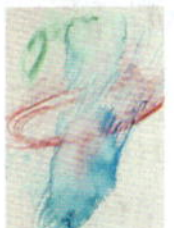

Untitled, 2022, watercolor on paper, 41 × 31 cm

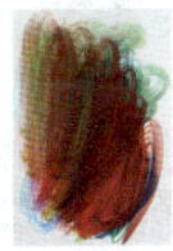

Untitled, 2021, watercolor on paper, 42 × 29 cm

Pages 549–51
Image of US airplane maneuvers between the wars (1918–39). They are practicing the bombing of warships.

Page 562

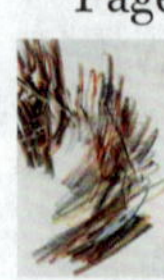

Katharina Grosse, *Untitled*, 2021, crayon on paper, 13 × 9 cm

Pages 570–73

"Ruins of Aleppo"

Pages 576–77

Time perspective versus space perspective

In painting, spatial perspective has been dominant since the Renaissance. In the younger art of film, the perspective of time remains the relevant element. The film still of a stone fragment from twenty-four-hundred years ago depicting Medea linked to a scissor-lift stage by Katharina Grosse—an installation that was on view in the exhibition *Die Oper: Tempel der Ernsthaftigkeit* at the Kunsthalle Weishaupt in Ulm and that clearly comes from the twenty-first century—forms just such a *time-trace*, or rather, perspective. The Separatrix Project attempts to enable a creative friction between spatial images and perspectives of time.

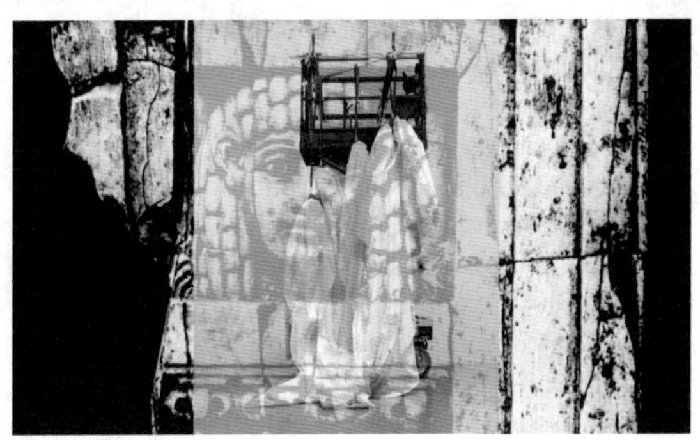

"Time-trace of the Medea"

FOR STATION 11—HERALDIC ANIMALS OF THE ENGLIGHTENMENT

Katharina Grosse and I debated all the different animals that the heraldic animals of the Enlightenment might contain. In effect, all of evolution: that of animals, plants, mushrooms, and microbes, up through the roots of liberty and the Enlightenment. That stated, there are a number of animals of admirable intelligence and even some creatures, such as flies, without which the history of progress is simply unthinkable. In the great species EXTINCTION of sixty-six million years ago (which ended the world of the dinosaurs), mollusks and snakes, creatures with unprotected or particularly sensitive skin, somehow survived. It is the fragility of the human being that reminds us of these evolutionary seams.

We can only guess at what the process of enlightenment, which humanity has by no means experienced universally, means in practice. Thus we can also apply the search term "Heraldic Animals of the Enlightenment" rather broadly.

According to a biologist, if you put a bee and a fly in a closed container with only one exit, the bee will carefully and methodically begin looking for it, but will starve to death before finding it. The fly, on the other hand, will zigzag up and down in a panic, thus increasing its chances of finding the exit to 99 percent. "The consideration of emergency exits is the beginning of philosophy."

Page 584

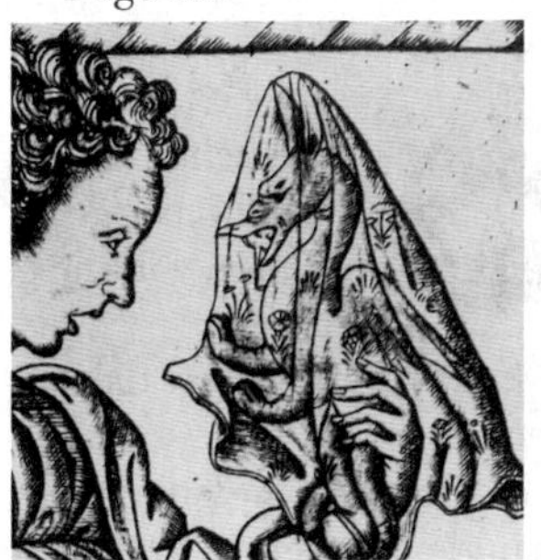

"Woman speaking to a snake with a cat-like body." Detail from table 50/51 in Aby Warburg's *Mnemosyne Atlas*, the so-called Mantegna Tarocchi (e-series *The Arts and the Muses*). From the year 1465. The allegory's name "logica" = "logic."

In the paradise narrative, the serpent is considered a provocateur. A master of questioning. Snakes listen with their jaws. They place them firmly on the ground and are thus able to register the vibrations of approaching prey. This kind of hearing has a wider radius than the human eye outfitted with infrared, night-seeing technology. The snakes' hearing organ, the jaw bone, has migrated into the ear in the evolution of humans. The ossicle distinguishes music and speech, and is responsible for balance and our upright gait.

Page 587

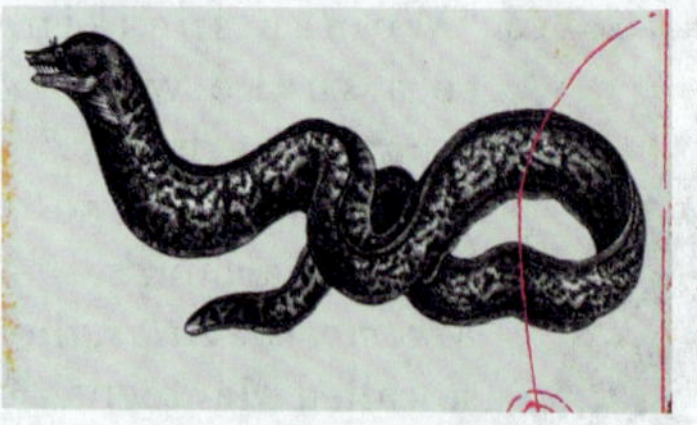

"Image of the snake" from: Bertuch's *Bilderbuch für Kinder*, volume 9, table 19: "Peculiar fishes." Here: the Surinamese eel.

The book says: "In this fish sex, the gill openings are united into a single one beneath the throat. The snakelike body is scaleless. The head is slightly thicker than the trunk, which lacks the pectoral and ventral fins. The dorsal side is olive, the ventral side yellowish-green. Its habitat is the sweet and marshy waters of Surinam."

Pages 588–89

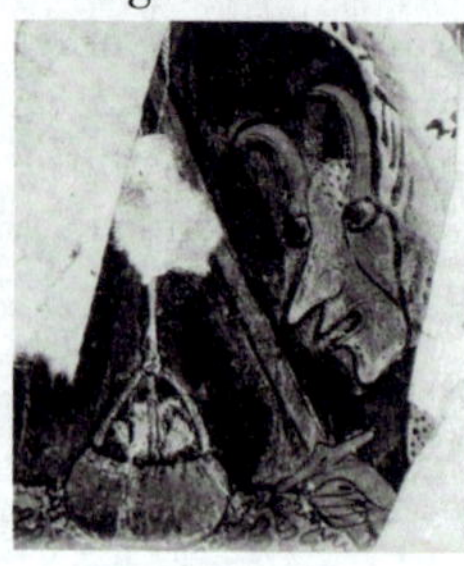

The devil in animal form. Keeping watch over his "children." They are "cooking" in an alchemical vessel. Miniature from Aby Warburg's *Mnemosyne Atlas*.

Pages 590–91

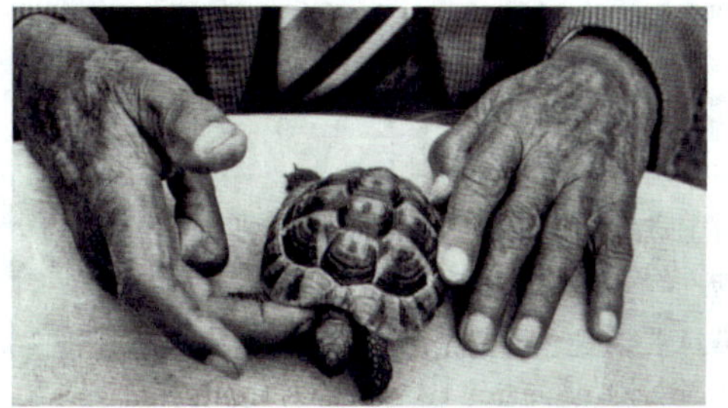

Turtle with Ernst Jünger's hands.
Photograph by Stefan Moses.
From: Stefan Moses / Alexander Kluge:
Le Moment fugitif, Nimbus Verlag.

Pages 592–93

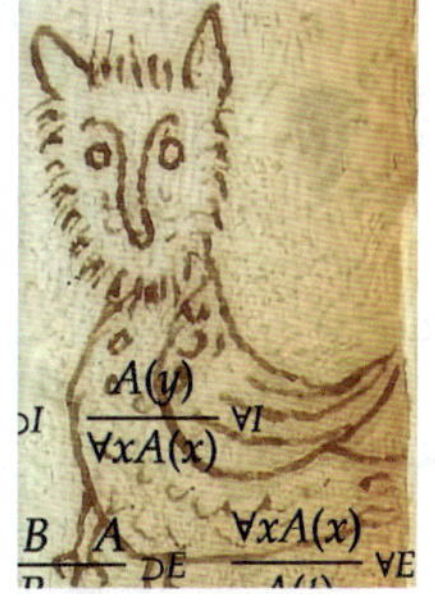

The Owl of Minerva

The Owl of Minerva
Film triptych
02:55

Page 596

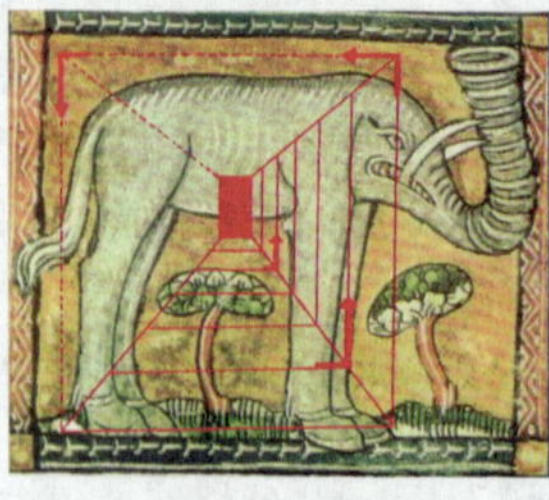

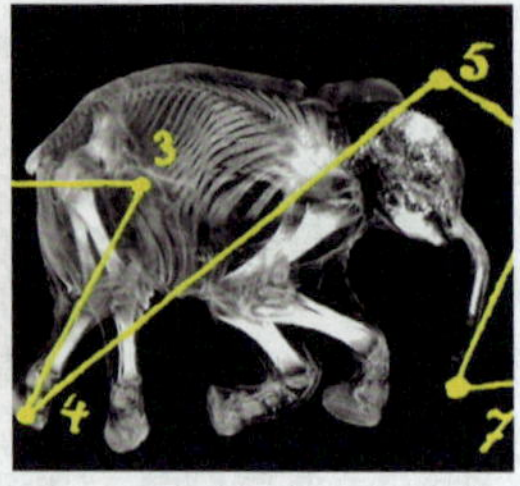

Left: book illustration of Charles the Great's elephant. *Right*: dwarf elephant, discovered on Sumatra.

Page 603

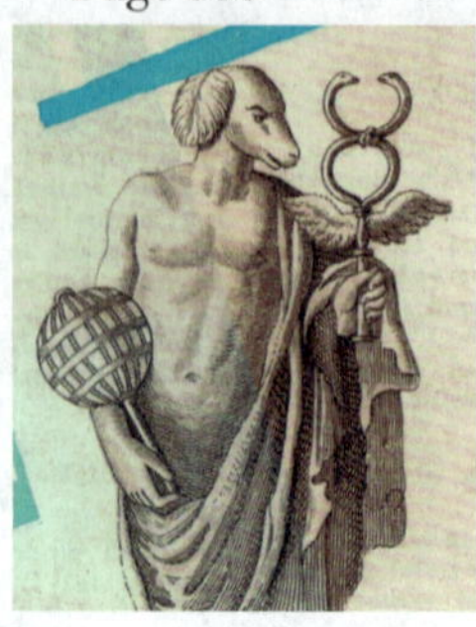

The doctor Asclepius, son of Apollo. Here in the form of the Egyptian Anubis, one of the sons of Osiris, also a doctor. In allegorical representation, he has been assigned the head of an animal. This is meant to signal the ART OF HEALING.

Page 604

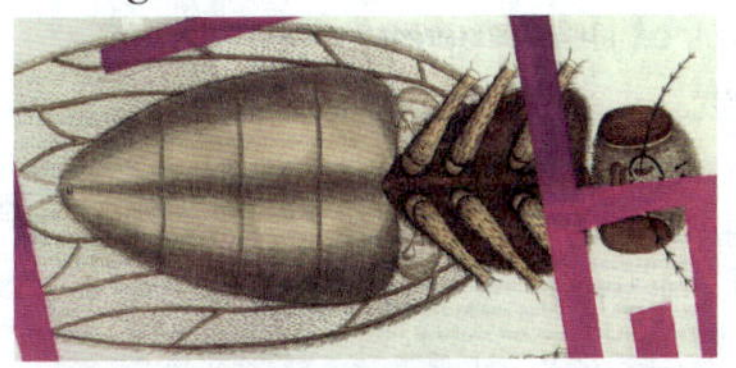

Schematic drawing of a fly from Bertuch's *Bilderbuch für Kinder*, 1807.

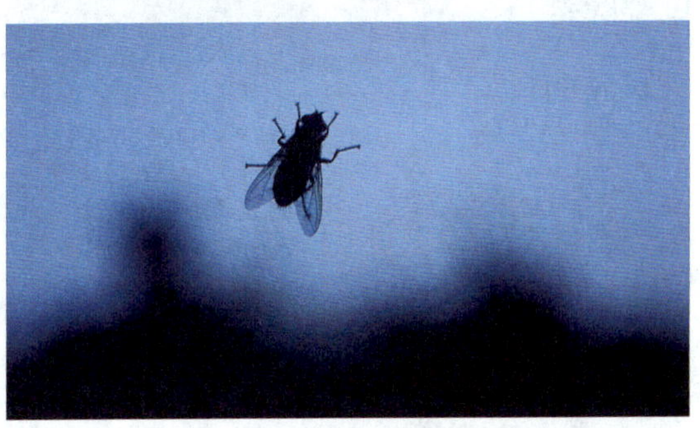

The fly in the Pernod glass. It doesn't seem to be moving. With my pencil eraser I lift it out of the green liquid and lay it onto the wickerwork. I assume it has died. But after a few seconds the animal begins to move violently about.
The next minute the ephemeral fly has vanished from my sight. Manifestly capable of flight.
It did not appear "drunk." A tough animal that has my respect. In the space of our brief encounter (as far as it is concerned), it has lived a number of years. Should it ever have any children, its line will outlive me. It has existed for eighteen million

years. Due to their favorable attitude toward chance, small flies of this type enjoy an almost eternal existence.

Fly in the Pernod Glass
01:29

Page 605

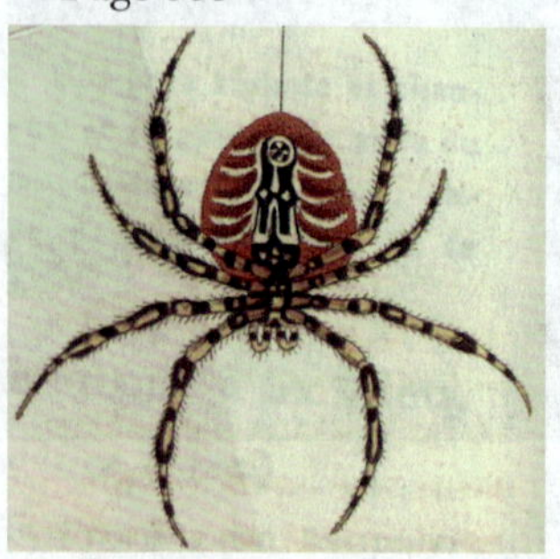

Arachne, the spider. In Greek *arachne* means "spider." Ovid's *Metamorphoses* describe a highly gifted weaver who wove the history of the world into clothes. The goddess Athena, Ovid continues, jealous of this rival in matters of art, transformed the young woman into a spider. Since then, the spider has been the symbol of the art of weaving and is today the patron saint of the World Wide Web.

Pages 612–13, 615

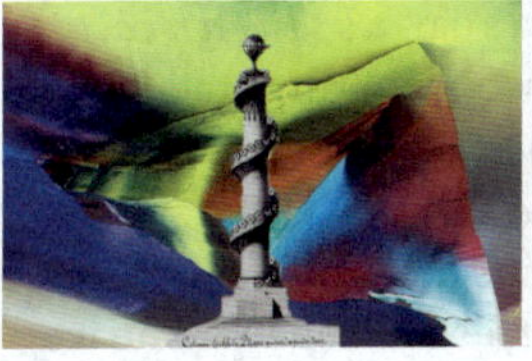

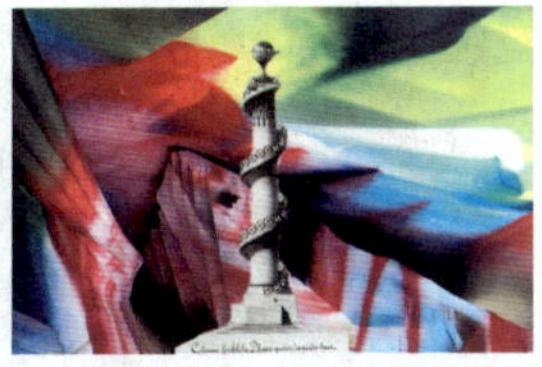

"Lighthouse for wanderers in the desert." Sculpture by the architect of the French Revolutionary period Lequeu. There is one single exemplar of the column at the Louvre in Paris. It never reached the deserts of Africa. Film still of the column against the background of a detail of Katharina Grosse's exhibition *It Wasn't Us*, 2020. Acrylic on floor, polystyrene, and bronze; paint on asphalt, concrete, bricks, and metal, 7×65×183 m, Hamburger Bahnhof—Museum für Gegenwart—Berlin

Page 614

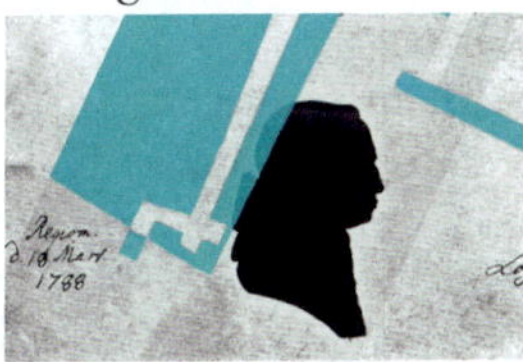

Silhouette of Immanuel Kant with a characteristic mark of the Bauhaus as homage.

Page 617

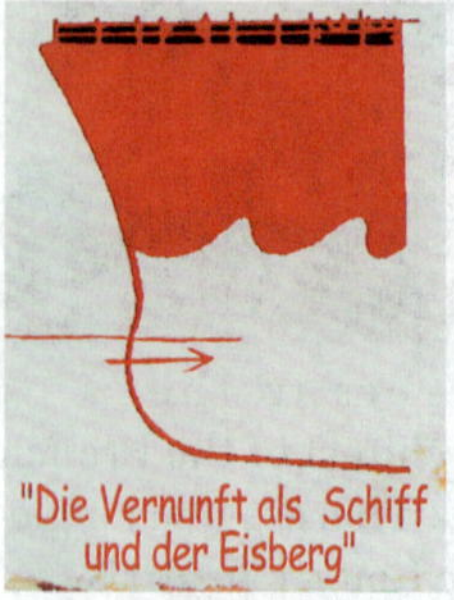

Reason as *Titanic*. Reason, represented here as a ship, is sailing toward man's forces of the soul, which are represented in turn as an iceberg. The iceberg's Italian inscription denotes consciousness, the unconscious, the preconscious, the symbolic representations of forgotten conflicts and other mechanisms that constitute people's inner make-up. The forces of the soul form a six-tiered vertical. Up to the groundwaters of man's subjective character, which have arrived to us unchanged from evolution. These forces know nothing of "good and evil." Watch out for a collision between steamer and iceberg!

Page 620

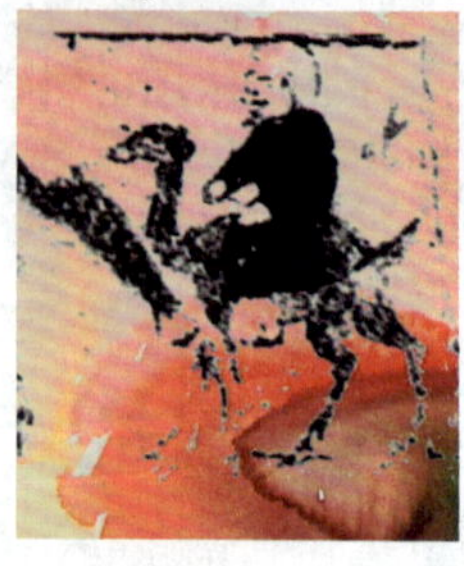

Arabic merchant on a dromedary camel. Detail from Aby Warburg's *Mnemosyne Atlas*.

First trade then bookkeeping. From this comes writing. Philosophy is the last in line.

Page 622

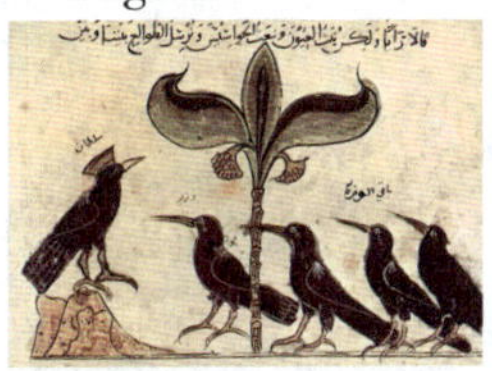

The king of the ravens teaching young ravens. Arabic emblem.

Bitter Cold, Rain, and Ravens
Triptych
01:58

Pages 626, 628

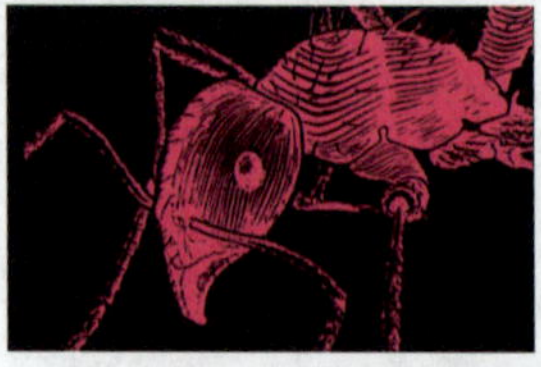

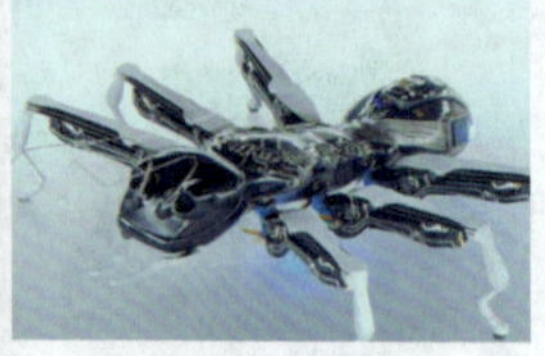

Ants. The high level of ants' social structure separates them from the other heraldic animals of the Enlightenment. Enlightenment has traditionally been associated with the process of individualization, and not the social collective. As corresponds to the self-conception of free labor and free enterprise. In point of fact, however, we must distinguish between the most diverse kinds of intelligence. The intelligence that evolution itself has produced in its long history forms a collective. For artificial intelligence—this has been insufficiently explored—the resources of this evolution and with it too the intelligence of ants could provide an important inflow. What poses a challenge to art's ability to foresee things is not so much academic intelligence, but the wide array of forms of knowledge—including that intelligence required to survive in the suburbs, crisis areas, and slums.

R as in Robot Ants
03:19

Page 631

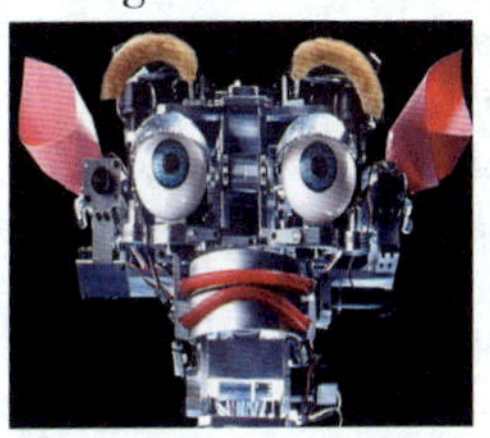

The robot Kismet. One of the first constructions in AI, it was created by Dr. Cynthia Breazeal at MIT's Artficial Intelligence Laboratory, directed by Rodney Brooks. The head can hear and respond. It has three eyes.

Page 634

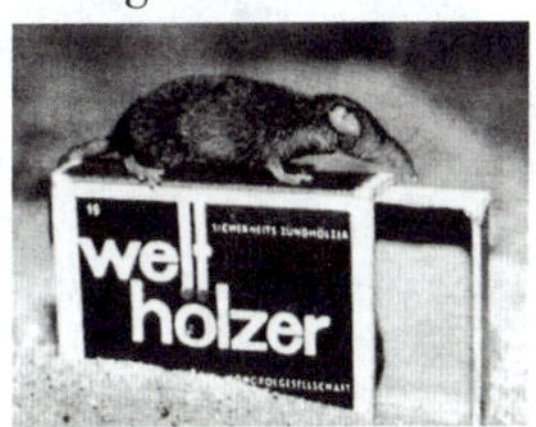

Etruscan harvest mouse. Placed on top of a matchbox to give an impression of its size. This species belongs to the line of ancestors that leads to humans. In order to maintain the proper functioning of their circulation, these animals must constantly be on the hunt.

Page 635

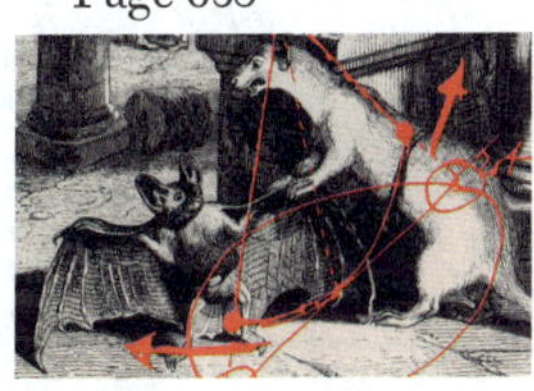

Conversation between weasel and bat. After an illustration by Grandville.

Pages 638–39

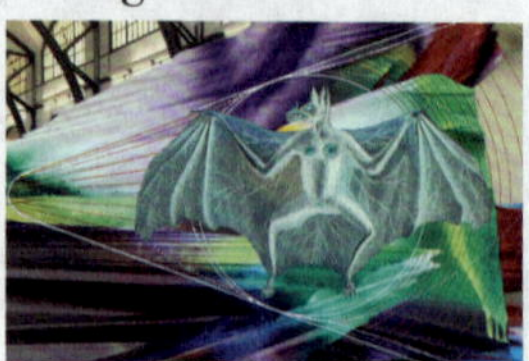

Bat from Bertuch's *Bilderbuch für Kinder*, volume 9, table 12. Placed over a detail from Katharina Grosse's exhibition *It Wasn't Us*, 2020. Hamburger Bahnhof—Museum für Gegenwart—Berlin.

Bertuch has the following to say about bats: "The true vampire. This vampire, the only one that really sucks blood from sleeping mammals, makes its home in South America and is the size of a squirrel. It is a pale gray color."

Page 656

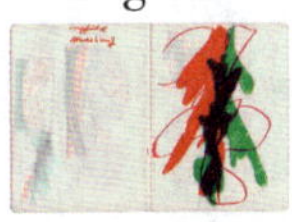

From: Katharina Grosse, *Sketchbook*, 2021, fiber pen on paper, 25×19×1.5 cm

IMPRESSUM
Volume #10 of the series *Volte expanded*, edited by Dorothee Elmiger, Mathias Zeiske, and Jan Wenzel

Katharina Grosse and Alexander Kluge: *The SEPARATRIX Project*

- Translations: Alexander Booth, Isabel Cole
- Proofreading: Mary Cason
- Graphic design: Wolfgang Schwärzler
- Color grading: Ralf Lenk, Scancolor Reprostudio Gmbh, Leipzig
- Typefaces: Walbaum B Regular, Walbaum 10 Italic
- Materials: Fancy Linen, Surbalin 115 g/m², Lonaopak 50 g/m²
- Printing and binding: Gutenberg Beuys Feindruckerei Gmbh, Langenhagen

Photo credits
- Pages 10–11, 14, 17, 28–37, 40–41, 75, 77, 194, 244–47, 250–51, 254–55, 258–61, 264–65, 270–77, 284, 300, 323, 375, 450–61, 467, 470, 478–88, 542, and 543: Photos by Jens Ziehe
- Pages 13, 15, 18–26, 39, 252, 253, 462, 472–76, 544–45, and 562: Photos by Sam Hartnett
- Pages 215–16, 234–35, 284, 304, 316, and 464: Photos by Katharina Grosse

Published by
Spector Books, Harkortstraße 10,
04107 Leipzig, Germany
www.spectorbooks.com

Distribution

- GERMANY, AUSTRIA: GVA, Gemeinsame Verlagsauslieferung Göttingen GmbH & Co. KG, www.gva-verlage.de
- SWITZERLAND: AVA Verlagsauslieferung AG, www.ava.ch France, Belgium: Interart Paris, www.interart.fr
- UK: Central Books Ltd, www.centralbooks.com
- USA, CANADA, CENTRAL and SOUTH AMERICA, AFRICA: ARTBOOK/D.A.P., www.artbook.com
- SOUTH KOREA: The Book Society, www.thebooksociety.org
- JAPAN: twelvebooks, www.twelve-books.com
- AUSTRALIA, NEW ZEALAND: Perimeter Distribution, www.perimeterdistribution.com

Supported by the Wunderblock Foundation

Wunderblock

First Edition: 2022
Printed in Germany
ISBN 978-3-95905-679-3

CONTENTS